studysync®

Reading & Writing Companion

GRADE 9 UNITS

Empathy • Leadership

Dreams and Aspirations • All for Love

∷studysync®

studysync.com

Send all inquiries to:
BookheadEd Learning, LLC
610 Daniel Young Drive
Sonoma, CA 95476

2015 G9

Table of Contents

Empathy

How do we develop compassion for others?

Leadership

What are the responsibilities of power?

Dreams and Aspirations

What makes a dream worth pursuing?

All for Love

How are we affected by the power of love?

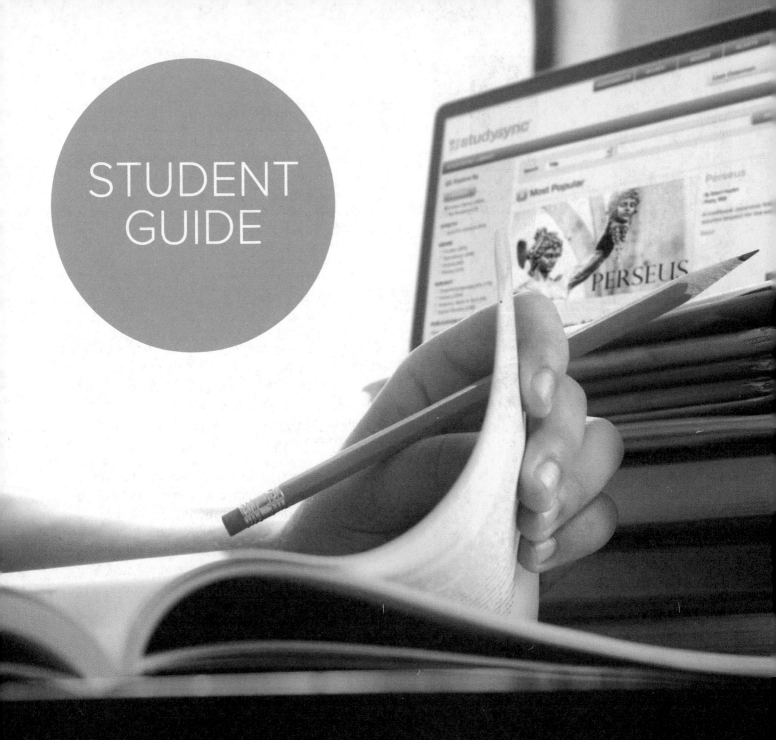

STUDENT GUIDE

GETTING STARTED

Welcome to the StudySync Reading and Writing Companion! In this booklet, you will find a collection of readings based on the theme of the unit you are studying. As you work through the readings, you will be asked to answer questions and perform a variety of tasks designed to help you closely analyze and understand each text selection. Read on for an explanation of

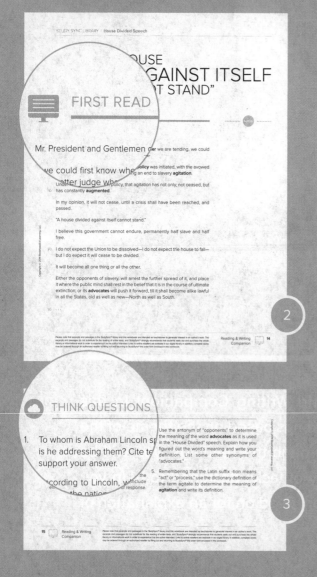

1 INTRODUCTION

An Introduction to each text provides historical context for your reading as well as information about the author. You will also learn about the genre of the excerpt and the year in which it was written.

2 FIRST READ

During your first reading of each excerpt, you should just try to get a general idea of the content and message of the reading. Don't worry if there are parts you don't understand or words that are unfamiliar to you. You'll have an opportunity later to dive deeper into the text.

Many times, while working through the Think Questions after your first read, you will be asked to **annotate** or **make annotations** about what you are reading. This means that you should use the "Notes" column to make comments or jot down any questions you may have about the text. You may also want to note any unfamiliar vocabulary words here.

3 THINK QUESTIONS

These questions will ask you to start thinking critically about the text, asking specific questions about its purpose, and making connections to your prior knowledge and reading experiences. To answer these questions, you should go back to the text and draw upon specific evidence that you find there to support your responses. You will also begin to explore some of the more challenging vocabulary words used in the excerpt.

4 CLOSE READ & FOCUS QUESTIONS

After you have completed the First Read, you will then be asked to go back and read the excerpt more closely and critically. Before you begin your Close Read, you should read through the Focus Questions to get an idea of the concepts you will want to focus on during your second reading. You should work through the Focus Questions by making annotations, highlighting important concepts, and writing notes or questions in the "Notes" column. Depending on instructions from your teacher, you may need to respond online or use a separate piece of paper to start expanding on your thoughts and ideas.

5 WRITING PROMPT

Your study of each excerpt or selection will end with a writing assignment. To complete this assignment, you should use your notes, annotations, and answers to both the Think and Focus Questions. Be sure to read the prompt carefully and address each part of it in your writing assignment.

6 EXTENDED WRITING PROJECT

After you have read and worked through all of the unit text selections, you will move on to a writing project. This project will walk you through steps to plan, draft, revise, edit, and finally publish an essay or other piece of writing about one or more of the texts you have studied in the unit. Student models and graphic organizers will provide guidance and help you organize your thoughts as you plan and write your essay. Throughout the project, you will also study and work on specific writing skills to help you develop different portions of your writing.

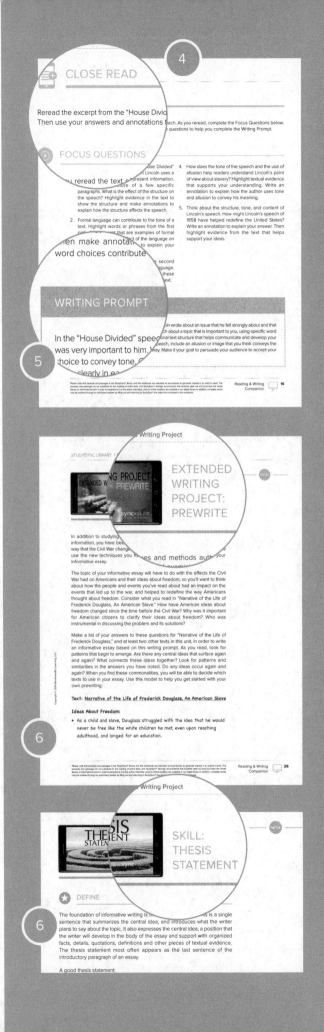

studysync®

Reading & Writing Companion

How do we develop compassion for others?

Empathy

UNIT 1   How do we develop compassion for others?

Empathy

 TEXTS

TEXTS

EXTENDED WRITING PROJECT

462

Text Fulfillment
through
StudySync

MARIGOLDS

FICTION
Eugenia Collier
1969

INTRODUCTION

In Eugenia Collier's powerful short story, "Marigolds," Lizabeth, the narrator, tells a story from her childhood in a dusty Depression-era town. Confused and amused by why the town outcast, Miss Lottie, puts so much care into the brilliantly colored patch of marigolds outside her crumbling gray shack, Lizabeth and her friends tease the old woman and throw rocks at her flowers. A later incident in the garden causes Lizabeth great shame, but leads to a deeper moral understanding, and a major change in her life.

"Miss Lottie's marigolds were perhaps the strangest part of the picture."

 FIRST READ

1   When I think of the hometown of my youth, all that I seem to remember is dust—the brown, crumbly dust of late summer—arid, sterile dust that gets into the eyes and makes them water, gets into the throat and between the toes of bare brown feet. I don't know why I should remember only the dust. Surely there must have been lush green lawns and paved streets under leafy shade trees somewhere in town; but memory is an abstract painting—it does not present things as they are, but rather as they *feel*. And so, when I think of that time and that place, I remember only the dry September of the dirt roads and grassless yards of the shantytown where I lived. And one other thing I remember, another incongruency of memory—a brilliant splash of sunny yellow against the dust—Miss Lottie's marigolds.

2   Whenever the memory of those marigolds flashes across my mind, a strange nostalgia comes with it and remains long after the picture has faded. I feel again the chaotic emotions of adolescence, illusive as smoke, yet as real as the potted geranium before me now. Joy and rage and wild animal gladness and shame become tangled together in the multicolored skein of fourteen-going-on-fifteen as I recall that devastating moment when I was suddenly more woman than child, years ago in Miss Lottie's yard. I think of those marigolds at the strangest times; I remember them vividly now as I desperately pass away the time.

3   I suppose that futile waiting was the sorrowful background music of our impoverished little community when I was young. The Depression that gripped the nation was no new thing to us, for the black workers of rural Maryland had always been depressed. I don't know what it was that we were waiting for; certainly not for the **prosperity** that was "just around the corner," for those were white folks' words, which we never believed. Nor did we wait for hard work and thrift to pay off in shining success, as the American Dream promised, for we knew better than that, too. Perhaps we waited for a miracle,

amorphous in concept but necessary if one were to have the grit to rise before dawn each day and labor in the white man's vineyard until after dark, or to wander about in the September dust offering one's sweat in return for some meager share of bread. But God was chary with miracles in those days, and so we waited—and waited.

4   We children, of course, were only vaguely aware of the extent of our poverty. Having no radios, few newspapers, and no magazines, we were somewhat unaware of the world outside our community. Nowadays we would be called culturally deprived and people would write books and hold conferences about us. In those days everybody we knew was just as hungry and ill clad as we were. Poverty was the cage in which we all were trapped, and our hatred of it was still the vague, undirected restlessness of the zoo-bred flamingo who knows that nature created him to fly free.

5   As I think of those days I feel most poignantly the tag end of summer, the bright, dry times when we began to have a sense of shortening days and the imminence of the cold.

6   By the time I was fourteen, my brother Joey and I were the only children left at our house, the older ones having left home for early marriage or the lure of the city, and the two babies having been sent to relatives who might care for them better than we. Joey was three years younger than I, and a boy, and therefore vastly inferior. Each morning our mother and father trudged wearily down the dirt road and around the bend, she to her domestic job, he to his daily unsuccessful quest for work. After our few chores around the tumbledown shanty, Joey and I were free to run wild in the sun with other children similarly situated.

7   For the most part, those days are ill-defined in my memory, running together and combining like a fresh watercolor painting left out in the rain. I remember squatting in the road drawing a picture in the dust, a picture which Joey gleefully erased with one sweep of his dirty foot. I remember fishing for minnows in a muddy creek and watching sadly as they eluded my cupped hands, while Joey laughed uproariously. And I remember, that year, a strange restlessness of body and of spirit, a feeling that something old and familiar was ending, and something unknown and therefore terrifying was beginning.

8   One day returns to me with special clarity for some reason, perhaps because it was the beginning of the experience that in some inexplicable way marked the end of innocence. I was loafing under the great oak tree in our yard, deep in some reverie which I have now forgotten, except that it involved some secret, secret thoughts of one of the Harris boys across the yard. Joey and a bunch of kids were bored now with the old tire suspended from an oak limb, which had kept them entertained for a while.

NOTES

9   "Hey, Lizbeth," Joey yelled. He never talked when he could yell. "Hey, Lizbeth, let's go somewhere."

10 I came reluctantly from my private world. "Where you want to go? What you want to do?"

11 The truth was that we were becoming tired of the formlessness of our summer days. The idleness whose prospect had seemed so beautiful during the busy days of spring now had **degenerated** to an almost desperate effort to fill up the empty midday hours.

12 "Let's go see can we find some locusts on the hill," someone suggested.

13 Joey was scornful. "Ain't no more locusts there. Y'all got 'em all while they was still green."

14 The argument that followed was brief and not really worth the effort. Hunting locust trees wasn't fun anymore by now.

15 "Tell you what," said Joey finally, his eyes sparkling. "Let's us go over to Miss Lottie's."

16 The idea caught on at once, for annoying Miss Lottie was always fun. I was still child enough to scamper along with the group over rickety fences and through bushes that tore our already raggedy clothes, back to where Miss Lottie lived. I think now that we must have made a tragicomic spectacle, five or six kids of different ages, each of us clad in only one garment—the girls in faded dresses that were too long or too short, the boys in patchy pants, their sweaty brown chests gleaming in the hot sun. A little cloud of dust followed our thin legs and bare feet as we tramped over the barren land.

17 When Miss Lottie's house came into view we stopped, ostensibly to plan our strategy, but actually to reinforce our courage. Miss Lottie's house was the most ramshackle of all our ramshackle homes. The sun and rain had long since faded its rickety frame siding from white to a sullen gray. The boards themselves seemed to remain upright not from being nailed together but rather from leaning together, like a house that a child might have constructed from cards. A brisk wind might have blown it down, and the fact that it was still standing implied a kind of enchantment that was stronger than the elements. There it stood and as far as I know is standing yet—a gray, rotting thing with no porch, no shutters, no steps, set on a cramped lot with no grass, not even any weeds—a monument to decay.

18 In front of the house in a squeaky rocking chair sat Miss Lottie's son, John Burke, completing the impression of decay. John Burke was what was known as queer-headed. Black and ageless, he sat rocking day in and day out in a

mindless stupor, lulled by the monotonous squeak-squawk of the chair. A battered hat atop his shaggy head shaded him from the sun. Usually John Burke was totally unaware of everything outside his quiet dream world. But if you disturbed him, if you intruded upon his fantasies, he would become enraged, strike out at you, and curse at you in some strange enchanted language which only he could understand. We children made a game of thinking of ways to disturb John Burke and then to elude his violent retribution.

19   But our real fun and our real fear lay in Miss Lottie herself. Miss Lottie seemed to be at least a hundred years old. Her big frame still held traces of the tall, powerful woman she must have been in youth, although it was now bent and drawn. Her smooth skin was a dark reddish brown, and her face had Indian-like features and the stern **stoicism** that one associates with Indian faces. Miss Lottie didn't like intruders either, especially children. She never left her yard, and nobody ever visited her. We never knew how she managed those necessities which depend on human interaction—how she ate, for example, or even whether she ate. When we were tiny children, we thought Miss Lottie was a witch and we made up tales that we half believed ourselves about her exploits. We were far too sophisticated now, of course, to believe the witch nonsense. But old fears have a way of clinging like cobwebs, and so when we sighted the tumbledown shack, we had to stop to reinforce our nerves.

20   "Look, there she is," I whispered, forgetting that Miss Lottie could not possibly have heard me from that distance. "She's fooling with them crazy flowers."

21   "Yeh, look at 'er."

22   Miss Lottie's marigolds were perhaps the strangest part of the picture. Certainly they did not fit in with the crumbling decay of the rest of her yard. Beyond the dusty brown yard, in front of the sorry gray house, rose suddenly and shockingly a dazzling strip of bright blossoms, clumped together in enormous mounds, warm and passionate and sun-golden. The old black witch-woman worked on them all summer, every summer, down on her creaky knees, weeding and cultivating and arranging, while the house crumbled and John Burke rocked. For some perverse reason, we children hated those marigolds. They interfered with the perfect ugliness of the place; they were too beautiful; they said too much that we could not understand; they did not make sense. There was something in the vigor with which the old woman destroyed the weeds that intimidated us. It should have been a comical sight—the old woman with the man's hat on her cropped white head, leaning over the bright mounds, her big backside in the air—but it wasn't comical, it was something we could not name. We had to annoy her by whizzing a pebble into her flowers or by yelling a dirty word, then dancing away from her rage, reveling in our youth and mocking her age. Actually, I think it was the

flowers we wanted to destroy, but nobody had the nerve to try it, not even Joey, who was usually fool enough to try anything.

23 "Y'all git some stones," commanded Joey now and was met with instant giggling obedience as everyone except me began to gather pebbles from the dusty ground. "Come on, Lizabeth."

24 I just stood there peering through the bushes, torn between wanting to join the fun and feeling that it was all a bit silly.

25 "You scared, Lizabeth?"

26 I cursed and spat on the ground—my favorite gesture of phony bravado. "Y'all children get the stones, I'll show you how to use 'em."

27 I said before that we children were not consciously aware of how thick were the bars of our cage. I wonder now, though, whether we were not more aware of it than I thought. Perhaps we had some dim notion of what we were, and how little chance we had of being anything else. Otherwise, why would we have been so preoccupied with destruction? Anyway, the pebbles were collected quickly, and everybody looked at me to begin the fun.

28 "Come on, y'all."

29 We crept to the edge of the bushes that bordered the narrow road in front of Miss Lottie's place. She was working placidly, kneeling over the flowers, her dark hand plunged into the golden mound. Suddenly *zing*—an expertly aimed stone cut the head off one of the blossoms.

30 "Who out there?" Miss Lottie's backside came down and her head came up as her sharp eyes searched the bushes. "You better git!"

31 We had crouched down out of sight in the bushes, where we stifled the giggles that insisted on coming. Miss Lottie gazed warily across the road for a moment, then cautiously returned to her weeding. *Zing*—Joey sent a pebble into the blooms, and another marigold was beheaded.

32 Miss Lottie was enraged now. She began struggling to her feet, leaning on a rickety cane and shouting. "Y'all git! Go on home!" Then the rest of the kids let loose with their pebbles, storming the flowers and laughing wildly and senselessly at Miss Lottie's impotent rage. She shook her stick at us and started shakily toward the road crying, "Git 'long! John Burke! John Burke, come help!"

33 Then I lost my head entirely, mad with the power of inciting such rage, and ran out of the bushes in the storm of pebbles, straight toward Miss Lottie,

NOTES

chanting madly, "Old witch, fell in a ditch, picked up a penny and thought she was rich!" The children screamed with delight, dropped their pebbles, and joined the crazy dance, swarming around Miss Lottie like bees and chanting, "Old lady witch!" while she screamed curses at us. The madness lasted only a moment, for John Burke, startled at last, lurched out of his chair, and we dashed for the bushes just as Miss Lottie's cane went whizzing at my head.

34 I did not join the merriment when the kids gathered again under the oak in our bare yard.

35 Suddenly I was ashamed, and I did not like being ashamed. The child in me sulked and said it was all in fun, but the woman in me flinched at the thought of the **malicious** attack that I had led. The mood lasted all afternoon. When we ate the beans and rice that was supper that night, I did not notice my father's silence, for he was always silent these days, nor did I notice my mother's absence, for she always worked until well into evening. Joey and I had a particularly bitter argument after supper; his exuberance got on my nerves. Finally I stretched out upon the pallet in the room we shared and fell into a fitful doze. When I awoke, somewhere in the middle of the night, my mother had returned, and I vaguely listened to the conversation that was audible through the thin walls that separated our rooms. At first I heard no words, only voices. My mother's voice was like a cool, dark room in summer— peaceful, soothing, quiet. I loved to listen to it; it made things seem all right somehow. But my father's voice cut through hers, shattering the peace.

36 "Twenty-two years, Maybelle, twenty-two years," he was saying, "and I got nothing for you, nothing, nothing."

37 "It's all right, honey, you'll get something. Everybody out of work now, you know that."

38 "It ain't right. Ain't no man ought to eat his woman's food year in and year out, and see his children running wild. Ain't nothing right about that."

39 "Honey, you took good care of us when you had it. Ain't nobody got nothing nowadays."

40 "I ain't talking about nobody else, I'm talking about *me*. God knows I try." My mother said something I could not hear, and my father cried out louder, "What must a man do, tell me that?"

41 "Look, we ain't starving. I git paid every week, and Mrs. Ellis is real nice about giving me things. She gonna let me have Mr. Ellis's old coat for you this winter—"

42   "Damn Mr. Ellis's coat! And damn his money! You think I want white folks' leavings?"

43   "Damn, Maybelle"—and suddenly he sobbed, loudly and painfully, and cried helplessly and hopelessly in the dark night. I had never heard a man cry before. I did not know men ever cried. I covered my ears with my hands but could not cut off the sound of my father's harsh, painful, despairing sobs. My father was a strong man who could whisk a child upon his shoulders and go singing through the house. My father whittled toys for us, and laughed so loud that the great oak seemed to laugh with him, and taught us how to fish and hunt rabbits. How could it be that my father was crying? But the sobs went on, unstifled, finally quieting until I could hear my mother's voice, deep and rich, humming softly as she used to hum to a frightened child.

44   The world had lost its boundary lines. My mother, who was small and soft, was now the strength of the family; my father, who was the rock on which the family had been built, was sobbing like the tiniest child. Everything was suddenly out of tune, like a broken accordion. Where did I fit into this crazy picture? I do not now remember my thoughts, only a feeling of great bewilderment and fear.

45   Long after the sobbing and humming had stopped, I lay on the pallet, still as stone with my hands over my ears, wishing that I too could cry and be comforted. The night was silent now except for the sound of the crickets and of Joey's soft breathing. But the room was too crowded with fear to allow me to sleep, and finally, feeling the terrible aloneness of 4 A.M., I decided to awaken Joey.

46   "Ouch! What's the matter with you? What you want?" he demanded disagreeably when I had pinched and slapped him awake.

47   "Come on, wake up."

48   "What for? Go 'way."

49   I was lost for a reasonable reply. I could not say, "I'm scared and I don't want to be alone," so I merely said, "I'm going out. If you want to come, come on."

50   The promise of adventure awoke him. "Going out now? Where to, Lizabeth? What you going to do?"

51   I was pulling my dress over my head. Until now I had not thought of going out. "Just come on," I replied tersely.

52   I was out the window and halfway down the road before Joey caught up with me.

NOTES

53   "Wait, Lizabeth, where you going?"

54   I was running as if the Furies were after me, as perhaps they were—running silently and furiously until I came to where I had half known I was headed: to Miss Lottie's yard.

55   The half-dawn light was more eerie than complete darkness, and in it the old house was like the ruin that my world had become—foul and crumbling, a grotesque caricature. It looked haunted, but I was not afraid, because I was haunted too.

56   "Lizabeth, you lost your mind?" panted Joey.

57   I had indeed lost my mind, for all the smoldering emotions of that summer swelled in me and burst—the great need for my mother who was never there, the hopelessness of our poverty and degradation, the bewilderment of being neither child nor woman and yet both at once, the fear unleashed by my father's tears. And these feelings combined in one great impulse toward destruction.

58   "Lizabeth!"

59   I leaped furiously into the mounds of marigolds and pulled madly, trampling and pulling and destroying the perfect yellow blooms. The fresh smell of early morning and of dew-soaked marigolds spurred me on as I went tearing and mangling and sobbing while Joey tugged my dress or my waist crying, "Lizabeth, stop, please stop!"

60   And then I was sitting in the ruined little garden among the uprooted and ruined flowers, crying and crying, and it was too late to undo what I had done. Joey was sitting beside me, silent and frightened, not knowing what to say. Then, "Lizabeth, look!'

61   I opened my swollen eyes and saw in front of me a pair of large, calloused feet; my gaze lifted to the swollen legs, the age-distorted body clad in a tight cotton nightdress, and then the shadowed Indian face surrounded by stubby white hair. And there was no rage in the face now, now that the garden was destroyed and there was nothing any longer to be protected.

62   "M-miss Lottie!" I scrambled to my feet and just stood there and stared at her, and that was the moment when childhood faded and womanhood began. That violent, crazy act was the last act of childhood. For as I gazed at the immobile face with the sad, weary eyes, I gazed upon a kind of reality which is hidden to childhood. The witch was no longer a witch but only a broken old woman who had dared to create beauty in the midst of ugliness and sterility. She had been born in squalor and lived in it all her life. Now at the end of that

Copyright © BookheadEd Learning, LLC

NOTES

life she had nothing except a falling down hut, a wrecked body, and John Burke, the mindless son of her passion. Whatever verve there was left in her, whatever was of love and beauty and joy that had not been squeezed out by life, had been there in the marigolds she had so tenderly cared for.

63 Of course I could not express the things that I knew about Miss Lottie as I stood there awkward and ashamed. The years have put words to the things I knew in that moment, and as I look back upon it, I know that that moment marked the end of innocence. Innocence involves an unseeing acceptance of things at face value, an ignorance of the area below the surface. In that humiliating moment I looked beyond myself and into the depths of another person. This was the beginning of **compassion**, and one cannot have both compassion and innocence.

64 The years have taken me worlds away from that time and that place, from the dust and squalor of our lives, and from the bright thing that I destroyed in a blind, childish striking out at God knows what. Miss Lottie died long ago and many years have passed since I last saw her hut, completely barren at last, for despite my wild contrition she never planted marigolds again. Yet, there are times when the image of those passionate yellow mounds returns with a painful poignancy. For one does not have to be ignorant and poor to find that his life is as barren as the dusty yards of our town. And I too have planted marigolds.

© 1994 by Eugenia Collier, Breeder and Other Stories. Reproduced by permission of Eugenia Collier. Originally published in the *Negro Digest,* November, 1969.

 THINK QUESTIONS

1. How do we know that Lizabeth is on the verge of becoming an adult? Refer to several details from the text.

2. Citing details from the text, how do you think Lizabeth's destruction of Miss Lottie's marigolds relates to her transition from adolescence to adulthood?

3. What does the narrator mean when she says, "... these days are ill-defined in my memory, running together and combining like a fresh watercolor painting left out in the rain"? What type of literary device is author using? Provide examples from the text to support your answer.

4. Use context to determine the meaning of the word **prosperity** as it is used in "Marigolds." Write your definition of *prosperity* and tell how you got it.

5. Remembering that the Latin root *mal* means "evil," and the suffix *-ious* means "full of," use the context clues provided in the passage to determine the meaning of **malicious**. Write your definition of *malicious* and tell how you got it.

CLOSE READ

Reread the short story "Marigolds." As you reread, complete the Focus Questions below. Then use your answers and annotations from the questions to help you complete the Writing Prompt.

 FOCUS QUESTIONS

1. As you reread "Marigolds," identify important details that reveal Lizabeth's character, especially from the middle to the end of the story. What makes her a complex character? Highlight textual evidence and make annotations to show how the details reveal Lizabeth's complexity.

2. One of the ways an author develops character is by describing how a character interacts with the setting. The narrator provides many details about the setting in the early part of the story. How does Lizabeth feel about her town? Highlight textual evidence and annotate to explain the effect the setting has on Lizabeth, and how Lizabeth interacts with the setting.

3. An author will sometimes use figurative language to develop a reader's understanding of a character and the setting. When Lizabeth begins to describe Miss Lottie's house in paragraph 18, she uses a simile, saying it "looks like a house a child might have constructed from cards." How do images like this help the reader understand Miss Lottie's situation? Highlight other descriptions of Miss Lottie and her house. Annotate to explain how these details help develop the ideas and advance the events in the story.

4. One way that authors develop complex characters is by showing how they interact with other characters. How does Lizabeth react when Joey suggests that they all go to Miss Lottie's house? How does Lizabeth feel later that afternoon as a result? Find evidence in the text to explain why Lizabeth does not join in the group's "merriment."

5. What in Lizabeth's life causes her to see Miss Lottie as an antagonist? Highlight textual evidence to help explain your ideas. How does Lizabeth deal with her rage against Miss Lottie? How does this action affect Lizabeth at the time and in the present? Identify details and explain how Lizabeth has changed since the story's beginning and the role empathy plays in how she changes. How do these elements help express the story's central idea, or theme?

WRITING PROMPT

How does Lizabeth's adolescence affect her decisions and actions in the story? Identify specific textual details, including key words and phrases, figurative language, and descriptions of the characters and setting, to discuss the changing character of Lizabeth. Which of Lizabeth's decisions and actions have the most significant impact on the plot? Which decisions and actions tell you the most about the theme of the story? Use a graphic organizer to organize the textual evidence you will use to form a response.

Please note that excerpts and passages in the StudySync® library and this workbook are intended as touchstones to generate interest in an author's work. The excerpts and passages do not substitute for the reading of entire texts, and StudySync® strongly recommends that students seek out and purchase the whole literary or informational work in order to experience it as the author intended. Links to online resellers are available in our digital library. In addition, complete works may be ordered through an authorized reseller by filling out and returning to StudySync® the order form enclosed in this workbook.

Reading & Writing Companion **15**

TO KILL A MOCKINGBIRD

FICTION

Harper Lee
1960

INTRODUCTION

studysync tv

Drawing from events in her own childhood, Harper Lee completed *To Kill A Mockingbird* just prior to the peak of the Civil Rights Movement. It created an immediate sensation, winning the Pulitzer Prize in 1961 and selling over fifteen million copies. Told through the eyes of a six-year old girl growing up in Alabama during the Great Depression, Lee's novel is renowned for its warmth and humor, despite dealing with the serious issue of racial injustice. In this excerpt, Scout, the narrator, learns a lesson about compassion.

"You never really understand a person until...you climb into his skin and walk around in it."

FIRST READ

Excerpt from Chapter 3

1 Walter looked as if he had been raised on fish food: his eyes, as blue as Dill Harris's, were red-rimmed and watery. There was no color in his face except at the tip of his nose, which was moistly pink. He fingered the straps of his overalls, nervously picking at the metal hooks.

2 Jem suddenly grinned at him. "Come on home to dinner with us, Walter," he said. "We'd be glad to have you."

3 Walter's face brightened, then darkened.

4 Jem said, "Our daddy's a friend of your daddy's. Scout here, she's crazy—she won't fight you any more."

5 "I wouldn't be too certain of that," I said. Jem's free dispensation of my pledge irked me, but precious noontime minutes were ticking away. "Yeah Walter, I won't jump on you again. Don't you like butterbeans? Our Cal's a real good cook."

6 Walter stood where he was, biting his lip. Jem and I gave up, and we were nearly to the Radley Place when Walter called, "Hey, I'm comin'!"

7 When Walter caught up with us, Jem made pleasant conversation with him. "A **hain't** lives there," he said cordially, pointing to the Radley house. "Ever hear about him, Walter?"

8 "Reckon I have," said Walter. "Almost died first year I come to school and et them pecans—folks say he pizened 'em and put 'em over on the school side of the fence."

NOTES

9   Jem seemed to have little fear of Boo Radley now that Walter and I walked beside him. Indeed, Jem grew boastful: "I went all the way up to the house once," he said to Walter.

10   "Anybody who went up to the house once oughta not to still run every time he passes it," I said to the clouds above.

11   "And who's runnin', Miss Priss?"

12   "You are, when ain't anybody with you."

13   By the time we reached our front steps Walter had forgotten he was a Cunningham. Jem ran to the kitchen and asked Calpurnia to set an extra plate, we had company.

     ...

14   After supper, Atticus sat down with the paper and called, "Scout, ready to read?" The Lord sent me more than I could bear, and I went to the front porch. Atticus followed me.

15   "Something wrong, Scout?"

16   I told Atticus I didn't feel very well and didn't think I'd go to school any more if it was all right with him.

17   Atticus sat down in the swing and crossed his legs. His fingers wandered to his watchpocket; he said that was the only way he could think. He waited in **amiable** silence, and I sought to reinforce my position: "You never went to school and you do all right, so I'll just stay home too. You can teach me like Granddaddy taught you 'n' Uncle Jack."

18   "No I can't," said Atticus. "I have to make a living. Besides, they'd put me in jail if I kept you at home—dose of **magnesia** for you tonight and school tomorrow."

19   "I'm feeling all right, really."

20   "Thought so. Now what's the matter?"

21   Bit by bit, I told him the day's misfortunes. "—and she said you taught me all wrong, so we can't ever read any more, ever. Please don't send me back, please sir."

22   Atticus stood up and walked to the end of the porch. When he completed his examination of the **wisteria** vine he strolled back to me.

NOTES

23   "First of all," he said, "if you can learn a simple trick, Scout, you'll get along a lot better with all kinds of folks. You never really understand a person until you consider things from his point of view—"

24   "Sir?"

25   "—until you climb into his skin and walk around in it."

Excerpt from Chapter 15

26   I looked around the crowd. It was a summer's night, but the men were dressed, most of them, in overalls and denim shirts buttoned up to the collars. I thought they must be cold-natured, as their sleeves were unrolled and buttoned at the cuffs. Some wore hats pulled firmly down over their ears. They were sullen-looking, sleepy-eyed men who seemed unused to late hours. I sought once more for a familiar face, and at the center of the semi-circle I found one.

27   "Hey, Mr. Cunningham."

28   The man did not hear me, it seemed.

29   "Hey, Mr. Cunningham. How's your **entailment** getting' along?"

30   Mr. Walter Cunningham's legal affairs were well known to me; Atticus had once described them at length. The big man blinked and hooked his thumbs in his overall straps. He seemed uncomfortable; he cleared his throat and looked away. My friendly overture had fallen flat.

31   Mr. Cunningham wore no hat, and the top half of his forehead was white in contrast to his sunscorched face, which led me to believe that he wore one most days. He shifted his feet, clad in heavy work shoes.

32   "Don't you remember me, Mr. Cunningham? I'm Jean Louise Finch. You brought us some hickory nuts one time, remember?" I began to sense the futility one feels when unacknowledged by a chance acquaintance.

33   "I go to school with Walter," I began again. "He's your boy, ain't he? Ain't he, sir?"

34   Mr. Cunningham was moved to a faint nod. He did know me, after all.

35   "He's in my grade," I said, "and he does right well. He's a good boy," I added, "a real nice boy. We brought him home for dinner one time. Maybe he told you about me, I beat him up one time but he was real nice about it. Tell him hey for me, won't you?"

NOTES

36 Atticus had said it was the polite thing to talk to people about what they were interested in, not about what you were interested in. Mr. Cunningham displayed no interest in his son, so I tackled his entailment once more in a last-ditch effort to make him feel at home.

37 "Entailments are bad," I was advising him, when I slowly awoke to the fact that I was addressing the entire aggregation. The men were all looking at me, some had their mouths half-open. Atticus had stopped poking at Jem: they were standing together beside Dill. Their attention amounted to fascination. Atticus's mouth, even, was half-open, an attitude he had once described as uncouth. Our eyes met and he shut it.

38 "Well, Atticus, I was just sayin' to Mr. Cunningham that entailments are bad an' all that, but you said not to worry, it takes a long time sometimes . . . that you all'd ride it out together . . ." I was slowly drying up, wondering what idiocy I had committed. Entailments seemed all right enough for livingroom talk.

39 I began to feel sweat gathering at the edges of my hair; I could stand anything but a bunch of people looking at me. They were quite still.

40 "What's the matter?" I asked.

41 Atticus said nothing. I looked around and up at Mr. Cunningham, whose face was equally impassive. Then he did a peculiar thing. He squatted down and took me by both shoulders.

42 "I'll tell him you said hey, little lady," he said.

43 Then he straightened up and waved a big paw. "Let's clear out," he called. "Let's get going, boys."

44 As they had come, in ones and twos the men shuffled back to their ramshackle cars. Doors slammed, engines coughed, and they were gone.

Excerpted from *To Kill a Mockingbird* by Harper Lee, published by Grand Central Publishing.

THINK QUESTIONS

1. Walter speaks in a Southern dialect that reveals not only where he grew up but other things about his character. Cite an example of Walter's dialect and explain what it tells about his character.

2. Reread the scene when Atticus asks Scout to read. Write a few sentences describing Scout's and Atticus's relationship. Cite details from the text to support your answer.

3. Citing details from the text, write a brief explanation of why Scout is successful in "breaking the spell" in front of the jailhouse.

4. Remembering that the Latin root *amicus* means "friend," use your knowledge of other sentence parts and context clues provided in the passage to determine the meaning of the word **amiable**.

5. What context clues help you determine the meaning of **magnesia** as it is used in the passage? Write your definition of *magnesia* and explain which context clues helped you determine its meaning.

Please note that excerpts and passages in the StudySync® library and this workbook are intended as touchstones to generate interest in an author's work. The excerpts and passages do not substitute for the reading of entire texts, and StudySync® strongly recommends that students seek out and purchase the whole literary or informational work in order to experience it as the author intended. Links to online resellers are available in our digital library. In addition, complete works may be ordered through an authorized reseller by filling out and returning to StudySync® the order form enclosed in this workbook.

Reading & Writing Companion   21

CLOSE READ

Reread the excerpts from *To Kill a Mockingbird*. As you reread, complete the Focus Questions below. Then use your answers and annotations from the questions to help you complete the Writing Prompt.

FOCUS QUESTIONS

1. In paragraphs 1–5 of the excerpt from chapter 3, what can you infer about Jem and Scout's relationship? What is Scout's reaction to Jem's behavior? Highlight textual evidence and make annotations to support your analysis of the relationship between these two characters.

2. Authors can develop characters through dialogue—the way they speak to other characters. How is the language Jem, Scout, and Walter use similar? How does Walter speak differently than Jem and Scout speak? How does dialect help develop the characters and enhance the story? Cite textual evidence to support your analysis.

3. Inferences based on textual evidence can support an interpretation or analysis as powerfully as evidence that is explicitly stated. What can you infer about how well or poorly Atticus understands Scout from his reaction to her request not to be sent to school the next day? What can you infer about their relationship as a result of this moment? Highlight your evidence and annotate to explain your answer.

4. When Scout attempts to engage Mr. Cunningham in conversation, what can you infer about her? Highlight textual evidence to show how this gesture connects to Atticus's advice about dealing with others. How does Scout feel about her attempts at conversation with Mr. Cunningham? Cite textual evidence to explain.

5. Sometimes you must make an inference about the meaning of the text from a single statement or action of one of the characters. Understanding why a character says something or does something should be evaluated in light of the context of the situation and the motivations of the character. In paragraph 17 of the excerpt from chapter 15, Mr. Cunningham says to Scout, "I'll tell him you said hey, little lady." What can you infer about Mr. Cunningham based on this dialogue? What subsequent plot event offers explicit evidence of your inference about the meaning of Mr. Cunningham's statement?

6. Examine the role empathy plays in each of these excerpts. How does Atticus try to instill the idea of empathy in Scout? How do other characters display, or try to display, empathy? Highlight evidence from the text to support your explanation.

WRITING PROMPT

In Chapter 15 of *To Kill a Mockingbird*, lawyer Atticus Finch is at a jailhouse protecting his client, Tom Robinson, a black man accused of raping a white woman in their Alabama town, from a lynch mob. In at least 200 words, explain how Scout's actions dispel the tension of the situation. How do the events that unfold in this scene relate to the theme of compassion developed in other sections of the excerpted novel? Cite textual evidence to support your inferences and analysis.

THE JUNGLE

FICTION

Upton Sinclair
1906

INTRODUCTION

For seven weeks, Upton Sinclair worked side-by-side with new immigrants in Chicago's meatpacking district to research his groundbreaking book, *The Jungle*. Considered a cornerstone of Marxist literature, his searing exposé of the dismal conditions in factories and the horrors of the industry itself led Theodore Roosevelt to call him a muckracker, but eventually paved the way to the passage of The Meat Inspection Act and The Pure Food and Drug Act of 1906. In this passage, new workers get their first taste of Chicago and the stockyards.

"They were tied to the great packing machine, and tied to it for life."

 ## FIRST READ

NOTES

Excerpt from Chapter 2

1   It was in the **stockyards** that Jonas' friend had gotten rich, and so to Chicago the party was bound. They knew that one word, Chicago and that was all they needed to know, at least, until they reached the city. Then, tumbled out of the cars without ceremony, they were no better off than before; they stood staring down the vista of Dearborn Street, with its big black buildings towering in the distance, unable to realize that they had arrived, and why, when they said "Chicago," people no longer pointed in some direction, but instead looked **perplexed**, or laughed, or went on without paying any attention. They were pitiable in their helplessness; above all things they stood in deadly terror of any sort of person in official uniform, and so whenever they saw a policeman they would cross the street and hurry by. For the whole of the first day they wandered about in the midst of deafening confusion, utterly lost; and it was only at night that, cowering in the doorway of a house, they were finally discovered and taken by a policeman to the station. In the morning an interpreter was found, and they were taken and put upon a car, and taught a new word—"stockyards." Their delight at discovering that they were to get out of this adventure without losing another share of their possessions it would not be possible to describe.

2   They sat and stared out of the window. They were on a street which seemed to run on forever, mile after mile—thirty-four of them, if they had known it— and each side of it one uninterrupted row of wretched little two-story frame buildings. Down every side street they could see, it was the same—never a hill and never a hollow, but always the same endless vista of ugly and dirty little wooden buildings. Here and there would be a bridge crossing a filthy creek, with hard-baked mud shores and dingy sheds and docks along it; here and there would be a railroad crossing, with a tangle of switches, and locomotives puffing, and rattling freight cars filing by; here and there would

be a great factory, a dingy building with innumerable windows in it, and immense volumes of smoke pouring from the chimneys, darkening the air above and making filthy the earth beneath. But after each of these interruptions, the **desolate** procession would begin again—the procession of dreary little buildings.

3   A full hour before the party reached the city they had begun to note the perplexing changes in the atmosphere. It grew darker all the time, and upon the earth the grass seemed to grow less green. Every minute, as the train sped on, the colors of things became dingier; the fields were grown parched and yellow, the landscape hideous and bare. And along with the thickening smoke they began to notice another circumstance, a strange, pungent odor. They were not sure that it was unpleasant, this odor; some might have called it sickening, but their taste in odors was not developed, and they were only sure that it was curious. Now, sitting in the trolley car, they realized that they were on their way to the home of it—that they had traveled all the way from Lithuania to it. It was now no longer something far off and faint, that you caught in whiffs; you could literally taste it, as well as smell it—you could take hold of it, almost, and examine it at your leisure. They were divided in their opinions about it. It was an elemental odor, raw and crude; it was rich, almost rancid, sensual, and strong. There were some who drank it in as if it were an intoxicant; there were others who put their handkerchiefs to their faces. The new emigrants were still tasting it, lost in wonder, when suddenly the car came to a halt, and the door was flung open, and a voice shouted— "Stockyards!"

Excerpt from Chapter 10

4   In the spring there were cold rains, that turned the streets into canals and bogs; the mud would be so deep that wagons would sink up to the hubs, so that half a dozen horses could not move them. Then, of course, it was impossible for any one to get to work with dry feet; and this was bad for men that were poorly clad and shod, and still worse for women and children. Later came midsummer, with the stifling heat, when the dingy killing beds of Durham's became a very purgatory; one time, in a single day, three men fell dead from sunstroke. All day long the rivers of hot blood poured forth, until, with the sun beating down, and the air motionless, the stench was enough to knock a man over; all the old smells of a generation would be drawn out by this heat—for there was never any washing of the walls and rafters and pillars, and they were caked with the filth of a lifetime. The men who worked on the killing beds would come to reek with foulness, so that you could smell one of them fifty feet away; there was simply no such thing as keeping decent, the most careful man gave it up in the end, and **wallowed** in uncleanness. There was not even a place where a man could wash his hands, and the men ate as much raw blood as food at dinnertime. When they were at work they could

not even wipe off their faces—they were as helpless as newly born babes in that respect; and it may seem like a small matter, but when the sweat began to run down their necks and tickle them, or a fly to bother them, it was a torture like being burned alive. Whether it was the slaughterhouses or the dumps that were responsible, one could not say, but with the hot weather there descended upon Packingtown a veritable Egyptian plague of flies; there could be no describing this—the houses would be black with them. There was no escaping; you might provide all your doors and windows with screens, but their buzzing outside would be like the swarming of bees, and whenever you opened the door they would rush in as if a storm of wind were driving them.

5   Perhaps the summertime suggests to you thoughts of the country, visions of green fields and mountains and sparkling lakes. It had no such suggestion for the people in the yards. The great packing machine ground on **remorselessly**, without thinking of green fields; and the men and women and children who were part of it never saw any green thing, not even a flower. Four or five miles to the east of them lay the blue waters of Lake Michigan; but for all the good it did them it might have been as far away as the Pacific Ocean. They had only Sundays, and then they were too tired to walk. They were tied to the great packing machine, and tied to it for life. The managers and superintendents and clerks of Packingtown were all recruited from another class, and never from the workers; they scorned the workers, the very meanest of them. A poor devil of a bookkeeper who had been working in Durham's for twenty years at a salary of six dollars a week, and might work there for twenty more and do no better, would yet consider himself a gentleman, as far removed as the poles from the most skilled worker on the killing beds; he would dress differently, and live in another part of the town, and come to work at a different hour of the day, and in every way make sure that he never rubbed elbows with a laboring man. Perhaps this was due to the repulsiveness of the work; at any rate, the people who worked with their hands were a class apart, and were made to feel it.

THINK QUESTIONS

1. How do we know that "the party" referred to in the opening sentence of the first paragraph has just arrived from another country and cannot speak English? Cite evidence from the text in your answer.

2. The author describes the scene the party sees out the window as it travels to the stockyards in a car. Citing details from the text, what does the landscape reveal about the living conditions of many people who live in and around Chicago?

3. What does the author mean when he describes the "great packing machine" at the beginning of the last paragraph? What type of literary device is the author using, and what does it add to the tone of the selection, or the attitude the author has toward a subject and his or her audience? Cite textual evidence in your response.

4. Use context to determine the meaning of the word **perplexed** in the first paragraph of Chapter 2 of *The Jungle*.

5. The word **remorselessly** is an adverb. The noun *remorse*, which means a "gnawing" feeling of guilt, comes from the Latin root *remordere*, meaning "to bite again". The suffix *-less* means "without." Using this knowledge, what does the adverb *remorselessly* mean?

CLOSE READ

Reread the excerpts from *The Jungle*. As you reread, complete the Focus Questions below. Then use your answers and annotations from the questions to help you complete the Writing Prompt.

FOCUS QUESTIONS

1. As you reread the excerpt of *The Jungle*, keep in mind that the meat-packing industry the narrator describes did not have the regulations that are in place today. The author uses descriptive details to help the reader visualize the horrors of factory life and the challenges the immigrant workers faced. Provide textual details to show how the party of Lithuanians reacted to the conditions at the factory.

2. Highlight three or four images that stand out for you in the excerpt. How might these images be symbolic, or serve to stand for larger ideas or concepts? Annotate to explain your ideas.

3. How does the narrator function as a tool to communicate the author's political message about this industry? Highlight textual details, including descriptions of the city, the factories, and the working conditions. Add an annotation that states the theme in a complete sentence, based on the text evidence you have highlighted.

4. Highlight one example from the text of figurative language and one example of language that has positive connotations. Identify your examples and explain how they help the reader better understand the conditions the factory workers endured at that time.

5. Think about the excerpt's narration, details, and theme. Which details does the author use to elicit compassion and empathy from you as a reader? Highlight evidence from the text that will help support your view.

WRITING PROMPT

Reread the excerpt from *The Jungle*, focusing on the last section, where immigrants work in the stockyards. Imagine that you are an immigrant worker at the end of your Sunday off, and you are preparing to return to work on Monday morning. Write a first-person narrative of at least 300 words explaining how you prepare for another week at the stockyard and the meat-packing plant. Use descriptive details to help you develop your narrative and allow the reader to visualize the scene. When you have finished, state the theme of your narrative in one sentence and list five details that show how you developed your theme.

LIFT EVERY VOICE AND SING

POETRY
James Weldon Johnson
1900

INTRODUCTION

James Weldon Johnson was an American poet and academic, as well as an early civil rights activist. He originally wrote "Lift Every Voice and Sing"—which celebrated the gains of African-Americans since the Civil War and offered hope for the future—as a poem. His brother set it to music, and before long it was known as the "Black National Anthem." By the 1920's, the song was pasted in the hymnals of black churches across the country.

"We have come over a way that with tears has been watered..."

FIRST READ

NOTES

1   Lift every voice and sing,
2   Till earth and heaven ring,
3   Ring with the harmonies of Liberty,
4   Let our rejoicing rise
5   High as the list'ning skies,
6   Let it **resound** loud as the rolling sea.
7   Sing a song full of the faith that the dark past has taught us
8   Sing a song full of the hope that the present has brought us
9   Facing the rising sun of our new day begun,
10 Let us march on till victory is won.

11 Stony the road we **trod**
12 Bitter the **chast'ning** rod,
13 Felt in the days when hope unborn had died;
14 Yet with a steady beat
15 Have not our weary feet
16 Come to the place for which our fathers sighed?
17 We have come over a way that with tears has been watered
18 We have come, treading our path thro' the blood of the **slaughtered**,
19 Out from the gloomy past, till now we stand at last
20 Where the white gleam of our bright star is cast.

21 God of our weary years,
22 God of our silent tears,
23 Thou who hast brought us thus far on the way;
24 Thou who hast by Thy might,
25 Led us into the light, Keep us forever in the path, we pray.
26 Lest our feet stray from the places, our God, where we meet Thee,
27 Lest, our hearts drunk with the wine of the world, we forget Thee;
28 Shadowed beneath Thy hand, may we forever stand,
29 True to our God, true to our **native** land.

THINK QUESTIONS

1. Reread the first section of the poem. What do you think the poem is celebrating? What is the "new day" the poet refers to? Cite text evidence to support your inference.

2. Reread the second section of the poem. Using textual evidence to support your answer, what can you infer about the journey forward from the "dark past"?

3. How can you infer that the people mentioned in the poem have believed in God for a long time? Use text evidence to support your answer.

4. Use context clues to determine the meaning of the word **chastening** as it is used in the selection. Write your definition of *chastening* and explain how you got it.

5. Remember that you can use what you know about one word to help you understand other words in the same word family. For example, the Latin prefix *re-* means "again," and you know that the base word *sound* refers to something audible, something that you can hear. What can you infer is the meaning of the word **resounding**?

CLOSE READ

Reread the poem "Lift Every Voice and Sing." As you reread, complete the Focus Questions below. Then use your answers and annotations from the questions to help you complete the Writing Prompt.

FOCUS QUESTIONS

1. As you reread the text of "Lift Every Voice and Sing," think about the subject of the poem. How does the language change and how does that change impact the tone over the course of the poem? Compare the tone of the first verse to the tone of the second verse. Remember that word choice, sound devices, the song's subject, and the poet's point of view all contribute to the tone. Highlight evidence from the text to support your answer.

2. A writer uses figurative language to appeal to readers' and listeners' senses and create emotional impact. In the second verse, the poet writes, "Where the white gleam of our bright star is cast." What kind of figurative language is being used? What meaning comes from this image? Look for other examples of figurative language, and think about how the language affects the meaning.

3. In the third and final verse, the writer includes the words *Thy, Thou,* and *Thee* for the first time. How would you describe effect of these words on the tone in the final verse? What other words or phrases influence the tone? Highlight textual evidence and annotate to explain your ideas. How does this verse relate to the rest of the poem?

4. What does the poet mean by the phrase "drunk with the wine of the world" in the third verse? Explain how the phrase is an example of figurative language. What is the poet calling on God's help to avoid? Look at the context of the poem to help you explain its meaning. Cite text evidence in your explanation.

5. In the second verse, the poet writes, "Bitter the chast'ning rod." Look at the context of the word *chast'ning,* (a short form of *chastening*) and the use of the word *rod*. How does the context of the line in which the word appears help you understand its meaning? What does the poet mean by a *chast'ning rod*? How does this choice of words in the poem help develop a reader or listener's empathy for the people being described?

WRITING PROMPT

Think about the title of the poem "Lift Every Voice and Sing" by James Weldon Johnson. What is the difference between "Lift Every Voice and Sing" and, for example, "Lift Your Voice and Sing?" How does that affect the appeal of the poem? How does the writer use figurative language and tone to explore his subject and create meaning? Include textual evidence to explain your ideas.

Please note that excerpts and passages in the StudySync® library and this workbook are intended as touchstones to generate interest in an author's work. The excerpts and passages do not substitute for the reading of entire texts, and StudySync® strongly recommends that students seek out and purchase the whole literary or informational work in order to experience it as the author intended. Links to online resellers are available in our digital library. In addition, complete works may be ordered through an authorized reseller by filling out and returning to StudySync® the order form enclosed in this workbook.

Reading & Writing Companion **33**

STATEMENT ON
THE ASSASSINATION OF
MARTIN LUTHER
KING, JR.

NON-FICTION
Robert F. Kennedy
1968

INTRODUCTION

studysync⒱

On April 4, 1968, in the midst of campaigning to become President of the
United States, Senator Robert F. Kennedy learned of the assassination of
Martin Luther King, Jr. Upon arriving in Indianapolis for a campaign rally,
instead of delivering a rousing political speech, Kennedy made some brief but
powerful remarks about King's death. During an extremely tense period in
American history, Kennedy's speech stands out as an eloquent and passionate

"...what we need in the United States is not violence and lawlessness, but is love..."

FIRST READ

NOTES

1 Ladies and Gentlemen,

2 I'm only going to talk to you just for a minute or so this evening, because I have—some very sad news for all of you—Could you lower those signs, please?—I have some very sad news for all of you, and, I think, sad news for all of our fellow citizens, and people who love peace all over the world; and that is that Martin Luther King was shot and was killed tonight in Memphis, Tennessee.

3 Martin Luther King **dedicated** his life to love and to justice between fellow human beings. He died in the cause of that effort. In this difficult day, in this difficult time for the United States, it's perhaps well to ask what kind of a nation we are and what direction we want to move in. For those of you who are black—considering the evidence evidently is that there were white people who were responsible—you can be filled with bitterness, and with hatred, and a desire for revenge.

4 We can move in that direction as a country, in greater **polarization**—black people amongst blacks, and white amongst whites, filled with hatred toward one another. Or we can make an effort, as Martin Luther King did, to understand, and to comprehend, and replace that violence, that stain of bloodshed that has spread across our land, with an effort to understand, compassion, and love.

5 For those of you who are black and are tempted to fill with—be filled with hatred and mistrust of the injustice of such an act, against all white people, I would only say that I can also feel in my own heart the same kind of feeling. I had a member of my family killed, but he was killed by a white man.

6 But we have to make an effort in the United States. We have to make an effort to understand, to get beyond, or go beyond these rather difficult times.

7   My favorite poem, my—my favorite poet was Aeschylus. And he once wrote:

8   *Even in our sleep, pain which cannot forget*
    falls drop by drop upon the heart,
    until, in our own despair,
    against our will,
    comes wisdom
    through the awful grace of God.

9   What we need in the United States is not division; what we need in the United States is not hatred; what we need in the United States is not violence and lawlessness, but is love, and wisdom, and compassion toward one another, and a feeling of justice toward those who still suffer within our country, whether they be white or whether they be black.

10 So I ask you tonight to return home, to say a prayer for the family of Martin Luther King—yeah, it's true—but more importantly to say a prayer for our own country, which all of us love—a prayer for understanding and that compassion of which I spoke.

11 We can do well in this country. We will have difficult times. We've had difficult times in the past, but we—and we will have difficult times in the future. It is not the end of violence; it is not the end of lawlessness; and it's not the end of **disorder**.

12 But the vast majority of white people and the vast majority of black people in this country want to live together, want to improve the quality of our life, and want justice for all human beings that **abide** in our land.

13 And let's dedicate ourselves to what the Greeks wrote so many years ago: to tame the **savageness** of man and make gentle the life of this world. Let us dedicate ourselves to that, and say a prayer for our country and for our people.

14 Thank you very much.

THINK QUESTIONS

1. In the first paragraph of his speech, Kennedy mentions three groups of people that he believes will be saddened by the news of King's assassination. One of them is the audience of listeners in front of him. Who are the other two groups? Support your answer with textual evidence.

2. In the first sentence of the second paragraph, Kennedy briefly explains what made King such an extraordinary figure. What does Kennedy state explicitly, and what can you infer about Kennedy's feelings for Martin Luther King, Jr. from reading his speech? Use details from the text to support your answer.

3. In the third and the fifth paragraphs, Kennedy repeats that Americans have to "make an effort." What does he want Americans to make an effort to do? Use textual evidence to support your answer.

4. Use context clues to determine the meaning of the word **polarization** as it is used in this speech. Write your definition here and explain how you used the context clues to figure out its meaning.

5. The suffix -*ness* added to a word turns it into a noun. Knowing this, use the context clues provided in the passage to determine the meaning of **savageness**. Write your definition of *savageness* and explain how you used the context clues to figure out its meaning.

CLOSE READ

Reread the text "Statement on the Assassination of Martin Luther King, Jr." As you reread, complete the Focus Questions below. Then use your answers and annotations from the questions to help you complete the Writing Prompt.

FOCUS QUESTIONS

1. As you reread the text "Statement on the Assassination of Martin Luther King, Jr.," remember that Kennedy gave this speech during a difficult time in history, just as the country lost one of the most influential leaders of the Civil Rights Movement in an act of violence and hatred. In paragraphs 1 and 2, how does Kennedy reveal his point of view about Martin Luther King, Jr. to the audience? Highlight evidence of his point of view in the text and make annotations to explain how his point of view is revealed in the sentences you've chosen.

2. In paragraph 2, Kennedy introduces his argument with a specific claim. Highlight the claim he makes in this paragraph. Also highlight Kennedy's reasons for suggesting that some people might be tempted to take revenge in response to King's death. Do his reasons for this assumption seem valid? Make annotations to explain why or why not.

3. Kennedy uses the rhetorical devices of repetition and figurative language in paragraph 3. What is he trying to emphasize through their use? Highlight Kennedy's rhetoric and make annotations to explain how his language reveals and communicates his purpose and point of view.

4. Kennedy states that he's only going to speak for a few minutes. He later asks his audience to go home and say two prayers, and he repeats the recommendation to say a prayer in his last paragraph. What is his purpose in recommending prayer? Highlight the specific prayers he suggests. Make annotations to explain why you think he suggests prayer. Support your answer with textual evidence.

5. What types of evidence does Kennedy use to elicit empathy from the audience? Do you think the evidence is relevant and sufficient to support Kennedy's specific claims about the pain of loss? Highlight and summarize four instances in which Kennedy supports his claims with evidence. Make annotations to identify the type of evidence. Evaluate whether Kennedy's reasoning based on the evidence elicits empathy from the reader.

WRITING PROMPT

How effectively does Robert F. Kennedy develop his argument in "Statement on the Assassination of Martin Luther King, Jr."? Does he support his claims with strong evidence? Does his rhetoric successfully communicate his purpose and point of view? Use your understanding of argument, claim, persuasion, author's purpose, and author's point of view to summarize Kennedy's argument and to evaluate whether it is persuasive. Support your writing with evidence from the text.

THE HARVEST GYPSIES

NON-FICTION
John Steinbeck
1936

WHAT HURTS BUSINESS HURTS ME

NATION'S BUSINESS
MAGAZINE

INTRODUCTION

n 1936, John Steinbeck wrote a series of seven articles, "The Harvest Gypsies," for a San Francisco newspaper. The series was later compiled into a short book that reported on the situation of unemployed migrants who were flooding into California, looking for jobs as agricultural workers. This excerpt from the second article in the series details the wretched living conditions that families were forced

"Dignity is all gone, and spirit has turned to sullen anger before it dies."

FIRST READ

Excerpt from Article II

1   This is a family of six; a man, his wife and four children. They live in a tent the color of the ground. Rot has set in on the canvas so that the flaps and the sides hang in tatters and are held together with bits of rusty baling wire. There is one bed in the family and that is a big **tick** lying on the ground inside the tent.

2   They have one quilt and a piece of canvas for bedding. The sleeping arrangement is clever. Mother and father lie down together and two children lie between them. Then, heading the other way; the other two children lie, the littler ones. If the mother and father sleep with their legs spread wide, there is room for the legs of the children.

3   There is more filth here. The tent is full of flies clinging to the apple box that is the dinner table, buzzing about the foul clothes of the children, particularly the baby; who has not been bathed nor cleaned for several days.

4   This family has been on the road longer than the builder of the paper house. There is no toilet here, but there is a clump of willows nearby where human feces lie exposed to the flies—the same flies that are in the tent.

5   Two weeks ago there was another child, a four year old boy. For a few weeks they had noticed that he was kind of lackadaisical, that his eyes had been feverish.

6   They had given him the best place in the bed, between father and mother. But one night he went into convulsions and died, and the next morning the coroner's wagon took him away. It was one step down.

7   They know pretty well that it was a diet of fresh fruit, beans and little else that caused his death. He had no milk for months. With this death there came a

NOTES

change of mind in his family. The father and mother now feel that paralyzed dullness with which the mind protects itself against too much sorrow and too much pain.

8   And this father will not be able to make a maximum of four hundred dollars a year any more because he is no longer alert; he isn't quick at piece-work, and he is not able to fight clear of the dullness that has settled on him. His spirit is losing **caste** rapidly.

9   The dullness shows in the faces of this family, and in addition there is a **sullenness** that makes them **taciturn**. Sometimes they still start the older children off to school, but the ragged little things will not go; they hide in ditches or wander off by themselves until it is time to go back to the tent, because they are scorned in the school.

10 The better-dressed children shout and jeer, the teachers are quite often impatient with these additions to their duties, and the parents of the "nice" children do not want to have disease carriers in the schools.

11 The father of this family once had a little grocery store and his family lived in back of it so that even the children could wait on the counter. When the drought set in there was no trade for the store any more.

12 This is the middle class of the squatters' camp. In a few months this family will slip down to the lower class.

13 Dignity is all gone, and spirit has turned to sullen anger before it dies.

14 The next door neighbor family of man, wife and three children of from three to nine years of age, have built a house by driving willow branches into the ground and wattling weeds, tin, old paper and strips of carpet against them.

15 A few branches are placed over the top to keep out the noonday sun. It would not turn water at all. There is no bed.

16 Somewhere the family has found a big piece of old carpet. It is on the ground. To go to bed the members of the family lie on the ground and fold the carpet up over them.

17 The three year old child has a gunny sack tied about his middle for clothing. He has the swollen belly caused by **malnutrition**.

18 He sits on the ground in the sun in front of the house, and the little black fruit flies buzz in circles and land on his closed eyes and crawl up his nose until he weakly brushes them away.

19   They try to get at the mucous in the eye-corners. This child seems to have the reactions of a baby much younger. The first year he had a little milk, but he has had none since.

20   He will die in a very short time. The older children may survive. Four nights ago the mother had a baby in the tent, on the dirty carpet. It was born dead, which was just as well because she could not have fed it at the breast; her own diet will not produce milk.

21   After it was born and she had seen that it was dead, the mother rolled over and lay still for two days. She is up today, tottering around. The last baby, born less than a year ago, lived a week. This woman's eyes have the glazed, far-away look of a sleep walker's eyes.

22   She does not wash clothes any more. The drive that makes for cleanliness has been drained out of her and she hasn't the energy. The husband was a **share-cropper** once, but he couldn't make it go. Now he has lost even the desire to talk.

23   He will not look directly at you for that requires will, and will needs strength. He is a bad field worker for the same reason. It takes him a long time to make up his mind, so he is always late in moving and late in arriving in the fields. His top wage, when he can find work now; which isn't often, is a dollar a day.

Excerpted from *The Harvest Gypsies* by John Steinbeck, published by Heyday.

THINK QUESTIONS

1. Identify three details in the text that point to the fact that physical decay and hardship can lead to mental decay and despair. Support your answer with evidence from the text.

2. How does the treatment of the older children at school help you understand that adults can have as much difficulty showing compassion toward others as children do? Support your answer with evidence from the text.

3. The author, John Steinbeck, states that the first family he writes about is in the middle class squatter's camp, but that in a few months they "will slip down to the lower class." What information from the text does the author use to support his prediction? Explain your reasoning with textual evidence.

4. Use context to determine the meaning of the word **sullenness** as it is used in *The Harvest Gypsies*. Write your definition of *sullenness* and identify the context clues that helped you define it.

5. Remembering that the Latin prefix *mal-* means "bad," "harmful," or "ill," use the context clues provided in the passage to determine the meaning of **malnutrition**. Write your definition of *malnutrition*.

CLOSE READ

Reread the excerpt from *The Harvest Gypsies*. Then use your answers and annotations from the questions to help you complete the Writing Prompt.

FOCUS QUESTIONS

1. How does Steinbeck organize the information he reveals about the first family? How is the family introduced, what does Steinbeck describe first, and what connections does he draw between their living conditions and the state of their health? Cite textual evidence in your response.

2. In the sixth paragraph, Steinbeck writes that when the father and mother saw that their four-year-old boy had eyes that were "feverish," they gave him the best place in the bed. But one night he went into convulsions and died and "it was one step down." What does Steinbeck mean by this phrase? What comparisons can you make between the first and second families the author describes that explains what Steinbeck means when he talks about the middle and lower class of the squatter's camp, and why this tragic event is "one step down?" Support your answer with textual evidence.

3. Make connections between what happens to the boy in the "middle class" family and the events that occur as a result. Annotate examples in the text and identify any transition words or phrases that signal interactions between individuals and events.

4. In addition to the actual horror of physical death, Steinbeck also describes the stages a family goes through before reaching the lower class and compares it to a kind of death. Evaluate his claim that falling from reasonable prosperity and self-sufficiency into abject poverty is a kind of death. Highlight evidence from the text that supports this idea.

5. In *The Harvest Gypsies*, Steinbeck presents facts and information about a historical event in U.S. history, the plight of migrant workers in the 1930s. He does not embellish his tale with sensational descriptions of the conditions he found in the migrant camps. What effect does Steinbeck's straightforward, expository style have on the level of empathy readers feel for the people he describes? Highlight evidence from the text that will help support your ideas.

WRITING PROMPT

What basic argument does Steinbeck make about the plight of the families living in migrant camps? Referring to the text for specific details, write an essay of 300 words in which you delineate, or explain, and evaluate his argument. How is the argument shaped and refined over the course of the passage? Support your analysis with evidence from the text.

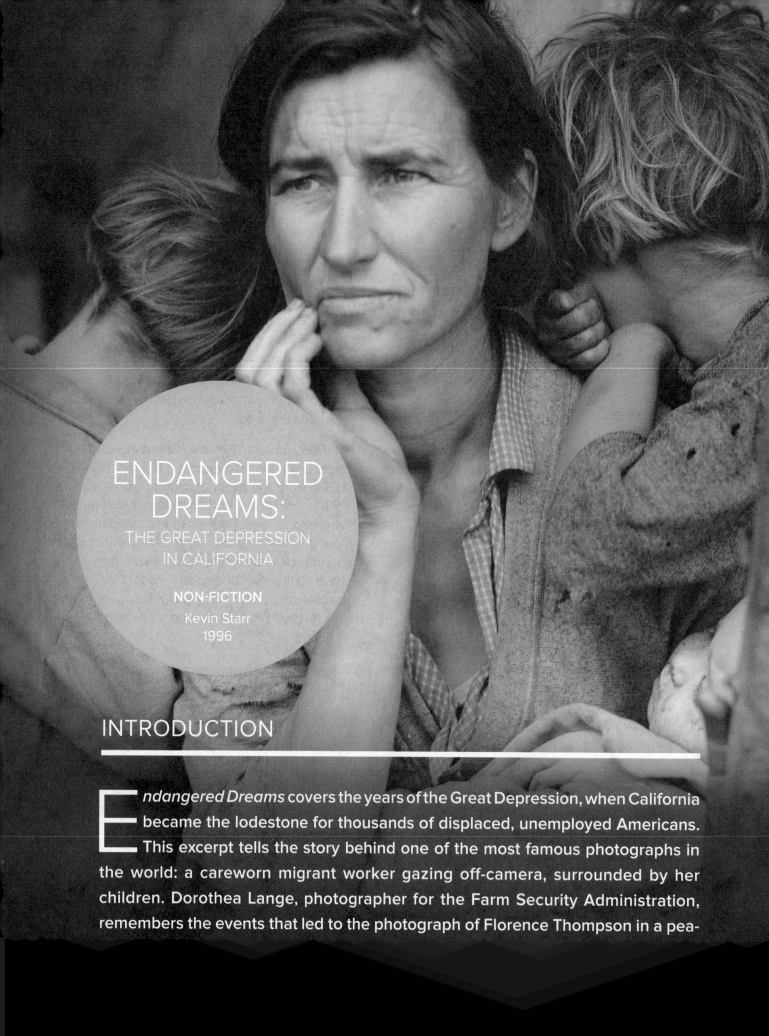

ENDANGERED DREAMS:

THE GREAT DEPRESSION IN CALIFORNIA

NON-FICTION
Kevin Starr
1996

INTRODUCTION

Endangered Dreams covers the years of the Great Depression, when California became the lodestone for thousands of displaced, unemployed Americans. This excerpt tells the story behind one of the most famous photographs in the world: a careworn migrant worker gazing off-camera, surrounded by her children. Dorothea Lange, photographer for the Farm Security Administration, remembers the events that led to the photograph of Florence Thompson in a pea-

"I saw and approached the hungry and desperate mother, as if drawn by a magnet."

 FIRST READ

 NOTES

1   Among the photographs Lange forwarded to Washington was one which soon achieved the **stature** of an American masterpiece. Subsequently entitled *Migrant Mother,* Lange's photograph has become not only the best-known image of the 270,000 plus **negatives** assembled by her Resettlement/Farm Security Administration team, but one of the most universally recognized and appreciated photographs of all time.

2   She almost missed taking it. Returning in March 1936 after a month in the field, Lange was heading north to San Francisco past Nipomo. On the side of the road, on a cold wet miserable day, she saw a sign that said "Pea Pickers Camp." She passed it. After all, at her side on the car seat rested a box containing rolls and packs of exposed film. Accompanied by the rhythmic hum of the windshield wipers, she debated over the next twenty miles the pros and cons of returning. In a sudden instinctive decision, she made a U-turn on the empty highway and returned to the pea pickers' camp. "I saw and approached the hungry and desperate mother, as if drawn by a magnet," she later recalled. "I do not remember how I explained my presence or my camera to her, but I do remember she asked me no questions. I made five **exposures**, working closer and closer from the same direction. I did not ask her name or her history. She told me her age, that she was thirty-two. She said that they had been living on frozen vegetables from surrounding fields, and birds that the children killed. She had just sold the tires from her car to buy food. There she sat in that lean-to tent with her children huddled around her, and seemed to know that my pictures might help her, and so she helped me. There was a sort of equality about it."

3   Some critics have made much of the fact that Lange did not learn the woman's name, which was Florence Thompson, taking this as proof of Lange's photographic **detachment**. In the woman and her three children, stranded in a roadside canvas lean-to, such critics suggest, Lange found a subject for her

NOTES

photographic art: a subject removed in time and circumstances from her prosperous clients in her previous practice; but she approached her nevertheless from a similarly detached **perspective.** The primary subject of *Migrant Mother,* from this perspective, is photography itself. Such a criticism ignores the fact that as soon as Lange returned to San Francisco and developed these Nipomo negatives (there were actually six, not five as she remembered), she rushed with them to George West at the San Francisco *News*, telling him that thousands of pea pickers in Nipomo were starving because of the frozen harvest. West got the story out in both the *News,* using two of Lange's photographs (but not *Migrant Mother*), and over the wires of the United Press. The federal government, meanwhile, rushed in twenty thousand pounds of food to feed the starving pea pickers.

Excerpted from *Endangered Dreams: The Great Depression in California* by Kevin Starr, published by Oxford University Press.

THINK QUESTIONS

1. Where did Lange find the woman who was the subject of *Migrant Mother*? Support your answer with textual evidence.

2. Why, according to Lange, did the woman cooperate fully without asking any questions? In which paragraph did you read this information? Support your answer with textual evidence.

3. Use textual evidence to explain why some critics have seen *Migrant Mother* as an example of Lange's photographic detachment. Give at least two reasons for the critics' theory.

4. Which words in the first sentence of the passage can be used as clues to the meaning of **stature**? Explain how you used them to figure out the definition of the word.

5. The word **detachment** in the third paragraph is a noun formed from the verb *detach*. In the same paragraph, the word *detached* is also formed from the verb *detach*. What do you think *detachment* means in the context of the paragraph?

CLOSE READ

Reread the excerpt from *Endangered Dreams.* As you reread, complete the Focus Questions below. Then use your answers and annotations from the questions to help you complete the Writing Prompt.

FOCUS QUESTIONS

1. The excerpt "Endangered Dreams" comes from a book with the same title. Which specific details in the excerpt fit the idea of dreams in danger? Highlight textual evidence to support your answer and write annotations to explain your choices.

2. Some critics view *Migrant Mother* as an example of Lange's photographic detachment. In the text, highlight two reasons someone might hold this opinion

3. Review each paragraph's central idea and key details. Ask yourself what these ideas and details explain, describe, and have in common. Notice how, together, they begin to develop and shape the central idea of the overall excerpt. Based on your analysis, write a sentence that states the central idea of the overall excerpt.

4. Write a five-sentence summary of the text. Include only the most important details in your summary. Do not include your opinions.

5. After closely examining the photograph *Migrant Mother,* write a list of at least five details you notice. Next to each detail, write a check mark if the detail is also mentioned in the text.

WRITING PROMPT

What have you learned about the migrant family shown in *Migrant Mother* from closely analyzing both the photograph itself and the text about the photograph? After considering the information, do you agree or disagree with the idea that Lange photographed the family from a detached perspective? Write a 300-word essay that argues for or against the idea that Lange's photograph shows a detached perspective. Use details from both mediums, photography and print, to support your argument.

Please note that excerpts and passages in the StudySync® library and this workbook are intended as touchstones to generate interest in an author's work. The excerpts and passages do not substitute for the reading of entire texts, and StudySync® strongly recommends that students seek out and purchase the whole literary or informational work in order to experience it as the author intended. Links to online resellers are available in our digital library. In addition, complete works may be ordered through an authorized reseller by filling out and returning to StudySync® the order form enclosed in this workbook.

Reading & Writing Companion   **49**

THE GRAPES OF WRATH

FICTION

John Steinbeck
1939

INTRODUCTION

studysync tv

American author John Steinbeck frequently featured downtrodden protagonists in his work, and his Pulitzer Prize-winning masterpiece, *The Grapes of Wrath,* was no exception. First published in 1939, the novel chronicles the fictional Joad family's difficult journey from Oklahoma's Dust Bowl to California during the Great Depression. The following excerpt, set in a typical roadside diner along Route 66, is an independent story, inserted into the midst of

"We got a thousan' miles to go, an' we don' know if we'll make it.

FIRST READ

NOTES

1   The man took off his dark, stained hat and stood with a curious **humility** in front of the screen. "Could you see your way to sell us a loaf of bread, ma'am?"

2   Mae said, "This ain't a grocery store. We got bread to make san'widges."

3   "I know, ma'am." His humility was **insistent**. "We need bread and there ain't nothin' for quite a piece, they say."

4   "'F we sell bread we gonna run out." Mae's tone was faltering.

5   "We're hungry," the man said.

6   "Whyn't you buy a san'widge? We got nice san'widges, hamburgs."

7   "We'd sure admire to do that, ma'am. But we can't. We got to make a dime do all of us." And he said embarrassedly, "We ain't got but a little."

8   Mae said, "You can't get no loaf a bread for a dime. We only got fifteen-cent loafs."

9   From behind her Al growled, "God Almighty, Mae, give 'em bread."

10 "We'll run out 'fore the bread truck comes."

11 "Run out then, goddamn it," said Al. He looked sullenly down at the potato salad he was mixing.

12 Mae shrugged her plump shoulders and looked to the truck drivers to show them what she was up against.

13 She held the screen door open and the man came in, bringing a smell of sweat with him. The boys edged behind him and they went immediately to

the candy case and stared in—not with craving or with hope or even with desire, but just with a kind of wonder that such things could be. They were alike in size and their faces were alike. One scratched his dusty ankle with the toe nails of his other foot. The other whispered some soft message and then they straightened their arms so that their clenched fists in the overall pockets showed through the thin blue cloth.

14   Mae opened a drawer and took out a long waxpaper-wrapped loaf. "This here is a fifteen-cent loaf."

15   The man put his hat back on his head. He answered with **inflexible** humility, "Won't you—can't you see your way to cut off ten cents' worth?"

16   Al said snarlingly, "Goddamn it, Mae. Give 'em the loaf."

17   The man turned toward Al. "No, we want ta buy ten cents' worth of it. We got it figgered awful close, mister, to get to California."

18   Mae said **resignedly**, "You can have this for ten cents."

19   "That'd be robbin' you, ma'am."

20   "Go ahead—Al says to take it." She pushed the waxpapered loaf across the counter. The man took a deep leather pouch from his rear pocket, untied the strings, and spread it open. It was heavy with silver and with greasy bills.

21   "May soun' funny to be so tight," he apologized. "We got a thousan' miles to go, an' we don' know if we'll make it."

22   He dug in the pouch with a forefinger, located a dime, and pinched in for it. When he put it down on the counter he had a penny with it. He was about to drop the penny back into the pouch when his eye fell on the boys frozen before the candy counter. He moved slowly down to them. He pointed in the case at big long sticks of striped peppermint.

23   "Is them penny candy, ma'am?"

24   Mae moved down and looked in. "Which ones?"

25   "There, them stripy ones."

26   The little boys raised their eyes to her face and they stopped breathing; their mouths were partly opened, their halfnaked bodies were rigid.

27   "Oh—them. Well, no—them's two for a penny."

28 "Well, gimme two then, ma'am." He placed the copper cent carefully on the counter. The boys **expelled** their held breath softly. Mae held the big sticks out.

Excerpted from *The Grapes of Wrath* by John Steinbeck, published by the Penguin Group.

 THINK QUESTIONS

1. Why does the man not use more money from his pouch to get more food that the family wants or needs? Use textual evidence to support your answer.

2. What does the children's reaction to the candy say about their experiences in life so far? How does this moment elicit the reader's empathy? Explain your answer with textual evidence.

3. The dialogue of the characters is written to show their dialect, or the particular way they pronounce words and use language based on their geographical location and other factors. How does the use of dialogue help the reader better understand the characters and the time in which they are living? Cite textual evidence from the passage to support your answer.

4. Use context to determine the meaning of the word **resignedly** as it is used in *The Grapes of Wrath* excerpt. Write your definition of *resignedly*.

5. Remembering that the prefix *in-* means "not" and the Latin root *flex* means "bend," use this information, along with clues from the text, to determine the meaning of the word **inflexible**. Write your definition of *inflexible* and explain how you got that definition.

Please note that excerpts and passages in the StudySync® library and this workbook are intended as stuchstones to generate interest in an author's work. The excerpts and passages do not substitute for the reading of entire texts, and StudySync® strongly recommends that students seek out and purchase the whole literary or informational work in order to experience it as the author intended. Links to online resellers are available in our digital library. In addition, complete works may be ordered through an authorized reseller by filling out and returning to StudySync® the order form enclosed in this workbook.

Reading & Writing Companion

53

CLOSE READ

Reread the excerpt from *The Grapes of Wrath*. As you reread, complete the Focus Questions below. Then use your answers and annotations from the questions to help you complete the Writing Prompt.

FOCUS QUESTIONS

1. As you reread the excerpt of *The Grapes of Wrath*, highlight descriptions and dialogue that make the characters and setting seem realistic. Who are the people who visit the diner, and how are they similar to and different from the workers there? Use textual evidence to support your ideas.

2. Think about other research you have done as well as other texts you have read in the unit, such as Steinbeck's magazine account of life during the Dust Bowl, *The Harvest Gypsies*, and Starr's *Endangered Dreams: The Great Depression in California*, which included information about one of Dorothea Lange's photographs of the time. What does Steinbeck's novel accomplish that is different from what an article or a photograph can do? Cite textual evidence to help explain your views.

3. What does the dialogue spoken by Al and Mae reveal about their characters? Do you think Mae changes as a result of this encounter with the man and his children? Highlight details and cite textual evidence to support your inference.

4. What central idea or theme is Steinbeck developing in this excerpt? Summarize the excerpt and explain, using textual evidence, what this small scene reveals about the problems of the migrant families during the Great Depression.

5. Why does the reader have empathy for the characters in the excerpt? Ask questions about their situation and why people would have sympathy for them, and then answer them using evidence from the text.

WRITING PROMPT

In *The Grapes of Wrath*, John Steinbeck tells a fictional story based on real events, the great migration of people from Oklahoma to California during the Dust Bowl that coincided with the Great Depression. Imagine you are a journalist sitting in the diner, and this scene unfolds before you. How would you write this same scene for a newspaper or radio story? Use the content of this excerpt to ask and answer questions about the scene and write a short informational article to explain how the Dust Bowl is affecting communities along Route 66. Finally, describe a photograph that you would like to see accompany this article. What moment would you like the photo to capture? Write a caption for the photo.

TUESDAY SIESTA

FICTION
Gabriel García Márquez
1962

INTRODUCTION

Gabriel García Márquez was a Colombian writer who earned international fame popularizing a literary style called magical realism. His most widely read work, the novel *One Hundred Years of Solitude*, has been translated into dozens of languages and has sold millions of copies worldwide. In 1982, García Márquez received the highest international award for writing—the Nobel Prize in Literature. Here, in "Tuesday Siesta," he tells the story a mother and daughter who ride a train to a distant village to visit the grave of a relative.

"'It's an emergency,' the woman insisted. Her voice showed a calm determination."

 FIRST READ

1   The train emerged from the quivering tunnel of sandy rocks, began to cross the symmetrical, interminable banana plantations, and the air became humid and they couldn't feel the sea breeze any more. A stifling blast of smoke came in the car window. On the narrow road parallel to the railway there were oxcarts loaded with green bunches of bananas. Beyond the road, in uncultivated spaces set at odd intervals there were offices with electric fans, red-brick buildings, and residences with chairs and little white tables on the terraces among dusty palm trees and rose-bushes. It was eleven in the morning, and the heat had not yet begun.

2   "You'd better close the window," the woman said. "Your hair will get full of soot." The girl tried to, but the shade wouldn't move because of the rust.

3   They were the only passengers in the lone third-class car. Since the smoke of the locomotive kept coming through the window, the girl left her seat and put down the only things they had with them: a plastic sack with some things to eat and a bouquet of flowers wrapped in newspaper. She sat on the opposite seat, away from the window, facing her mother. They were both in severe and poor mourning clothes.

4   The girl was twelve years old, and it was the first time she'd ever been on a train. The woman seemed too old to be her mother, because of the blue veins on her eyelids and her small, soft, and shapeless body, in a dress cut like a cassock. She was riding with her spinal column braced firmly against the back of the seat, and held a peeling patent-leather handbag in her lap with both hands. She bore the conscientious serenity of someone accustomed to poverty.

5   By twelve the heat had begun. The train stopped for ten minutes to take on water at a station where there was no town. Outside, in the mysterious silence

of the plantations, the shadows seemed clean. But the still air inside the car smelled like untanned leather. The train did not pick up speed. It stopped at two identical towns with wooden houses painted bright colors. The woman's head nodded and she sank into sleep. The girl took off her shoes. Then she went to the washroom to put the bouquet of flowers in some water.

6 When she came back to her seat, her mother was waiting to eat. She gave her a piece of cheese, half a cornmeal pancake, and a cookie, and took an equal portion out of the plastic sack for herself. While they ate, the train crossed an iron bridge very slowly and passed a town just like the ones before, except that in this one there was a crowd in the plaza. A band was playing a lively tune under the oppressive sun. At the other side of town the plantations ended in a plain which was cracked from the drought.

7 The woman stopped eating.

8 "Put on your shoes," she said.

9 The girl looked outside. She saw nothing but the **deserted** plain, where the train began to pick up speed again, but she put the last piece of cookie into the sack and quickly put on her shoes. The woman gave her a comb.

10 "Comb your hair," she said.

11 The train whistle began to blow while the girl was combing her hair. The woman dried the sweat from her neck and wiped the oil from her face with her fingers. When the girl stopped combing, the train was passing the outlying houses of a town larger but sadder than the earlier ones.

12 "If you feel like doing anything, do it now," said the woman. "Later, don't take a drink anywhere even if you're dying of thirst. Above all, no crying."

13 The girl nodded her head. A dry, burning wind came in the window, together with the locomotive's whistle and the clatter of the old cars. The woman folded the plastic bag with the rest of the food and put it in the handbag.

14 For a moment a complete picture of the town, on that bright August Tuesday, shone in the window. The girl wrapped the flowers in the soaking-wet newspapers, moved a little farther away from the window, and stared at her mother. She received a pleasant expression in return. The train began to whistle and slowed down. A moment later it stopped.

15 There was no one at the station. On the other side of the street, on the sidewalk shaded by the almond trees, only the pool hall was open. The town was floating in the heat. The woman and the girl got off the train and crossed

Please note that excerpts and passages in the StudySync® library and this workbook are intended as touchstones to generate interest in an author's work. The excerpts and passages do not substitute for the reading of entire texts, and StudySync® strongly recommends that students seek out and purchase the whole literary or informational work in order to experience it as the author intended. Links to online resellers are available in our digital library. In addition, complete works may be ordered through an authorized reseller by filling out and returning to StudySync® the order form enclosed in this workbook.

Reading & Writing
Companion   57

the abandoned station—the tiles split apart by the grass growing up between— and over to the shady side of the street.

16   It was almost two. At that hour, weighted down by drowsiness, the town was taking a **siesta**. The stores, the town offices, the public school were closed at eleven, and didn't reopen until a little before four, when the train went back. Only the hotel across from the station, with its bar and pool hall, and the telegraph office at one side of the plaza stayed open. The houses, most of them built on the banana company's model, had their doors locked from inside and their blinds drawn. In some of them it was so hot that the residents ate lunch in the patio. Others leaned a chair against the wall, in the shade of the almond trees, and took their siesta right out in the street.

17   Keeping to the protective shade of the almond trees, the woman and the girl entered the town without disturbing the siesta. They went directly to the parish house. The woman scratched the metal grating on the door with her fingernail, waited a moment, and scratched again. An electric fan was humming inside. They did not hear the steps. They hardly heard the slight creaking of a door, and immediately a cautious voice, right next to the metal grating: "Who is it?" The woman tried to see through the grating.

18   "I need the priest," she said.

19   "He's sleeping now."

20   "It's an emergency," the woman insisted. Her voice showed a calm determination.

21   The door was opened a little way, noiselessly, and a plump, older woman appeared, with very pale skin and hair the color of iron. Her eyes seemed too small behind her thick eyeglasses.

22   "Come in," she said, and opened the door all the way.

23   They entered a room permeated with an old smell of flowers. The woman of the house led them to a wooden bench and signaled them to sit down. The girl did so, but her mother remained standing, absentmindedly, with both hands clutching the handbag. No noise could be heard above the electric fan.

24   The woman of the house reappeared at the door at the far end of the room. "He says you should come back after three," she said in a very low voice. "He just lay down five minutes ago."

25   "The train leaves at three thirty," said the woman.

26   It was a brief and self-assured reply, but her voice remained pleasant, full of undertones. The woman of the house smiled for the first time.

27   "All right," she said.

28   When the far door closed again, the woman sat down next to her daughter. The narrow waiting room was poor, neat, and clean. On the other side of the wooden railing which divided the room, there was a worktable, a plain one with an oilcloth cover, and on top of the table a primitive typewriter next to a vase of flowers. The parish records were beyond. You could see that it was an office kept in order by a **spinster**.

29   The far door opened and this time the priest appeared, cleaning his glasses with a handkerchief. Only when he put them on was it evident that he was the brother of the woman who had opened the door.

30   "How can I help you?" he asked.

31   "The keys to the cemetery," said the woman.

32   The girl was seated with the flowers in her lap and her feet crossed under the bench. The priest looked at her, then looked at the woman, and then through the wire mesh of the window at the bright, cloudless sky.

33   "In this heat," he said. "You could have waited until the sun went down."

34   The woman moved her head silently. The priest crossed to the other side of the railing, took out of the cabinet a notebook covered in oilcloth, a wooden penholder, and an inkwell, and sat down at the table. There was more than enough hair on his hands to account for what was missing on his head.

35   "Which grave are you going to visit?" he asked.

36   "Carlos Centeno's," said the woman.

37   "Who?"

38   "Carlos Centeno," the woman repeated.

39   The priest still did not understand.

40   "He's the thief who was killed here last week," said the woman in the same tone of voice. "I am his mother."

41   The priest **scrutinized** her. She stared at him with quiet self-control, and the Father blushed. He lowered his head and began to write. As he filled the page, he asked the woman to identify herself, and she replied unhesitatingly,

with precise details, as if she were reading them. The Father began to sweat. The girl unhooked the buckle of her left shoe, slipped her heel out of it, and rested it on the bench rail. She did the same with the right one.

42   It had all started the Monday of the previous week, at three in the morning, a few blocks from there. Rebecca, a lonely widow who lived in a house full of odds and ends, heard above the sound of the drizzling rain someone trying to force the front door from outside. She got up, rummaged around in her closet for an ancient revolver that no one had fired since the days of Colonel Aureliano Buendia, and went into the living room without turning on the lights. Orienting herself not so much by the noise at the lock as by a terror developed in her by twenty eight years of loneliness, she fixed in her imagination not only the spot where the door was but also the exact height of the lock. She clutched the weapon with both hands, closed her eyes, and squeezed the trigger. It was the first time in her life that she had fired a gun. Immediately after the explosion, she could hear nothing except the murmur of the drizzle on the galvanized roof. Then she heard a little metallic bump on the cement porch, and a very low voice, pleasant but terribly exhausted: "Ah, Mother." The man they found dead in front of the house in the morning, his nose blown to bits, wore a flannel shirt with colored stripes, everyday pants with a rope for a belt, and was barefoot. No one in town knew him.

43   "So his name was Carlos Centeno," murmured the Father when he finished writing.

44   "Centeno Ayala," said the woman. "He was my only boy."

45   The priest went back to the cabinet. Two big rusty keys hung on the inside of the door; the girl imagined, as her mother had when she was a girl and as the priest himself must have imagined at some time, that they were Saint Peter's keys. He took them down, put them on the open notebook on the railing, and pointed with his forefinger to a place on the page he had just written, looking at the woman.

46   "Sign here."

47   The woman scribbled her name, holding the handbag under her arm. The girl picked up the flowers, came to the railing shuffling her feet, and watched her mother attentively.

48   The priest sighed.

49   "Didn't you ever try to get him on the right track?"

50   The woman answered when she finished signing.

51   "He was a very good man."

52   The priest looked first at the woman and then at the girl, and realized with a kind of pious amazement that they were not about to cry. The woman continued in the same tone:

53   "I told him never to steal anything that anyone needed to eat, and he minded me. On the other hand, before, when he used to box, he used to spend three days in bed, exhausted from being punched."

54   "All his teeth had to be pulled out," interrupted the girl.

55   "That's right," the woman agreed. "Every mouthful I ate those days tasted of the beatings my son got on Saturday nights."

56   "God's will is **inscrutable**," said the Father.

57   But he said it without much conviction, partly because experience had made him a little skeptical and partly because of the heat. He suggested that they cover their heads to guard against sunstroke. Yawning, and now almost completely asleep, he gave them instructions about how to find Carlos Centeno's grave. When they came back, they didn't have to knock. They should put the key under the door; and in the same place, if they could, they should put an offering for the Church. The woman listened to his directions with great attention, but thanked him without smiling.

58   The Father had noticed that there was someone looking inside, his nose pressed against the metal grating, even before he opened the door to the street. Outside was a group of children. When the door was opened wide, the children scattered. Ordinarily, at that hour there was no one in the street. Now there were not only children. There were groups of people under the almond trees. The Father scanned the street swimming in the heat and then he understood. Softly, he closed the door again.

59   "Wait a moment," he said without looking at the woman.

60   His sister appeared at the far door with a black jacket over her nightshirt and her hair down over her shoulders. She looked silently at the Father.

61   "What was it?" he asked.

62   "The people have noticed," murmured his sister.

63   "You'd better go out by the door to the patio," said the Father.

64   "It's the same there," said his sister. "Everybody is at the windows."

Reading & Writing
Companion

NOTES

65 The woman seemed not to have understood until then. She tried to look into the street through the metal grating. Then she took the bouquet of flowers from the girl and began to move toward the door. The girl followed her.

66 "Wait until the sun goes down," said the Father.

67 "You'll melt," said his sister, motionless at the back of the room. "Wait and I'll lend you a parasol."

68 "Thank you," replied the woman. "We're all right this way."

69 She took the girl by the hand and went into the street.

Gabriel García Márquez. "La siesta del martes," LOS FUNERALES DE LA MAMÁ GRANDE © Gabriel García Márquez, 1962 y Herederos de Gabriel García Márquez.

THINK QUESTIONS

1. Identify details from the text to explain from what social class the mother and daughter come. Why might the author want readers to know about their social class?

2. What is the mother in this story like? Cite textual details to show how the author reveals the character of the mother and to explain your inferences.

3. The author chooses not to explain what has happened to the woman's son until halfway through the story. What hints does the narrator provide as to why the mother and daughter have come to this town? Cite textual evidence and explain your inferences.

4. Use context to determine the meaning of the word **spinster** as it is used in "Tuesday Siesta." Write your definition of *spinster*.

5. The words *inscrutable, scrutiny,* and *scrutinize* have the same root, from the Latin *scrutari*, meaning "to examine or search." What part of speech is **scrutinized**? How do you know?

CLOSE READ

Reread the excerpt from *Tuesday Siesta*. As you reread, complete the Focus Questions below. Then use your answers and annotations from the questions to help you complete the Writing Prompt.

FOCUS QUESTIONS

1. As you reread the beginning of "Tuesday Siesta," think about how the author structures the early paragraphs by describing the setting and the characters. Think about what the author includes, and what he leaves out. What effect does the author achieve? Highlight evidence to support your ideas and write annotations to explain your choices.

2. The mother makes certain demands on her daughter throughout the story. Why does she make these demands? What do they tell you about her? Highlight textual evidence to support your ideas and write annotations to explain your choices.

3. Religion is part of the cultural context of the story. What is the role of the priest in the village? Highlight textual evidence that shows his role. How does the priest function in the story's plot and structure? Highlight evidence, including things he says and does, as well as his interactions with the woman and her daughter. Annotate to explain your ideas.

4. The author reveals something that happened to the woman's son in a flashback. Why do you think the author chose to use the structure of a flashback? What effect does it have on your understanding of all the events that have come before? Highlight your evidence and make annotations to explain the effect.

5. Use your understanding of cultural context and story structure in these chapters to identify the central message, or theme, that emerges in the story. Highlight evidence from the text that will help support your ideas.

6. Do you think the author wants the reader to feel empathy for the main characters? Why or why not? Do any of the other characters demonstrate empathy toward them? Use details from the story to support your answer.

WRITING PROMPT

Think about the way García Márquez reveals the cultural context of "Tuesday Siesta," as well as how he structures the story, including the use of flashback. Use your understanding of story structure and cultural context to determine the story's theme, or central idea. Support your writing with evidence from the text.

Please note that excerpts and passages in the StudySync® library and this workbook are intended as touchstones to generate interest in an author's work. The excerpts and passages do not substitute for the reading of entire texts, and StudySync® strongly recommends that students seek out and purchase the whole literary or informational work in order to experience it as the author intended. Links to online resellers are available in our digital library. In addition, complete works may be ordered through an authorized reseller by filling out and returning to StudySync® the order form enclosed in this workbook.

Reading & Writing Companion   **63**

LIVING TO TELL THE TALE

NON-FICTION
Gabriel García Márquez
2003

INTRODUCTION

I n this excerpt from his autobiography, Gabriel García Márquez recounts the real-life events that inspired him to write "Tuesday Siesta." On a trip back to his hometown, which is poor and in disrepair, García Márquez is reminded of an incident years ago in which a thief was shot and killed trying to break into a house—an event that left a profound and lasting impact on the author.

"Everything was identical to my memories, but smaller and poorer, and leveled by a windstorm of fatality."

 FIRST READ

NOTES

Excerpt from Chapter 1

1   While the train stood there I had the sensation that we were not altogether alone. But when it pulled away, with an immediate, heart-wrenching blast of its whistle, my mother and I were left forsaken beneath the infernal sun, and all the heavy grief of the town came down on us. But we did not say anything to each other. The old wooden station with its tin roof and running balcony was like a tropical version of the ones we knew from westerns. We crossed the deserted station whose tiles were beginning to crack under the pressure of grass, and we sank into the **torpor** of siesta as we sought the protection of the almond trees.

2   Since I was a boy I had despised those **inert** siestas because we did not know what to do. "Be quiet, we're sleeping," the sleepers would murmur without waking. Stores, public offices, and schools closed at twelve and did not open again until a little before three. The interiors of the houses floated in a limbo of lethargy. In some it was so unbearable that people would hang their hammocks in the courtyard or place chairs in the shade of the almond trees and sleep sitting up in the middle of the street. Only the hotel across from the station, with its bar and billiard room, and the telegraph office behind the church remained open. Everything was identical to my memories, but smaller and poorer, and leveled by a windstorm of fatality: the decaying houses themselves, the tin roofs perforated by rust, the levee with its crumbling granite benches and **melancholy** almond trees, and all of it transfigured by the invisible burning dust that deceived the eye and calcinated the skin. On the other side of the train tracks the private paradise of the banana company, stripped now of its electrified wire fence, was a vast thicket with no palm trees, ruined houses among the poppies, and the rubble of the hospital destroyed by fire. There was not a single door, a crack in a wall, a human trace that did not find a supernatural resonance in me.

3   My mother held herself very erect as she walked with her light step, almost not perspiring in her funereal dress, and in absolute silence, but her mortal pallor and sharpened profile revealed what was happening to her on the inside.

4   When we turned the corner, the dust burned my feet through the weave of my sandals. The feeling of being forsaken became unbearable. Then I saw myself and I saw my mother, just as I saw, when I was a boy, the mother and sister of the thief whom Maria Consuegra had killed with a single shot one week earlier, when he tried to break into her house.

5   At three in the morning the sound of someone trying to force the street door from the outside had wakened her. She got up without lighting the lamp, felt around in the armoire for an archaic revolver that no one had fired since the War of a Thousand Days, and located in the darkness not only the place where the door was but also the exact height of the lock. Then she aimed the weapon with both hands, closed her eyes, and squeezed the trigger. She had never fired a gun before, but the shot hit its target through the door.

6   He was the first dead person I had seen. When I passed by at seven in the morning on my way to school, the body was still lying on the sidewalk in a patch of dried blood, the face destroyed by the lead that had shattered its nose and come out one ear. He was wearing a sailor's T-shirt with colored stripes and ordinary trousers held up by a rope instead of a belt, and he was barefoot. At his side, on the ground, they found the homemade picklock with which he had tried to jimmy the lock.

7   The town dignitaries came to Maria Consuegra's house to offer her their condolences for having killed the thief. I went that night with Papalelo, and we found her sitting in an armchair from Manila that looked like an enormous wicker peacock, surrounded by the fervor of her friends who listened to the story she had repeated a thousand times. Everyone agreed with her that she had fired out of sheer fright. It was then that my grandfather asked her if she had heard anything after the shot, and she answered that the first she had heard a great silence, then the metallic sound of the picklock falling on the cement, and then a faint, anguished voice: "Mother, help me!" Maria Consuegra, it seemed, had not been conscious of this heart-breaking **lament** until my grandfather asked her the question. Only then did she burst into tears.

8   This happened on a Monday. On Tuesday of the following week, during siesta, I was playing tops with Luis Carmelo Correa, my oldest friend in life, when we were surprised by the sleepers waking before it was time and looking out the windows. Then we saw in the deserted street a woman dressed in strict mourning and a girl about twelve years old who was carrying

a bouquet of faded flowers wrapped in newspaper. They protected themselves from the burning sun with a black umbrella and were quite oblivious to the **effrontery** of the people who watched them pass by. They were the mother and younger sister of the dead thief, bringing flowers for his grave.

9   That vision pursued me for many years, like a single dream that the entire town watched through its windows as it passed, until I managed to exorcise it in a story. But the truth is that I did not become aware of the drama of the woman and the girl, or their **imperturbable** dignity, until the day I went with my mother to sell the house and surprised myself walking down the same deserted street at the same lethal hour.

10 "I feel as if I were the thief," I said.

11 My mother did not understand me. In fact, when we passed the house of Maria Consuegra she did not even glance at the door where you could still see the patched bullet hole in the wood. Years later, recalling that trip with her, I confirmed that she did remember the tragedy but would have given her soul to forget it.

Excerpted from *Living to Tell the Tale* by Gabriel García Márquez, published by Vintage Books.

 THINK QUESTIONS

1. This excerpt is from an autobiography. Highlight details from the text that signal to the reader that the author is writing a memoir. How is this writing similar to fiction? Use the textual evidence to explain how the siesta connects to memories discussed in the excerpt.

2. The author describes an incident that affected him deeply as a child. What happened and why did it affect him so strongly? Refer to one or more details from the text to support your answer.

3. Why did Maria Consuegra burst into tears when she spoke to the author's grandfather? Refer to one or more details from the text to support your answer.

4. Use context to determine the meaning of the word **torpor** as it is used in *Living to Tell the Tale*. Write your definition of *torpor*.

5. The author uses the phrase "melancholy almond trees" in describing his town. What clues from the text help you to determine the meaning of **melancholy**? Write your definition of *melancholy*.

CLOSE READ

Reread the excerpt from *Living to Tell the Tale*. As you reread, complete the Focus Questions below. Then use your answers and annotations from the questions to help you complete the Writing Prompt.

FOCUS QUESTIONS

1. As you reread the beginning of this excerpt from the autobiography *Living to Tell the Tale*, look back to see how Gabriel García Márquez began his short story "Tuesday Siesta." How are the details similar in each version of events? How are the details different? What does the author emphasize most in each version? Highlight textual evidence to support your ideas and write annotations to explain your choices.

2. How does García Márquez develop the events in this autobiography? What overall shape does he give the story structure by unfolding events in a certain order? Highlight images, phrases, and moments that stand out for you. Annotate to explain your choices.

3. In paragraph 3 of *Living to Tell the Tale*, Gabriel García Márquez describes his mother. How does the image connect to the events he describes? Compare this description with that of the mother in "Tuesday Siesta." What evidence in the two texts reveals the importance of this image of the mother? Highlight textual evidence and annotate to explain your inferences.

4. What do you think is the central idea of this excerpt? Highlight evidence from the autobiography that will help support your statement, and then explain how the evidence supports the central idea.

5. Near the end of this excerpt, García Márquez says to his mother, "I feel as if I were the thief." What makes him develop this empathy for the thief, and with whom else does he empathize? Annotate to explain your ideas. Highlight evidence from the text that helps support your explanation.

WRITING PROMPT

Author Gabriel García Márquez wrote a short story, "Tuesday Siesta," based on real events he later recounted in his autobiography, *Living to Tell the Tale*. How does the author transform a boyhood memory into a story? Write a response in which you compare and contrast this excerpt from the autobiography with the story "Tuesday Siesta." In your response, analyze what is emphasized or absent in each treatment. Finally, compare the text structure and order of events in the autobiography with the structure and order of the short story. Support your analysis with textual evidence.

THE ELEPHANT MAN

DRAMA
Bernard Pomerance
1979

INTRODUCTION

Bernard Pomerance's award-winning play was based on the life of Joseph (also known as John) Merrick, a Victorian-era British man born with a bone disease that caused his limbs and skull to become grossly oversized. His condition made him a freak show attraction and a witty favorite of the aristocracy,

"The deformities rendered the face utterly incapable of the expression of any emotion..."

 FIRST READ

SCENE II: ART IS AS NOTHING TO NATURE

1 *[Whitechapel Rd. A storefront. A large advertisement of a creature with an elephant's head. ROSS, his manager.]*

2 ROSS: **Tuppence** only, step in and see: This side of the grave, John Merrick has no hope nor expectation of relief. In every sense his situation is desperate. His physical agony is exceeded only by his mental anguish, a despised creature without consolation. Tuppence only, step in and see! To live with his physical hideousness, incapacitating deformities and **unremitting** pain is trial enough, but to be exposed to the cruelly lacerating expressions of horror and disgust by all who behold him—is even more difficult to bear. Tuppence only, step in and see! For in order to survive, Merrick forces himself to suffer these humiliations, in order to survive, thus he exposes himself to crowds who pay to gape and **yawp** at this freak of nature, the Elephant Man.

3 *[Enter TREVES who looks at advertisement.]*

4 ROSS: See Mother Nature uncorseted and in **malignant** rage! Tuppence.

5 TREVES: The sign's absurd. Half-elephant, half-man is not possible. Is he foreign?

6 ROSS: Right, from Leicester. But nothing to fear.

7 TREVES: I'm at the London across the road. I would be curious to see him if there is more genuine disorder. If he is a mass of papier-maché and paint however—

8 ROSS: Then pay me nothing. Enter sir. Merrick, stand up. Ya bloody donkey, up, up.

9 *[They go in, then emerge. TREVES pays.]*

10 TREVES: I must examine him further at the hospital. Here is my card. I'm Treves. I will have a cab pick him up and return him. My card will gain him admittance.

11 ROSS: Five bob he's yours for the day.

12 TREVES: I wish to examine him in the interests of science, you see.

13 ROSS: Sir, I'm Ross. I look out for him, get him his living. Found him in Leicester workhouse. His own ma put him there age of three. Couldn't bear the sight, well you can see why. We—he and I—are in business. He is our capital, see. Go to a bank. Go anywhere. Want to borrow capital, you pay interest. Scientists even. He's good value though. You won't find another like him.

14 TREVES: Fair enough. *[He pays.]*

15 ROSS: Right. Out here, Merrick. Ya bloody donkey, out!

16 *[Lights fade out.]*

SCENE III: WHO HAS SEEN THE LIKE OF THIS?

17 [TREVES *lectures.* MERRICK *contorts himself to approximate projected slides of the real Merrick.*]

18 TREVES: The most striking feature about him was his enormous head. Its circumference was about that of a man's waist. From the brow there projected a huge bony mass like a loaf, while from the back of his head hung a bag of spongy fungous-looking skin, the surface of which was comparable to brown cauliflower. On the top of the skull were a few long lank hairs. The **osseous** growth on the forehead, at this stage about the size of a tangerine, almost occluded one eye. From the upper jaw there projected another mass of bone. It protruded from the mouth like a pink stump, turning the upper lip inside out, and making the mouth a wide slobbering aperture. The nose was merely a lump of flesh, only recognizable as a nose from its position. The deformities rendered the face utterly incapable of the expression of any emotion whatsoever. The back was horrible because from it hung, as far down as the middle of the thigh, huge sacklike masses of flesh covered by the same loathsome cauliflower stain. The right arm was of enormous size and shapeless. It suggested but was not elephantiasis, and was overgrown also with pendant masses of the same cauliflower-like skin. The right hand was large and clumsy—a fin or paddle rather than a hand. No distinction existed between the palm and back, the thumb was like a radish, the fingers like thick **tuberous** roots. As a limb it was useless. The other arm was

NOTES

remarkable by contrast. It was not only normal but was moreover a delicately shaped limb covered with a fine skin and provided with a beautiful hand which any woman might have envied. From the chest hung a bag of the same repulsive flesh. It was like a dewlap suspended from the neck of a lizard. The lower limbs had the characters of the deformed arm. They were unwieldy, dropsical-looking, and grossly misshapen. There arose from the fungous skin growths a very sickening stench which was hard to tolerate. To add a further burden to his trouble, the wretched man when a boy developed hip disease which left him permanently lame, so that he could only walk with a stick. [*to* MERRICK] Please. [MERRICK *walks*.] He was thus denied all means of escape from his tormenters.

19   VOICE: Mr. Treves, you have shown a profound and unknown disorder to us. You have said when he leaves here it is for his exhibition again. I do not think it ought to be permitted. It is a disgrace. It is a pity and a disgrace. It is an indecency in fact. It may be a danger in ways we do not know. Something ought to be done about it.

20   TREVES: I am a doctor. What would you have me do?

21   VOICE: Well. I know what to do. I know.

22   *[Silence. A policeman enters as lights fade out.]*

Excerpted from *The Elephant Man* by Bernard Pomerance, published by Grove Press.

 THINK QUESTIONS

1. To what is Ross beckoning customers? Cite details from the text to explain how you drew your inference.

2. What details provide clues about the time and place this play is set? Highlight and make annotations to identify the textual evidence that provides clues.

3. Use textual evidence to make an inference as to why the author ended the scene (indicated by the stage direction "lights fade out") with the arrival of the police officer.

4. Use context to determine the meaning of the word **yawp** as it is used in *The Elephant Man*. Write your definition here. Why do you think the author used *yawp* in this line?

5. Considering that the prefix *mal-* means "bad," what other context clues can you find to help you determine the meaning of the word **malignant** as it is used in the passage? Write your definition of the word *malignant*.

CLOSE READ

Reread the scenes from "The Elephant Man." As you reread, complete the Focus Questions below. Then use your answers and annotations from the questions to help you complete the Writing Prompt.

FOCUS QUESTIONS

1. Reread the first speech of Scene II. How might this beginning help the audience visualize John Merrick? Highlight textual evidence and write an annotation to explain your answer.

2. As you reread the excerpt from *The Elephant Man*, remember that the author communicates the tone through dialogue and stage directions. In Scene II, highlight a sentence or phrase in Ross's first speech that describes how people react when they see Merrick. Then write an annotation to explain how this text contributes to the tone.

3. How does the character of VOICE create a sense of uncertainty or mystery in the play? Highlight this character and lines that help establish this tone. Then write an annotation to explain how this character's arrival might look when produced for the stage. What kind of entrance might help reinforce the tone of mystery?

4. In Scene II, highlight words or phrases from the first five sentences of Treves's long speech that are examples of academic or technical language that contribute to the tone of the text. Then make annotations to explain your choices.

5. In their speeches, both Ross and Treves describe John Merrick and express a point of view about him. How do they describe him and what are their perspectives? How might their descriptions and perspectives affect the attitude of the audience toward Merrick? In what way might this play demonstrate how we develop empathy for others? Write an annotation to explain your response.

WRITING PROMPT

When *The Elephant Man* was performed live on stage, the actor playing John Merrick typically had a natural appearance without elaborate makeup. Instead, the actor would contort his body to portray Merrick's physical challenges. However, in the movie version, the actor was made up to match the descriptions given in the play. Based on the short excerpt you have read, which choice do you think would be more effective in staying true to the author's tone? Write a short response to state your opinion. Support your claim with valid reasons and relevant textual evidence.

Please note that excerpts and passages in the StudySync® library and this workbook are intended as touchstones to generate interest in an author's work. The excerpts and passages do not substitute for the reading of entire texts, and StudySync® strongly recommends that students seek out and purchase the whole literary or informational work in order to experience it as the author intended. Links to online resellers are available in our digital library. In addition, complete works may be ordered through an authorized reseller by filling out and returning to StudySync® the order form enclosed in this workbook.

Reading & Writing Companion

73

MENDING WALL

POETRY
Robert Frost
1914

INTRODUCTION

A four-time winner of the Pulitzer Prize for Poetry, Robert Frost was one of the most popular and critically acclaimed poets the 20th century. Much of his work is set in rural New England, vividly evoking pastoral life in all its trials and beauty. Here, in "Mending Wall," he examines one of the more difficult boundaries to navigate in such a life.

"We keep the wall between us as we go."

FIRST READ

NOTES

1 Something there is that doesn't love a wall,
2 That sends the frozen-ground-swell under it,
3 And spills the upper boulders in the sun,
4 And makes gaps even two can pass **abreast**.
5 The work of hunters is another thing:
6 I have come after them and made repair
7 Where they have left not one stone on a stone,
8 But they would have the rabbit out of hiding,
9 To please the **yelping** dogs. The gaps I mean,
10 No one has seen them made or heard them made,
11 But at spring **mending**-time we find them there.
12 I let my neighbor know beyond the hill;
13 And on a day we meet to walk the line
14 And set the wall between us once again.
15 We keep the wall between us as we go.
16 To each the boulders that have fallen to each.
17 And some are loaves and some so nearly balls
18 We have to use a spell to make them balance:
19 "Stay where you are until our backs are turned!"
20 We wear our fingers rough with handling them.
21 Oh, just another kind of outdoor game,
22 One on a side. It comes to little more:
23 He is all pine and I am apple-orchard.
24 My apple trees will never get across
25 And eat the cones under his pines, I tell him.
26 He only says, "Good fences make good neighbors."
27 Spring is the mischief in me, and I wonder
28 If I could put a notion in his head:
29 "*Why* do they make good neighbors? Isn't it

Please note that excerpts and passages in the StudySync® library and this workbook are intended as touchstones to generate interest in an author's work. The excerpts and passages do not substitute for the reading of entire texts, and StudySync® strongly recommends that students seek out and purchase the whole literary or informational work in order to experience it as the author intended. Links to online resellers are available in our digital library. In addition, complete works may be ordered through an authorized reseller by filling out and returning to StudySync® the order form enclosed in this workbook.

Reading & Writing Companion **75**

30 Where there are cows? But here there are no cows.
31 Before I built a wall I'd ask to know
32 What I was walling in or walling out,
33 And to whom I was like to give **offense**.
34 Something there is that doesn't love a wall,
35 That wants it down!" I could say "Elves" to him,
36 But it's not elves exactly, and I'd rather
37 He said it for himself. I see him there,
38 Bringing a stone grasped firmly by the top
39 In each hand, like an old-stone **savage** armed.
40 He moves in darkness as it seems to me,
41 Not of woods only and the shade of trees.
42 He will not go behind his father's saying,
43 And he likes having thought of it so well
44 He says again, "Good fences make good neighbors."

 THINK QUESTIONS

1. What task is the author of "Mending Wall" describing in this poem? Why does the job have to be done every year? Highlight and annotate textual evidence to explain your answer.

2. What do you think the neighbor means by the expression "Good fences make good neighbors"? Find evidence in the poem to explain.

3. What lines from the poem show that the speaker does not completely believe that this task needs to be done every year? How can you tell that the speaker disagrees with his neighbor's statement that "Good fences make good neighbors"? Use textual evidence to explain.

4. Read the lines that include "To please the yelping dogs." What clues from the passage help you understand the meaning of **yelping**? Also, identify the part of speech of the word.

5. Use context to determine the meaning of the word **abreast** as it is used in the poem. Write your definition of *abreast* and identify the context clues that helped you define it.

CLOSE READ

Reread the poem "Mending Wall." As you reread, complete the Focus Questions below. Then use your answers and annotations from the questions to help you complete the Writing Prompt.

FOCUS QUESTIONS

1. As you read the poem, it becomes clear that the wall has a larger meaning for the author. How does the description of the wall contribute to the author's theme concerning the separations between people? What textual evidence supports your answer?

2. The author writes that "Spring is the mischief in me." What does he mean by this metaphor? And what details does he include in the poem to develop the metaphor?

3. The author repeats both sides of the argument for and against building the wall. Explain his position on the wall and his neighbor's position. How does the structure of the poem emphasize these positions?

4. What does the author mean by the phrase "he is all pine and I am apple-orchard"? Why does the author include this detail in the poem, and how does it support the author's theme? What text evidence can you cite to support your answer?

5. The author includes details in his poetry that suggest, whether earnestly or not, a supernatural power. Give examples of these references and explain how they relate to the themes of the poem.

6. Do you think the speaker feels empathy for his neighbor? Why or why not? Use text evidence to support your claim.

WRITING PROMPT

Read the poem once through and apply your knowledge of figurative language and theme to each line as you read. Do you agree or disagree with the statement "Good fences make good neighbors"? Write a short essay of 250–300 words to develop your response. Quote textual evidence from the poem, including explanations of metaphors and symbols, to support your ideas.

Please note that excerpts and passages in the StudySync® library and this workbook are intended as touchstones to generate interest in an author's work. The excerpts and passages do not substitute for the reading of entire texts, and StudySync® strongly recommends that students seek out and purchase the whole literary or informational work in order to experience it as the author intended. Links to online resellers are available in our digital library. In addition, complete works may be ordered through an authorized reseller by filling out and returning to StudySync® the order form enclosed in this workbook.

Reading & Writing Companion   **77**

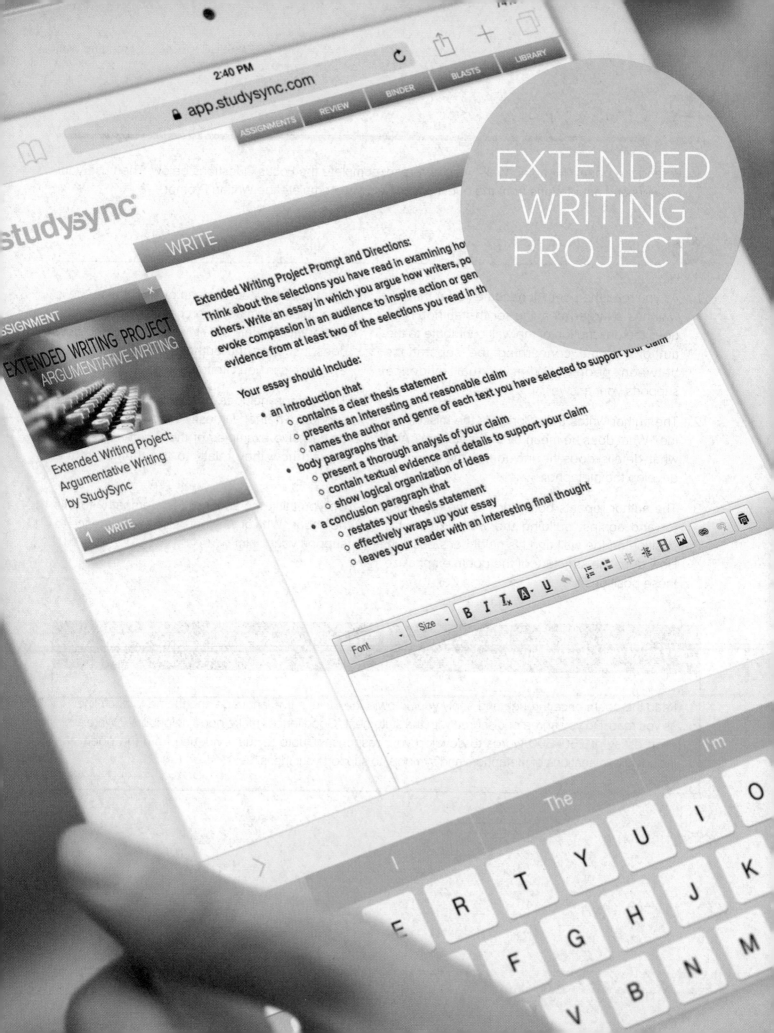

EXTENDED WRITING PROJECT

studysync®

WRITE

ASSIGNMENT

EXTENDED WRITING PROJECT
ARGUMENTATIVE WRITING

Extended Writing Project:
Argumentative Writing
by StudySync

1   WRITE

Extended Writing Project Prompt and Directions:

Think about the selections you have read in examining ho[w]
others. Write an essay in which you argue how writers, po[...]
evoke compassion in an audience to inspire action or gen[...]
evidence from at least two of the selections you read in th[...]

Your essay should include:

- an introduction that
  - contains a clear thesis statement
  - presents an interesting and reasonable claim
  - names the author and genre of each text you have selected to support your claim
- body paragraphs that
  - present a thorough analysis of your claim
  - contain textual evidence and details to support your claim
  - show logical organization of ideas
- a conclusion paragraph that
  - restates your thesis statement
  - effectively wraps up your essay
  - leaves your reader with an interesting final thought

ARGUMENTATIVE
WRITING

WRITING PROMPT

Think about the selections you have read in examining how we develop empathy for others. Write an essay in which you argue how writers, poets, artists, or politicians best evoke compassion in an audience to inspire action or generate understanding. Use textual evidence from at least two of the selections you read in this unit to support your claim.

Your essay should include:

- An introduction that

  › contains a clear thesis statement.

  › presents an interesting and reasonable claim.

  › names the author and genre of each text you have selected to support your claim.

- Body paragraphs that

  › present a thorough analysis of your claim.

  › contain textual evidence and details to support your claim.

  › show logical organization of ideas.

- A conclusion paragraph that

  › restates your thesis statement.

  › effectively wraps up your essay.

  › leaves your reader with an interesting final thought.

Argumentative writing is a type of non-fiction writing in which a writer establishes a strong position about a topic and develops it with paragraphs that support that position with evidence. The purpose of argumentative writing is to persuade an audience to agree that the writer's claim is sound and true. Argumentative writing can appear in many forms, including essays, papers, speeches, debates, and letters to the editor of a newspaper.

Copyright © BookheadEd Learning, LLC

NOTES

The most important part of a strong argumentative essay is a clear **claim**. A claim is a writer's central argument or thesis. It communicates the main focus of the writing and allows readers to understand exactly what a writer is arguing. The claim should appear in the introductory paragraph, to help readers understand what will come next.

An argumentative essay should stay focused on the main claim and present information in a logical order that is easy for a reader to follow. Transition words help connect ideas and build the argument point by point. Effective argument writing includes strong evidence that supports the writer's reasoning and demonstrates the claim. It also presents a formal tone that is appropriate to the purpose and style of argumentative writing. A strong argumentative conclusion restates the writer's claim, effectively wraps up the argument, and leaves readers with a lasting final thought. The features of argumentative writing include:

- Clear and logical organizational structure
- An introduction with a clear thesis statement
- Supporting details, including valid reasoning and textual evidence
- A formal tone
- A concluding restatement of the claim

As you continue with this extended writing project, you'll receive more instructions and practice to help you craft each of the elements of argumentative writing in your own essay.

 STUDENT MODEL

You will learn skills of the writer's craft as you follow the writing process steps of Prewrite, Plan, Draft, and Revise before the final step of Edit, Proofread, and Publish. Before you get started on your own argumentative essay, begin by reading this essay that one student wrote in response to the writing prompt. As you read this student model, highlight and annotate the features of argumentative writing that the student included in her essay.

Words to Change the World

One of the key messages an author or artist can convey to people is the need for human compassion in order to make the world a better place to live. Precise word choice and sensory details are an author's keys to unlocking a reader's deepest emotions, but startling photographs can also move people. Through an article or broadcast, words can raise public awareness of social problems, but so can photographs. Which are more effective, words or pictures? The excerpt from the informational text *Endangered Dreams: The Great Depression in California* by Kevin Starr and the article "The Harvest Gypsies" by John Steinbeck both inform readers about migrant life during the Great Depression; the photographs of artists like Dorothea Lange, as explained in Starr's article, allow viewers to visualize that life. While the photographs of Dorothea Lange and artists like her provide important insights into those conditions, it is the deeper human stories provided by writers like John Steinbeck that are more effective in bringing about social change.

In *Endangered Dreams: The Great Depression in California*, the author, Kevin Starr, shows the world that photographer Dorothea Lange captured information that the pictures themselves cannot contain, providing readers with insights into the subjects of Lange's pictures. Sensory details such as "cold wet miserable day" give context for the moment when she debates the importance of turning around to visit the pea pickers camp (Starr 250). Her "instinctive" decision to turn around leads her back to the camp, where she encounters the subject of a photograph that will eventually help change the fate of many starving Americans during the Great Depression in California. Starr describes the mother Lange meets as "hungry" and "desperate" (Starr 250). He explains Lange's own empathy for the woman by revealing Lange's thoughts that she "seemed to know that my pictures might help her, and so she helped me. There was a sort of equality about it" (Starr 250). While the picture went on to become known around the world, this commentary by Lange is absent from the image.

Starr points out that people often want words to accompany an image. "Some critics have made much of the fact that Lange did not learn the woman's name," and Starr would seem to support that criticism when he adds that she and her children were "stranded in a roadside canvas lean-to..." (Starr 250). However, Starr defends Lange: "Such criticism," Starr explains, "ignores the fact that as soon as Lange returned to San Francisco, and developed these negatives," she told her editor "that thousands of pea pickers in Nipomo were starving because of the frozen harvest" (Starr 250). Starr shows the energy of the moment, as Lange "rushed" her film to the paper. It was her editor, George West, who "got the story out," using two of Lange's other photographs to explain what happened. The result of getting the word out was "twenty thousand pounds of food to feed the starving pea pickers" (Starr 250). A combination of

Please note that excerpts and passages in the StudySync® library and this workbook are intended as touchstones to generate interest in an author's work. The excerpts and passages do not substitute for the reading of entire texts, and StudySync® strongly recommends that students seek out and purchase the whole literary or informational work in order to experience it as the author intended. Links to online resellers are available in our digital library. In addition, complete works may be ordered through an authorized reseller by filling out and returning to StudySync® the order form enclosed in this workbook.

Reading & Writing Companion   81

NOTES

photographs and news copy alerted the government, and action was taken. Words as well as photographs, Starr shows, changed America in those times of human need.

In addition to images, then, powerful words are needed to gain a public's interest in important issues. With the powerful words of his article "The Harvest Gypsies," Steinbeck presents a vivid account of the plight of families migrating through California during the Great Depression. His organization of the precise details he reveals about two particular families leads readers to a deeper understanding of the dangerous difficulties many families faced during this time in America. For example, Steinbeck begins his article by introducing precise words to describe a family's home: the "rot" in the "tattered" canvas held in place with "rusty" wire; the "filth" of the tent and the "exposed" human feces covered in flies that fill the tent with their "buzzing"; the "foul" clothes of the children and "the baby, who has not been bathed or cleaned for several days" (Steinbeck 29). The emphasis on the time passing in the camp, "for several days," is something a photograph could not show. When Steinbeck reveals that a four-year-old boy who was sick for weeks from lack of nourishment has died, his words capture a problem that developed over time. Steinbeck uses words to gain compassion for the parents, who now live in "paralyzed dullness" (Steinbeck 29). Steinbeck's repetition of "dullness" throughout the excerpt creates a continuous feeling that a single photograph, which only captures a specific moment in time, cannot communicate or express.

During his article, there are particular words Steinbeck does *not* include: Steinbeck does not name any of the people he describes. While people criticized Lange for not learning the names of her subjects, Steinbeck deliberately omits the names. The decision to use only generic terms, such as "the father," "the mother," or "the boy," helps readers see that these things could happen to anyone. Select details tell us that this family was once much better off—"the father of this family once had a little grocery store and his family lived in back of it so that even the children could wait on the counter"—but that the drought has caused their current extreme poverty and loss (Steinbeck 29). As readers, we are reminded that any of us could fall into tough times that change our lives drastically, and we are compelled to feel greater empathy for this family. Additionally, Steinbeck describes the family's current state as "the middle class of the squatters' camp," revealing that other families in the camp are even worse off (Steinbeck 29–30). The writer's many details about these circumstances could not be captured in a photograph. When Steinbeck introduces us to the three-year-old son, the details he also offers could be shown in a photo: "The three year old child has a gunny sack tied about his middle for clothing. He has the swollen belly caused by malnutrition" (Steinbeck 30). However, providing details of agonies over time, such as being too weak to "try to get at the mucous in the eye-corners" and allowing flies to "crawl up his nose," are unique to the writer's craft (Steinbeck 30).

Certainly a powerful image crafted by a photographer, such as Dorothea Lange's *Migrant Mother*, draws a viewer in and makes it hard to look away. However, as the news story that accompanied her photos indicates, images alone are not enough to bring about social change. In addition, writers like John Steinbeck can do things that a photographer cannot, such as provide context or offer commentary on a situation he is writing about. Steinbeck says of one migrant, "He will not look directly at you for that requires will, and will needs strength" (Steinbeck 30). The writer interprets a moment for a reader, based on evidence he himself has provided. Together the craft of the photographer and the craft of the writer can influence the ways citizens respond to the needs of society, but it is words that change the world.

 THINK QUESTIONS

1. What is the author's claim in the student model essay? What introductory explanation does the author of the essay offer to support this claim?

2. How does the author support her claim? Is her reasoning sound? Are there any false statements? Include examples from the student model in your answer to explain whether the author has sufficiently supported her claim in this essay.

3. Has the student author presented information in a logical organization that shows how her claim and evidence are related? Explain how the author has organized her essay and determine whether the organization is logical.

4. Thinking about the writing prompt, which selections or other resources would you like to use to create your own argumentative essay? What are some ideas that you may want to develop into your own essay?

5. Based on what you have read, listened to, or researched, how would you answer the question *How do writers, poets, artists, or politicians best evoke compassion in an audience in order to inspire action or generate understanding?* What are some selections you might explore in your essay to answer this question, and what might your focus be?

Please note that excerpts and passages in the StudySync® library and this workbook are intended as touchstones to generate interest in an author's work. The excerpts and passages do not substitute for the reading of entire texts, and StudySync® strongly recommends that students seek out and purchase the whole literary or informational work in order to experience it as the author intended. Links to online resellers are available in our digital library. In addition, complete works may be ordered through an authorized reseller by filling out and returning to StudySync® the order form enclosed in this workbook.

Reading & Writing Companion   83

PREWRITE

WRITING PROMPT

Think about the selections you have read in examining how we develop empathy for others. Write an essay in which you argue how writers, poets, artists, or politicians best evoke compassion in an audience to inspire action or generate understanding. Use textual evidence from at least two of the selections you read in this unit to support your claim.

Your essay should include:
- An introduction that
  - › contains a clear thesis statement.
  - › presents an interesting and reasonable claim.
  - › names the author and genre of each text you have selected to support your claim.

- Body paragraphs that
  - › present a thorough analysis of your claim.
  - › contain textual evidence and details to support your claim.
  - › show logical organization of ideas.

- A conclusion paragraph that
  - › restates your thesis statement.
  - › effectively wraps up your essay.
  - › leaves your reader with an interesting final thought.

In addition to studying techniques authors use to make arguments, you have been reading and learning about stories that evoke compassion in readers. In the extended writing project, you will use those argumentative writing techniques to compose your own argumentative essay.

As you begin to brainstorm for your essay, think back to the selections you've read in this unit. How do these selections show how writers, poets, artists, or

Copyright © BookheadEd Learning, LLC

politicians best evoke compassion in an audience? What claim can you make based on these selections? What reasons can you think of to support your claim? How will audience and purpose affect the way you develop your ideas?

Then complete a prewriting road map such as this one, completed by the author of the student model:

My Claim: A writer's words evoke stronger empathy in others than an artist's photographs do.

Selections I Will Cite to Support My Claim:
Endangered Dreams: The Great Depression in California by Kevin Starr
"The Harvest Gypsies" by John Steinbeck

Reasons and Evidence That Support My Claim:

- <u>Reason</u>: Starr's description of Lange's trip to the pea pickers camp contains empathy-evoking details that are not present in the photograph.
- <u>Evidence</u>: "cold wet miserable day" (sensory detail), the "hungry" and "desperate" mother, that she "seemed to know that my pictures might help her, and so she helped me. There was a sort of equality about it" (Lange's own commentary)
- <u>Reason</u>: Steinbeck's words provide readers with a deeper understanding of the dangerous difficulties faced by families during the Great Depression.
- <u>Evidence</u>: "buzzing" flies and "foul" clothes (sensory details), repetition of "dullness" and mention of the baby who has not been bathed "for several days" (illustrates the length of time in which the families suffered, which can't be captured by a photograph)
- <u>Reason</u>: Steinbeck's word choices remind readers that any of us could face these difficulties, creating greater reader empathy.
- Evidence: use of "the father," "the mother," "the boy" (rather than names; creates ambiguity and a universal feeling)
- <u>Reason</u>: Words and photographs can work in harmony to produce empathy, but words have a greater impact when inspiring action or generating understanding.
- <u>Evidence</u>: Lange "rushed" her film to the paper, but her editor "got the story out," prompting the government to take action to help

Considerations for Audience and Purpose: I should use strong, persuasive language and a formal tone to help persuade my audience.

SKILL:
THESIS
STATEMENT

 DEFINE

The **thesis statement** is the most important sentence in an argumentative essay because it introduces what the writer is going to explore and attempt to prove in the essay or analysis. The thesis statement expresses the writer's **central or main idea about** that topic, or the **claim** the writer will develop in the body of the essay. In this way, the thesis statement of an essay acts as a road map, giving readers a view of what they will encounter throughout the essay. The thesis statement appears in the essay's introductory paragraph and is often the introduction's last sentence. The body paragraphs of the essay all support the thesis statement with specific ideas, as well as evidence to support the ideas. The thesis statement should reappear in some form in the essay's concluding paragraph.

 IDENTIFICATION AND APPLICATION

A thesis statement

- makes a clear statement about the central idea of the essay.
- lets the reader know what to expect in the body of the essay.
- responds fully and completely to an essay prompt.
- is presented in the introductory paragraph and restated in the conclusion.
- is a work in progress and should be revised and improved, as needed, during the early stages of the writing process.

 MODEL

The following is the introductory paragraph from the student model essay "Words to Change the World":

One of the key messages an author or artist can convey to people is the need for human compassion in order to make the world a better place to

NOTES

live. Precise word choice and sensory details are an author's keys to unlocking a reader's deepest emotions, but startling photographs can also move people. Through an article or broadcast, words can raise public awareness of social problems, but so can photographs. Which are more effective, words or pictures? The excerpt from the informational text *Endangered Dreams: The Great Depression in California* by Kevin Starr and the article "The Harvest Gypsies" by John Steinbeck both inform readers about migrant life during the Great Depression; the photographs of artists like Dorothea Lange, as explained in Starr's article, allow viewers to visualize that life. **While the photographs of Dorothea Lange and artists like her provide important insights into those conditions, it is the deeper human stories provided by writers like John Steinbeck that are more effective in bringing about social change.**

Notice the bold-faced thesis statement. This student's thesis statement responds to the prompt, identifying the works she will analyze in the essay, the authors and creators of those selections, and the point she will be making about the selections. It reminds readers of the topic of the essay, in this case, how authors and artists make the world a better place. It also specifically states the writer's particular central or main idea about that topic. In this writer's view, words are more effective than images in bringing about social change.

 ## PRACTICE

Using a pen and paper, draft a thesis statement for your argumentative essay that states your main idea in a clear and engaging way. Be sure that your thesis statement addresses the prompt. When you are done writing, switch papers with a partner to evaluate each other's work. How clearly did your partner state the main point? Does the thesis statement answer the question or topic posed in the prompt? Does the thesis statement clearly state the focus of the rest of the essay? Offer suggestions, and remember that they are most helpful when they are informative and constructive.

NOTES

SKILL: ORGANIZE ARGUMENTATIVE WRITING

DEFINE

Argumentative essays intend to convince readers of an author's position or point of view on a subject. To build an argument, authors introduce **claims**, or arguments, they will support with logical and valid reasoning and relevant evidence from reliable sources. The author's claim is stated in an **argumentative thesis statement**. In order to make a convincing argument, authors must distinguish their claims from **opposing claims**, or **counterclaims**—those that are contrary to the author's position or point of view. Authors then organize the claims, reasons, supporting evidence, and counterclaims into an effective argument.

IDENTIFICATION AND APPLICATION

The author of an argumentative essay takes a position on the topic and states a claim.

- The claim is the author's point of view or opinion about a topic.

- The claim is stated in a thesis statement and is supported by logical reasoning.

- The claim is clearly stated in the first paragraph of the argumentative essay.

- A restatement of the claim is usually found in the concluding paragraph.

- The author uses a formal style and a tone that is objective, or that shows no emotional bias.

- Text evidence is factual information from the text that supports the author's claim. Some evidence is strong because it can be verified in other sources as true. Strong text evidence may be in the form of:
  - › Numbers or statistics
  - › Quotes from experts
  - › Names or dates

 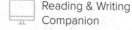

NOTES

› Other facts
› References to other credible sources

- Weaker text evidence cannot always be proven to be true. It may be in the form of:
  › Opinions
  › Personal beliefs
  › Emotional appeals
  › Biased, or one-sided, statements

 MODEL

"Words to Change the World" is an example of an argumentative essay written by a student. The author states her first claim—that the need for human compassion is an essential message for writers and artists to communicate—in her first sentence. She then raises an interesting question: Are words or pictures more effective in conveying compassion and motivating change? The writer indicates that her position on the topic will be supported with strong textual evidence from two reliable sources: the excerpt from *Endangered Dreams* by Kevin Starr and the article "The Harvest Gypsies," by John Steinbeck, both texts about the Great Depression. She goes on, in the final sentence of her introduction, to state her position.

> While the photographs of Dorothea Lange and artists like her provide important insights into those conditions, **it is the deeper human stories provided by writers like John Steinbeck that are more effective in bringing about social change.**

The writer is asserting that words are more effective than photographs. This is her thesis statement, the most important claim that she will make in her essay. This claim sets up what will follow in the body of the text.

In the second paragraph of her essay "Words to Change the World," the writer references *Endangered Dreams* to begin to support her argument.

> In ***Endangered Dreams: The Great Depression in California,*** the author, Kevin Starr, shows the world that photographer Dorothea Lange captured **information that the pictures themselves cannot contain,** providing readers with insights into the subjects of Lange's pictures. Sensory details such as "cold wet miserable day" give context for the moment when she debates the importance of turning around to visit the pea pickers camp (Starr 250).

Her "instinctive" decision to turn around leads her back to the camp, where she encounters the subject of a photograph that will eventually help change the fate of many starving Americans during the Great Depression in California. Starr describes the mother Lange meets as "hungry" and "desperate" (Starr 250). He explains Lange's own empathy for the woman by revealing Lange's thoughts that she "seemed to know that my pictures might help her, and so she helped me. There was a sort of equality about it" (Starr 250). While the picture went on to become known around the world, this commentary by Lange is absent from the image.

The writer argues against the counterclaim that pictures are more important by presenting evidence from Starr's text. He provides "information that the pictures themselves cannot contain." She includes details from Starr's text to show how the background information he provides serves to enhance an audience's appreciation of Lange's work. For example, familiarity with Lange's quotes can heighten the experience of viewing the photograph *Migrant Mother*. By the end of the third paragraph, she also points out that Starr's own evidence shows how a combination of photographs and news copy was needed to spur government action to help the migrants.

Words as well as photographs, Starr shows, changed America in those times of human need.

By the beginning of her fourth paragraph, the writer has successfully used a combination of claims, logical reasoning, and evidence to effectively argue that "powerful words are needed to gain a public's interest in important issues."

 PRACTICE

Go back to the thesis statement you crafted for your argumentative essay. Draft one or two paragraphs in which you present this thesis statement, offer evidence to support the claim it contains, and argue against a counterclaim. Exchange papers with a partner and offer each other feedback. Is it clear what is being proved or disproved?

SUPPORTING DETAILS

sync•skills
Writing

SKILL: SUPPORTING DETAILS

DEFINE

Before beginning an argumentative essay, writers must search for relevant **supporting details** to support their claims. Relevant information includes facts, statistics, definitions, textual evidence, examples, or quotations that are directly related to the writer's thesis statement, or main idea.

Writers must evaluate source information to determine its reliability before using it to support a claim. Information that comes from a credible source and is directly related to the writer's main idea provides strong support for a claim.

IDENTIFICATION AND APPLICATION

- Supporting evidence helps writers develop and strengthen claims in an argumentative essay.
- All supporting details in an argumentative essay should directly relate to the essay's main claim, or thesis statement.
- Writers often introduce and refute counterclaims to support their own claims.
- A writer's own reasoning can provide support for a claim when it is valid and relevant.
- When planning an argumentative essay, writers should choose details that are appropriate to a particular audience.

MODEL

In this excerpt from *Endangered Dreams: The Great Depression in California,* author Kevin Starr presents his thesis statement in the first paragraph:

> Among the photographs Lange forwarded to Washington was one which soon achieved the stature of an American masterpiece.

Please note that excerpts and passages in the StudySync® library and this workbook are intended as touchstones to generate interest in an author's work. The excerpts and passages do not substitute for the reading of entire texts, and StudySync® strongly recommends that students seek out and purchase the whole literary or informational work in order to experience it as the author intended. Links to online resellers are available in our digital library. In addition, complete works may be ordered through an authorized reseller by filling out and returning to StudySync® the order form enclosed in this workbook.

Reading & Writing Companion

91

Subsequently entitled *Migrant Mother,* **Lange's photograph has become not only the best-known image of the 270,000 plus negatives assembled by her Resettlement/Farm Security Administration team, but one of the most universally recognized and appreciated photographs of all time.**

In the third paragraph, Starr introduces a counterclaim questioning the universal appreciation of Lange's photograph and then refutes the counterclaim in support of his thesis statement:

> **Some critics have made much of the fact** that Lange did not learn the woman's name, which was Florence Thompson, **taking this as proof of Lange's photographic detachment.** In the woman and her three children, stranded in a roadside canvas lean-to, **such critics suggest,** Lange found a subject for her photographic art: a subject removed in time and circumstances from her prosperous clients in her previous practice; **but she approached her nevertheless from a similarly detached perspective.** The primary subject of *Migrant Mother,* from this perspective, is photography itself. **Such a criticism ignores the fact that as soon as Lange returned to San Francisco and developed these Nipomo negatives (there were actually six, not five as she remembered), she rushed with them to George West at the San Francisco News, telling him that thousands of pea pickers in Nipomo were starving because of the frozen harvest.** West got the story out in both the News, using two of Lange's photographs (but not *Migrant Mother*), and over the wires of the United Press. The federal government, meanwhile, rushed in twenty thousand pounds of food to feed the starving pea pickers.

The counterclaim introduced in this third paragraph is "Some critics have made much of the fact that Lange did not learn the woman's name, which was Florence Thompson, taking this as proof of Lange's photographic detachment." He continues to build the counterclaim with the idea that Lange's "critics suggest" she "approached her subjects" with the same "detached perspective" she used when taking portrait photographs of paying clients.

Starr then goes on to refute the counterclaim with the statement "Such a claim ignores the fact" and then presents factual details contrary to the claim. He reveals that "as Lange returned to San Francisco and developed these Nipomo negatives ... she rushed with them to George West at the San Francisco News, telling him that thousands of pea pickers in Nipomo were starving because of the frozen harvest." His addition of the parenthetical note "(there were actually six, not five as she remembered)" lends legitimacy to his refutation, showing readers that he has worked to uncover the facts. The

details weaken the criticism of Lange's photograph as "detached" and support Starr's claim that the photograph is "appreciated."

 PRACTICE

Go back to your prewriting road map, reread your main claim or replace it with your revised thesis, and evaluate the strength and relevance of the reasons and evidence you included in the road map. Copy your main claim or thesis on a new sheet, and under it, write a list of the strongest, most relevant supporting details from the road map or other sources you found after creating the road map. When you have finished, exchange lists with a partner and offer each other feedback. Which supporting detail is the most persuasive? Which is the least persuasive? Which reasons seem clear, and which seem confusing?

PLAN

WRITING PROMPT

Think about the selections you have read in examining how we develop empathy for others. Write an essay in which you argue how writers, poets, artists, or politicians best evoke compassion in an audience to inspire action or generate understanding. Use textual evidence from at least two of the selections you read in this unit to support your claim.

Your essay should include:
- An introduction that
  › contains a clear thesis statement.
  › presents an interesting and reasonable claim.
  › names the author and genre of each text you have selected to support your claim.

- Body paragraphs that
  › present a thorough analysis of your claim.
  › contain textual evidence and details to support your claim.
  › show logical organization of ideas.

- A conclusion paragraph that
  › restates your thesis statement.
  › effectively wraps up your essay.
  › leaves your reader with an interesting final thought.

As you begin to plan your argumentative essay, use your prewriting road map and list of possible supporting details to assemble your sources, your claim, and the relevant evidence you will be using to support your claim. Create an outline in preparation for writing your extended argumentative essay. At the top, state the claim you will argue. List the main topics you will address. Underneath each topic, list reasons and supporting evidence from the selections you have chosen to support your claim. Check that your outline

Copyright © BookheadEd Learning, LLC

follows logical organization for an argumentative essay. If you wish to do additional research to develop your ideas, be sure to keep a record of your sources as you place the information in the outline.

The author of the student model essay, "Words to Change the World," used an outline to organize her ideas before she started writing her essay. The outline divides evidence from the two articles the student references in the order in which these details are presented in the articles. Note that all of the evidence cited addresses the original claim. Outlines help writers eliminate information that is not relevant to the argument.

Look at the outline example and think about how you will outline and organize the information in your argumentative essay:

Essay Outline:

Essay Claim: While photographs can provide important insights into the human condition, it is the deeper human stories provided by writers that are more effective in bringing about social change.

Logical reasoning (to support the claim): The most important part of an outline is an explanation of the reasoning behind the argument. To support an argument, writers need to present credible, provable evidence in the form of facts, statistics, studies, and other documented research to back up any claims they make.

1. Claim: Photographs can provide important insights into the human condition, but writers are more effective in bringing about social change.
    a. Compare and contrast the photographs of Dorothea Lange in *Endangered Dreams: The Great Depression in California* and John Steinbeck's "The Harvest Gypsies."
        i. Which are more effective, words or pictures?
        ii. Word choice and sensory details can unlock a reader's emotions and raise public awareness
        iii. Startling photographs can also move people

2. Textual evidence from *Endangered Dreams*
    a. Starr provides insight into the subject of Lange's photographs that the photos alone cannot provide.
        i. Lange's decision to turn around and visit the pea pickers camp
        ii. Explanation of Lange's empathy for her subject
        iii. Relationship between Lange and her subject
    b. Effects of Lange's photograph *Migrant Mother*
        i. Lange developed the negatives as soon as she returned to San Francisco

Please note that excerpts and passages in the StudySync® library and this workbook are intended as touchstones to generate interest in an author's work. The excerpts and passages do not substitute for the reading of entire texts, and StudySync® strongly recommends that students seek out and purchase the whole literary or informational work in order to experience it as the author intended. Links to online resellers are available in our digital library. In addition, complete works may be ordered through an authorized reseller by filling out and returning to StudySync® the order form enclosed in this workbook.

Reading & Writing Companion

95

NOTES

      ii. Tells editor about the plight of pea pickers in Nipomo

      iii. Lange's editor "gets the story out" with two of Lange's photographs

      iv. The government acts and delivers food to the pea pickers camp.

      v. Powerful words needed in addition to photographs to spark action

3. Textual evidence from "The Harvest Gypsies"

    a. Steinbeck's use of precise details reveals plight of migrant families in California during the Great Depression.

      i. "rot" in the "tattered" canvas held in place with "rusty" wire

      ii. "filth" of the tent, "exposed" human feces, "buzzing" of flies

      iii. emphasis on time passing

      iv. words capture problems that develop over time; photo only captures a single moment

    b. Details that Steinbeck deliberately omits create empathy and a sense that this could be anyone's situation at any time.

      i. Steinbeck omits names; uses only generic terms such as "mother" and "father"

      ii. Points out how family fell on hard times

      iii. Certain details that happen over time can only be revealed through a writer's craft

4. Conclusion

    a. Images alone are not enough to bring about social change

      i. A news story accompanied Lange's photos to alert people about the conditions in Nipomo

      ii. Writers provide context or offer commentary on a situation that a photograph cannot

      iii. The craft of the photographer and writer can influence society, but it is words that can change the world.

SKILL:
INTRODUCTIONS

 DEFINE

The **introduction** is the opening paragraph or section of an essay or other non-fiction text. To begin an argumentative essay, writers identify the **topic,** or what the essay will be about. For an argumentative essay, the most important part of the introduction is the **thesis statement,** which contains the writer's main claim. An essay introduction should also include a **hook,** a statement or detail that grabs the reader's attention and generates reader interest in the topic.

 IDENTIFICATION AND APPLICATION

- To set up the argument and introduce the topic, authors may offer descriptions, anecdotes, and other information to prepare the reader.
- A thesis statement often appears as the last sentence of an introduction.
- A thesis statement is not based on an author's immediate, unconsidered opinion of a topic but is instead a statement based on reasons and evidence.
- The claim in the thesis statement must be proven in the body of the essay with relevant evidence and clear reasoning.
- The introduction should leave the reader with no doubt about the author's intention.
- The introduction should engage the reader and create interest that will encourage him or her to keep reading.

 MODEL

To introduce an argument, writers need to prepare readers for the subject, the claim that will be made, and the kinds of evidence the writer will be using. The student author of the argumentative essay "Words to Change the World" has opened her argument with this introductory paragraph.

Copyright © BookheadEd Learning, LLC

One of the key messages an **author or artist can convey to people is the need for human compassion in order to make the world a better place to live.** Precise word choice and sensory details are an author's keys to unlocking a reader's deepest emotions, but startling photographs can also move people. Through **an article or broadcast, words can raise public awareness of social problems, but so can photographs.** Which are more effective, words or pictures? The excerpt **from the informational text *Endangered Dreams: The Great Depression in California* by Kevin Starr and the article "The Harvest Gypsies" by John Steinbeck** both inform readers about migrant life during the Great Depression; the photographs of artists like Dorothea Lange allow viewers to visualize that life. **While the photographs of Dorothea Lange and artists like her provide important insights into those conditions, it is the deeper human stories provided by writers like John Steinbeck that are more effective in bringing about social change.**

The opening sentence states the reasons for her interest in the subject: Authors and artists communicate to people "the need for human compassion in order to make the world a better place to live." She sees this as a "key message," and offers her reason for believing this, saying that articles and photographs "can raise public awareness of social problems." She also cites the two selections she will use as source material to provide textual evidence for her essay: "The excerpt from the informational text *Endangered Dreams: The Great Depression* by Kevin Starr and the article "The Harvest Gypsies" by John Steinbeck." All of this builds up to the writer's claim, which is contained in the thesis statement. The writer's mention of the "deeper human stories" is intended to hook readers, so they will keep reading to find out more about how the words of writers can bring about social change. A strong introduction draws the readers into the topic, leaving no room for doubt about the writer's intentions.

 PRACTICE

Write an introduction for your informative essay that introduces the topic, presents the thesis statement and the sources that will be discussed in the essay, and includes a hook. When you are finished, trade introductions with a partner and offer each other feedback. How clear is the topic? How strong is the claim made in the thesis statement? How effective was the hook in drawing you into the topic? Offer each other suggestions for improvement, and remember that they are most helpful when they are constructive.

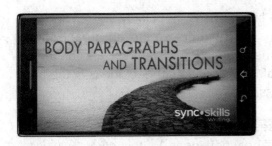

SKILL: BODY PARAGRAPHS AND TRANSITIONS

 DEFINE

Body paragraphs are the section of the essay between the introduction and conclusion paragraphs. Body paragraphs reveal a writer's **main points** and **claims.** They also present **evidence,** or information that supports the author's claim. Each body paragraph of an essay typically presents one main point or claim, to avoid confusing the reader. The main point of each body paragraph must support the **thesis statement,** the main claim of the essay.

Each body paragraph of an argumentative essay should contain the following structure:

Topic sentence: The topic sentence is the first sentence of a body paragraph. It should state the main point of the paragraph and support the thesis statement or main claim of the essay.

Evidence #1: A topic sentence is followed by evidence that supports the main point. Evidence can be relevant facts, statistics, definitions, quotations, examples, or other information used to support a claim.

Reasoning #1: Evidence should be followed by reasoning, or an explanation of how that evidence supports the main point of the paragraph. This explanation should also reveal how the evidence supports the overall thesis statement, or main claim of the essay.

Evidence #2: Writers can provide further support for their main points by introducing a second piece of evidence.

Reasoning #2: Again, evidence should be followed by reasoning, or an explanation of how that evidence supports the main point, and overall, the thesis statement.

Concluding sentence: The concluding sentence of a paragraph wraps up the main idea and transitions to the next paragraph.

Transitions are connecting words and phrases that clarify the relationships among ideas in a text. Transitions help writers create an organizational structure and show readers how the information in the essay is connected. Writers use many different types of transitions to connect ideas in the body paragraphs of an argumentative essay:

- **Introductory phrases and clauses,** which begin a sentence and end in a comma, help create connections between ideas. Writers commonly use introductory phrases and clauses such as "Because of these events," "As the results showed," or "According to experts" to introduce evidence and explain how the evidence supports the main point.
- **Cause-and-effect transitions** present a cause-and-effect relationship between ideas. Words such as *since, because, so, therefore, thus, hence,* and *consequently* allow writers to show how one idea leads to another, or to explain how a piece of evidence supports a point.
- **Problem and solution transitions** help writers build claims. Writers use transitions such as "so that" and "in order to" to propose solutions and support the claims in an argumentative essay.
- **Illustration transitions** help writers present evidence. Transitions such as *Such as, For example, For instance,* and *To illustrate* connect a writer's main point in the previous sentence to the evidence that will support it.

The most effective argumentative essays will achieve their aim—to persuade a reader to agree with the author's main claim—by containing well-structured body paragraphs that use strong transitions to connect ideas.

 IDENTIFICATION AND APPLICATION

- The body paragraphs of an argumentative essay provide the reasons, evidence, and arguments that support the claim made in the thesis statement.
- Writers typically develop one main idea or claim per body paragraph.
- Each body paragraph contains:
  › A topic sentence to present the main idea of the paragraph
  › Evidence to support the topic sentence
  › Reasoning to explain how the evidence supports the main idea of the paragraph and main claim of the essay

- A body paragraph may present a counterclaim that is contrary to the thesis statement. The writer then refutes the counterclaim to support the main claim of the essay.

- The conclusion sentence of a body paragraph wraps up the main idea or claim and transitions to the following body paragraph.
- Writers use transition words and phrases to connect and clarify the relationships among ideas in a text.

 MODEL

As writers craft an argument, the way they connect ideas and information—claims, logical reasoning, and evidence—will determine whether their readers will be convinced. The writer of the student model essay "Words to Change the World" uses a logical structure to present the information that supports her main claim.

Look at the third paragraph of the essay:

> **Starr points out that people often want words to accompany an image.** "Some critics have made much of the fact that Lange did not learn the woman's name," and **Starr would seem to support that criticism when he adds that she and her children were "stranded in a roadside canvas lean-to..."** (Starr 250). **However,** Starr defends Lange: "Such criticism," Starr explains, "ignores the fact that as soon as Lange returned to San Francisco, and developed these negatives," she told her editor "that thousands of pea pickers in Nipomo were starving because of the frozen harvest" (Starr 250). **Starr shows the energy of the moment,** as Lange **"rushed"** her film to the paper. It was her editor, George West, who **"got the story out,"** using two of Lange's other photographs to explain what happened. The result of getting the word out was "twenty thousand pounds of food to feed the starving pea pickers" (Starr 250). **A combination of photographs and news copy alerted the government, and action was taken. Words as well as photographs, Starr shows, changed America in those times of human need.**

This body paragraph begins with a topic sentence: "Starr points out that people often want words to accompany an image." The writer of the student model then introduces evidence from the text to suggest that "Starr would seem to support that criticism when he adds that she and her children were 'stranded in a roadside canvas lean-to.'" She then uses the transition word *However* to present the explanation of the evidence: that Starr actually defends Lange by refuting her critics.

The writer then introduces further evidence that Starr presents to explain that Lange "rushed" to the paper with her negatives and details of the pea pickers' plight, to help her editor craft the written news story that would accompany the photographs and eventually cause the government to take action. The writer's concluding sentence returns to the ideas presented in the topic sentence: "Words as well as photographs, Starr shows, changed America in those times of human need."

Now read the next paragraph of the essay:

> **In addition to images, then, powerful words are needed to gain a public's interest in important issues.** With the powerful words of his article *"The Harvest Gypsies,"* Steinbeck presents a vivid account of the plight of families migrating through California during the Great Depression. His organization of the precise details he reveals about two particular families leads readers to a deeper understanding of the dangerous difficulties many families faced during this time in America. **For example,** Steinbeck begins his article by introducing precise words to describe a family's home: the "rot" in the "tattered" canvas held in place with "rusty" wire; the "filth" of the tent and the "exposed" human feces covered in flies that fill the tent with their "buzzing"; the "foul" clothes of the children and "the baby, who has not been bathed or cleaned for several days" (Steinbeck 29). The emphasis on the time passing in the camp, "for several days," is something a photograph could not show. When Steinbeck reveals that a four-year-old boy who was sick for weeks from lack of nourishment has died, his words capture a problem that developed over time. Steinbeck uses words to gain compassion for the parents, who now live in "paralyzed dullness" (Steinbeck 29). **Steinbeck's repetition of "dullness" throughout the excerpt creates a continuous feeling that a single photograph, which only captures a specific moment in time, cannot communicate or express.**

The writer presents the topic sentence that will introduce the ideas of the new paragraph: "In addition to images, then, powerful words are needed to gain a public's interest in important issues." Here the writer uses the transition "In addition to images, then" to signal a connection between ideas in the third and fourth paragraphs of the essay. The transition "For example" allows readers to understand that the writer will now introduce evidence to support the main idea of the paragraph. As in the previous paragraph, the writer then wraps up the main idea with a strong concluding statement that explains how the textual evidence supports her thesis.

PRACTICE

Write two body paragraphs for your argumentative essay that follow the suggested format. When you are finished, trade with a partner and offer each other feedback. How effective is the topic sentence at stating the main idea of the paragraph? How strong is the evidence used to support the main idea? Does the reasoning for the evidence thoroughly support the main idea? Do the paragraphs contain strong transitions to connect and clarify ideas? Offer each other suggestions and remember that they are most helpful when they are constructive.

Please note that excerpts and passages in the StudySync® library and this workbook are intended as touchstones to generate interest in an author's work. The excerpts and passages do not substitute for the reading of entire texts, and StudySync® strongly recommends that students seek out and purchase the whole literary or informational work in order to experience it as the author intended. Links to online resellers are available in our digital library. In addition, complete works may be ordered through an authorized reseller by filling out and returning to StudySync® the order form enclosed in this workbook.

Reading & Writing
Companion

103

SKILL:
CONCLUSIONS

DEFINE

No argument can be considered "won" without a strong conclusion. The **conclusion** of an argumentative essay effectively brings together the points the writer makes by summarizing or restating the thesis found in the introduction. The thesis contains the claim the writer has made, while the body of the text has offered evidence to prove that claim. The conclusion gives the final statement of the argument. For this reason, conclusions should not introduce new information. A conclusion should remind readers of the main points in the argument and support the claim in the thesis statement.

IDENTIFICATION AND APPLICATION

- Writers often use phrases and clauses such as *Because of these events, As the results showed,* or *According to experts,* to help introduce summary items in a conclusion.

- The conclusion of an argumentative essay should contain a restatement of the thesis statement.

- The conclusion of an argumentative essay should convince readers that the writer has effectively proven his or her claim.

- An essay conclusion should end in a summary statement that wraps up the ideas in the concluding paragraph.

- A writer may choose to leave the reader with a final thought, to create a lasting impression on the reader.

MODEL

Read these concluding paragraphs from Robert Kennedy's "Statement on the Assassination of Martin Luther King, Jr."

We can do well in this country. We will have difficult times. We've had difficult times in the past, but we—and we will have difficult times in the future. It is not the end of violence; it is not the end of lawlessness; and it's not the end of disorder.

But **the vast majority of white people and the vast majority of black people in this country want to live together,** want to improve the quality of our life, and **want justice for all human beings that abide in our land.**

And let's **dedicate ourselves** to what the Greeks wrote so many years ago: **to tame the savageness of man** and make gentle the life of this world. Let us dedicate ourselves to that, and say a prayer for our country and for our people.

To frame his conclusion, Robert Kennedy returns to the themes of polarization and division that he used to open his statement, noting that this act of senseless violence will not in fact be the end of violence, and will not ultimately be the end of disorder, but that, even so, "the vast majority of white people and the vast majority of black people in this country want to live together . . . .and want justice for all human beings that abide in our land." The final paragraph asks readers to "dedicate ourselves . . . to tame the savageness of man." This ties in with the opening of the second paragraph, in which Kennedy recalls that "Martin Luther King dedicated his life to love and to justice between fellow human beings." Kennedy' s final thought—his call to tame savageness and create a gentle life for all—inspires readers to re-dedicate themselves to the goals of a fallen leader.

 PRACTICE

Write a conclusion for your argumentative essay. When you are finished, trade with a partner and offer each other feedback. How well did the writer restate the thesis statement? How effectively did the writer restate the main points of the essay in the conclusion? Did the writer include a summary statement to wrap up the concluding paragraph? What final thought did the writer leave you with? Offer each other suggestions, and remember that they are most helpful when they are constructive.

NOTES

DRAFT

WRITING PROMPT

Think about the selections you have read in examining how we develop empathy for others. Write an essay in which you argue how writers, poets, artists, or politicians best evoke compassion in an audience to inspire action or generate understanding. Use textual evidence from at least two of the selections you read in this unit to support your claim.

Your essay should include:
- An introduction that
  › contains a clear thesis statement.
  › presents an interesting and reasonable claim.
  › names the author and genre of each text you have selected to support your claim.

- Body paragraphs that
  › present a thorough analysis of your claim.
  › contain textual evidence and details to support your claim.
  › show logical organization of ideas.

- A conclusion paragraph that
  › restates your thesis statement.
  › effectively wraps up your essay.
  › leaves your reader with an interesting final thought.

You've already made progress toward writing your own argumentative essay. You've thought about the experiences of the characters in the texts. You've figured out how authors have used their writing to create empathy in readers. You've decided how to organize your information and gathered supporting details. Now it's time to write a draft. Use the prewriting and planning you have done—including your road map, outline, and drafted paragraphs—to

Copyright © BookheadEd Learning, LLC

NOTES

draft your argumentative essay. Be sure to include an introduction with a clear thesis statement that states your claim. Identify textual evidence and include sources of information throughout the essay. Draft a concluding paragraph that restates or reinforces your thesis statement and leaves a lasting impression on your readers. Finally, work to maintain a formal writing style. Before you submit your draft, read it over carefully. You want to be sure that you've responded to all aspects of the prompt.

When drafting, ask yourself these questions:

- How can I improve my hook to make it more appealing?
- What can I do to clarify my thesis statement?
- Which relevant facts, strong details, and interesting quotations in each body paragraph support the thesis statement?
- Would more precise language or different details about each character's experiences make the text more exciting and vivid?
- How well have I communicated how the author has used these experiences to create empathy?
- What final thought do I want to leave with my readers?

Please note that excerpts and passages in the StudySync® library and this workbook are intended as touchstones to generate interest in an author's work. The excerpts and passages do not substitute for the reading of entire texts, and StudySync® strongly recommends that students seek out and purchase the whole literary or informational work in order to experience it as the author intended. Links to online resellers are available in our digital library. In addition, complete works may be ordered through an authorized reseller by filling out and returning to StudySync® the order form enclosed in this workbook.

Reading & Writing
Companion

107

REVISE

You have written a draft of your argumentative essay. You have also received input from your peers about how to improve it. Now you are going to revise your draft.

Here are some recommendations to help you revise:

- Reread your draft before beginning your revision.
- Review the suggestions made by your peers. Make any adjustments you feel are necessary and warranted.
- Evaluate the strength of your introduction and revise as needed.
- Revise your thesis statement, if needed, to more clearly state your claim.
- Devise a strong conclusion that summarizes your ideas and restates the thesis.
- Consult a style manual to check guidelines for formatting and the placement of in-text as well as bibliographical citations (Works Cited).
  - › For in-text citations, be sure that you have applied quotation marks and parentheses correctly and included accurate page numbers.
  - › For bibliographical citations, be sure that every source contains all essential information and is formatted according to the style manual's guidelines.

- Focus on maintaining a formal style. A formal style suits your purpose—arguing for the use of a certain technique to create empathy in readers. It also fits your audience—students, teachers, and other readers interested in learning more about your topic.
  - › As you revise, eliminate any slang.
  - › Remove any first-person pronouns such as *I, me,* or *mine* or instances of addressing readers as *you*. These are more suitable to a writing style that is informal, personal, and conversational.
  - › If you include your personal opinions, remove them. Your essay should be clear, direct, and unbiased.

- After you have revised elements of style, think about whether there is anything else you can do to improve your essay's information or organization.

  › Do you need to add any new details to your essay? Is there a detail about someone's experiences that you haven't included yet that readers might empathize with?

  › Did one of your subjects say something special that you forgot to quote? Quotations can add life to your essay. Be sure to cite your sources.

  › Can you substitute a more precise word for a word that is general or dull?

  › Consider your organization. Would your essay flow better if you strengthened the transitions between paragraphs?

- As you add new details or change information, check your punctuation.

  › Be sure to punctuate restrictive and nonrestrictive phrases and clauses correctly.

  › Check that you use the proper pronoun case and number.

  › Check that you use possessives correctly.

Please note that excerpts and passages in the StudySync® library and this workbook are intended as touchstones to generate interest in an author's work. The excerpts and passages do not substitute for the reading of entire texts, and StudySync® strongly recommends that students seek out and purchase the whole literary or informational work in order to experience it as the author intended. Links to online resellers are available in our digital library. In addition, complete works may be ordered through an authorized reseller by filling out and returning to StudySync® the order form enclosed in this workbook.

Reading & Writing Companion   **109**

EDIT,
PROOFREAD
AND PUBLISH

WRITING PROMPT

Think about the selections you have read in examining how we develop empathy for others. Write an essay in which you argue how writers, poets, artists, or politicians best evoke compassion in an audience to inspire action or generate understanding. Use textual evidence from at least two of the selections you read in this unit to support your claim.

Your essay should include:
- An introduction that
  › contains a clear thesis statement.
  › presents an interesting and reasonable claim.
  › names the author and genre of each text you have selected to support your claim.

- Body paragraphs that
  › present a thorough analysis of your claim.
  › contain textual evidence and details to support your claim.
  › show logical organization of ideas.

- A conclusion paragraph that
  › restates your thesis statement.
  › effectively wraps up your essay.
  › leaves your reader with an interesting final thought.

You have revised your argumentative essay and received input from your peers on that revision. Now it's time to edit and proofread your essay to produce a final version. Have you included all the valuable suggestions from your peers? Ask yourself: Have I fully developed my thesis statement with strong textual evidence? Have I accurately cited my sources? What more can I do to improve my essay's information and organization?

When you are satisfied with your work, move on to proofread it for errors. For example, check that you have used correct punctuation for quotations and citations. Have you used possessives correctly? Have you styled italics properly according to style conventions for academic writing? Have you spelled compound words correctly? Be sure to correct any misspelled words.

Once you have made all your corrections, you are ready to submit and publish your work. You can distribute your writing to family and friends, hang it on a bulletin board, or post it on your blog. If you publish online, create links to your sources and citations. That way, readers can follow up on what they've learned from your essay and read more on their own.

studysync®

Reading & Writing Companion

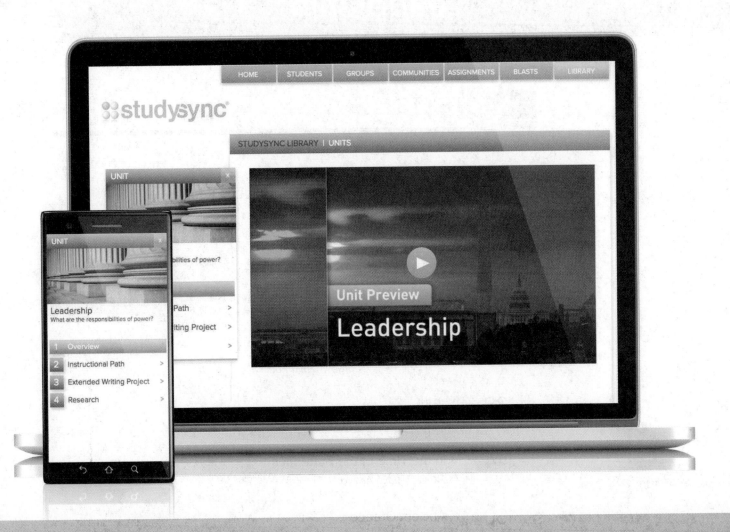

What are the responsibilities of power?

Leadership

Leadership

TEXTS

TEXTS

EXTENDED WRITING PROJECT

462

Text Fulfillment
through
StudySync

THE LADY, OR THE TIGER?

FICTION
Frank R. Stockton
1882

INTRODUCTION

rank Stockton, an engraver by trade, was said to have been influenced at an early age by the royalty and mythical creatures in fairytales, as well as by a fourteen-year-old servant girl who amused him by reading blood-curdling stories aloud in his kitchen. Both influences are evident in "The Lady, or the Tiger," the most famous of all his work. The ambiguity of the story is the likely reason its

"And yet, that awful tiger, those shrieks, that blood!"

FIRST READ

1   In the very olden time, there lived a semi-**barbaric** king, whose ideas, though somewhat polished and sharpened by the progressiveness of distant Latin neighbors, were still large, florid, and **untrammeled,** as became the half of him which was barbaric. He was a man of exuberant fancy, and, withal, of an authority so irresistible that, at his will, he turned his varied fancies into facts. He was greatly given to self-communing, and when he and himself agreed upon anything, the thing was done. When every member of his domestic and political systems moved smoothly in its appointed course, his nature was bland and genial; but whenever there was a little hitch, and some of his orbs got out of their orbits, he was blander and more genial still, for nothing pleased him so much as to make the crooked straight, and crush down uneven places.

2   Among the borrowed notions by which his barbarism had become semified was that of the public arena, in which, by exhibitions of manly and beastly valor, the minds of his subjects were refined and cultured.

3   But even here the exuberant and barbaric fancy asserted itself. The arena of the king was built, not to give the people an opportunity of hearing the rhapsodies of dying gladiators, nor to enable them to view the inevitable conclusion of a conflict between religious opinions and hungry jaws, but for purposes far better adapted to widen and develop the mental energies of the people. This vast amphitheatre, with its encircling galleries, its mysterious vaults, and its unseen passages, was an agent of poetic justice, in which crime was punished, or virtue rewarded, by the decrees of an impartial and incorruptible chance.

4   When a subject was accused of a crime of sufficient importance to interest the king, public notice was given that on an appointed day the fate of the accused person would be decided in the king's arena—a structure which well deserved its name; for, although its form and plan were borrowed from afar,

NOTES

its purpose **emanated** solely from the brain of this man, who, every barleycorn a king, knew no tradition to which he owed more allegiance than pleased his fancy, and who ingrafted on every adopted form of human thought and action the rich growth of his barbaric idealism.

5   When all the people had assembled in the galleries, and the king, surrounded by his court, sat high up on his throne of royal state on one side of the arena, he gave a signal, a door beneath him opened, and the accused subject stepped out into the amphitheatre. Directly opposite him, on the other side of the enclosed space, were two doors, exactly alike and side by side. It was the duty and the privilege of the person on trial to walk directly to these doors and open one of them. He could open either door he pleased. He was subject to no guidance or influence but that of the aforementioned impartial and incorruptible chance. If he opened the one, there came out of it a hungry tiger, the fiercest and most cruel that could be procured, which immediately sprang upon him, and tore him to pieces, as a punishment for his guilt. The moment that the case of the criminal was thus decided, doleful iron bells were clanged, great wails went up from the hired mourners posted on the outer rim of the arena, and the vast audience, with bowed heads and downcast hearts, wended slowly their homeward way, mourning greatly that one so young and fair, or so old and respected, should have merited so dire a fate.

6   But if the accused person opened the other door, there came forth from it a lady, the most suitable to his years and station that his Majesty could select among his fair subjects; and to this lady he was immediately married, as a reward of his innocence. It mattered not that he might already possess a wife and family, or that his affections might be engaged upon an object of his own selection. The king allowed no such subordinate arrangements to interfere with his great scheme of retribution and reward. The exercises, as in the other instance, took place immediately, and in the arena. Another door opened beneath the king, and a priest, followed by a band of choristers, and dancing maidens blowing joyous airs on golden horns and treading an **epithalamic** measure, advanced to where the pair stood side by side, and the wedding was promptly and cheerily solemnized. Then the gay brass bells rang forth their merry peals, the people shouted glad hurrahs, and the innocent man, preceded by children strewing flowers on his path, led his bride to his home.

7   This was the king's semi-barbaric method of administering justice. Its perfect fairness is obvious. The criminal could not know out of which door would come the lady. He opened either he pleased, without having the slightest idea whether, in the next instant, he was to be devoured or married. On some occasions the tiger came out of one door, and on some out of the other. The decisions of this tribunal were not only fair—they were positively determinate.

The accused person was instantly punished if he found himself guilty, and if innocent he was rewarded on the spot, whether he liked it or not. There was no escape from the judgments of the king's arena.

8   The institution was a very popular one. When the people gathered together on one of the great trial days, they never knew whether they were to witness a bloody slaughter or a hilarious wedding. This element of uncertainty lent an interest to the occasion which it could not otherwise have attained. Thus the masses were entertained and pleased, and the thinking part of the community could bring no charge of unfairness against this plan; for did not the accused person have the whole matter in his own hands?

9   This semi-barbaric king had a daughter as blooming as his most florid fancies, and with a soul as fervent and **imperious** as his own. As is usual in such cases, she was the apple of his eye, and was loved by him above all humanity. Among his courtiers was a young man of that fineness of blood and lowness of station common to the conventional heroes of romance who love royal maidens. This royal maiden was well satisfied with her lover, for he was handsome and brave to a degree unsurpassed in all this kingdom, and she loved him with an ardor that had enough of barbarism in it to make it exceedingly warm and strong. This love affair moved on happily for many months, until, one day, the king happened to discover its existence. He did not hesitate nor waver in regard to his duty in the premises. The youth was immediately cast into prison, and a day was appointed for his trial in the king's arena. This, of course, was an especially important occasion, and his Majesty, as well as all the people, was greatly interested in the workings and development of this trial. Never before had such a case occurred—never before had a subject dared to love the daughter of a king. In after years such things became commonplace enough, but then they were, in no slight degree, novel and startling.

10 The tiger cages of the kingdom were searched for the most savage and relentless beasts, from which the fiercest monster might be selected for the arena, and the ranks of maiden youth and beauty throughout the land were carefully surveyed by competent judges, in order that the young man might have a fitting bride in case fate did not determine for him a different destiny. Of course, everybody knew that the deed with which the accused was charged had been done. He had loved the princess, and neither he, she, nor any one else thought of denying the fact. But the king would not think of allowing any fact of this kind to interfere with the workings of the tribunal, in which he took such great delight and satisfaction. No matter how the affair turned out, the youth would be disposed of, and the king would take an aesthetic pleasure in watching the course of events which would determine whether or not the young man had done wrong in allowing himself to love the princess.

NOTES

11 The appointed day arrived. From far and near the people gathered, and thronged the great galleries of the arena, while crowds, unable to gain admittance, massed themselves against its outside walls. The king and his court were in their places, opposite the twin doors—those fateful portals, so terrible in their similarity!

12 All was ready. The signal was given. A door beneath the royal party opened, and the lover of the princess walked into the arena. Tall, beautiful, fair, his appearance was greeted with a low hum of admiration and anxiety. Half the audience had not known so grand a youth had lived among them. No wonder the princess loved him! What a terrible thing for him to be there!

13 As the youth advanced into the arena, he turned, as the custom was, to bow to the king. But he did not think at all of that royal personage; his eyes were fixed upon the princess, who sat to the right of her father. Had it not been for the moiety of barbarism in her nature, it is probable that lady would not have been there. But her intense and fervid soul would not allow her to be absent on an occasion in which she was so terribly interested. From the moment that the decree had gone forth that her lover should decide his fate in the king's arena, she had thought of nothing, night or day, but this great event and the various subjects connected with it. Possessed of more power, influence, and force of character than any one who had ever before been interested in such a case, she had done what no other person had done—she had possessed herself of the secret of the doors. She knew in which of the two rooms behind those doors stood the cage of the tiger, with its open front and in which waited the lady. Through these thick doors, heavily curtained with skins on the inside, it was impossible that any noise or suggestion should come from within to the person who should approach to raise the latch of one of them. But gold, and the power of a woman's will, had brought the secret to the princess.

14 Not only did she know in which room stood the lady, ready to emerge, all blushing and radiant, should her door be opened, but she knew who the lady was. It was one of the fairest and loveliest of the damsels of the court who had been selected as the reward of the accused youth, should he be proved innocent of the crime of aspiring to one so far above him; and the princess hated her. Often had she seen, or imagined that she had seen, this fair creature throwing glances of admiration upon the person of her lover, and sometimes she thought these glances were perceived and even returned. Now and then she had seen them talking together. It was but for a moment or two, but much can be said in a brief space. It may have been on most unimportant topics, but how could she know that? The girl was lovely, but she had dared to raise her eyes to the loved one of the princess, and, with all the intensity of the savage blood transmitted to her through long lines of wholly barbaric ancestors, she hated the woman who blushed and trembled behind that silent door.

15 When her lover turned and looked at her, and his eye met hers as she sat there paler and whiter than any one in the vast ocean of anxious faces about her, he saw, by that power of quick perception which is given to those whose souls are one, that she knew behind which door crouched the tiger, and behind which stood the lady. He had expected her to know it. He understood her nature, and his soul was assured that she would never rest until she had made plain to herself this thing, hidden to all other lookers-on, even to the king. The only hope for the youth in which there was any element of certainty was based upon the success of the princess in discovering this mystery, and the moment he looked upon her, he saw she had succeeded, as in his soul he knew she would succeed.

16 Then it was that his quick and anxious glance asked the question, "Which?" It was as plain to her as if he shouted it from where he stood. There was not an instant to be lost. The question was asked in a flash; it must be answered in another.

17 Her right arm lay on the cushioned parapet before her. She raised her hand, and made a slight, quick movement toward the right. No one but her lover saw her. Every eye but his was fixed on the man in the arena.

18 He turned, and with a firm and rapid step he walked across the empty space. Every heart stopped beating, every breath was held, every eye was fixed immovably upon that man. Without the slightest hesitation, he went to the door on the right, and opened it.

19 Now, the point of the story is this: Did the tiger come out of that door, or did the lady?

20 The more we reflect upon this question, the harder it is to answer. It involves a study of the human heart which leads us through devious mazes of passion, out of which it is difficult to find our way. Think of it, fair reader, not as if the decision of the question depended upon yourself, but upon that hot-blooded, semi-barbaric princess, her soul at a white heat beneath the combined fires of despair and jealousy. She had lost him, but who should have him?

21 How often, in her waking hours and in her dreams, had she started in wild horror and covered her face with her hands as she thought of her lover opening the door on the other side of which waited the cruel fangs of the tiger!

22 But how much oftener had she seen him at the other door! How in her grievous reveries had she gnashed her teeth and torn her hair when she saw his start of rapturous delight as he opened the door of the lady! How her soul had burned in agony when she had seen him rush to meet that woman, with her flushing cheek and sparkling eye of triumph; when she had seen him lead

NOTES

her forth, his whole frame kindled with the joy of recovered life; when she had heard the glad shouts from the multitude, and the wild ringing of the happy bells; when she had seen the priest, with his joyous followers, advance to the couple, and make them man and wife before her very eyes; and when she had seen them walk away together upon their path of flowers, followed by the tremendous shouts of the hilarious multitude, in which her one despairing shriek was lost and drowned!

23 Would it not be better for him to die at once, and go to wait for her in the blessed regions of semi-barbaric futurity?

24 And yet, that awful tiger, those shrieks, that blood!

25 Her decision had been indicated in an instant, but it had been made after days and nights of anguished deliberation. She had known she would be asked, she had decided what she would answer, and, without the slightest hesitation, she had moved her hand to the right.

26 The question of her decision is one not to be lightly considered, and it is not for me to presume to set up myself as the one person able to answer it. So I leave it with all of you: Which came out of the opened door—the lady or the tiger?

THINK QUESTIONS

1. What kind of person is the king? How do you know? Cite textual evidence to support your answer.

2. How are people in the kingdom treated when they are accused of a crime? What do the king and his people think of this treatment? Cite textual evidence to support your response.

3. At the end of the story, it isn't clear as to which door the king's daughter will send the youth. What does the fact that it was a hard choice for the princess imply about her character? Cite textual evidence to support your answer.

4. In the first sentence, the author writes, "In the very olden time, there lived a semi-barbaric king, whose ideas, though somewhat polished and sharpened by the progressiveness of distant Latin neighbors, were still large, florid, and **untrammelled,** as became the half of him which was barbaric." What context clues help you determine the meaning of the word *"untrammeled"* in this sentence? What additional clues might come from the fact that "untrammeled" begins with the prefix *un-*, which means "not"?

5. The author describes the king as **barbaric** several times. The adjective *"barbaric"* has Latin and Greek roots that actually go back to even older languages like Sanskrit. It is believed that these roots developed from the sound *bar-bar,* which ancient people made to imitate the words of an unfamiliar language that they regarded as primitive and inferior. How might the use of *"barbaric"* in "The Lady, or the Tiger?" connect to the word's history?

CLOSE READ

Reread the short story "The Lady, or the Tiger?" As you reread, complete the Focus Questions below. Then use your answers and annotations from the questions to help you complete the Writing Prompt.

FOCUS QUESTIONS

1. As you reread the beginning of "The Lady, or the Tiger?" think about how the author structures the early paragraphs by describing the character of the king. What effect do these descriptions have? Highlight evidence to support your ideas and write annotations to explain your choices.

2. In paragraph 9, the king discovers his daughter's love affair. What part of the story structure is this discovery? What impact does this discovery have on the rest of the text? Highlight your evidence and annotate to explain your ideas.

3. What is the central problem in "The Lady, or the Tiger?" Which character faces the problem? Highlight evidence to support your ideas and write annotations to explain your choices.

4. The author uses the word **semi-barbaric** to describe both the king and his daughter. Use a print or online dictionary to look up the prefix *semi-* and write annotations to define it. Then explain in what ways the princess is both barbaric and civilized, highlighting evidence and writing annotations to support your ideas.

5. The structure of "The Lady, or the Tiger?" works to create suspense for the reader. In what ways does the structure create this tension? Highlight evidence from the text that will help support your ideas.

6. What ideas does the author convey about power? Consider the power held by both the king and the princess. Use evidence from the text to support your answer.

WRITING PROMPT

What came out of the door, the lady or the tiger? Create a resolution to Stockton's story, since he deliberately left out that element of story structure. In an essay of 400 words or more, answer the question that comprises the last sentence of this short story, drawing upon your understanding of the princess's complex character and of human nature in general. Use textual evidence to support your views and defend your response.

Please note that excerpts and passages in the StudySync® library and this workbook are intended as touchstones to generate interest in an author's work. The excerpts and passages do not substitute for the reading of entire texts, and StudySync® strongly recommends that students seek out and purchase the whole literary or informational work in order to experience it as the author intended. Links to online resellers are available in our digital library. In addition, complete works may be ordered through an authorized reseller by filling out and returning to StudySync® the order form enclosed in this workbook.

Reading & Writing Companion   **123**

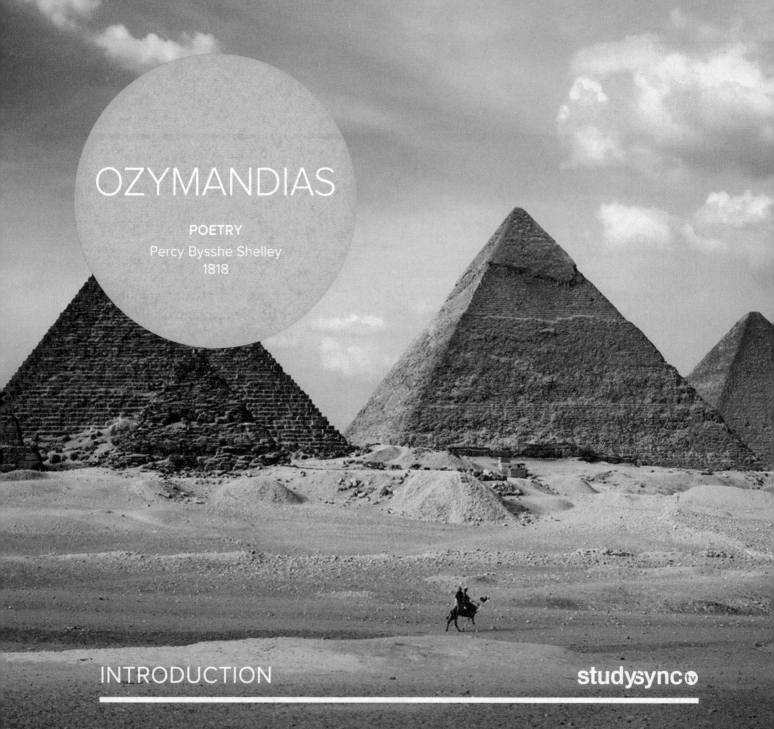

OZYMANDIAS

POETRY
Percy Bysshe Shelley
1818

INTRODUCTION

Percy Bysshe Shelley (1792-1822), one of the most famous of English romantic poets, was known for his radical ideas and unconventional lifestyle. Like *Frankenstein*, which was written by his second wife Mary Shelley, the poem *Ozymandias* was composed in response to a challenge. Shelley and his friend, poet Horace Smith, submitted poems to the *The Examiner* on the occasion of the statue of the Pharaoh Rameses II being transported from Egypt to London. Shelley's fourteen-line sonnet appeared in the paper first in January 1818. The imaginative poet invented a traveler and a sculptor's inscription, evoking the ancient relic's

"Look on my works, ye Mighty, and despair!"

 FIRST READ

 NOTES

1   I met a traveller from an antique land
2   Who said: 'Two vast and trunkless legs of stone
3   Stand in the desert. Near them, on the sand,
4   Half sunk, a shattered **visage** lies, whose frown,
5   And wrinkled lip, and sneer of cold command,
6   Tell that its sculptor well those passions read
7   Which yet survive, stamped on these lifeless things,
8   The hand that **mocked** them and the heart that fed.
9   And on the **pedestal** these words appear --
10 "My name is Ozymandias, king of kings:
11 Look on my works, ye Mighty, and **despair!"**
12 Nothing beside remains. Round the decay
13 Of that **colossal** wreck, boundless and bare
14 The lone and level sands stretch far away.

 THINK QUESTIONS

1. How does the traveler in the poem describe the statue and the area that surrounds it? Use details from the text to support your answer.

2. In the inscription on the pedestal, what does the term *works* refer to? Use details from the text to support your answer.

3. What does the inscription on the pedestal suggest about the kind of person Ozymandias was? Include details from the text in your response.

4. Use context to determine the meaning of the word **visage** as it is used in "Ozymandias." Write your definition of *visage* and tell how you got it. What might be a synonym for this term?

5. Use context to determine the meaning of the word **colossal** as it is used in the poem. Write your definition of *colossal* and tell how you got it.

Reading & Writing
Companion

CLOSE READ

Reread the poem "Ozymandias." As you reread, complete the Focus Questions below. Then use your answers and annotations from the questions to help you complete the Writing Prompt.

FOCUS QUESTIONS

1. As you reread "Ozymandias," think about the fact that the traveler narrates most of the poem. What do you think his point of view is toward Ozymandias? Highlight and annotate words in the poem's first four lines that provide clues to what the narrator thinks and feels about the statue. How are these words clues to the poem's theme? How would the poem be different if the poet substituted the words a "regal and commanding smile" for "sneer of cold command"?

2. How do word sounds contribute to the meaning and tone of the poem? Highlight one example each of assonance, consonance, and alliteration in the poem. Explain how each sound contributes to the reader's understanding of the poem's setting and theme.

3. The poem's theme is underscored by a comparison between the inscription on the pedestal and the emptiness of the landscape. What other details in the poem point to this comparison? Highlight and annotate textual evidence in the poem that shows the degree of contrast between this ruler's expectations and his fate. You might focus your analysis on the words *colossal wreck*.

4. One theme in the poem is the idea that worldly expectations can lead nowhere, and that great pride can be followed by a great fall. Another related theme is the idea that art endures while all else passes away. What details in the poem are clues to this theme? Use textual evidence to support the idea that this is one of the poem's themes.

5. Think of a famous person's statue with which you're familiar. It might be standing in your neighborhood, or it might be one you've seen on a trip or in a movie, read about in books, or heard about from a friend or relative. How would you compare this statue with the one portrayed in the poem? Highlight and annotate elements in the poem "Ozymandias" that you would want to include in any comparison. For example, highlight the facial features of the statue of Ozymandias in the poem. Make notes on how they differ from the features of the statue you've chosen.

6. What does the tone of "Ozymandias" suggest about the speaker's attitude toward power, and people in power? Use evidence from the text to support your ideas about how the speaker's attitude is conveyed in the poem.

WRITING PROMPT

Imagine that the main theme of "Ozymandias" was "great power requires great responsibility." How would the poem be different? Would the language of the poem be altered with the change in main theme, and if so, how? How might the traveler's point of view change? Which details from the text would remain the same and which might change? Address these questions in a written response of at least 300 words. Support your claim with valid reasons and relevant textual support.

THANKSGIVING PROCLAMATION

NON-FICTION
George Washington
1789

INTRODUCTION

Following a resolution of Congress, President George Washington proclaimed November 26, 1789, as a day of "public thanksgiving and prayer," honoring a tradition that traces back in America to the Pilgrims and their 1621 celebration at Plymouth Plantation. Washington declared another Thanksgiving in 1795, but it wasn't until 1863 and the Civil War that it became a federal holiday, when Abraham Lincoln called for a national day of "Thanksgiving and Praise."

"That we may then all unite in rendering unto him our sincere and humble thanks..."

NOTES

FIRST READ

1 By the President of the United States of America, a Proclamation.

2 Whereas it is the duty of all Nations to acknowledge the **providence** of Almighty God, to obey his will, to be grateful for his benefits, and humbly to implore his protection and favor—and whereas both Houses of Congress have by their joint Committee requested me to recommend to the People of the United States a day of public thanksgiving and prayer to be observed by acknowledging with grateful hearts the many signal favors of Almighty God especially by affording them an opportunity peaceably to establish a form of government for their safety and happiness.

3 Now therefore I do recommend and assign Thursday the 26th day of November next to be devoted by the People of these States to the service of that great and glorious Being, who is the beneficent Author of all the good that was, that is, or that will be—That we may then all unite in **rendering** unto him our sincere and humble thanks—for his kind care and protection of the People of this Country previous to their becoming a Nation—for the signal and **manifold** mercies, and the favorable interpositions of his Providence which we experienced in the course and conclusion of the late war—for the great degree of tranquility, union, and plenty, which we have since enjoyed—for the peaceable and rational manner, in which we have been enabled to establish constitutions of government for our safety and happiness, and particularly the national One now lately instituted—for the civil and religious liberty with which we are blessed; and the means we have of acquiring and diffusing useful knowledge; and in general for all the great and various favors which he hath been pleased to confer upon us.

4 And also that we may then unite in most humbly offering our prayers and **supplications** to the great Lord and Ruler of Nations and beseech him to pardon our national and other transgressions—to enable us all, whether in

public or private stations, to perform our several and relative duties properly and punctually—to render our national government a blessing to all the people, by constantly being a Government of wise, just, and constitutional laws, discreetly and faithfully executed and obeyed—to protect and guide all Sovereigns and Nations (especially such as have shewn kindness unto us) and to bless them with good government, peace, and **concord**—To promote the knowledge and practice of true religion and virtue, and the encrease of science among them and us—and generally to grant unto all Mankind such a degree of temporal prosperity as he alone knows to be best.

5   Given under my hand at the City of New York the third day of October in the year of our Lord 1789.

 THINK QUESTIONS

1. To whom or what does Washington give credit for America's victory in the Revolution? Cite textual evidence to support your answer.

2. What was the capital of the United States when Washington issued his Proclamation? How can you tell? Cite textual evidence to support your answer.

3. According to Washington, what is the primary purpose for this day of thanksgiving? Cite textual evidence to support your answer.

4. Use context clues to determine the meaning of the word **supplications** in the third paragraph of the "Thanksgiving Proclamation." Write your definition of *supplications*.

5. If *accord* means "agreement," and *discord* means "conflict," what do you suppose the word **concord** might mean? Use your knowledge of roots and prefixes to help you decide.

Please note that excerpts and passages in the StudySync® library and this workbook are intended as touchstones to generate interest in an author's work. The excerpts and passages do not substitute for the reading of entire texts, and StudySync® strongly recommends that students seek out and purchase the whole literary or informational work in order to experience it as the author intended. Links to online resellers are available in our digital library. In addition, complete works may be ordered through an authorized reseller by filling out and returning to StudySync® the order form enclosed in this workbook.

Reading & Writing Companion   **129**

CLOSE READ

Reread "Thanksgiving Proclamation." As you reread, complete the Focus Questions below. Then use your answers and annotations from the questions to help you complete the Writing Prompt.

FOCUS QUESTIONS

1. As you reread the text of "Thanksgiving Proclamation," think about why Washington is making this announcement. What does he hope to accomplish? What are his reasons? Highlight evidence to support your ideas and write annotations to explain your choices in detail.

2. Because this is a proclamation, it is written with a degree of formality. Where can we see that in the text? Which words or phrases indicate the importance and seriousness of the proclamation? Highlight your evidence and record your ideas in annotations.

3. How does Washington indicate that this special day, the 26th of November, is a day set aside specifically for giving thanks? Highlight your evidence and annotate to explain your ideas.

4. What is Washington's attitude toward his God? Highlight words and phrases that indicate his feelings and make annotations to explain your choices.

5. If you were to summarize this text in a sentence or two, what would you say? Highlight specific ideas in the text that you might include in a summary.

6. How does the text of the "Thanksgiving Proclamation" reveal Washington's attitude toward the responsibilities of power? Highlight evidence from the text that supports your answer.

WRITING PROMPT

Rewrite this proclamation in modern English, as it might be presented by a modern president. Keep the main idea and tone in mind as you write.

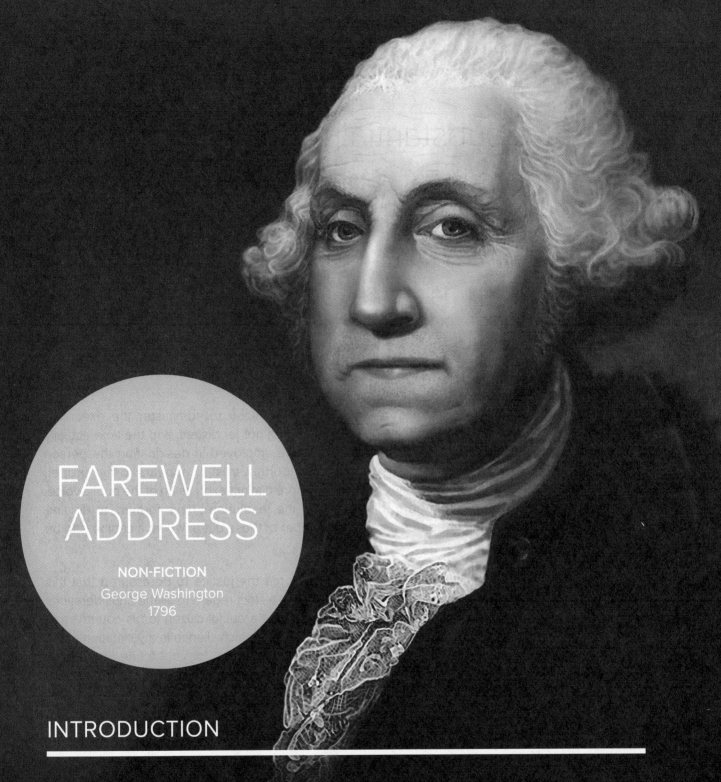

FAREWELL ADDRESS

NON-FICTION
George Washington
1796

INTRODUCTION

I n 1796, after serving eight years as President of the United States, George Washington disappointed supporters by refusing to run for a third term in office. Instead, Washington announced his retirement and reiterated his political philosophies in a public letter that is now considered one of America's most important historical documents. In the following excerpt, Washington discusses the importance of preserving the union, adhering to the doctrines of religion and morality, and maintaining peaceful relationships with other nations.

"It is substantially true that virtue or morality is a necessary spring of popular government."

 FIRST READ

1 Friends and Citizens:

2 The period for a new election of a citizen to administer the executive government of the United States being not far distant, and the time actually arrived when your thoughts must be employed in designating the person who is to be clothed with that important trust, it appears to me proper, especially as it may conduce to a more distinct expression of the public voice, that I should now apprise you of the resolution I have formed, to decline being considered among the number of those out of whom a choice is to be made.

3 I beg you, at the same time, to do me the justice to be assured that this resolution has not been taken without a strict regard to all the considerations appertaining to the relation which binds a dutiful citizen to his country; and that in withdrawing the tender of service, which silence in my situation might imply, I am influenced by no **diminution** of zeal for your future interest, no deficiency of grateful respect for your past kindness, but am supported by a full conviction that the step is compatible with both.

...

4 Interwoven as is the love of liberty with every ligament of your hearts, no recommendation of mine is necessary to fortify or confirm the attachment.

5 The unity of government which constitutes you one people is also now dear to you. It is justly so, for it is a main pillar in the **edifice** of your real independence, the support of your tranquility at home, your peace abroad; of your safety; of your prosperity; of that very liberty which you so highly prize. But as it is easy to foresee that, from different causes and from different quarters, much pains will be taken, many artifices employed to weaken in your minds the conviction of this truth; as this is the point in your political fortress against which the

batteries of internal and external enemies will be most constantly and actively (though often covertly and insidiously) directed, it is of infinite moment that you should properly estimate the immense value of your national union to your collective and individual happiness; that you should cherish a cordial, habitual, and immovable attachment to it; accustoming yourselves to think and speak of it as of the palladium of your political safety and prosperity; watching for its preservation with jealous anxiety; discountenancing whatever may suggest even a suspicion that it can in any event be abandoned; and indignantly frowning upon the first dawning of every attempt to alienate any portion of our country from the rest, or to enfeeble the sacred ties which now link together the various parts.

6   For this you have every inducement of sympathy and interest. Citizens, by birth or choice, of a common country, that country has a right to concentrate your affections. The name of American, which belongs to you in your national capacity, must always exalt the just pride of patriotism more than any **appellation** derived from local discriminations. With slight shades of difference, you have the same religion, manners, habits, and political principles. You have in a common cause fought and triumphed together; the independence and liberty you possess are the work of joint counsels, and joint efforts of common dangers, sufferings, and successes.

...

7   While, then, every part of our country thus feels an immediate and particular interest in union, all the parts combined cannot fail to find in the united mass of means and efforts greater strength, greater resource, proportionably greater security from external danger, a less frequent interruption of their peace by foreign nations; and, what is of inestimable value, they must derive from union an exemption from those broils and wars between themselves, which so frequently afflict neighboring countries not tied together by the same governments, which their own rival ships alone would be sufficient to produce, but which opposite foreign alliances, attachments, and intrigues would stimulate and embitter. Hence, likewise, they will avoid the necessity of those overgrown military establishments which, under any form of government, are **inauspicious** to liberty, and which are to be regarded as particularly hostile to republican liberty. In this sense it is that your union ought to be considered as a main prop of your liberty, and that the love of the one ought to endear to you the preservation of the other.

8   These considerations speak a persuasive language to every reflecting and virtuous mind, and exhibit the continuance of the Union as a primary object of patriotic desire. Is there a doubt whether a common government can embrace so large a sphere? Let experience solve it. To listen to mere speculation in such a case were criminal. We are authorized to hope that a proper

organization of the whole with the auxiliary agency of governments for the respective subdivisions, will afford a happy issue to the experiment. It is well worth a fair and full experiment. With such powerful and obvious motives to union, affecting all parts of our country, while experience shall not have demonstrated its impracticability, there will always be reason to distrust the patriotism of those who in any quarter may endeavor to weaken its bands.

9   In contemplating the causes which may disturb our Union, it occurs as matter of serious concern that any ground should have been furnished for characterizing parties by geographical discriminations, Northern and Southern, Atlantic and Western; whence designing men may endeavor to excite a belief that there is a real difference of local interests and views. One of the expedients of party to acquire influence within particular districts is to misrepresent the opinions and aims of other districts. You cannot shield yourselves too much against the jealousies and heartburnings which spring from these misrepresentations; they tend to render alien to each other those who ought to be bound together by fraternal affection.

...

10   Of all the dispositions and habits which lead to political prosperity, religion and morality are indispensable supports. In vain would that man claim the tribute of patriotism, who should labor to subvert these great pillars of human happiness, these firmest props of the duties of men and citizens. The mere politician, equally with the pious man, ought to respect and to cherish them. A volume could not trace all their connections with private and public felicity. Let it simply be asked: Where is the security for property, for reputation, for life, if the sense of religious obligation desert the oaths which are the instruments of investigation in courts of justice? And let us with caution indulge the supposition that morality can be maintained without religion. Whatever may be conceded to the influence of refined education on minds of peculiar structure, reason and experience both forbid us to expect that national morality can prevail in exclusion of religious principle.

11   It is substantially true that virtue or morality is a necessary spring of popular government. The rule, indeed, extends with more or less force to every species of free government. Who that is a sincere friend to it can look with indifference upon attempts to shake the foundation of the fabric?

...

12   Observe good faith and justice towards all nations; cultivate peace and harmony with all. Religion and morality enjoin this conduct; and can it be, that good policy does not equally enjoin it - It will be worthy of a free, enlightened, and at no distant period, a great nation, to give to mankind the magnanimous and too novel example of a people always guided by an exalted justice and

benevolence. Who can doubt that, in the course of time and things, the fruits of such a plan would richly repay any temporary advantages which might be lost by a steady adherence to it? Can it be that Providence has not connected the permanent felicity of a nation with its virtue? The experiment, at least, is recommended by every sentiment which ennobles human nature. Alas! is it rendered impossible by its vices?

...

13 Though, in reviewing the incidents of my administration, I am unconscious of intentional error, I am nevertheless too sensible of my defects not to think it probable that I may have committed many errors. Whatever they may be, I fervently beseech the Almighty to avert or mitigate the evils to which they may tend. I shall also carry with me the hope that my country will never cease to view them with indulgence; and that, after forty five years of my life dedicated to its service with an upright zeal, the faults of incompetent abilities will be consigned to oblivion, as myself must soon be to the mansions of rest.

14 Relying on its kindness in this as in other things, and actuated by that fervent love towards it, which is so natural to a man who views in it the native soil of himself and his progenitors for several generations, I anticipate with pleasing expectation that retreat in which I promise myself to realize, without **alloy,** the sweet enjoyment of partaking, in the midst of my fellow-citizens, the benign influence of good laws under a free government, the ever-favorite object of my heart, and the happy reward, as I trust, of our mutual cares, labors, and dangers.

THINK QUESTIONS

1. Explain what Washington means when he says the following about the military establishment: "...avoid the necessity of those overgrown military establishments, which, under any form of government, are inauspicious to liberty, and which are to be regarded as particularly hostile to Republican Liberty." Support your explanation by citing specific words from this quotation.

2. What are Washington's views about the role of morality and religion in the life of a nation? What is his opinion about the relationship between morality and religion? Cite textual evidence that supports your inference about his views.

3. What can you infer about the problems Washington faced as president from his appeals to people to put their loyalty to the United States over their loyalty to their own state or region? Cite textual evidence to support your answer.

4. What context clues in this sentence help you understand the meaning of the word **appellation**? "The name of American, which belongs to you in your national capacity, must always exalt the just pride of patriotism more than any *appellation* derived from local discriminations."

5. The word **diminution** contains the noun-forming suffix *-tion*. Using your knowledge of suffixes—and a print or online dictionary, if necessary—determine and write the form that *diminution* would have if it were (1) an adjective and (2) a verb.

CLOSE READ

Reread the text *Farewell Address*. As you reread, complete the Focus Questions below. Then use your answers and annotations from the questions to help you complete the Writing Prompt.

FOCUS QUESTIONS

1. Washington makes an argument that resembles the adage *The whole is stronger than its individual parts*. Highlight textual evidence and make annotations showing how he builds and supports this argument.

2. Highlight the text in the ninth paragraph in which Washington states his strong belief that religion is an important part of the political structure. How might his position on religion and morality shape his thinking about conflicts in his day? Can you think of other ways in which Washington's ideas about religion may have shaped his leadership? Cite textual evidence to explain your answers.

3. Why in paragraph 12 do you think Washington includes an apology for any mistakes he might have made? Highlight this apologetic language and then write annotations to explain his possible motive for including it. Would a modern president apologize in this way? Make additional annotations to explain why or why not.

4. Highlight this comment in paragraph 9: "It is substantially true that virtue or morality is a necessary spring of popular government." What does he mean by this statement? Do you agree or disagree with the statement? Use the annotation tool to explain your answer.

5. A little more than halfway through the excerpt, Washington comments on the idea that Americans might identify with the region of the country in which they live, rather than with the nation as a whole. Highlight the sentence in which he names some of those regions. Then make annotations to explain Washington's opinion about focusing on regional differences rather than national unity and how it might relate to his feelings about power and responsibility.

WRITING PROMPT

How would a modern-day president give an address like this? Would a president today use the same rhetoric that Washington used? Would he or she use similar language and sentence structure? Washington wrote his address as a letter, which was quickly reprinted in newspapers and in pamphlets all over the nation. How would a modern president share the address, and who would be the audience? Reread the selection, comparing Washington's rhetoric with the style you might hear in political speeches today. Then rewrite the excerpt from Washington's *Farewell Address* in contemporary English. Present the same arguments that Washington sets forth, but use the language that a modern president would use.

Please note that excerpts and passages in the StudySync® library and this workbook are intended as touchstones to generate interest in an author's work. The excerpts and passages do not substitute for the reading of entire texts, and StudySync® strongly recommends that students seek out and purchase the whole literary or informational work in order to experience it as the author intended. Links to online resellers are available in our digital library. In addition, complete works may be ordered through an authorized reseller by filling out and returning to StudySync® the order form enclosed in this workbook.

Reading & Writing Companion **137**

1984

FICTION
George Orwell
1949

INTRODUCTION

Written in the aftermath of World War II, amidst the invasion of technology into all aspects of human existence, George Orwell's *1984* sounds the alarm against the dangers of totalitarianism and constant surveillance. The dystopian novel explores the psychological landscape of power, and how language can be manipulated to control people and their sense of reality. The book opens with the thirteenth chime, introducing readers to a world of inverted truths and intimidation.

"BIG BROTHER IS WATCHING YOU,
the caption beneath it ran."

 FIRST READ

 NOTES

One

1   It was a bright cold day in April, and the clocks were striking thirteen. Winston Smith, his chin nuzzled into his breast in an effort to escape the vile wind, slipped quickly through the glass doors of Victory Mansions, though not quickly enough to prevent a swirl of gritty dust from entering along with him.

2   The hallway smelt of boiled cabbage and old rag mats. At one end of it a coloured poster, too large for indoor display, had been tacked to the wall. It depicted simply an enormous face, more than a metre wide: the face of a man of about forty-five, with a heavy black moustache and ruggedly handsome features. Winston made for the stairs. It was no use trying the lift. Even at the best of times it was seldom working, and at present the electric current was cut off during daylight hours. It was part of the economy drive in preparation for Hate Week. The flat was seven flights up, and Winston, who was thirty-nine and had a varicose ulcer above his right ankle, went slowly, resting several times on the way. On each landing, opposite the lift-shaft, the poster with the enormous face gazed from the wall. It was one of those pictures which are so **contrived** that the eyes follow you about when you move. BIG BROTHER IS WATCHING YOU, the caption beneath it ran.

3   Inside the flat a fruity voice was reading out a list of figures which had something to do with the production of pig iron. The voice came from an oblong metal plaque like a dulled mirror which formed part of the surface of the right-hand wall. Winston turned a switch and the voice sank somewhat, though the words were still distinguishable. The instrument (the telescreen, it was called) could be dimmed, but there was no way of shutting it off completely. He moved over to the window: a smallish, frail figure, the meagreness of his body merely emphasized by the blue overalls which were the uniform of the party. His hair was very fair, his face naturally **sanguine**, his

NOTES

skin roughened by coarse soap and blunt razor blades and the cold of the winter that had just ended.

4   Outside, even through the shut window-pane, the world looked cold. Down in the street little eddies of wind were whirling dust and torn paper into spirals, and though the sun was shining and the sky a harsh blue, there seemed to be no colour in anything, except the posters that were plastered everywhere. The black-moustachio'd face gazed down from every commanding corner. There was one on the house-front immediately opposite. BIG BROTHER IS WATCHING YOU, the caption said, while the dark eyes looked deep into Winston's own. Down at street level another poster, torn at one corner, flapped fitfully in the wind, alternately covering and uncovering the single word INGSOC. In the far distance a helicopter skimmed down between the roofs, hovered for an instant like a bluebottle, and darted away again with a curving flight. It was the police patrol, snooping into people's windows. The patrols did not matter, however. Only the Thought Police mattered.

5   Behind Winston's back the voice from the telescreen was still babbling away about pig iron and the overfulfillment of the Ninth Three-Year Plan. The telescreen received and transmitted simultaneously. Any sound that Winston made, above the level of a very low whisper, would be picked up by it, moreover, so long as he remained within the field of vision which the metal plaque commanded, he could be seen as well as heard. There was of course no way of knowing whether you were being watched at any given moment. How often, or on what system, the Thought Police plugged in on any individual wire was guesswork. It was even conceivable that they watched everybody all the time. But at any rate they could plug in your wire whenever they wanted to. You had to live -- did live, from habit that became instinct -- in the assumption that every sound you made was overheard, and, except in darkness, every movement scrutinized.

6   Winston kept his back turned to the telescreen. It was safer; though, as he well knew, even a back can be revealing. A kilometre away the Ministry of Truth, his place of work, towered vast and white above the grimy landscape. This, he thought with a sort of vague distaste -- this was London, chief city of Airstrip One, itself the third most **populous** of the provinces of Oceania. He tried to squeeze out some childhood memory that should tell him whether London had always been quite like this. Were there always these vistas of rotting nineteenth-century houses, their sides shored up with baulks of timber, their windows patched with cardboard and their roofs with corrugated iron, their crazy garden walls sagging in all directions? And the bombed sites where the plaster dust swirled in the air and the willow-herb straggled over the heaps of rubble; and the places where the bombs had cleared a larger patch and there had sprung up sordid colonies of wooden dwellings like chicken-houses? But it was no use, he could not remember: nothing remained

Copyright © BookheadEd Learning, LLC

of his childhood except a series of bright-lit tableaux, occurring against no background and mostly unintelligible.

7   The Ministry of Truth -- Minitrue, in Newspeak -- was startlingly different from any other object in sight. It was an enormous pyramidal structure of glittering white concrete, soaring up, terrace after terrace, 300 metres into the air. From where Winston stood it was just possible to read, picked out on its white face in elegant lettering, the three slogans of the Party:

8
WAR IS PEACE
FREEDOM IS SLAVERY
IGNORANCE IS STRENGTH...

9   It was a peculiarly beautiful book. Its smooth creamy paper, a little yellowed by age, was of a kind that had not been manufactured for at least forty years past. He could guess, however, that the book was much older than that. He had seen it lying in the window of a frowsy little junk-shop in a slummy quarter of the town (just what quarter he did not now remember) and had been stricken immediately by an overwhelming desire to possess it. Party members were supposed not to go into ordinary shops ('dealing on the free market', it was called), but the rule was not strictly kept, because there were various things, such as shoelaces and razor blades, which it was impossible to get hold of in any other way. He had given a quick glance up and down the street and then had slipped inside and bought the book for two dollars fifty. At the time he was not conscious of wanting it for any particular purpose. He had carried it guiltily home in his briefcase. Even with nothing written in it, it was a **compromising** possession.

10 The thing that he was about to do was to open a diary. This was not illegal (nothing was illegal, since there were no longer any laws), but if detected it was reasonably certain that it would be punished by death, or at least by twenty-five years in a forced-labour camp. Winston fitted a nib into the penholder and sucked it to get the grease off. The pen was an **archaic** instrument, seldom used even for signatures, and he had procured one, furtively and with some difficulty, simply because of a feeling that the beautiful creamy paper deserved to be written on with a real nib instead of being scratched with an ink-pencil. Actually he was not used to writing by hand. Apart from very short notes, it was usual to dictate everything into the speakwrite which was of course impossible for his present purpose. He dipped the pen into the ink and then faltered for just a second. A tremor had gone through his bowels. To mark the paper was the decisive act. In small clumsy letters he wrote:

11 April 4th, 1984.

Please note that excerpts and passages in the StudySync® library and this workbook are intended as touchstones to generate interest in an author's work. The excerpts and passages do not substitute for the reading of entire texts, and StudySync® strongly recommends that students seek out and purchase the whole literary or informational work in order to experience it as the author intended. Links to online resellers are available in our digital library. In addition, complete works may be ordered through an authorized reseller by filling out and returning to StudySync® the order form enclosed in this workbook.

Reading & Writing
Companion

141

Excerpted from *1984* by George Orwell, published by Signet Classic.

 THINK QUESTIONS

1. What textual details show that Winston is curious about the past and may even yearn for it?

2. The author describes a poster that says BIG BROTHER IS WATCHING YOU. Identify textual evidence that either supports or refutes this statement about Winston's world.

3. How does Winston feel about the world he lives in and how it is run? What clues can you find that show how he feels? Use textual evidence to support your answer.

4. Use context to determine the meaning of the word **archaic** as it is used in *1984*. Write your definition of *archaic* and tell how you got it.

5. Use context to determine the meaning of the word **sanguine** as it is used in *1984*. Write your definition of *sanguine* and tell how you got it.

CLOSE READ

Reread the excerpt from *1984.* As you reread, complete the Focus Questions below. Then use your answers and annotations from the questions to help you complete the Writing Prompt.

FOCUS QUESTIONS

1. As you reread the text of *1984,* remember that the story is told from a third-person limited point of view. Readers see and experience the world through the eyes of one character, Winston Smith. What details in paragraph 4 reveal Winston's thoughts about his surroundings? Highlight the words in the text that show opinions and feelings.

2. In paragraph 6, Winston sees the building where he works on the horizon. How do the descriptions of the building show Winston's thoughts and feelings about London? Does Winston have a positive or negative feeling about the city? Mark places in the text that show how Winston feels about London.

3. Choose one of the sentences in the party's slogans—*War Is Peace; Freedom Is Slavery; Ignorance Is Strength*—and explain why it is an oxymoron. Look at the paragraph above the slogans. Examine the description of the building where the slogans are displayed. How is this description similar to the earlier description of the posters? Highlight your evidence and annotate to explain your ideas.

4. Look at the description of memories in paragraph 6 and the way the author describes the old book and pen in paragraph 8. How do these descriptions help readers understand what's happening to history and memories under this government? Highlight your evidence and annotate to explain your ideas.

5. In paragraph 9, examine the sentence that begins "This was not illegal . . ." How is this sentence an example of the paradoxical quality of the government in 1984? What words and phrases in paragraph 9 reveal Winston's feelings about starting a diary? Highlight the words and phrases and annotate to explain your ideas.

6. Analyze the caption BIG BROTHER IS WATCHING YOU for its impact on the society in 1984. What does the meaning behind the caption reveal about this government's view of power? What can you infer from details in the passage about how individual citizens might feel about this level of power? Support your response with examples from the text.

WRITING PROMPT

What do the three Party slogans—*War Is Peace; Freedom Is Slavery; Ignorance Is Strength*— say about the Party's point of view on controlling thought for its people? Using your understanding of point of view and paradox, write an essay of at least 300 words explaining why individuals expressing unique points of view threaten the government in 1984. Support your writing with evidence from the text.

IN THE TIME OF THE BUTTERFLIES

FICTION

Julia Álvarez
1995

INTRODUCTION

studysync tv

I n 1960, three sisters were found at the bottom of a 150-foot cliff on the north coast of the Dominican Republic. The state newspaper reported that their deaths were accidental. A fourth sister knows differently, in Julia Alvarez's historical novel, *In the Time of the Butterflies*. The excerpt below foreshadows the girls' fate.

"You know, Enrique, that I don't believe in fortunes..."

FIRST READ

Excerpt from Dedi

1994
and
circa 1943

1   She remembers a clear moonlit night before the future began. They are sitting in the cool darkness under the anacahuita tree in the front yard, in the rockers, telling stories, drinking guanabana juice. Good for the nerves, Mamá always says.

2   They're all there, Mamá, Papá, Patria-Minerva-Dedé. Bang-bang-bang, their father likes to joke, aiming a finger pistol at each one, as if he were shooting them, not boasting about having **sired** them. Three girls, each born within a year of the other! And then, nine years later, María Teresa, his final desperate attempt at a boy misfiring.

3   Their father has his slippers on, one foot hooked behind the other. Every once in a while Dedé hears the clink of the rum bottle against the rim of his glass.

4   Many a night, and this night is no different, a shy voice calls out of the darkness, begging their pardon. Could they spare a calmante for a sick child out of their stock of kindness? Would they have some tobacco for a tired old man who spent the day grating yucca?

5   Their father gets up, swaying a little with drink and tiredness, and opens up the store. The campesino goes off with his medicine, a couple of cigars, a few mints for the godchildren. Dedé tells her father that she doesn' know how they do as well as they do, the way he gives everything away. But her father

Please note that excerpts and passages in the StudySync® library and this workbook are studyed as touchstones to generate interest in an author's work. The excerpts and passages do not substitute for the reading of entire texts, and StudySync® strongly recommends that students seek out and purchase the whole literary or informational work in order to experience it as the author intended. Links to online resellers are available in our digital library. In addition, complete works may be ordered through an authorized reseller by filling out and returning to StudySync® the order form enclosed in this workbook.

Reading & Writing
Companion

145

NOTES

just puts his arm around her, and says, "Ay, Dedé, that's why I have you. Every soft foot needs a hard shoe."

6   "She'll bury us all," her father adds, laughing, "in silk and pearls." Dedé hears again the clink of the rum bottle. "Yes, for sure, our Dedé here is going to be the millionaire in the family."

7   "And me, Papá, and me?" María Teresa pipes up in her little girl's voice, not wanting to be left out of the future.

8   "You, mi ñapita, you'll be our little coquette. You'll make a lot of men's--"

9   Their mother coughs her correcting-your-manners cough.

10   "--a lot of men's mouths water?" their father concludes.

11   María Teresa groans. At eight years old, in her long braids and checkered blouse, the only future the baby wants is one that will make her own mouth water, sweets and gifts in big boxes that clatter with something fun inside when she shakes them.

12   "What of me, Papá?" Patria asks more quietly. It is difficult to imagine Patria unmarried without a baby on her lap, but Dedé's memory is playing dolls with the past. She has sat them down that clear, cool night before the future begins, Mamá and Papá and their four pretty girls, no one added, no one taken away Papá calls on Mamá to help him out with his fortune-telling. Especially—though he doesn't say this—if she's going to censor the **clairvoyance** of his several glasses of rum. "What would you say, Mamá, about our Patria?"

13   "You know, Enrique, that I don't believe in fortunes," Mama says evenly. "Padre Ignacio says fortunes are for those without faith." In her mother's tone, Dedé can already hear the distance that will come between her parents. Looking back, she thinks, Ay, Mama, ease up a little on those commandments. Work out the Christian math of how you give a little and you get it back a hundredfold. But thinking about her own divorce, Dedé admits the math doesn't always work out. If you multiply by zero, you still get zero, and a thousand heartaches.

14   "I don't believe in fortunes either," Patria says quickly. She's as religious as Mamá, that one. "But Papá isn't really telling fortunes."

15   Minerva agrees. "Papa's just confessing what he thinks are our strengths." She stresses the verb confessing as if their father were actually being **pious** in looking ahead for his daughters. "Isn't that so, Papá?"

16   "Sí, señorita," Papá burps, slurring his words. It's almost time to go in.

17 "Also," Minerva adds, "Padre Ignacio condemns fortunes only if you believe a human being knows what only God can know." That one can't leave well enough alone.

18 "Some of us know it all," Mamá says curtly.

19 María Teresa defends her adored older sister. "It isn't a sin, Mamá, it isn't. Berto and Raúl have this game from New York. Padre Ignacio played it with us. It's a board with a little glass you move around, and it tells the future!" Everybody laughs, even their mother, for María Teresa's voice is bursting with **gullible** excitement. The baby stops, suddenly, in a pout. Her feelings get hurt so easily. On Minerva's urging, she goes on in a little voice. "I asked the talking board what I would be when I grew up, and it said a lawyer."

20 They all hold back their laughter this time, for of course, María Teresa is parroting her big sister's plans. For years Minerva has been **agitating** to go to law school.

21 "Ay, Dios mío, spare me." Mama sighs, but playfulness has come back into her voice. "Just what we need, skirts in the law!"

22 "It is just what this country needs." Minerva's voice has the steely sureness it gets whenever she talks politics. She has begun talking politics a lot. Mama says she's running around with the Perozo girl too much. "It's about time we women had a voice in running our country."

23 "You and Trujillo," Papa says a little loudly, and in this clear peaceful night they all fall silent. Suddenly, the dark fills with spies who are paid to hear things and report them down at Security. Don Enrique claims Trujillo needs help in running this country. Don Enrique's daughter says it's about time women took over the government. Words repeated, distorted, words recreated by those who might bear them a grudge, words stitched to words until they are the winding sheet the family will be buried in when their bodies are found dumped in a ditch, their tongues cut off for speaking too much.

24 Now, as if drops of rain had started falling—though the night is as clear as the sound of a bell—they hurry in, gathering their shawls and drinks, leaving the rockers for the yardboy to bring in. Maria Teresa squeals when she steps on a stone. "I thought it was el cuco," she moans.

25 As Dedé is helping her father step safely up the stairs of the galería, she realizes that hers is the only future he really told. María Teresa's was a tease, and Papá never got to Minerva's or Patria's on account of Mamá's disapproval. A chill goes through her, for she feels it in her bones, the future is now beginning. By the time it is over, it will be the past, and she doesn't want to be the only one left to tell their story.

Excerpted from *In the Time of the Butterflies* by Julia Álvarez, published by the Penguin Group.

 THINK QUESTIONS

1. What sort of store does Dede's father run? What clues in the text give you this idea? Cite textual evidence to support your answer.

2. What can you infer about the father's character from the comments he makes about his daughters' futures in paragraphs 5–8? What can you infer about the mother from her objections in paragraph 13 and the narrator's follow-up comment? Cite textual evidence to support your answer.

3. Explain why the discussion of Minerva's interests in paragraphs 20–23 could endanger the family, according to the narrator's comment in paragraph 24. Cite textual evidence to support your answer.

4. Use context clues to determine the meaning of the word **gullible** as it is used in paragraph 19 of the selection from *In the Time of Butterflies*. Write your definition of *gullible* and explain how you got this meaning.

5. The noun **clairvoyance** was originally French, combining the French words *clair,* meaning "clear," and *voyant,* meaning "seeing." To go back even further, the Latin roots for the French word are *clarus* ("clear") and *video* ("to see"). List two more words based on the Latin roots, one for *clarus* and one for *video*. Note that words based on the root *video* may change the *d* to *s*.

CLOSE READ

Reread the excerpt from *In the Time of the Butterflies*. Then use your answers and annotations from the questions to help you complete the Writing Prompt.

FOCUS QUESTIONS

1. As you reread the text of *In the Time of Butterflies*, use the strategies you learned about making inferences and identifying the story's cultural context. Based on the introduction and the first paragraph of the text, what can you infer about the setting of the story and the culture of its characters? Highlight evidence to support your ideas and make annotations to explain your choices.

2. Does the father actually own the store or simply work in it? Highlight evidence from paragraphs 3 and 4 of the story, and cite textual evidence that supports your inference. Write a few sentences to explain your thoughts.

3. How would you describe the father's behavior toward his daughters Dedé and María Teresa in paragraphs 5–11? What might the father's interactions with these daughters reveal about the culture's view of female children? Highlight your evidence and write an annotation to explain your ideas.

4. How does Mamá respond to Papá's request for help when Patria asks for a prediction about her future? Based on this interaction and other evidence from the text, what inferences can you make about the attitudes of the mother and her daughters regarding the role of women? Highlight evidence from paragraphs 12 through 16 that support your inferences, and write a brief annotation to explain your answers.

5. How might Minerva's personality and views seem different from those of the other three daughters in the story? What do her interactions with her parents reveal about Minerva's view of the culture she lives in? Highlight evidence from paragraphs 17–22 that supports your response and write an annotation to explain your answers.

6. How does Trujillo's power make itself felt in this passage? Who else has an unusual amount of power in this situation? In what way are the characters' actions controlled by this power, even though nothing has actually happened? Highlight evidence from the text and use the annotation tool to explain how the evidence supports your response.

WRITING PROMPT

Do our memories of past events determine, or have a controlling effect on, our future actions? Write an essay of at least 300 words in which you state your position. Use examples from your own experience and quotations from the text to support your ideas.

ANCIENT GREECE:
A POLITICAL, SOCIAL, AND CULTURAL HISTORY

NON-FICTION
Pomeroy, Burstein,
Donlan, and Roberts
1998

INTRODUCTION

Written by four leading classical scholars, *Ancient Greece: A Political, Social, and Cultural History* offers a comprehensive understanding of ancient Greek history and civilization. The excerpt provided addresses the role of warrior-leaders, such as Odysseus in the world of Homer's epics.

"To a chief, being called 'greedy' is almost as devastating an insult as being called 'cowardly.'"

 FIRST READ

From: Society in the Early Dark Age
The Basileus

1   The Greek word *basileus* is usually translated as "king" wherever it appears
in literature, including in the *Iliad* and *Odyssey.* It would be misleading,
however, to call the Dark Age leaders "kings," a title that conjures up in the
modern mind visions of monarchs with **autocratic** powers. A more appropriate
name for the Dark Age basileus is the anthropological term "chief," which
suggests a man with far less power than a king. The basileus, nevertheless,
was a man of great stature and importance in his community.

From: Late Dark Age (Homeric) Society
Chiefs and Followers

2   Because epic poetry concentrates almost exclusively on the activities of
basileis and their families (largely ignoring the mass of the ordinary people),
the *Iliad* and *Odyssey* provide a fairly detailed description of chieftainship. As
is common among chiefdom societies everywhere, the office and title of
basileus passes from father to son. But inheritance alone is not enough; the
young chief must also be competent to fulfill his role, which is to lead his
people in war and peace. For the successor of the **paramount** basileus, there
is an additional challenge—to secure the compliance of the local chiefs in the
demos. A paramount basileus should have the capabilities of man like Thoas,
who was

3   by far the best of the Aetolians, skilled with the throwing spear,
        and a good man in the close-in fighting, and in the assembly
        few of the Achaeans
        surpassed him, whenever the young men competed in debate.

                                                            (*Iliad* 15.282–284)

4　The two prime **requisites** of leadership, skill in battle and the ability to persuade, are encapsulated in the advice that the basileus Peleus gives to his young son Achilles as he sends him off to the Trojan War: "Be both a speaker of words and a doer of deeds." Above all, it is the deeds, "the works of war," that make a man the leader. In Homer, as in many chieftain societies worldwide, a chief's status is measured by the number of warriors who follow him. A chief who does not show himself a good warrior will find few who are willing to follow his lead. For example, in the Catalogue of the Ships, we are told that Nireus, the son of the basileus on the island of Syme, led only three ships to the Trojan War. Although he was the handsomest of the Greeks at Troy (next to Achilles), Nireus was "a weak man, and few people followed him" (*Iliad* 2.671-675). By contrast, Agamemnon was acknowledged as the leader of the entire Greek army at Troy, because, as commander of one hundred ships from the region around Mycenae, "he led by far the most troops."

5　All basileis, both local chiefs and the paramount, have their own personal followings. The men who follow a chief are called by him and call each other *hetairoi* ("companions"), a word that conveys a deep feeling of mutual loyalty. Thus the "army" of a demos is composed of several individual hetairoi bands, each under the command of its own basileus, and all under the command of the paramount. However, the entire fighting force of the demos is mustered together under the paramount basileus only when there is an all-out war, usually for defense of the demos when an outside enemy has attacked in force. Otherwise, a local or a paramount chief is free to raise his own following and go on raiding expeditions against villages of another demos, either to even the score in some ongoing quarrel or just to steal or plunder their livestock, valuables, and women. Commonly, a chief recruits his followers with a large feast, showing that he is a generous leader and thereby binding his followers to him. For instance, Odysseus (posing as a warrior-leader from Crete), describes how he made a raiding expedition into Egypt. Having fitted out nine ships, he says, he gathered a following,

6　and for six days my trusty companions (hetairoi)
feasted, and I gave them many animal victims
both to sacrifice to the gods and to make a feast for themselves,
and on the seventh we got on board and set sail from broad Crete. . . .

(*Odyssey* 14.247–252)

7　Raiding is a way of life in Homeric society. Booty raids not only enrich the raid-leader and his men, but also serve as a test of their manliness, skill, and courage, and thus bring honor and glory. Whether on a raid or in a war, the basileus is the one most severely tested, for he is literally the leader, stationing himself "among the front-fighters." The leader is obliged to risk his life fighting at the front of his army (a custom that persisted throughout ancient Greek

history). In return for his leadership, the demos is under obligation to provide the basileus with honors and material gifts.

...

8   Reciprocity—mutual and fair exchange—which governs all social relationships in the Homeric world, is the core of the leader-people relationship. The giving and the receiving should ideally balance one another. So, too, fairness is the rule in the **apportionment** of the spoils of war. Following a raid, the booty is gathered together. First the leader takes his share (and something extra as the leader's "prize") and, under his supervision, special rewards for **valor** are given out. The rest is then given to the men "to divide up, so that no one may go cheated of an equal share."

9   A leader who keeps more than he deserves or distributes prizes unfairly risks losing the respect of his followers. To a chief, being called "greedy" is almost as devastating an insult as being called "cowardly." In short, a basileus cannot afford not to appear generous and openhanded. Similarly, Homeric chiefs engage in a constant exchange of gifts and feasts with other chiefs and important men. This is both a way of showing off their wealth and a means to cement friendships, win new friends, and collect obligations through a display of generosity.

10   Despite the great authority given him by his position, a basileus has limited ability to coerce others to follow his lead. He is only a chief, not a king. Thus in the Odyssey, there are several occasions when Odysseus' hetairoi simply refuse to obey him. Once, when his followers decide to do exactly the opposite of what he has ordered them, Odysseus can only say that as "one man alone" he must abide by the will of the many. Odysseus' helplessness illustrates the fundamental fragility of leadership authority in this type of low-level chieftainship.

Excerpted from *Ancient Greece: A Political, Social, and Cultural History* by Pomeroy, Burstein, Donlan, and Roberts, published by Oxford University Press.

THINK QUESTIONS

1. According to what the text states and what you can infer from it, why was raiding "a way of life" in ancient Greece? Cite textual evidence to support your answer.

2. Write two or three sentences explaining what you can infer about the values of the ancient Greeks from the following quotation: "A leader who keeps more than he deserves or distributes prizes unfairly risks losing the respect of his followers. To a chief, being called 'greedy' is almost as devastating an insult as being called "cowardly."" Provide another example from the text to develop your inference and cite textual evidence to support your answers.

3. Why was the ability to persuade important for a basileus? Cite textual evidence to support your answer.

4. Use context clues to determine the meaning of the word **apportionment** as it is used in the text. Write your definition and cite text evidence that supports it.

5. The word **autocrat** is based on two Greek roots: *autos*, meaning "self," and *kratos*, which refers to "strength" or "power." How might this information help you determine the meaning of the word *autocrat?* Give examples of other words that have these roots.

CLOSE READ

Reread the excerpt from *Ancient Greece: A Political, Social, and Cultural History.* As you reread, complete the Focus Questions below. Then use your answers and annotations from the questions to help you complete the Writing Prompt.

FOCUS QUESTIONS

1. As you reread the text of *Ancient Greece: A Political, Social, and Cultural History,* consider the headings. Identify the main idea of the first paragraph under the heading "Chiefs and Followers." What does the main idea tell readers about the characteristics of a basileus? How does the quotation from the *Iliad* illustrate this main idea? Make annotations to record your answers.

2. Highlight the key details in paragraphs 4 and 5 that develop the idea that courage is essential for a basileus. Which of these key details do you think is the best support for this idea? Make annotations to explain your choices.

3. How do the authors develop the idea that a basileus who wants to gain followers must be generous? Highlight the place where this idea is first mentioned. Then highlight two supporting details. Add any annotations that you think are helpful.

4. Identify another important idea that the authors develop about the relationship between a basileus and his followers. Where is this idea first mentioned? How is the idea developed in the selection? Highlight your evidence and make annotations to explain your answers.

5. Determine a central idea that emerges from the selection about the responsibilities of power and leadership. Write that idea and make annotations to explain how it covers the most important points in the text about the role of the basileus. Highlight text evidence that supports your explanation.

WRITING PROMPT

Write a response in which you explain why the translation of *basileus* as "king" is misleading. Use your understanding of key details to provide support for why "king" is not an accurate name for this level of leader.

Please note that excerpts and passages in the StudySync® library and this workbook are intended as touchstones to generate interest in an author's work. The excerpts and passages do not substitute for the reading of entire texts, and StudySync® strongly recommends that students seek out and purchase the whole literary or informational work in order to experience it as the author intended. Links to online resellers are available in our digital library. In addition, complete works may be ordered through an authorized reseller by filling out and returning to StudySync® the order form enclosed in this workbook.

Reading & Writing Companion   **155**

THE ODYSSEY
(BOOK XII - BUTLER TRANSLATION)

FICTION

Homer
8th Century, BCE

INTRODUCTION

After fighting in the Trojan War for a decade, the Greek hero, Odysseus, sails for his home island of Ithaca. However, as he later tells his rescuers, the voyage turned into a series of catastrophic adventures—often as a result of his crew's greed and recklessness. Early in the voyage, within sight of Ithaca, the men unwisely open a leather bag that has been given to Odysseus, thinking it contains gold. In fact, it holds captive the world's most dangerous winds, which promptly blow Odysseus's ship far off course. What follows are perilous encounters with a one-eyed giant, a transforming sorceress, a six-headed monster, a deadly whirlpool, and the Sirens, whose sweet songs lure sailors to their death. Odysseus's homecoming will face further delays on the island of the nymph, Calypso. But before that, he and his crew make port at the island of the sun god, Helios. They have been warned to keep away from Helios's prized herd of cattle, but one crewmate, the headstrong and persuasive Eurylochus, is not convinced

"I stuck to the ship till the sea knocked her sides from her keel…"

FIRST READ

1   As long as corn and wine held out the men did not touch the cattle when they were hungry; when, however, they had eaten all there was in the ship, they were forced to go further afield, with hook and line, catching birds, and taking whatever they could lay their hands on; for they were starving. One day, therefore, I went up inland that I might pray heaven to show me some means of getting away. When I had gone far enough to be clear of all my men, and had found a place that was well sheltered from the wind, I washed my hands and prayed to all the gods in Olympus till by and by they sent me off into a sweet sleep.

2   "Meanwhile Eurylochus had been giving evil **counsel** to the men. 'Listen to me,' said he, 'my poor comrades. All deaths are bad enough but there is none so bad as famine. Why should not we drive in the best of these cows and offer them in sacrifice to the immortal gods? If we ever get back to Ithaca, we can build a fine temple to the sun-god and enrich it with every kind of ornament; if, however, he is determined to sink our ship out of revenge for these horned cattle, and the other gods are of the same mind, I for one would rather drink salt water once for all and have done with it, than be starved to death by inches in such a desert island as this is.'

3   "Thus spoke Eurylochus, and the men approved his words. Now the cattle, so fair and goodly, were feeding not far from the ship; the men, therefore, drove in the best of them, and they all stood round them saying their prayers, and using young oak-shoots instead of barley-meal, for there was no barley left. When they had done praying they killed the cows and dressed their carcasses; they cut out the thigh bones, wrapped them round in two layers of fat, and set some pieces of raw meat on top of them. They had no wine with which to make drink-offerings over the sacrifice while it was cooking, so they kept pouring on a little water from time to time while the inward meats were being grilled; then, when the thigh bones were burned and they had tasted the inward meats, they cut the rest up small and put the pieces upon the spits.

4   "By this time my deep sleep had left me, and I turned back to the ship and to the sea shore. As I drew near I began to smell hot roast meat, so I groaned out a prayer to the immortal gods. 'Father Jove,' I exclaimed, 'and all you other gods who live in everlasting bliss, you have done me a cruel mischief by the sleep into which you have sent me; see what fine work these men of mine have been making in my absence.'

5   "Meanwhile Lampetie went straight off to the sun and told him we had been killing his cows, whereon he flew into a great rage, and said to the immortals, 'Father Jove, and all you other gods who live in everlasting bliss, I must have **vengeance** on the crew of Ulysses' ship: they have had the **insolence** to kill my cows, which were the one thing I loved to look upon, whether I was going up heaven or down again. If they do not square accounts with me about my cows, I will go down to Hades and shine there among the dead.'

6   "'Sun,' said Jove, 'go on shining upon us gods and upon mankind over the fruitful earth. I will shiver their ship into little pieces with a bolt of white lightning as soon as they get out to sea.'

7   "I was told all this by Calypso, who said she had heard it from the mouth of Mercury.

8   "As soon as I got down to my ship and to the sea shore I rebuked each one of the men separately, but we could see no way out of it, for the cows were dead already. And indeed the gods began at once to show signs and wonders among us, for the hides of the cattle crawled about, and the joints upon the spits began to low like cows, and the meat, whether cooked or raw, kept on making a noise just as cows do.

9   "For six days my men kept driving in the best cows and feasting upon them, but when Jove the son of Saturn had added a seventh day, the fury of the gale **abated;** we therefore went on board, raised our masts, spread sail, and put out to sea. As soon as we were well away from the island, and could see nothing but sky and sea, the son of Saturn raised a black cloud over our ship, and the sea grew dark beneath it. We did not get on much further, for in another moment we were caught by a terrific squall from the West that snapped the forestays of the mast so that it fell aft, while all the ship's gear tumbled about at the bottom of the vessel. The mast fell upon the head of the helmsman in the ship's stern, so that the bones of his head were crushed to pieces, and he fell overboard as though he were diving, with no more life left in him.

10 "Then Jove let fly with his thunderbolts, and the ship went round and round, and was filled with fire and brimstone as the lightning struck it. The men all fell into the sea; they were carried about in the water round the ship, looking like

so many sea-gulls, but the god presently deprived them of all chance of getting home again.

11   "I stuck to the ship till the sea knocked her sides from her keel (which drifted about by itself) and struck the mast out of her in the direction of the keel; but there was a backstay of stout ox-thong still hanging about it, and with this I lashed the mast and keel together, and getting astride of them was carried wherever the winds chose to take me.

12   "The gale from the West had now spent its force, and the wind got into the South again, which frightened me lest I should be taken back to the terrible whirlpool of Charybdis. This indeed was what actually happened, for I was borne along by the waves all night, and by sunrise had reached the rock of Scylla, and the whirlpool. She was then sucking down the salt sea water, but I was carried aloft toward the fig tree, which I caught hold of and clung on to like a bat. I could not plant my feet anywhere so as to stand securely, for the roots were a long way off and the boughs that overshadowed the whole pool were too high, too vast, and too far apart for me to reach them; so I hung patiently on, waiting till the pool should discharge my mast and raft again— and a very long while it seemed. A jury-man is not more glad to get home to supper, after having been long detained in court by troublesome cases, than I was to see my raft beginning to work its way out of the whirlpool again. At last I let go with my hands and feet, and fell heavily into the sea, hard by my raft on to which I then got, and began to row with my hands. As for Scylla, the father of gods and men would not let her get further sight of me—otherwise I should have certainly been lost.

13   "**Hence** I was carried along for nine days till on the tenth night the gods stranded me on the Ogygian island, where dwells the great and powerful goddess Calypso. She took me in and was kind to me, but I need say no more about this, for I told you and your noble wife all about it yesterday, and I hate saying the same thing over and over again."

Please note that excerpts and passages in the StudySync® library and this workbook are intended as touchstones to generate interest in an author's work. The excerpts and passages do not substitute for the reading of entire texts, and StudySync® strongly recommends that students seek out and purchase the whole literary or informational work in order to experience it as the author intended. Links to online resellers are available in our digital library. In addition, complete works may be ordered through an authorized reseller by filling out and returning to StudySync® the order form enclosed in this workbook.

Reading & Writing Companion   **159**

THINK QUESTIONS

1. What do people in *The Odyssey* think of the gods? How do you know? Refer to relevant details in the text to support your answer.

2. How does Jove respond to the threat the sun makes? Why do you think he responds this way? Cite textual evidence to support your response.

3. What can you infer about the gods by the way they behave? Cite evidence to support your response.

4. Use context clues to determine the meaning of the word **counsel** as it is used in *The Odyssey*. Write your definition of *counsel* and explain how you got it.

5. Remembering that the root of **vengeance** is the same as the root of *revenge*, use the context clues provided in the passage to determine the meaning of *vengeance*. Write your definition of *vengeance* and tell how you got it.

CLOSE READ

Reread the excerpt from *The Odyssey, Book XII*. As you reread, complete the Focus Questions below. Then use your answers and annotations from the questions to help you complete the Writing Prompt.

 FOCUS QUESTIONS

1. As you reread the beginning of the excerpt from *The Odyssey,* think about how the author reveals Odysseus' character. What kind of person is Odysseus? What are his positive attributes? What, if any, indication is there that Odysseus might also have some character flaws? What could he have done differently? Highlight textual evidence both in paragraph 1 and in the paragraph that begins "As soon as I got down to my ship" to support your ideas. Include detailed annotations to explain your choices.

2. Paragraph 2 introduces the character of Eurylochus. What kind of character is he? What role does he play in the passage? Highlight your textual evidence and annotate to explain your how your annotations demonstrate the character traits of Eurylochus.

3. What is Odysseus' central problem in this excerpt? How is the problem resolved? In what ways is this resolution satisfactory or unsatisfactory? Highlight textual evidence to support your ideas and write annotations to explain your choices.

4. In what ways do the gods work against Odysseus' goals? What might the gods represent to the people of ancient Greece? Highlight textual evidence and write annotations to support your ideas.

5. What character traits of Odysseus help him to survive the adventure? What does the final paragraph of the excerpt reveal about plot and Odysseus' character? Highlight relevant evidence from the text that will help support your ideas.

6. How does Odysseus lead his men in this excerpt? How well does he fulfill his responsibilities toward them, and what character traits do his actions reveal? Highlight relevant evidence and annotate to support your ideas.

WRITING PROMPT

What does this excerpt indicate about the purpose of *The Odyssey?* Is the work's chief aim to inform—to teach history? Or is the aim to entertain—to tell an exciting and memorable tale? Could the purpose be to serve as a moral compass, to guide listeners and readers as they make their way in the world? What contribution does the character of Odysseus make to the overall the purpose and meaning of the text? How might the work's purpose reflect the cultural context in which this extraordinary adventure tale was first told and then put into writing several thousand years ago? Write an essay of 300 words or more explaining what you think *The Odyssey's* main purpose is, using textual evidence to support your claim.

Please note that excerpts and passages in the StudySync® library and this workbook are intended as touchstones to generate interest in an author's work. The excerpts and passages do not substitute for the reading of entire texts, and StudySync® strongly recommends that students seek out and purchase the whole literary or informational work in order to experience it as the author intended. Links to online resellers are available in our digital library. In addition, complete works may be ordered through an authorized reseller by filling out and returning to StudySync® the order form enclosed in this workbook.

Reading & Writing Companion   **161**

THE ODYSSEY
(A GRAPHIC NOVEL)

FICTION
Gareth Hinds
2010

INTRODUCTION

In Gareth Hinds's vivid retelling of *The Odyssey*, words yield to wordless illustration the way oarsmen might yield to a strong current. This excerpt, mainly from Book 12, covers the same events as the SyncTV episode of *The Odyssey*. Odysseus is telling his hosts, the Phaeacians, about his seven-year homeward journey from Troy. He has just finished recounting his escape with his crewmen from Scylla and Charybdis, a deadly whirlpool and monster. Next he tells about their ill-fated stay on the island of Helios, where the sun-god's cattle tempt the starving men into a

"They were mutinous, and I saw that fate had us by the leash."

FIRST READ

The Odyssey (A Graphic Novel) by Gareth Hinds
Based on Homer's epic poem

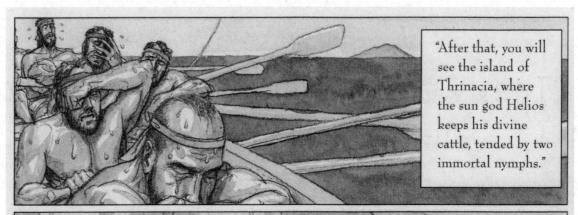

"After that, you will see the island of Thrinacia, where the sun god Helios keeps his divine cattle, tended by two immortal nymphs."

"Remember Tiresias's words — steer clear of that island, and before long you'll make landfall in Ithaca."

I remembered it well, and told the crew repeatedly. But when we came in sight of that sunny island, with its green meadows and bubbling streams, my exhausted men clamored to land.

They were mutinous, and I saw that fate had us by the leash. Before I would let them land, I made them swear that they would eat only the provisions Circe had given us and never touch Helios's cattle.

Just as we beached our ship, a storm blew up. This cursed wind blew continuously by day and night for thirty days, trapping us on the island.

As long as Circe's food and wine held out, the men were content. But when at last it was gone, and starvation began to wrack their bodies, all eyes turned toward those magnificent cattle.

I reminded them of their oath, then went to climb the highest peak and ask the gods for help.

I prayed to all the gods of Olympus, but their answer was to close my eyes with an accursed sleep, while down on the shore Eurylochus hatched a fateful plan.

Comrades, hear me! All men fear death, but the worst death of all is starvation. It is repugnant, painful, and slow. We should not die pitifully on this beach, with these fat, majestic cattle so near at hand. We'll make sacrifices to the Sun God, promise him a grand temple on Ithaca, and ask his forgiveness. If he destroys us instead, at least we'll go down fighting!

Please note that excerpts and passages in the StudySync® library and this workbook are intended as touchstones to generate interest in an author's work. The excerpts and passages do not substitute for the reading of entire texts, and StudySync® strongly recommends that students seek out and purchase the whole literary or informational work in order to experience it as the author intended. Links to online resellers are available in our digital library. In addition, complete works may be ordered through an authorized reseller by filling out and returning to StudySync® the order form enclosed in this workbook.

Reading & Writing Companion

165

I knew we were doomed, and soon fearful omens confirmed it.

The hides began to crawl, and the meat on the spits to bellow like a herd of oxen.

The wind turned, and we launched our ship once more onto the wine-dark sea.

No sooner was the island out of sight behind us than giant thunderheads began to mass overhead, and the sun was blotted out.

Please note that excerpts and passages in the StudySync® library and this workbook are intended as touchstones to generate interest in an author's work. The excerpts and passages do not substitute for the reading of entire texts, and StudySync® strongly recommends that students seek out and purchase the whole literary or informational work in order to experience it as the author intended. Links to online resellers are available in our digital library. In addition, complete works may be ordered through an authorized reseller by filling out and returning to StudySync® the order form enclosed in this workbook.

Reading & Writing
Companion

169

I drifted for nine days before the gods cast me up on Ogygia, the island home of the nymph Calypso, Atlas's daughter.

There I was stranded for seven long years. Calypso wanted to keep me there forever, make me immortal — but I wept every day for my home, and at last she set me free.

I sailed my raft on the open sea for seventeen days, before Poseidon wrecked me within sight of your shore.

Now your troubles are ended. My friend, we've kept you here long enough. The ship is ready. Come, princes, let's go and stow noble Odysseus's goods beneath the benches, pile up rugs so he may rest in the bow.

You'll be home soon, king of Ithaca.

Please note that excerpts and passages in the StudySync® library and this workbook are intended as touchstones to generate interest in an author's work. The excerpts and passages do not substitute for the reading of entire texts, and StudySync® strongly recommends that students seek out and purchase the whole literary or informational work in order to experience it as the author intended. Links to online resellers are available in our digital library. In addition, complete works may be ordered through an authorized reseller by filling out and returning to StudySync® the order form enclosed in this workbook.

Reading & Writing **173**
Companion

THINK QUESTIONS

1. Why do Odysseus' men refrain at first from eating the cattle? How does the situation change while they are on the island? Use textual evidence to support your answer.

2. What do readers learn about Odysseus by reading the text on page 52? What additional information can readers infer by analyzing the pictures on page 52?

3. How do the words and the images on page 53 work together to create a feeling of doom and horror? Use specific details from the text and the pictures to support your answer.

4. Use clues from the pictures and text to explain the meaning of the word **mutinous.** Write your definition of *mutinous* and tell how you got it.

5. The word **immortal** appears on page 50 and again on page 58. Remembering that the Latin prefix *im-* means "not," use the context clues provided in the passage and your prior knowledge to determine the meaning of *immortal*. Write your definition of *immortal* and tell how you got it.

CLOSE READ

Reread the excerpt from *The Odyssey (A Graphic Novel)*. As you reread, complete the Focus Questions below. Then use your answers and annotations from the questions to help you complete the Writing Prompt.

FOCUS QUESTIONS

1. Reread the first page of the graphic novel *The Odyssey* by Hinds. What information about Odysseus and his men does Hinds communicate in words and pictures on this page? How does this information help you understand how the men feel, and what happens next when they see the island? Cite textual and visual evidence to support your answer.

2. Look at the first illustration on page 51. Highlight the caption. Then reread the first two sentences of the excerpt from Book XII of Homer's *The Odyssey*. Compare and contrast what you learn from these two sentences with what you learn from the illustration and caption. What details are emphasized or omitted in each version? Make annotations to support your answers.

3. Which paragraph from the text of Book XII is illustrated in the first four pictures on page 52? What details are emphasized or omitted in each version? Why do you think Hinds made certain choices in using and transforming the source material? Highlight your evidence and make annotations to explain your choices.

4. Compare and contrast the description of the shipwreck from Book XII with the description of it in the graphic novel, starting when the squall hits the ship and ending when the helmsman dies. Which do you think is more effective—the description in words or in pictures? What is the function of the caption in this section of the graphic novel? Highlight and annotate visual and textual evidence to support your ideas.

5. Do you learn anything new or different about Odysseus as a leader, or his attitude toward his power, from analyzing the graphic novel's pictures and captions along with reading the excerpt from Book XII? Support your answers with visual and textual evidence from both versions.

WRITING PROMPT

Write an essay of at least 400 words comparing and contrasting this graphic novel segment of *The Odyssey* by Hinds with the same section from Book XII of Homer's *The Odyssey* in the StudySync Library (SyncTV episode). Analyze the positive or negative features of the graphic novel compared with the Book XII version. Think about such categories as story, character, setting, and tone as you make your comparison.

Please note that excerpts and passages in the StudySync® library and this workbook are intended as touchstones to generate interest in an author's work. The excerpts and passages do not substitute for the reading of entire texts, and StudySync® strongly recommends that students seek out and purchase the whole literary or informational work in order to experience it as the author intended. Links to online resellers are available in our digital library. In addition, complete works may be ordered through an authorized reseller by filling out and returning to StudySync® the order form enclosed in this workbook.

Reading & Writing
Companion

175

HISTORY OF THE PELOPONNESIAN WAR:
PERICLES' FUNERAL ORATION

NON-FICTION
Thucydides
circa 404 BCE

INTRODUCTION

Great rivals and bitter enemies, Athens and Sparta came to blows during the Peloponnesian War, with Sparta emerging victorious. No two Greek city-states could have been more opposite than democratic Athens and oligarchic Sparta, and Athenian politician Pericles made sure to elaborate the differences in his address at a public funeral honoring Athens' war dead. As friends and family gathered to mourn, Pericles assured them that their loved ones died for the noblest of causes—to protect the Athenian democratic way of life.

"Comfort, therefore, not condolence, is what I have to offer to the parents of the dead..."

 FIRST READ

 NOTES

Excerpt from From Book II, Chapter VI:

1   "Our constitution does not copy the laws of neighboring states; we are rather a pattern to others than imitators ourselves. Its administration favors the many instead of the few; this is why it is called a democracy. If we look to the laws, they afford equal justice to all in their private differences; if no social standing, advancement in public life falls to reputation for **capacity,** class considerations not being allowed to interfere with merit; nor again does poverty bar the way, if a man is able to serve the state, he is not hindered by the obscurity of his condition. The freedom which we enjoy in our government extends also to our ordinary life. There, far from exercising a jealous surveillance over each other, we do not feel called upon to be angry with our neighbor for doing what he likes, or even to indulge in those injurious looks which cannot fail to be offensive, although they inflict no positive penalty. But all this ease in our private relations does not make us lawless as citizens. Against this fear is our chief safeguard, teaching us to obey the magistrates and the laws, particularly such as regard the protection of the injured, whether they are actually on the statute book, or belong to that code which, although unwritten, yet cannot be broken without acknowledged disgrace.

2   "Further, we provide plenty of means for the mind to refresh itself from business. We celebrate games and sacrifices all the year round, and the elegance of our private establishments forms a daily source of pleasure and helps to banish the spleen; while the magnitude of our city draws the produce of the world into our harbor, so that to the Athenian the fruits of other countries are as familiar a luxury as those of his own.

3   "If we turn to our military policy, there also we differ from our antagonists. We throw open our city to the world, and never by alien acts exclude foreigners from any opportunity of learning or observing, although the eyes of an enemy may occasionally profit by our liberality; trusting less in system and policy

than to the native spirit of our citizens; while in education, where our rivals from their very cradles by a painful discipline seek after manliness, at Athens we live exactly as we please, and yet are just as ready to encounter every legitimate danger. In proof of this it may be noticed that the Lacedaemonians do not invade our country alone, but bring with them all their confederates; while we Athenians advance unsupported into the territory of a neighbor, and fighting upon a foreign soil usually vanquish with ease men who are defending their homes. Our united force was never yet encountered by any enemy, because we have at once to attend to our marine and to dispatch our citizens by land upon a hundred different services; so that, wherever they engage with some such fraction of our strength, a success against a detachment is magnified into a victory over the nation, and a defeat into a reverse suffered at the hands of our entire people. And yet if with habits not of labor but of ease, and courage not of art but of nature, we are still willing to encounter danger, we have the double advantage of escaping the experience of hardships in anticipation and of facing them in the hour of need as fearlessly as those who are never free from them.

4   "Nor are these the only points in which our city is worthy of admiration. We cultivate refinement without extravagance and knowledge without **effeminacy;** wealth we employ more for use than for show, and place the real disgrace of poverty not in owning to the fact but in declining the struggle against it. Our public men have, besides politics, their private affairs to attend to, and our ordinary citizens, though occupied with the pursuits of industry, are still fair judges of public matters; for, unlike any other nation, regarding him who takes no part in these duties not as unambitious but as useless, we Athenians are able to judge at all events if we cannot originate, and, instead of looking on discussion as a stumbling-block in the way of action, we think it an indispensable preliminary to any wise action at all. Again, in our enterprises we present the singular spectacle of daring and deliberation, each carried to its highest point, and both united in the same persons; although usually decision is the fruit of ignorance, hesitation of reflection. But the palm of courage will surely be adjudged most justly to those, who best know the difference between hardship and pleasure and yet are never tempted to shrink from danger. In generosity we are equally singular, acquiring our friends by conferring, not by receiving, favors. Yet, of course, the doer of the favor is the firmer friend of the two, in order by continued kindness to keep the recipient in his debt; while the debtor feels less keenly from the very consciousness that the return he makes will be a payment, not a free gift. And it is only the Athenians, who, fearless of consequences, confer their benefits not from calculations of expediency, but in the confidence of liberality.

5   "In short, I say that as a city we are the school of Hellas, while I doubt if the world can produce a man who, where he has only himself to depend upon, is equal to so many emergencies, and graced by so happy a versatility, as the

Athenian. And that this is no mere boast thrown out for the occasion, but plain matter of fact, the power of the state acquired by these habits proves. For Athens alone of her contemporaries is found when tested to be greater than her reputation, and alone gives no occasion to her assailants to blush at the antagonist by whom they have been worsted, or to her subjects to question her title by merit to rule. Rather, the admiration of the present and succeeding ages will be ours, since we have not left our power without witness, but have shown it by mighty proofs; and far from needing a Homer for our panegyrist, or other of his craft whose verses might charm for the moment only for the impression which they gave to melt at the touch of fact, we have forced every sea and land to be the highway of our daring, and everywhere, whether for evil or for good, have left imperishable monuments behind us. Such is the Athens for which these men, in the assertion of their resolve not to lose her, nobly fought and died; and well may every one of their survivors be ready to suffer in her cause.

6 "Indeed if I have dwelt at some length upon the character of our country, it has been to show that our stake in the struggle is not the same as theirs who have no such blessings to lose, and also that the **panegyric** of the men over whom I am now speaking might be by definite proofs established. That panegyric is now in a great measure complete; for the Athens that I have celebrated is only what the heroism of these and their like have made her, men whose fame, unlike that of most Hellenes, will be found to be only **commensurate** with their deserts. And if a test of worth be wanted, it is to be found in their closing scene, and this not only in cases in which it set the final seal upon their merit, but also in those in which it gave the first intimation of their having any. For there is justice in the claim that **steadfastness** in his country's battles should be as a cloak to cover a man's other imperfections; since the good action has blotted out the bad, and his merit as a citizen more than outweighed his demerits as an individual. But none of these allowed either wealth with its prospect of future enjoyment to unnerve his spirit, or poverty with its hope of a day of freedom and riches to tempt him to shrink from danger. No, holding that vengeance upon their enemies was more to be desired than any personal blessings, and reckoning this to be the most glorious of hazards, they joyfully determined to accept the risk, to make sure of their vengeance, and to let their wishes wait; and while committing to hope the uncertainty of final success, in the business before them they thought fit to act boldly and trust in themselves. Thus choosing to die resisting, rather than to live submitting, they fled only from dishonor, but met danger face to face, and after one brief moment, while at the summit of their fortune, escaped, not from their fear, but from their glory.

7 "So died these men as became Athenians. You, their survivors, must determine to have as unfaltering a resolution in the field, though you may pray that it may have a happier issue. And not contented with ideas derived only from

Please note that excerpts and passages in the StudySync® library and this workbook are intended as touchstones to generate interest in an author's work. The excerpts and passages do not substitute for the reading of entire texts, and StudySync® strongly recommends that students seek out and purchase the whole literary or informational work in order to experience it as the author intended. Links to online resellers are available in our digital library. In addition, complete works may be ordered through an authorized reseller by filling out and returning to StudySync® the order form enclosed in this workbook.

Reading & Writing Companion

179

words of the advantages which are bound up with the defense of your country, though these would furnish a valuable text to a speaker even before an audience so alive to them as the present, you must yourselves realize the power of Athens, and feed your eyes upon her from day to day, till love of her fills your hearts; and then, when all her greatness shall break upon you, you must reflect that it was by courage, sense of duty, and a keen feeling of honor in action that men were enabled to win all this, and that no personal failure in an enterprise could make them consent to deprive their country of their valor, but they laid it at her feet as the most glorious contribution that they could offer. For this offering of their lives made in common by them all they each of them individually received that renown which never grows old, and for a sepulcher, not so much that in which their bones have been deposited, but that noblest of shrines wherein their glory is laid up to be eternally remembered upon every occasion on which deed or story shall call for its commemoration. For heroes have the whole earth for their tomb; and in lands far from their own, where the column with its epitaph declares it, there is enshrined in every breast a record unwritten with no tablet to preserve it, except that of the heart. These take as your model and, judging happiness to be the fruit of freedom and freedom of valor, never decline the dangers of war. For it is not the miserable that would most justly be unsparing of their lives; these have nothing to hope for: it is rather they to whom continued life may bring reverses as yet unknown, and to whom a fall, if it came, would be most tremendous in its consequences. And surely, to a man of spirit, the degradation of cowardice must be immeasurably more grievous than the unfelt death which strikes him in the midst of his strength and patriotism!

8   "Comfort, therefore, not condolence, is what I have to offer to the parents of the dead who may be here. Numberless are the chances to which, as they know, the life of man is subject; but fortunate indeed are they who draw for their lot a death so glorious as that which has caused your mourning, and to whom life has been so exactly measured as to terminate in the happiness in which it has been passed. Still I know that this is a hard saying, especially when those are in question of whom you will constantly be reminded by seeing in the homes of others blessings of which once you also boasted: for grief is felt not so much for the want of what we have never known, as for the loss of that to which we have been long accustomed. Yet you who are still of an age to beget children must bear up in the hope of having others in their stead; not only will they help you to forget those whom you have lost, but will be to the state at once a reinforcement and a security; for never can a fair or just policy be expected of the citizen who does not, like his fellows, bring to the decision the interests and apprehensions of a father. While those of you who have passed your prime must congratulate yourselves with the thought that the best part of your life was fortunate, and that the brief span that remains will be cheered by the fame of the departed. For it is only the love of honor

that never grows old; and honor it is, not gain, as some would have it, that rejoices the heart of age and helplessness.

9   "Turning to the sons or brothers of the dead, I see an arduous struggle before you. When a man is gone, all are wont to praise him, and should your merit be ever so transcendent, you will still find it difficult not merely to overtake, but even to approach their renown. The living have envy to contend with, while those who are no longer in our path are honored with a goodwill into which rivalry does not enter. On the other hand, if I must say anything on the subject of female excellence to those of you who will now be in widowhood, it will be all comprised in this brief exhortation. Great will be your glory in not falling short of your natural character; and greatest will be hers who is least talked of among the men, whether for good or for bad.

10 "My task is now finished. I have performed it to the best of my ability, and in word, at least, the requirements of the law are now satisfied. If deeds be in question, those who are here interred have received part of their honors already, and for the rest, their children will be brought up till manhood at the public expense: the state thus offers a valuable prize, as the garland of victory in this race of valor, for the reward both of those who have fallen and their survivors. And where the rewards for merit are greatest, there are found the best citizens.

11 "And now that you have brought to a close your lamentations for your relatives, you may depart."

  THINK QUESTIONS

1. Why is Pericles giving this speech? To whom is he speaking? Cite textual evidence to support your answer.

2. Why would Pericles want to show that Athens is superior to other city-states? What information does he use to back up this claim about Athens? Cite textual evidence to support your answer.

3. Pericles claims that Athens' military is superior to that of its enemies and gives details to support this idea. What information does he use to support his argument and do you think his claim is justified by this information? Cite textual evidence to support your answer.

4. What advice does Pericles give to the parents of the deceased soldiers? What is the purpose of his advice? Cite textual evidence to support your answer.

5. By what actions might a soldier demonstrate **steadfastness?** Base your answer on the word's context in paragraph 6 of Pericles' Funeral Oration.

6. Note that *com-* is a Latin prefix denoting "with" and *mensura* is a Latin root meaning "to measure." Use this information to determine what Pericles means when he says in paragraph 6 that the Athenian soldiers' fame is "only **commensurate** with their deserts" [worth].

CLOSE READ

Reread the excerpt from *History of the Peloponnesian War: Pericles' Funeral Oration.* As you reread, complete the Focus Questions below. Then use your answers and annotations from the questions to help you complete the Writing Prompt.

FOCUS QUESTIONS

1. In paragraph 1, highlight details that develop Pericles' key idea that Athens is superior to Sparta.

2. Highlight some of the key ideas in paragraph 3. Then use your highlights to write a summary of the main idea of the paragraph.

3. Consider the connections between Pericles' ideas and the way in which these ideas build upon one another in the first five paragraphs. Highlight three examples of his ideas and write an explanation of how the order in which these ideas are presented helps Pericles to develop the central idea of his speech.

4. Highlight two examples of Pericles' use of emotional language used to convince his audience that Athens is superior to Sparta. Annotate to indicate what emotions Pericles is trying to evoke.

5. Highlight three examples of Pericles' use of persuasive language. Annotate to indicate what Pericles is trying to persuade his audience of with this language.

6. Explain how the central idea of the text addresses the idea of the responsibilities that come with power. Support your response with highlights from the text.

WRITING PROMPT

Which of Athens' qualities seem most important to Pericles? What is the Athenian ideal of a good life? Your response should also address the techniques Pericles uses to convey these ideas. Respond in an essay of at least 400 words, making sure to support your ideas with evidence from the text.

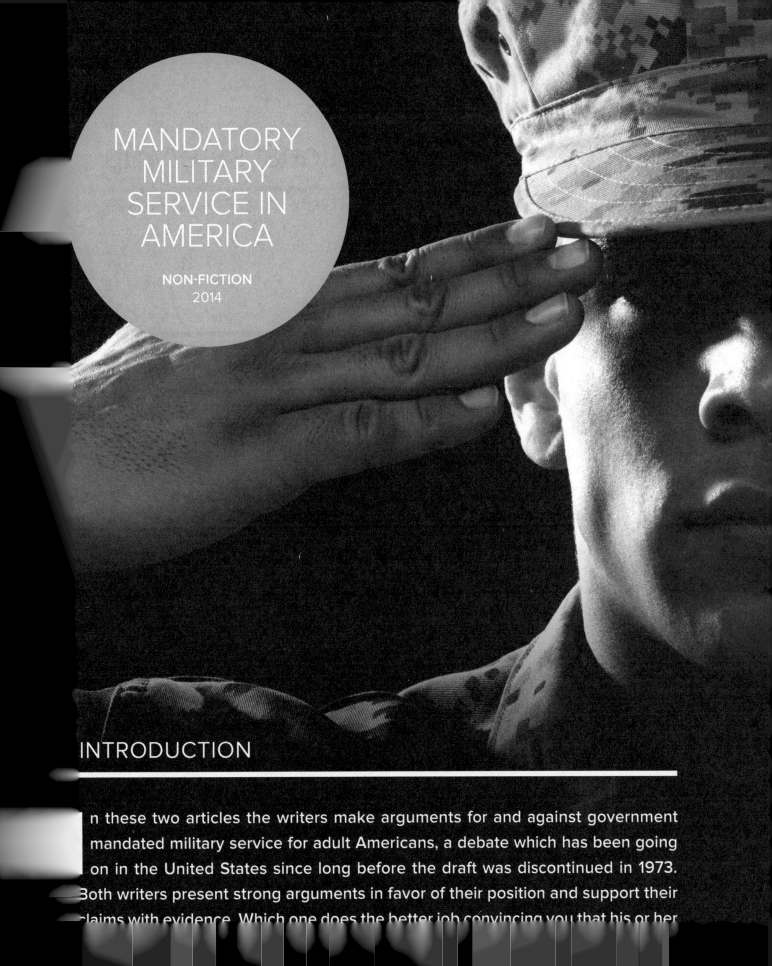

MANDATORY MILITARY SERVICE IN AMERICA

NON-FICTION
2014

INTRODUCTION

n these two articles the writers make arguments for and against government mandated military service for adult Americans, a debate which has been going on in the United States since long before the draft was discontinued in 1973. Both writers present strong arguments in favor of their position and support their claims with evidence. Which one does the better job convincing you that his or her

"Why leave our national safety up to chance?"

FIRST READ

Military Service: An Obligation or a Choice?

Point: Fight for Your Right to Be Free: Every American Should Be Required to Serve in the Military.

1 Are you 18–25 and male? If so, the law mandates that you register with the government for military service. Registering doesn't mean that you have to actually fight in the military—or even join it. This is because mandatory military conscription—known commonly as "the draft"—ended in 1973, when America removed the service requirement and created an all-volunteer army. Now, during these globally troubled times, it's time for the U.S. government to reinstate the draft. Having everyone serve in the armed forces will bring Americans together, despite our individual political views and personal agendas, as we fight together to ensure freedom of the world's citizens.

2 Some people believe that the voluntary army is sufficient and therefore we do not need every American to serve in the military. This is not an exceptional argument. It is **mediocre** at best. A volunteer army relies on people making the choice to join the army; if people stop volunteering, our country will be left unprotected. Why leave our national safety up to chance?

3 First, compulsory national service would strengthen American citizenship. During World War I and II especially, Americans took pride in serving their country by fighting for it. Some boys even lied about their ages, claiming they were older than they were, so they could enlist early! These **stalwart** men (and some women) helped us win freedom at home as well as abroad. Few people dispute that our current system of using a volunteer army has been a success, as its soldiers are highly trained and skilled. Nonetheless, in making military service optional for American men, a gulf has now formed between professional soldiers and civilians. In a sharp contrast to the past, most of today's leaders have never served in the military—nor have their children. Writing in

U.S. News & World Report, William A. Galston, a former adviser to President Clinton, stated, "For most of us, defending our country is something we watch on television. Little in the lives of young Americans helps them understand that citizenship is more than a list of rights to which they are entitled."

4   Second, reinstating compulsory military service is only fair. As Americans, we all share in our freedoms. Isn't it only just that we all shoulder the obligations to uphold those freedoms? National defense should be a citizenship duty, with risks shared equally across the board. Stanford University history professor David M. Kennedy argued that the people who are not in any danger of being on the firing line are paying the poorest Americans to "... do some of their most dangerous business while they go on with their affairs unbloodied and undistracted." Requiring everyone to join the armed forces will ensure that the American military truly represents all Americans.

5   Finally, compulsory military service would unite the country and serve as a rite of passage. Most Americans live in narrow communities, where people tend to dress, think, and act alike. Joining the military would allow young adults to leave their sheltered communities and meet people who are different—people they otherwise likely would never have met. In an article entitled "The End of the Draft and More," published in the *National Review,* noted historian Stephen Ambrose wrote, "Today, Cajuns from the Gulf Coast have never met a black person from Chicago. Kids from the ghetto don't know a middle-class white. Mexican-Americans have no contact with Jews. Muslim Americans have few Christian acquaintances. And so on." But during our world wars, everyone had to fight, including famous people. Ice-T, Bill Cosby, Clint Eastwood, and Elvis Presley all served in the military! In the past, serving as a soldier was a rite of passage, as young adults grew up together in the face of war. Whatever divided them—race, religion, language—was not as strong as the patriotism that united them. This broadening of our experience breaks down walls and builds tolerance.

6   Of course, serving in the military is not the only way to **bolster** American citizenship, ensure fairness, unite Americans, and safeguard our freedoms. People can volunteer to work in soup kitchens, clean up parks, or build homes for others, for instance. But the key word here is *volunteer,* as people can choose not to act in support of our country. An abundance of evidence strongly suggests the need for mandatory national service. America's freedoms come at a price, and to keep these freedoms, we must all serve in the military.

Counterpoint:
No, No—We Won't Go! Mandatory Military Service Is Not Necessary in America

7   A large number of Americans believe that the draft is **obsolete,** an outdated practice from decades ago. They believe that in this modern day and age, we

Please note that excerpts and passages in the StudySync® library and this workbook are intended as touchstones to generate interest in an author's work. The excerpts and passages do not substitute for the reading of entire texts, and StudySync® strongly recommends that students seek out and purchase the whole literary or informational work in order to experience it as the author intended. Links to online resellers are available in our digital library. In addition, complete works may be ordered through an authorized reseller by filling out and returning to StudySync® the order form enclosed in this workbook.

no longer need everyone to serve in the armed forces. These Americans argue that some people would not serve in the military even if they were drafted and forced into service, and I agree. I wouldn't want to be a soldier, and I know a lot of my friends wouldn't either.

8   History tells us that forced conscription would likely result in widespread resistance and civil unrest. Further, America has not had a draft in more than forty years. This means that more than a generation of people has no memory of the entire male population being called up to fight. My 62-year-old neighbor Mr. Walton, a Vietnam veteran, told me about the widespread resistance to the draft in the mid-1960's and early 1970's. He explained that there were anti-war protests and even riots! Part of the problem came from the "exemptions." These were ways to get out of serving in the military, granted by the government. Some exemptions included young men enrolled in college, men working on farms, or those preparing for a career as religious leaders. Conscientious objectors—people who refused to fight on moral or religious grounds—could also apply for an exemption from serving in the military.

9   Protesters said that mandatory military service was not fair because many of the exemptions meant that less-privileged Americans would be most likely to fight and die. Responding to these concerns, the government halted just about all of the exemptions in the late 1960's. Instead, the government set up a lottery system for the draft. This did not stop the protests; in fact, they got worse. Some young men who knew from their lottery number that they would be drafted ran away. Others went to jail rather than fight in the war. Do we want to have widespread protests like this again? Reinstituting the draft could result in such upheavals.

10   Next, compulsory national service would weaken American citizenship. Writing in *U.S. News & World Report,* Matthew Spaulding, the director of the B. Kenneth Simon Center for American Studies at the Heritage Foundation, argued that serving your country should be an individual choice, not one mandated by the government. He believes that volunteer organizations, private service groups, and people working on their own help the country better than being forced to serve in the army could. He cited statistics to back up his assertion: "[In 2009,] 63.4 million Americans volunteered, well exceeding the 500,000 involved in national service. Total private giving is estimated to exceed $300 billion a year, with individuals accounting for 75 percent of that... One organization, the Knights of Columbus, made charitable contributions of over $150 million and generated some 70 million volunteer service hours." Therefore, he concludes that Americans should reject the draft. Instead, we should do more volunteer work. By becoming more involved in the community, we would become better citizens, Spaulding believes.

11   But Spaulding goes even further. He thinks that mandatory military conscription would funnel away time from volunteering. This, in turn, "undermines the

American character and threatens to weaken private associations," he says. The draft would harm our country far more than it would ever help it.

12 Further, compulsory national service would not be fair to all Americans—and it never was. People against the draft argue that the mandatory military service was never fair because mainly poor people served. The all-volunteer army is fair because people of all races, religions, and backgrounds serve. Besides, how can something be fair if it is forced? With a draft, people are required to serve. They lose their free will. Walter Y. Oi, an economics professor who served on President Richard M. Nixon's Commission on an All-Volunteer Armed Force, believes the only good way to create an army is with volunteers. "Maintaining freedom of occupational choice and relying on incentives to attract qualified individuals for our national defense," Oi stated in *National Service,* "is surely the most equitable method of procuring military manpower."

13 Last but not least, compulsory military service would be very expensive. It costs a great deal of money to train soldiers. People who volunteer to join the military often make it their career, serving twenty years or longer. In contrast, people who are drafted serve their time and then usually leave the military to pursue civilian careers. Why spend the money to train someone who is only going to stay in the armed forces for two years? "People in the military get a lot of expensive training, and it's cost-effective to try to get a fairly long return on that investment," explains Beth Asch, a senior economist who specializes in defense manpower at the Rand Corporation.

14 We would be **naïve** to think that bringing back the draft would be fair. It would not strengthen our ties to our country, either. Society's problems are not that easily solved. Rather, bringing back the draft would more likely bring greater inequality and widespread protests. It would cost the country a great deal of money, too. For these reasons, America should continue with an all-volunteer army.

Please note that excerpts and passages in the StudySync® library and this workbook are intended as touchstones to generate interest in an author's work. The excerpts and passages do not substitute for the reading of entire texts, and StudySync® strongly recommends that students seek out and purchase the whole literary or informational work in order to experience it as the author intended. Links to online resellers are available in our digital library. In addition, complete works may be ordered through an authorized reseller by filling out and returning to StudySync® the order form enclosed in this workbook.

Reading & Writing Companion   **187**

THINK QUESTIONS

1. The author of "Fight for Your Right to Be Free: Every American Should Be Required to Serve in the Military" (the pro essay) says, "Now, during these globally troubled times, it's time for the U.S. government to reinstate the draft." What does the author mean by "globally troubled times"? Cite textual evidence to support your answer.

2. What is one reason the author of "No, No—We Won't Go! Mandatory Military Service Is Not Necessary in America" (the con essay) believes that military service should not be mandatory? Use textual evidence to support your answer.

3. The author of the pro essay says, "In a sharp contrast to the past, most of today's leaders have never served in the military—nor have their children." Why do you think the author says this? What is the author implying about military service? Cite textual evidence in your answer.

4. Use context to determine the meaning of the word **mediocre** as it is used in the pro essay. Write your definition of *mediocre*.

5. **Naïve,** which means "showing a lack of experience," is a word that came into English from French. Although originally this word meant "inborn" or "natural," to call someone *naïve* now is meant as a criticism. Suggest several more kind or complimentary terms that mean the opposite of *naïve*.

CLOSE READ

Reread the text *Mandatory Military Service in America*. As you reread, complete the Focus Questions below. Then use your answers and annotations from the questions to help you complete the Writing Prompt.

 FOCUS QUESTIONS

1. Highlight the sentence in each essay that states the author's opinion, introducing readers to the author's argument.

2. What is the claim in paragraph 3 of "Fight for Your Right to Be Free"? Highlight at least two pieces of evidence from the paragraph. Make annotations to explain how well the pieces of evidence support the claim.

3. What conclusion does the author draw in paragraph 5 of the pro essay? Highlight any examples of weak evidence or fallacious reasoning. Annotate these highlights with notes as to why they are weak or faulty.

4. Highlight three pieces of evidence in the con essay and write an annotation about what claim they support. Mention in the annotation what kind of evidence is being offered (testimony from an expert, statistics, a fact, and so on).

5. What conclusion are drawn by the author of the con essay in paragraphs 10 and 11? Highlight any examples of weak evidence or fallacious reasoning. Annotate these highlights with notes as to why they are weak or faulty.

6. What ideas does each essay express about individual power and national power? What responsibilities come with each of these kinds of power? Highlight examples in the text to support your response.

WRITING PROMPT

Write your own 300-word response about whether "Fight for Your Right to Be Free" or "No, No—We Won't Go!" makes a stronger argument for its case. Consider what you've learned about what makes a good argument: a strong introduction that clearly states the author's claim about the issue and conclusions/claims supported by strong evidence (including facts, expert testimony, statistics, and so on). Arguments should avoid false statements or faulty reasoning. Be sure to include strong textual evidence to support your response.

Please note that excerpts and passages in the StudySync® library and this workbook are intended as touchstones to generate interest in an author's work. The excerpts and passages do not substitute for the reading of entire texts, and StudySync® strongly recommends that students seek out and purchase the whole literary or informational work in order to experience it as the author intended. Links to online resellers are available in our digital library. In addition, complete works may be ordered through an authorized reseller by filling out and returning to StudySync® the order form enclosed in this workbook.

Reading & Writing Companion **189**

FOUR FREEDOMS INAUGURAL ADDRESS

NON-FICTION
Franklin Delano Roosevelt
1941

INTRODUCTION

I n 1941, World War II had been raging across Europe for over a year. President Franklin Delano Roosevelt, beginning an unprecedented third term of office, understood that that the U.S. could no longer stay neutral while Britain and other American allies suffered at the hands of Nazi aggression. In his State of the Union Address on January 6, broadcast to the American public, Roosevelt asked Congress for the authority and funding to support the allies' cause, calling upon all Americans to sacrifice to secure and defend the "four essential human freedoms."

"To that high concept there can be no end save victory."

 FIRST READ

1 The nation takes great satisfaction and much strength from the things which have been done to make its people conscious of their individual stake in the preservation of democratic life in America. Those things have toughened the **fiber** of our people, have renewed their faith and strengthened their devotion to the institutions we make ready to protect.

2 Certainly this is no time for any of us to stop thinking about the social and economic problems which are the root cause of the social revolution which is today a supreme factor in the world. For there is nothing mysterious about the foundations of a healthy and strong democracy.

3 The basic things expected by our people of their political and economic systems are simple. They are:

4 Equality of opportunity for youth and for others. Jobs for those who can work. Security for those who need it.

5 The ending of special privilege for the few.

6 The preservation of **civil** liberties for all.

7 The enjoyment of the fruits of scientific progress in a wider and constantly rising standard of living.

8 These are the simple, basic things that must never be lost sight of in the turmoil and unbelievable complexity of our modern world. The inner and abiding strength of our economic and political systems is dependent upon the degree to which they fulfill these expectations.

9 Many subjects connected with our social economy call for immediate improvement. As examples:

10   We should bring more citizens under the coverage of old-age pensions and unemployment insurance.

11   We should widen the opportunities for adequate medical care.

12   We should plan a better system by which persons deserving or needing gainful employment may obtain it.

13   I have called for personal sacrifice. I am assured of the willingness of almost all Americans to respond to that call. A part of the sacrifice means the payment of more money in taxes. In my budget message I shall recommend that a greater portion of this great defense program be paid for from taxation than we are paying today. No person should try, or be allowed, to get rich out of this program; and the principle of tax payments in **accordance** with ability to pay should be constantly before our eyes to guide our legislation.

14   If the Congress maintains these principles, the voters, putting patriotism ahead of pocketbooks, will give you their applause.

15   In the future days, which we seek to make secure, we look forward to a world founded upon four essential human freedoms.

16   The first is freedom of speech and expression—everywhere in the world.

17   The second is freedom of every person to worship God in his own way—everywhere in the world.

18   The third is freedom from want—which, translated into world terms, means economic understandings which will secure to every nation a healthy peacetime life for its inhabitants—everywhere in the world.

19   The fourth is freedom from fear—which, translated into world terms, means a world-wide reduction of armaments to such a point and in such a thorough fashion that no nation will be in a position to commit an act of physical aggression against any neighbor—anywhere in the world.

20   That is no vision of a distant millennium. It is a definite basis for a kind of world attainable in our own time and generation. That kind of world is the very **antithesis** of the so-called "new order" of tyranny which the dictators seek to create with the crash of a bomb.

21   To that new order we oppose the greater conception—the moral order. A good society is able to face schemes of world domination and foreign revolutions alike without fear.

22   Since the beginning of our American history we have been engaged in change, in a perpetual, peaceful revolution, a revolution which goes on steadily, quietly, adjusting itself to changing conditions without the concentration camp or the quicklime in the ditch. The world order which we seek is the cooperation of free countries, working together in a friendly, civilized society.

23   This nation has placed its destiny in the hands and heads and hearts of its millions of free men and women, and its faith in freedom under the guidance of God. Freedom means the **supremacy** of human rights everywhere. Our support goes to those who struggle to gain those rights and keep them. Our strength is our unity of purpose.

24   To that high concept there can be no end save victory.

 THINK QUESTIONS

1.   In his inaugural address, Roosevelt discusses the "basic things" which he believes Americans expect. He then moves on to identify immediate improvements needed in American society. What specific improvements does Roosevelt call for in the American social economy of his time? Support your answer with textual evidence.

2.   Roosevelt proposes the four freedoms as the basis for "a kind of world" that he sees as very different from what he calls "the new order"? What are the attributes of "the new order"? Use textual evidence to support your answer.

3.   What does Roosevelt mean by "freedom from fear"? After describing freedom from fear, why does he enter immediately into a discussion of the "new order" of tyranny in the next paragraph? Support your answer with details from the text.

4.   Use context to determine the meaning of the word **accordance** as Roosevelt uses it in this speech. Write your definition of *accordance* and explain how you arrived at your definition.

5.   Use your knowledge of word parts to determine the meaning of **supremacy** as it is used in the text. Write your definition and explain how you arrived at it.

Please note that excerpts and passages in the StudySync® library and this workbook are intended as touchstones to generate interest in an author's work. The excerpts and passages do not substitute for the reading of entire texts, and StudySync® strongly recommends that students seek out and purchase the whole literary or informational work in order to experience it as the author intended. Links to online resellers are available in our digital library. In addition, complete works may be ordered through an authorized reseller by filling out and returning to StudySync® the order form enclosed in this workbook.

Reading & Writing Companion   **193**

CLOSE READ

Reread the text "Four Freedoms Inaugural Address." As you reread, complete the Focus Questions below. Then use your answers and annotations from the questions to help you complete the Writing Prompt.

FOCUS QUESTIONS

1. Early on in his speech, Roosevelt states that Americans should continue thinking about the social and economic problems causing so much turmoil around the world. What social and economic improvements and solutions does he present in the course of his speech to help America avoid such problems and difficulties? Highlight and annotate textual evidence that supports your answer.

2. After calling for sacrifice, Roosevelt uses a strong alliterative phrase (a phrase with a repeated consonant sound) to indicate that the American people will understand the need for higher taxes. Highlight that phrase and annotate to explain its meaning.

3. Toward the end of his speech, Roosevelt defines what he means by the turmoil and complexity of the world at that time when he talks about a "new order." What "new order" is he referring to? Highlight and annotate textual evidence to support your answer.

4. The "four freedoms" section of the address opens up discussion of the world as a whole, not just the United States. Highlight the four freedoms. Then annotate the text as you answer these questions: What is it that Roosevelt hopes to make secure? How does he use a list to explain his thoughts?

5. Toward the end of the excerpt, Roosevelt contrasts two different kinds of world order. Highlight the text that describes them and write annotations to explain how they differ. How do his comments reveal his view on the responsibilities of power?

WRITING PROMPT

The four freedoms articulated in Roosevelt's speech are valued by many Americans. Roosevelt also believes that they are crucial to the establishment of a better world. Why did Roosevelt choose to present these four freedoms as the basis for a good society "able to face schemes of world domination and foreign revolutions alike without fear?" Write a 300-word essay explaining what these specific freedoms are, and why they are needed to sustain democracy. Use textual evidence from the speech to support your ideas.

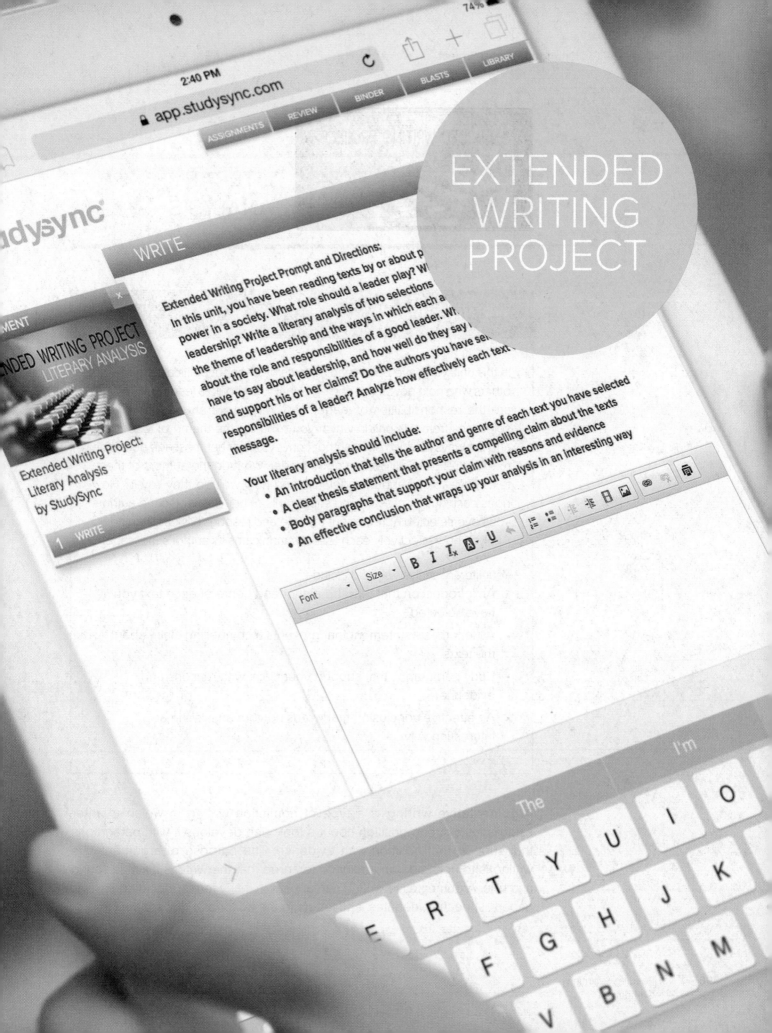

EXTENDED WRITING PROJECT

studysync®

WRITE

EXTENDED WRITING PROJECT
LITERARY ANALYSIS

Extended Writing Project:
Literary Analysis
by StudySync

1 WRITE

Extended Writing Project Prompt and Directions:

In this unit, you have been reading texts by or about p
power in a society. What role should a leader play? W
leadership? Write a literary analysis of two selections
the theme of leadership and the ways in which each a
about the role and responsibilities of a good leader. Wh
have to say about leadership, and how well do they say
and support his or her claims? Do the authors you have se
responsibilities of a leader? Analyze how effectively each text
message.

Your literary analysis should include:
- An introduction that tells the author and genre of each text you have selected
- A clear thesis statement that presents a compelling claim about the texts
- Body paragraphs that support your claim with reasons and evidence
- An effective conclusion that wraps up your analysis in an interesting way

LITERARY ANALYSIS

WRITING PROMPT

In this unit, you have been reading texts by or about political leaders and others who hold power in a society. What role should a leader play? What are the responsibilities of leadership? Write a literary analysis of two selections from this unit in which you examine the theme of leadership and the ways in which each author conveys his or her message about the role and responsibilities of a good leader. What do the authors of these texts have to say about leadership, and how well do they say it? How does each author present and support his or her claims? Do the authors you have selected agree about the role and responsibilities of a leader? Analyze how effectively each text communicates its author's message.

Your literary analysis should include:

- An introduction that tells the author and genre of each text you have selected

- A clear thesis statement that presents a compelling claim about the texts

- Body paragraphs that support your claim with reasons and evidence

- An effective conclusion that wraps up your analysis in an interesting way

Argumentative writing is a type of nonfiction writing in which a writer establishes a strong position about a topic and develops it with paragraphs that support that position with evidence. The purpose of argumentative writing is to persuade an audience to agree that the writer's claim is sound and true. Argumentative writing can appear in many forms, including essays, papers, speeches, debates, and letters to the editor of a newspaper.

NOTES

The most important part of a strong argumentative essay is a clear **claim.** A claim is a writer's central argument or thesis. It communicates the main focus of the writing and allows readers to understand exactly what a writer is arguing. The claim should appear in the introductory paragraph, to help readers understand what will come next.

An argumentative essay should stay focused on the main claim and present information in a logical order that is easy for a reader to follow. Transition words help connect ideas and build the argument point by point. Effective argument writing includes strong evidence that supports the writer's reasoning and demonstrates the claim. It also presents a formal tone that is appropriate to the purpose and style of argumentative writing. A strong argumentative conclusion restates the writer's claim, effectively wraps up the argument, and leaves readers with a lasting final thought. The features of argumentative writing include:

- clear and logical organizational structure
- an introduction with a clear thesis statement
- supporting details, including valid reasoning and textual evidence
- a formal tone
- a concluding restatement of the claim

As you continue with this extended writing project, you'll receive more instructions and practice to help you craft each of the elements of argumentative writing in your own essay.

 STUDENT MODEL

You will learn skills of the writer's craft as you follow the writing process steps of Prewrite, Plan, Draft, and Revise, before the final step of Edit, Proofread, and Publish. Before you get started on your own argumentative essay, begin by reading this essay that one student wrote in response to the writing prompt. As you read this student model, highlight and annotate the features of argumentative writing that the student included in her essay.

The Responsibilities of Power

People with power to do whatever they want also have a responsibility to use that power wisely. The question is: how do you balance power and responsibility? This question is answered differently by Homer in *The Odyssey Book XII* and George Orwell in the excerpt from *1984*. Orwell's novel is set in a futuristic society, and he portrays a world in which a totalitarian government tells people everything they should do. He presents a model of what leadership should <u>not</u> be. Homer, on the other hand, sets his story in times that even then were the distant past, drawing upon history, myth, and legend. He shows how a good leader can tell right from wrong but still allow his people to make decisions for themselves. Homer presents a model of what leadership, however imperfect, <u>can</u> be. Each book presents its ideas about the degree of control leaders can exert over their people's freedom, and how leaders should communicate with their people. However, *The Odyssey's* message, and the ways that Homer communicates his ideas, are more compelling than the vision Orwell presents in the excerpt from *1984*.

Although control is an essential part of power, Homer shows readers in *The Odyssey Book XII* that Odysseus does not try to exercise complete control over his men. Instead, Odysseus asks them to swear an oath not to kill the cattle on the island. For a while, as long "as corn and wine held out," they obey him (Homer). But even when the men are hungry and tempted to eat, Odysseus does not intervene directly. He prays to the gods for help. Afterwards, he is obviously upset by what the men do in his absence, but he seems resigned to their bad choices. In fact, after he sees what has happened, he says, "we could see no way out of it, for the cows were dead already" (Homer). Homer seems to be saying that Odysseus did his job by telling the men not to kill the cows, and that it was the crew's job to practice some self-control. Perhaps Odysseus did not make a good decision in allowing the men to continue "driving in the best cows and feasting upon them" (Homer). Still, Homer shows that, like leaders in real life, Odysseus has his weaknesses as well as strengths.

In *1984,* the situation is very different. The government controls what everyone does. The narrator says "nothing was illegal, since there were no longer any laws" (Orwell), but it is clear that people are not allowed to think for themselves. "Big Brother" spies on people everywhere. The police patrol goes "snooping into people's windows" (Orwell) and there's even a "Thought Police" that monitors people's thoughts. Though Orwell creates this society as a warning against totalitarian governments, he doesn't show the reader what a good leader should do.

Having control over people depends a lot on how a leader communicates with them. Homer's version of good communication is more convincing than Orwell's because in *The Odyssey Book XII* Odysseus communicates personally and individually with the men he leads. After his men killed the cattle, he "rebuked each one of the men separately" (Homer). Odysseus speaks honestly and directly. This is a great way to communicate with people because it makes them feel like individuals and feel respected.

Conversely, the communication of the government in *1984* is generic and bends the truth. The government communicates with people by constantly telling them things through their "telescreens." The government also uses the same Doublespeak and oxymorons for talking to everyone: "WAR IS PEACE, FREEDOM IS SLAVERY, IGNORANCE IS STRENGTH" (Orwell). The communication in *1984* is designed to be generalized and to manipulate people. There is no truth in it. Though Orwell is exaggerating what propaganda looks like here, he doesn't give any good ideas in this excerpt from *1984* for how to improve the situation.

In the end, both Homer and Orwell seem to suggest that leaders need to let people make their own decisions. Orwell makes this point through a negative example of what happens when leadership controls all thought and speech. However, this excerpt from Orwell's *1984* only shows people what <u>not</u> to do, not how to do it right. Homer, on the other hand, presents ideas about how leaders should behave. True, bad things can happen, and Odysseus isn't perfect, but Homer seems to suggest that the job of a leader is to have a clear moral compass and to do his best to give advice and guidance to his people. Homer's message is more compelling than Orwell's because *The Odyssey*'s author not only tells his readers what leaders should <u>not</u> do, he also presents ideas about how they <u>should</u> behave.

 THINK QUESTIONS

1. What is the main idea of this literary analysis? In which sentence or sentences does it appear?

2. How does the writer arrange the ideas in "The Responsibilities of Power"? Does the author introduce and connect his or her points in a particular order?

3. The writer discusses each author's point of view about how a leader should communicate with the people. How does the writer develop the idea that Homer's point of view is more compelling than Orwell's?

4. Thinking about the writing prompt, which selections or other resources would you like to use to create your own argumentative essay? What are some ideas that you may want to develop into your own piece?

5. Based on what you have read, listened to, or researched, how would you answer the question: *What are the responsibilities of power*? Which text from this unit presents the most compelling argument about the responsibilities of power?

Please note that excerpts and passages in the StudySync® library and this workbook are intended as touchstones to generate interest in an author's work. The excerpts and passages do not substitute for the reading of entire texts, and StudySync® strongly recommends that students seek out and purchase the whole literary or informational work in order to experience it as the author intended. Links to online resellers are available in our digital library. In addition, complete works may be ordered through an authorized reseller by filling out and returning to StudySync® the order form enclosed in this workbook.

Reading & Writing Companion **199**

PREWRITE

WRITING PROMPT

In this unit, you have been reading texts by or about political leaders and others who hold power in a society. What role should a leader play? What are the responsibilities of leadership? Write a literary analysis of two selections from this unit in which you examine the theme of leadership and the ways in which each author conveys his or her message about the role and responsibilities of a good leader. What do the authors of these texts have to say about leadership, and how well do they say it? How does each author present and support his or her claims? Do the authors you have selected agree about the role and responsibilities of a leader? Analyze how effectively each text communicates its author's message.

Your literary analysis should include:

- An introduction that tells the author and genre of each text you have selected
- A clear thesis statement that presents a compelling claim about the texts
- Body paragraphs that support your claim with reasons and evidence
- An effective conclusion that wraps up your analysis in an interesting way

In addition to studying techniques authors use to make an argument, you have been reading and discussing stories about the roles and responsibilities of leaders in various societies. In the extended writing project, you will use some of the techniques for argument writing that you have studied to compose a literary analysis.

Since the topic of your literary analysis has to do with what it means to hold power, you will want to think about how the various authors in this unit have

Copyright © BookheadEd Learning, LLC

NOTES

portrayed the roles and responsibilities of those in power. Think back to what you read about Odysseus as a leader in *The Odyssey Book XII*. How much control did he exert over his people? How did he communicate with them? What do his character traits and his actions tell you about the author's beliefs regarding the responsibilities of a leader?

Make a list of the answers to these questions for Odysseus and at least one other leader, ruler, or governing force you've encountered in this unit. As you write down your ideas, consider:

1. whether the author of a particular selection presents a compelling vision of leadership.
   a. Do you agree with him/her? Why or why not?
   b. Determining this will help you craft the claim of your literary analysis.
2. looking for patterns to emerge. Looking for these patterns may help you to solidify the reasons and evidence you use to support your claim when writing your essay.
   a. Do the leaders portrayed in the selections have anything in common?
   b. What important differences do they have?

Use the following model to help you get started with your own prewriting:

Text: *The Odyssey Book XII* by Homer

Extent of Control Exerted: *Odysseus asks his men to take an oath and stick to it, but he doesn't police their actions. He lets them make their own decisions.*
Method of Communication: *He talks to his men individually, addressing each on a personal level.*

Other Notes about Leadership Method: *Odysseus shows strengths and weaknesses.*
Author's Beliefs about Leadership: *A good leader is someone who guides his people in the right direction but doesn't make them do anything.*

Do you agree or disagree with him? Why?: *Yes, I do agree because people should be free to make their own decisions.*

Please note that excerpts and passages in the StudySync® library and this workbook are intended as touchstones to generate interest in an author's work. The excerpts and passages do not substitute for the reading of entire texts, and StudySync® strongly recommends that students seek out and purchase the whole literary or informational work in order to experience it as the author intended. Links to online resellers are available in our digital library. In addition, complete works may be ordered through an authorized reseller by filling out and returning to StudySync® the order form enclosed in this workbook.

Reading & Writing Companion   **201**

SKILL:
THESIS
STATEMENT

DEFINE

In informative writing, a thesis statement expresses a writer's main idea about a topic. In argument writing, the thesis statement takes the form of a claim. The claim is the writer's opinion about the topic he or she is writing about. When composing a literary analysis, a writer expresses an opinion about the themes or central ideas of one or more pieces of literature or informational texts. The claim typically appears in the introduction of the literary analysis, often as its last sentence. Support for the claim, such as text quotations, descriptions, and other details appears in the body of the argumentative essay.

IDENTIFICATION AND APPLICATION

A thesis statement:

- presents the essay's topic
- lets presents a main idea or claim about how literary or informational texts approach the topic
- reviews what will appear in the body of the literary analysis
- addresses the literary analysis prompt
- appears in the introduction paragraph

MODEL

The following is the introduction paragraph from the Student Model literary analysis "The Responsibilities of Power":

> *People with power to do whatever they want also have a responsibility to use that power wisely. The question is: how do you balance power and responsibility? This question is answered differently by Homer in*

The Odyssey Book XII and George Orwell in the excerpt from *1984*. Orwell's novel is set in a futuristic society, and he portrays a world in which a totalitarian government tells people everything they should do. He presents a model of what leadership should not be. Homer, on the other hand, sets his story in times that even then were the distant past, drawing upon history, myth and legend. He shows how a good leader can tell right from wrong but still allow his people to make decisions for themselves. Homer presents a model of what leadership, however imperfect, can be. Each book presents its ideas about the degree of control leaders can exert over their people's freedom, and how leaders should communicate with their people. **However, *The Odyssey's* message, and the ways that Homer communicates his ideas, are more compelling than the vision Orwell presents in the excerpt from *1984*.**

 ## PRACTICE

Draft a thesis statement with pen and paper that states your main idea in a clear and engaging way. Be sure that your thesis statement addresses the prompt. When you are done writing, switch papers with a partner and evaluate each other's work. How clearly did the writer state the main point? Does the thesis statement answer the question or topic posed in the prompt? Does the thesis statement clearly state the focus of the rest of the essay? Offer suggestions, and remember that they are most helpful when they are informative and constructive.

SKILL:
ORGANIZE
ARGUMENTATIVE
WRITING

 ## DEFINE

A literary analysis is a form of argumentative writing that tries to persuade readers to accept the writer's interpretation of the theme of a literary text or the central idea of an informative text. To do so, the writer must organize and present the reasons and relevant evidence—the details and quotations from the text or texts—in a logical and convincing way. The writer must select an **organizational structure** that best suits the argument.

The writer of a literary analysis can choose from a number of organizational structures, including **compare and contrast, order of importance, problem and solution, cause-effect, and chronological order.** Experienced writers use an outline or another graphic organizer to decide how to order and convey their ideas most persuasively.

 ## IDENTIFICATION AND APPLICATION

The author of an argumentative essay takes a position on the topic and states a claim.

- The claim is the author's point of view or opinion about a topic.

- The claim is stated in a thesis statement and is supported by logical reasoning.

- The claim is clearly stated in the first paragraph of the argumentative essay.

- A restatement of the claim is usually found in the concluding paragraph.

- The author uses a formal style and a tone that is objective, or that shows no emotional bias.

- Text evidence is factual information from the text that supports the author's claim. Some evidence is strong because it can be verified in other sources as true. Strong text evidence may be in the form of:

NOTES

> › numbers or statistics
> › quotes from experts
> › names or dates
> › other facts
> › references to other credible sources

- Weaker text evidence cannot always be proven to be true. It may be in the form of:
  > › opinions
  > › personal beliefs
  > › emotional appeals
  > › biased, or one-sided, statements

 ## MODEL

After reviewing prewriting notes, the writer of the Student Model decided to focus on two texts, *1984* and *The Odyssey Book XII,* because the methods of leadership portrayed in the two pieces seemed completely opposite. The writer determined from the prewriting materials that the two texts could be compared and contrasted based on two important points: degree of control and method of communication. Comparing these points would provide a foundation for evaluating each author's beliefs about power.

In the Student Model, the writer makes the organizational structure clear with the thesis statement's word choice:

> However, *The Odyssey's* message, and the ways that Homer communicates his ideas are more compelling than the vision Orwell presents in the excerpt from *1984.*

The writer uses the phrase *more compelling than* both to state the claim of the literary analysis and to signal that Homer's beliefs will be compared with Orwell's.

The writer of the Student Model, "The Responsibilities of Power," used a three-column chart to organize the ideas that were developed during the prewriting process.

Please note that excerpts and passages in the StudySync® library and this workbook are intended as touchstones to generate interest in an author's work. The excerpts and passages do not substitute for the reading of entire texts, and StudySync® strongly recommends that students seek out and purchase the whole literary or informational work in order to experience it as the author intended. Links to online resellers are available in our digital library. In addition, complete works may be ordered through an authorized reseller by filling out and returning to StudySync® the order form enclosed in this workbook.

Reading & Writing Companion **205**

Point of Comparison	The Odyssey Book XII	1984
degree of control	Odysseus trusts his men to do what is right. Doesn't control everything the men do.	The government monitors the people's movements and thoughts to make sure they don't do anything wrong.
method of communicating	personal, individual, truthful	impersonal, constant, and filled with propaganda

 PRACTICE

Use an *Organize Argumentative Writing* Three Column Chart like the one you have just studied to fill in the information you gathered in the prewrite stage of crafting your essay.

SUPPORTING DETAILS

sync•skills
Writing

SKILL:
SUPPORTING
DETAILS

 DEFINE

Because a literary analysis makes a claim about themes in literature or the central ideas in informative texts, it is a form of argument writing. To make his or her argument effective, the writer of a literary analysis must provide **supporting details** in the form of reasons and relevant textual evidence to add credibility to the claim. Reasons are statements that answer the question "Why?" Writers provide reasons to support a claim and to help readers understand their interpretation of the theme or central idea in a text. Relevant evidence includes definitions, quotations, observations, and examples from the text or texts being analyzed. Relevant evidence is the key to the success of the argument as it makes the reasons more credible and persuasive to the reader, develops the ideas, and clarifies the writer's understanding and interpretation of the text. Without reasons and relevant evidence, the writer would simply be stating his or her opinion about a theme or a central idea.

Because writers want to convince readers that their interpretations of a text's themes or central ideas are credible, they carefully select and present the evidence. Evidence is relevant only if it supports the claim and helps build the argument. If the evidence—a detail, an example, or a quotation—does not support the claim or validate the argument, it is irrelevant and should not be used.

 IDENTIFICATION AND APPLICATION

Step 1:

Review your claim. To identify supporting details that are relevant to your claim, ask the following question: What am I trying to persuade my audience to believe? For example, in the informational text *Ancient Greece: A Political, Social, and Cultural History*, the writers make a claim:

Reciprocity—mutual and fair exchange—which governs all social relationships in the Homeric world **is the core of the leader-people relationship.**

Step 2:

Ask what a reader needs to know about the topic in order to understand the claim about the theme or central idea. What are some of the reasons the authors make their claim? Additional details provide greater depth of understanding:

A leader who keeps more than he deserves or distributes prizes unfairly **risks losing the respect** of his followers.

Why is this important? The writers provide relevant evidence:

Homeric chiefs engage in a **constant exchange of gifts and feasts with other chiefs and important men.** This is both a way of **showing off their wealth** and a means to **cement friendships,** win new friends, and c**ollect obligations through a display of generosity.**

Step 3:

Look for definitions, quotations, examples, and descriptions to reinforce your claim. Use supporting details like these to build on information you've already provided, but remember to evaluate their relevance to your claim. To do this, ask yourself the following questions:

- Does this information help the reader understand the topic?
- Does this information support my claim?
- Does this information help build my argument?
- Is there stronger evidence that makes the same point?

 MODEL

In the following excerpt from George Washington's "Thanksgiving Proclamation," Washington's central idea is that the nation should observe a day of public thanksgiving:

Whereas **it is the duty of all Nations to acknowledge the providence of Almighty God,** to obey his will, to be grateful for his benefits, and humbly to implore his protection and favor—and whereas both Houses of Congress have by **their joint Committee requested me to recommend to the People of the United States a day of public thanksgiving and prayer** to be observed by acknowledging with grateful hearts the many signal favors of Almighty God especially by affording them an opportunity peaceably to establish a form of government for their safety and happiness.

Now therefore I do recommend and assign Thursday the 26th day of November next to be devoted by the People of these States to the service of that great and glorious Being, who is the beneficent Author of all the good that was, that is, or that will be—That we may then all unite in rendering unto him our sincere and humble thanks—**for his kind care and protection of the People of this Country** previous to their becoming a Nation—**for the signal and manifold mercies, and the favorable interpositions of his Providence which we experienced in the course and conclusion of the late war—for the great degree of tranquility, union, and plenty, which we have since enjoyed**—for the peaceable and rational manner, in which **we have been enabled to establish constitutions of government** for our safety and happiness, and particularly the national One now lately instituted—for the civil and religious liberty with which we are blessed; and the means we have of acquiring and diffusing useful knowledge; and in general for all the great and various favors which he hath been pleased to confer upon us.

In paragraph 1, Washington states that he has been asked "to recommend to the People of the United States a day of public thanksgiving and prayer." His thesis is that "it is the duty of all Nations to acknowledge the providence of Almighty God" and to show gratitude.

In paragraph 2, the reasons and details stated support the request for a national day of thanksgiving. These include the following conclusions:

- that God has protected "the People of this Country" before the war
- that God influenced "the course and conclusion of the late war"
- that God has provided "tranquility, union, and plenty" since the war

Washington goes on to include relevant evidence to support his reasons that the nation should show gratitude, including that the "constitutions of government" provide for people's safety and happiness.

PLAN

WRITING PROMPT

In this unit, you have been reading texts by or about political leaders and others who hold power in a society. What role should a leader play? What are the responsibilities of leadership? Write a literary analysis of two selections from this unit in which you examine the theme of leadership and the ways in which each author conveys his or her message about the role and responsibilities of a good leader. What do the authors of these texts have to say about leadership, and how well do they say it? How does each author present and support his or her claims? Do the authors you have selected agree about the role and responsibilities of a leader? Analyze how effectively each text communicates its author's message.

Your literary analysis should include:

- An introduction that tells the author and genre of each text you have selected

- A clear thesis statement that presents a compelling claim about the texts

- Body paragraphs that support your claim with reasons and evidence

- An effective conclusion that wraps up your analysis in an interesting way

Review the information you recorded in your *Organize Argumentative Writing Three Column Chart*. The chart stated the texts you will address, the points of comparison you will analyze between them, and details that explain what each text suggests about the responsibilities of power. This chart, along with your thesis statement, will help you to create a "road map" to use for writing your essay.

Consider the following questions as you develop topics and supporting details to include on your road map. This information will help you plan the content for each body paragraph of your literary analysis:

- How does the leader in this text behave toward the people he has power over?
- Do the leader's actions cause something good to happen? Why or why not?
- Do the leader's actions cause something bad to happen? Why or why not?
- How do the people view their leader?
- Does the author approve or disapprove of the way the leader behaves? How can you tell?
- Which author presents a more compelling argument about the responsibilities of power?

Use this model to get started with your road map:

Literary Analysis Road Map

Thesis statement: However, *The Odyssey's* message, and the ways that Homer communicates his ideas are more compelling than the vision Orwell presents in the excerpt from *1984*.

Body Paragraph 1 Topic: Odysseus does not exert complete control over his men.
    Supporting Detail #1: In *The Odyssey Book XII*, Odysseus asks his men not to kill the cattle.
    Supporting Detail #2: He does not stop them from continuing to feast.

Body Paragraph 2 Topic: The government in *1984* exercises control over citizens.
    Supporting Detail #1: The government spies on people's actions.
    Supporting Detail #2: The government monitors people's thoughts.

Body Paragraph 3 Topic: Homer presents a more compelling vision of how a leader should communicate with his people.
    Supporting Detail #1: Odysseus talks to his men one-on-one.
    Supporting Detail #2: He "rebukes" them, which shows honesty and directness.

Body Paragraph 4 Topic: The government in *1984* communicates in confusing and deceptive ways.

    Supporting Detail #1: The government speaks to the people constantly through their telescreens, telling them nothing but generalized propaganda.
    Supporting Detail #2: The government uses Doublespeak and oxymorons.

SKILL: INTRODUCTIONS

 DEFINE

The **introduction** is the opening paragraph or section of a literary analysis or other nonfiction text. The introduction of a literary analysis **identifies the texts and the topic to be discussed.** It almost always **states the writer's thesis,** the central claim that will be developed in the remainder of the essay. However, in some cases the thesis may be implicit in the introduction, rather than directly stated, and then stated explicitly later in the essay. The introduction **previews the relevant evidence** that will support the thesis and appear in the body of the text. The introduction is also the place where most writers include a **"hook"** that is intended to connect with and engage readers.

 IDENTIFICATION AND APPLICATION

- In a literary analysis, the introduction is the section in which the writer **identifies the texts and topic to be discussed.** Remember, a literary analysis examines a theme of one or more literary texts or the central idea of one or more nonfiction texts. The writer must let readers know what the focus of the analysis will be. Once readers have that information, they can concentrate on the writer's claim.

- A literary analysis is a form of argument, so the writer's claim is an important part of the introduction. The claim is a direct statement of the writer's opinion about, or interpretation of, the texts under discussion. By **stating the thesis or claim** in the introduction, the writer lets readers know the ideas he or she will explore in the body of the analysis. Establishing a claim here also allows readers to form their own opinions, which they can then measure against the writer's thesis or claim as they read the literary analysis.

- Sometimes a thesis statement or claim will be implicit in the introduction and stated explicitly later. This may happen when a writer wishes to establish a foundation of evidence for the thesis before introducing it. Usually, the thesis is expressed as part of the introduction, often as the last sentence of the introductory paragraph or section.

- Another use of the introduction is to provide a **preview of the supporting evidence** that will follow in the body of the text. By using the introduction to hint at key details, the writer can establish an effective argument, increasing the likelihood that readers will agree with his or her claim.

- The introduction's **"hook"** leaves readers with a first impression about what to expect from the writer. Good hooks engage readers' interest and make them want to keep reading. The hook should appeal to the audience and help readers connect to the topic in a meaningful way so that they will take the writer's claim seriously. The hook might include:
  › a quotation
  › a question
  › a brief anecdote
  › a strong statement
  › a connection to the reader or to life
  › a shocking statistic

 ## MODEL

Take a look at the following excerpt from Pericles' "Funeral Oration":

> **Our constitution does not copy the laws of neighboring states; we are rather a pattern to others than imitators ourselves. Its administration favors the many instead of the few; this is why it is called a democracy.** If we look to the laws, they afford equal justice to all in their private differences; if no social standing, advancement in public life falls to reputation for capacity, class considerations not being allowed to interfere with merit; nor again does poverty bar the way, if a man is able to serve the state, he is not hindered by the obscurity of his condition. **The freedom which we enjoy in our government extends also to our ordinary life.** There, far from exercising a jealous surveillance over each other, we do not feel called upon to be angry with our neighbor for doing what he likes, or even to indulge in those injurious looks which cannot fail to be offensive, although they inflict no positive penalty. But all this ease in our private relations does not make us lawless as citizens. Against this fear is our chief safeguard, teaching us to obey the magistrates and the laws, particularly such as regard the protection of the injured, whether they are actually on the statute book, or belong to that code which, although unwritten, yet cannot be broken without acknowledged disgrace.

Pericles starts readers off with a hook. The opening sentence makes a strong statement: Athens is a city-state that other places want to imitate — "we are rather a pattern to others than imitators ourselves." This is an effective hook because it raises two questions in the mind of the reader. First, why is Athens

NOTES

so admirable? Second, why does Pericles say this at the beginning of a speech given at a funeral?

Pericles moves on to make a claim about what is admirable about the Athenian form of government: "Its administration favors the many instead of the few; this is why it is called a democracy." Pericles' listeners understood that he was giving a funeral oration to honor the dead. In his introduction, Pericles' claim that Athens is exceptional implies his thesis: that the Athenian way of life is, therefore, worth every sacrifice. The heroes who died in war died for a worthy cause. The remainder of the introduction extolls the virtues that, in Pericles' opinion, make Athens worthy of its heroes. Pericles explains that its laws, giving "equal justice to all in their private differences," are remarkable. The introduction previews the virtues of Athens and establishes the foundation for showing that the sacrifice made by men who fought on the battlefield was not in vain. Their efforts help to maintain Athens' superiority. Near the end of the speech, Pericles confirms what he implies in the introduction: "fortunate indeed are they who draw for their lot a death so glorious as that which has caused your mourning."

 PRACTICE

Write an introduction for your essay that explicitly states the thesis you have already worked on and includes a hook to capture your readers' interest. Trade with a peer review partner when you are finished and offer feedback on each other's introductions. Remember that suggestions for improvement are most helpful when they are supportive and kind.

DEFINE

Body paragraphs are the section of a literary analysis between the introduction and conclusion paragraphs. These paragraphs are where you support the claim in your thesis statement by developing your supporting reasons with evidence from the texts and analysis. Typically, each body paragraph will focus on one main supporting reason. This makes your essay easy to follow for readers. The main supporting reason of each body paragraph must support the claim you make in your thesis statement.

Structuring the body paragraphs clearly is important. One strategy for structuring a body paragraph for a literary analysis is the following:

Topic sentence: The topic sentence is the first sentence of your body paragraph and clearly states the main supporting reason of the paragraph. It is important that your topic sentence supports the main claim you made in your thesis statement.

Evidence #1: It is essential to support your topic sentence with evidence. Evidence can be relevant facts, definitions, concrete details, quotations, or other valid information and examples.

Analysis/Explanation #1: After presenting evidence to support your topic sentence, you will need to analyze that evidence and explain how it supports your topic sentence and, in turn, the claim in your thesis.

Evidence #2: Continue to develop your topic sentence with a second piece of evidence.

Analysis/Explanation #2: Analyze this second piece of evidence and explain how it supports your topic sentence and, in turn, the claim in your thesis statement.

Concluding sentence: After presenting your evidence, it's a good idea to wrap up either by restating your topic sentence or transitioning to the next paragraph in your concluding sentence.

Transitions are words and phrases that connect and clarify the relationships among ideas in a text. Transitions work at three different levels: within a sentence, between paragraphs, and to indicate organizational structure.

Authors of argumentative texts, including literary analysis, use transitions to help readers recognize the overall organizational structure. Transitions also help readers make connections between the claim and supporting reasons, between a supporting reason and evidence, and between claims and counterclaims. Also, by adding transition words or phrases to the beginning or end of a paragraph, authors guide readers smoothly through the text.

In addition, transition words and phrases help authors make connections between words within a sentence. Conjunctions such as *and, or,* and *but* as well as prepositions such as *with, beyond,* and *inside* show the relationships between words. Transitions help readers understand how words fit together to create an overall meaning.

 IDENTIFICATION AND APPLICATION

- Body paragraphs are the section of the essay between the introduction and conclusion paragraphs. The body paragraphs provide the supporting reasons, evidence, and analysis/explanation needed to support the claim made in the thesis statement. Typically, writers develop one main idea per body paragraph.
  - › Topic sentences clearly state the main supporting reason of that paragraph.
  - › Evidence consists of relevant facts, definitions, concrete details, quotations, or other valid information and examples.
  - › Analysis and explanation are needed to explain how the evidence validates the supporting reason in the topic sentence and to point out its strengths and weaknesses.
  - › The conclusion sentence wraps up the main supporting reason and transitions to the next body paragraph.
- Transition words are a necessary element of a successful piece of literary analysis.
  - › Transition words help readers understand the text structure of an argumentative text. Here are some transition words and phrases that are frequently used in three different text structures:
    - » Cause and effect: *so, for, since, because, accordingly, in effect, as a result*
    - » Compare and contrast: *also, both, while, but, yet, still, like, unlike, meanwhile, although, however, similarly, whereas, conversely, as opposed to, on the contrary*
    - » Chronological order: *first, next, then, last, initially, subsequently, finally, ultimately*
  - › Transition words help readers understand the flow of ideas and concepts in a text. Some of the most useful transitions are words that indicate that the ideas in one paragraph are building on or adding to

those in another. Examples include: *furthermore, therefore, consequently, in addition, moreover, by extension, in order to.*

 MODEL

The Student Model uses a compare-and-contrast body paragraph structure to develop reasons that support the thesis statement. The model uses transitions to help the reader understand the relationships among the claim, supporting reasons, and evidence in the essay.

Read the first two body paragraphs from the Student Model essay, "The Responsibilities of Power." Look closely at the structure and note the transition words in bold. Think about the purpose of the information presented. Are supporting reasons stated in each body paragraph? Does relevant evidence support the reasons? How do the transition words help you to understand the information within and between paragraphs?

> Although control is an essential part of power, Homer shows readers in *The Odyssey Book XII* that Odysseus does not try to exercise complete control over his men. **Instead,** Odysseus asks them to swear an oath not to kill the cattle on the island. For a while, as long "as corn and wine held out," they obey him (Homer). **But** even when the men are hungry and tempted to eat, Odysseus does not intervene directly. He prays to the gods for help. **Afterwards,** he is obviously upset by what the men do in his absence, but he seems resigned to their bad choices. In fact, after he sees what has happened, he says, "we could see no way out of it, for the cows were dead already" (Homer). Homer seems to be saying that Odysseus did his job by telling the men not to kill the cows and that it was the crew's job to practice some self-control. Perhaps Odysseus did not make a good decision in allowing the men to continue "driving in the best cows and feasting upon them." **Still,** Homer shows that, like leaders in real life, Odysseus has his weaknesses as well as strengths.

> In *1984,* the situation is way **different.** The government controls what everyone does. The narrator says, "nothing was illegal, since there were no longer any laws" (Orwell), but it is clear that people are not allowed to think for themselves. "Big Brother" spies on people everywhere. The police patrol goes "snooping into people's windows" (Orwell) and there's even a "Thought Police" that monitors people's thoughts. Though Orwell creates this society as a warning against totalitarian governments, he doesn't show the reader what a good leader should do.

NOTES

*Having control over people depends a lot on how a leader communicates with them. Homer's version of good communication is **more convincing** than Orwell's because in The Odyssey Book XII Odysseus communicates personally and individually with the men he leads. After his men killed the cattle, he "rebuked each one of the men separately" (Homer). Odysseus speaks honestly and directly. This is a great way to communicate with people because it makes them feel like individuals and feel respected.*

In body paragraph 1, the Student Model begins by stating, "Although control is an essential part of power, Homer shows readers in *The Odyssey Book XII* that Odysseus does not try to exercise complete control over his men." This **topic sentence** clearly establishes one reason for the writer's claim that Homer is more compelling than Orwell, a reason that will be developed by body paragraph 1.

The topic sentence is immediately followed by the transition word *instead,* which indicates that the writer will define exactly what he or she means in the topic sentence. The writer goes on to provide **evidence** to support the idea that Odysseus does not exercise too much control. The writer explains that Odysseus asks the men to make a promise and that the men obey Odysseus until they become desperate. The writer supports this point with relevant evidence in the form of a quotation from the excerpt. The writer then uses the word *but* as a transition to a second piece of evidence: Odysseus doesn't intervene even when the men disobey him. The transition word *afterwards* helps readers understand the sequence of events. The writer goes on to explain that not interfering might or might not have been a wise decision.

Body paragraph 2 uses the word *different* to signal that the structure of this literary analysis will be compare and contrast.

 PRACTICE

Write one body paragraph for your literary analysis essay that follows the suggested format. When you are finished, trade with a partner and offer each other feedback. How effective is the topic sentence at stating the main point of the paragraph? How strong is the evidence used to support the topic sentence? Does the analysis thoroughly support the topic sentence? Does the analysis contain good organization and strong transitions to connect and clarify ideas? Offer each other suggestions, and remember that they are most helpful when they are constructive.

SKILL: CONCLUSIONS

⭐ DEFINE

A **conclusion** is the closing statement or section of a nonfiction text. In a literary analysis, the conclusion brings the writer's argument or interpretation to a close. It follows directly from the introduction's claim and the reasons and relevant evidence provided in the body of the text. The conclusion of a literary analysis text should restate the claim the writer is making about the text or texts in the analysis and also summarize the writer's main ideas. In some types of writing, the conclusion might also include a recommendation, a call to action, or an insightful comment.

••• IDENTIFICATION AND APPLICATION

- An effective conclusion of a literary analysis text will restate the writer's claim about the themes or central ideas of one or more texts.

- The conclusion should briefly summarize the strongest and most convincing reasons and evidence from the body paragraphs. Focusing on the strongest points makes it more likely that readers will agree with the writer's views.

- Some conclusions offer a recommendation or some form of insight relating to the analysis. This may take any of the following forms:

  › An answer to a question first posed in the introduction
  › A question designed to elicit reflection on the part of the reader
  › A memorable or inspiring message
  › A last compelling example
  › A suggestion that readers learn more

MODEL

In the concluding paragraph of the student model "The Responsibilities of Power," the writer reinforces the thesis statement, reminds the reader of relevant details about the two texts, and ends with a final thought.

Please note that excerpts and passages in the StudySync® library and this workbook are intended as touchstones to generate interest in an author's work. The excerpts and passages do not substitute for the reading of entire texts, and StudySync® strongly recommends that students seek out and purchase the whole literary or informational work in order to experience it as the author intended. Links to online resellers are available in our digital library. In addition, complete works may be ordered through an authorized reseller by filling out and returning to StudySync® the order form enclosed in this workbook.

 Reading & Writing Companion **219**

*In the end, both Homer and Orwell seem to suggest that leaders need to let people make their own decisions. Orwell makes this point through **a negative example of what happens when leadership controls all thought and speech.** However, this excerpt from Orwell's 1984 only shows people what <u>not</u> to do, not how to do it right. Homer, on the other hand, presents ideas about how leaders should behave. True, bad things can happen, and Odysseus isn't perfect, but Homer seems to suggest that **the job of a leader is to have a clear moral compass and to do his best to give advice** and guidance to his people. **Homer's message is more compelling than** Orwell's because The Odyssey's author not only tells his readers what leaders should <u>not</u> do, he also presents ideas about how they <u>should</u> behave.*

This conclusion begins by showing what Homer and Orwell have in common. It then returns to the thesis statement by indicating the flaws in what Orwell has to say, along with the strengths of what Homer has to say. The conclusion reminds readers of details from the literary analysis: Homer suggests that a leader's job "is to have a clear moral compass and give advice to his people," while in *1984* the leaders control all thought, speech, and actions. The writer of the Student Model restates and elaborates on the thesis statement by noting that Homer's vision of a leader is more compelling than Orwell's because Homer presents positive ideas about what leaders can and should be. This is an effective final thought. By comparing Odysseus with the government in *1984,* the writer of the Student Model helps answer the question posed in the introduction: "How do you balance power and responsibility?"

 PRACTICE

Write a conclusion for your essay. Your essay should include reinforcement or a restatement of the thesis you have already worked on and a final thought you want to leave with readers. Trade with a peer review partner and offer feedback on each other's conclusion.

DRAFT

WRITING PROMPT

In this unit, you have been reading texts by or about political leaders and others who hold power in a society. What role should a leader play? What are the responsibilities of leadership? Write a literary analysis of two selections from this unit in which you examine the theme of leadership and the ways in which each author conveys his or her message about the role and responsibilities of a good leader. What do the authors of these texts have to say about leadership, and how well do they say it? How does each author present and support his or her claims? Do the authors you have selected agree about the role and responsibilities of a leader? Analyze how effectively each text communicates its author's message.

Your literary analysis should include:

- An introduction that tells the author and genre of each text you have selected
- A clear thesis statement that presents a compelling claim about the texts
- Body paragraphs that support your claim with reasons and evidence
- An effective conclusion that wraps up your analysis in an interesting way

You've already made progress toward writing your own literary analysis. You have thought about your purpose, audience, and topic. You have carefully examined the unit's texts and selected the two you want to discuss. Based on your analysis of textual evidence, you have identified what you want to say about the authors' differing portrayals of the responsibilities of leadership and which portrayal you find more compelling. You have decided how to

Please note that excerpts and passages in the StudySync® library and this workbook are intended as touchstones to generate interest in an author's work. The excerpts and passages do not substitute for the reading of entire texts, and StudySync® strongly recommends that students seek out and purchase the whole literary or informational work in order to experience it as the author intended. Links to online resellers are available in our digital library. In addition, complete works may be ordered through an authorized reseller by filling out and returning to StudySync® the order form enclosed in this workbook.

Reading & Writing Companion   **221**

organize information, and generated supporting reasons. Now it is time to write a draft of your literary analysis.

Use your graphic organizers and your other prewriting materials to help you as you write. Remember that a literary analysis begins with an introduction and presents a claim in the form of a thesis statement. Body paragraphs develop the claim in the thesis statement with supporting reasons, details, quotations, and other relevant information and explanations drawn from the texts. Transitions help the reader understand the relationship among the thesis statement, supporting reasons, and evidence. They also help readers follow the flow of information. A concluding paragraph restates or reinforces the claim in your thesis statement. An effective conclusion can also do more— it can leave a lasting impression on your readers. When drafting, ask yourself these questions:

- How can I improve my hook to make it more appealing?
- What can I do to clarify the claim in my thesis statement?
- What textual evidence—including relevant facts, strong details, and interesting quotations in each body paragraph—supports the claim made in the thesis statement?
- Would more precise language or different details about the treatment of leadership in these two texts make my literary analysis more exciting and vivid?
- How well have I communicated each writer's portrayal of the responsibilities of power and my opinion about which portrayal is more compelling?
- What final thought do I want to leave with my readers?

Before you submit your draft, read it over carefully. You want to be sure that you have responded to all aspects of the prompt.

REVISE

WRITING PROMPT

In this unit, you have been reading texts by or about political leaders and others who hold power in a society. What role should a leader play? What are the responsibilities of leadership? Write a literary analysis of two selections from this unit in which you examine the theme of leadership and the ways in which each author conveys his or her message about the role and responsibilities of a good leader. What do the authors of these texts have to say about leadership, and how well do they say it? How does each author present and support his or her claims? Do the authors you have selected agree about the role and responsibilities of a leader? Analyze how effectively each text communicates its author's message.

Your literary analysis should include:

- An introduction that tells the author and genre of each text you have selected
- A clear thesis statement that presents a compelling claim about the texts
- Body paragraphs that support your claim with reasons and evidence
- An effective conclusion that wraps up your analysis in an interesting way

You have written a draft of your literary analysis. You have also received input from your peers about how to improve it. Now you are going to revise your draft.

Here are some recommendations to help you revise:

- Review the suggestions made by your peers.
- Focus on maintaining a formal style. A formal style suits your purpose—making a claim about academic texts. It also fits your audience—students,

Please note that excerpts and passages in the StudySync® library and this workbook are intended as touchstones to generate interest in an author's work. The excerpts and passages do not substitute for the reading of entire texts, and StudySync® strongly recommends that students seek out and purchase the whole literary or informational work in order to experience it as the author intended. Links to online resellers are available in our digital library. In addition, complete works may be ordered through an authorized reseller by filling out and returning to StudySync® the order form enclosed in this workbook.

Reading & Writing Companion   **223**

NOTES

teachers, and other readers interested in learning more about the texts you will discuss.

> As you revise, eliminate any slang.

> Remove any first-person pronouns such as *I*, *me*, or *mine* or instances of addressing readers as *you*. These are more suitable to a writing style that is informal, personal, and conversational. Check that you have used all pronouns correctly.

> If you include your personal opinions, remove them. Though your essay is making a claim, that claim is based on textual evidence, not your personal opinion. Argumentative writing should be clear, direct, and unbiased.

- After you have revised elements of style, think about whether there is anything else you can do to improve your essay's information or organization.

> Do you need to add any new textual evidence to fully support the claim in your thesis statement?

> Do you need to add more analysis of the textual evidence in your body paragraphs? In other words, have you adequately explained how your evidence supports your reasons and ultimately your claim?

> Do you need to evaluate the strength or weaknesses of any of the evidence you used?

> Can you substitute a more precise word for a word that is general or dull?

> Consider your organization. Would your essay flow better if you strengthen the transitions between paragraphs?

SKILL:
SOURCES AND
CITATIONS

 DEFINE

Sources are the documents and information that an author uses to research his or her writing. Some sources are **primary sources.** A primary source is a first-hand account of thoughts or events by the individual who experienced them. Other sources are **secondary sources.** A secondary source analyzes and interprets primary sources. **Citations** are notes that give information about the sources an author used in his or her writing. Citations are required whenever authors quote others' words or refer to others' ideas in their writing. Citations let readers know who originally came up with those words and ideas.

 IDENTIFICATION AND APPLICATION

- Sources can be primary or secondary in nature. Primary sources are first-hand accounts, artifacts, or other original materials. Examples of primary sources include:
  › Letters or other correspondence
  › Photographs
  › Official documents
  › Diaries or journals
  › Autobiographies or memoirs
  › Eyewitness accounts and interviews
  › Audio recordings and radio broadcasts
  › Works of art
  › Artifacts
- Secondary sources are usually text. Secondary sources are the written interpretation and analysis of primary source materials. Some examples of secondary sources include:
  › Encyclopedia articles
  › Textbooks
  › Commentary or criticisms
  › Histories

Please note that excerpts and passages in the StudySync® library and this workbook are intended as touchstones to generate interest in an author's work. The excerpts and passages do not substitute for the reading of entire texts, and StudySync® strongly recommends that students seek out and purchase the whole literary or informational work in order to experience it as the author intended. Links to online resellers are available in our digital library. In addition, complete works may be ordered through an authorized reseller by filling out and returning to StudySync® the order form enclosed in this workbook.

Reading & Writing
Companion

225

NOTES

› Documentary films
› News analyses
- Whether sources are primary or secondary, they must be credible and accurate. Writers of argumentative/informative/explanatory texts look for sources from experts in the topic they are writing about.
  › When researching online, they look for URLs that contain .gov (government agencies), .edu (colleges and universities), and .org (museums and other non-profit organizations).
  › Writers also use respected print and online news and information sources.

Anytime a writer uses words from another source exactly as they are written, the words must appear in quotation marks. Quotation marks show that the words are not the author's own words but are borrowed from another source. In the student model essay, the writer uses quotation marks around words taken directly from the source *1984*:

> **The narrator says, "nothing was illegal, since there were no longer any laws" (Orwell).**

- A writer includes a citation to give credit to any source, whether primary or secondary, that is quoted exactly. There are several different ways to cite a source.
  › One way is to put the author's last name in parenthesis at the end of the sentence in which the quote appears. This is what the writer of the student model essay does after the quotation above.
  › Another way to give credit is to cite the author's name in the context of the sentence. For example, the student could also have written the sentence above like so:

> **Orwell wrote, "nothing was illegal, since there were no longer any laws."**

- Citations are also necessary when a writer borrows ideas from another source, even if the writer paraphrases, or puts those ideas in his or her own words. For instance, if you write about another writer's analysis of the text you are writing about, you would include the author's name just as in the example above, even if you do not directly quote the text. Citations credit the source, but they also help readers discover where they can learn more.

  MODEL

In this excerpt from the student model essay, the writer uses quotations from literary texts and includes parenthetical citations.

Having control over people depends a lot on how a leader communicates with them. Homer's version of good communication is more convincing than Orwell's because in *The Odyssey Book XII* Odysseus communicates personally and individually with the men he leads. After his men killed the cattle, he "rebuked each one of the men separately" (Homer). Odysseus speaks honestly and directly. This is a great way to communicate with people because it makes them feel like individuals and feel respected.

Conversely, the communication of the government in *1984* is generic and bends the truth. The government communicates with people by constantly telling them things through their "telescreens." The government also uses the same Doublespeak and oxymorons for talking to everyone: "WAR IS PEACE, FREEDOM IS SLAVERY, IGNORANCE IS STRENGTH" (Orwell). The communication in *1984* is designed to be generalized and to manipulate people. There is no truth in it. Though Orwell is exaggerating what propaganda looks like here, he doesn't give any good ideas in this excerpt from *1984* for how to improve the situation.

Notice that each sentence begins with the Student Model writer's own words. When the writer uses portions of text from the source material, that text appears in quotations. The student has cited material with the author's last name in parenthesis after each quotation.

 PRACTICE

Write citations for quoted information in your literary analysis essay. When you are finished, trade with a partner and offer each other feedback. How successful was the writer in citing sources for the essay? How well did the writer make use of varied sources? Offer each other suggestions, and remember that they are most helpful when they are constructive.

EDIT,
PROOFREAD
AND PUBLISH

WRITING PROMPT

In this unit, you have been reading texts by or about political leaders and others who hold power in a society. What role should a leader play? What are the responsibilities of leadership? Write a literary analysis of two selections from this unit in which you examine the theme of leadership and the ways in which each author conveys his or her message about the role and responsibilities of a good leader. What do the authors of these texts have to say about leadership, and how well do they say it? How does each author present and support his or her claims? Do the authors you have selected agree about the role and responsibilities of a leader? Analyze how effectively each text communicates its author's message.

Your literary analysis should include:

- An introduction that tells the author and genre of each text you have selected

- A clear thesis statement that presents a compelling claim about the texts

- Body paragraphs that support your claim with reasons and evidence

- An effective conclusion that wraps up your analysis in an interesting way

You have revised your literary analysis and received input from your peers on that revision. Now it's time to edit and proofread your work to produce a final version. Have you included all the valuable suggestions from your peers? Ask yourself: "Have I fully developed the claim in my thesis statement with strong supporting reasons and relevant textual evidence? Have I accurately cited my sources? What more can I do to improve my essay's information and organization?"

When you are satisfied with your literary analysis, move on to proofread it for errors. For example, check that you have used correct punctuation for quotations, citations, restrictive/nonrestrictive phrases and clauses, and compound sentences. Have you used correct parallel structure in sentences with series? Have you misspelled any words?

Once you have made all your corrections, you are ready to submit and publish your work. You can distribute your writing to family and friends, hang it on a bulletin board, or post it on your blog. If you publish online, create links to your sources and citations. That way, readers can follow-up on what they have learned from your literary analysis and read more on their own.

studysync®

Reading & Writing Companion

What makes a dream worth pursuing?

Dreams and Aspirations

UNIT 3 What makes a dream worth pursuing?

Dreams and Aspirations

TEXTS

TEXTS

EXTENDED WRITING PROJECT

462

Text Fulfillment
through
StudySync

Please note that excerpts and passages in the StudySync® library and this workbook are intended as touchstones to generate interest in an author's work. The excerpts and passages do not substitute for the reading of entire texts, and StudySync® strongly recommends that students seek out and purchase the whole literary or informational work in order to experience it as the author intended. Links to online resellers are available in our digital library. In addition, complete works may be ordered through an authorized reseller by filling out and returning to StudySync® the order form enclosed in this workbook.

Reading & Writing
Companion
233

THE NECKLACE

FICTION
Guy de Maupassant
1884

INTRODUCTION

Guy de Maupassant ranks among the world's greatest short story writers. The child of wealthy parents, Maupassant grew up among the families of peasants and sailors who lived near his mother's estate in northwestern France. His own life experiences are reflected in his work, and he often wrote of peasants, soldiers, and ordinary people caught in disastrous or demeaning situations. Maupassant described his subject as life's "inexplicable, illogical, and contradictory catastrophes" and said that writing should aim not at "telling a story or entertaining us or touching our hearts, but at forcing us to think and understand the deeper, hidden meaning of events."

"She had no gowns, no jewels, nothing. And she loved nothing but that."

FIRST READ

1   The girl was one of those pretty and charming young creatures who sometimes are born, as if by a slip of fate, into a family of clerks. She had no dowry, no expectations, no way of being known, understood, loved, married by any rich and distinguished man; so she let herself be married to a little clerk of the Ministry of Public Instruction.

2   She dressed plainly because she could not dress well, but she was unhappy as if she had really fallen from a higher station; since with women there is neither caste nor rank, for beauty, grace and charm take the place of family and birth. Natural **ingenuity**, instinct for what is elegant, a supple mind are their sole hierarchy, and often make of women of the people the equals of the very greatest ladies.

3   Mathilde suffered ceaselessly, feeling herself born to enjoy all delicacies and all luxuries. She was distressed at the poverty of her dwelling, at the bareness of the walls, at the shabby chairs, the ugliness of the curtains. All those things, of which another woman of her rank would never even have been conscious, tortured her and made her angry. The sight of the little Breton peasant who did her humble housework aroused in her despairing regrets and bewildering dreams. She thought of silent antechambers hung with Oriental tapestry, illumined by tall bronze candelabra, and of two great footmen in knee breeches who sleep in the big armchairs, made drowsy by the oppressive heat of the stove. She thought of long reception halls hung with ancient silk, of the dainty cabinets containing priceless curiosities and of the little coquettish perfumed reception rooms made for chatting at five o'clock with intimate friends, with men famous and sought after, whom all women envy and whose attention they all desire.

4   When she sat down to dinner, before the round table covered with a tablecloth in use three days, opposite her husband, who uncovered the soup tureen

and declared with a delighted air, "Ah, the good soup! I don't know anything better than that," she thought of dainty dinners, of shining silverware, of tapestry that peopled the walls with ancient personages and with strange birds flying in the midst of a fairy forest; and she thought of delicious dishes served on marvelous plates and of the whispered gallantries to which you listen with a sphinxlike smile while you are eating the pink meat of a trout or the wings of a quail.

5   She had no gowns, no jewels, nothing. And she loved nothing but that. She felt made for that. She would have liked so much to please, to be envied, to be charming, to be sought after.

6   She had a friend, a former schoolmate at the convent, who was rich, and whom she did not like to go to see any more because she felt so sad when she came home.

7   But one evening her husband reached home with a triumphant air and holding a large envelope in his hand.

8   "There," said he, "there is something for you."

9   She tore the paper quickly and drew out a printed card which bore these words:

10   *The Minister of Public Instruction and Madame Georges Ramponneau*
     request the honor of M. and Madame Loisel's company
     at the palace of the Ministry on Monday evening, January 18th.

11   Instead of being delighted, as her husband had hoped, she threw the invitation on the table crossly, muttering:

12   "What do you wish me to do with that?"

13   "Why, my dear, I thought you would be glad. You never go out, and this is such a fine opportunity. I had great trouble to get it. Everyone wants to go; it is very select, and they are not giving many invitations to clerks. The whole official world will be there."

14   She looked at him with an irritated glance and said impatiently:

15   "And what do you wish me to put on my back?"

16   He had not thought of that. He stammered:

17   "Why, the gown you go to the theatre in. It looks very well to me."

NOTES

18 He stopped, distracted, seeing that his wife was weeping. Two great tears ran slowly from the corners of her eyes toward the corners of her mouth.

19 "What's the matter? What's the matter?" he answered.

20 By a violent effort she conquered her grief and replied in a calm voice, while she wiped her wet cheeks:

21 "Nothing. Only I have no gown, and, therefore, I can't go to this ball. Give your card to some colleague whose wife is better equipped than I am."

22 He was in despair. He resumed:

23 "Come, let us see, Mathilde. How much would it cost, a suitable gown, which you could use on other occasions—something very simple?"

24 She reflected several seconds, making her calculations and wondering also what sum she could ask without drawing on herself an immediate refusal and a frightened exclamation from the economical clerk.

25 Finally she replied hesitating:

26 "I don't know exactly, but I think I could manage it with four hundred francs."

27 He grew a little pale, because he was laying aside just that amount to buy a gun and treat himself to a little shooting next summer on the plain of Nanterre, with several friends who went to shoot larks there of a Sunday.

28 But he said:

29 "Very well. I will give you four hundred francs. And try to have a pretty gown."

30 The day of the ball drew near and Madame Loisel seemed sad, uneasy, anxious. Her frock was ready, however. Her husband said to her one evening:

31 "What is the matter? Come, you have seemed very queer these last three days."

32 And she answered:

33 "It annoys me not to have a single piece of jewelry, not a single ornament, nothing to put on. I shall look poverty-stricken. I would almost rather not go at all."

34 "You might wear natural flowers," said her husband. "They're very stylish at this time of year. For ten francs you can get two or three magnificent roses."

35 She was not convinced.

36 "No; there's nothing more humiliating than to look poor among other women who are rich."

37 "How stupid you are!" her husband cried. "Go look up your friend, Madame Forestier, and ask her to lend you some jewels. You're intimate enough with her to do that."

38 She uttered a cry of joy:

39 "True! I never thought of it."

40 The next day she went to her friend and told her of her distress.

41 Madame Forestier went to a wardrobe with a mirror, took out a large jewel box, brought it back, opened it and said to Madame Loisel:

42 "Choose, my dear."

43 She saw first some bracelets, then a pearl necklace, then a Venetian gold cross set with precious stones, of admirable workmanship. She tried on the ornaments before the mirror, hesitated and could not make up her mind to part with them, to give them back. She kept asking:

44 "Haven't you anymore?"

45 "Why, yes. Look further; I don't know what you like."

46 Suddenly she discovered, in a black satin box, a superb diamond necklace, and her heart throbbed with an **immoderate** desire. Her hands trembled as she took it. She fastened it round her throat, outside her high-necked waist, and was lost in ecstasy at her reflection in the mirror.

47 Then she asked, hesitating, filled with anxious doubt:

48 "Will you lend me this, only this?"

49 "Why, yes, certainly."

50 She threw her arms round her friend's neck, kissed her passionately, then fled with her treasure.

51 The night of the ball arrived. Madame Loisel was a great success. She was prettier than any other woman present, elegant, graceful, smiling and wild with joy. All the men looked at her, asked her name, sought to be introduced.

All the attaches of the Cabinet wished to waltz with her. She was remarked by the minister himself.

52   She danced with **rapture**, with passion, intoxicated by pleasure, forgetting all in the triumph of her beauty, in the glory of her success, in a sort of cloud of happiness comprised of all this homage, admiration, these awakened desires and of that sense of triumph which is so sweet to woman's heart.

53   She left the ball about four o'clock in the morning. Her husband had been sleeping since midnight in a little deserted anteroom with three other gentlemen whose wives were enjoying the ball.

54   He threw over her shoulders the wraps he had brought, the modest wraps of common life, the poverty of which contrasted with the elegance of the ball dress. She felt this and wished to escape so as not to be remarked by the other women, who were enveloping themselves in costly furs.

55   Loisel held her back, saying: "Wait a bit. You will catch cold outside. I will call a cab."

56   But she did not listen to him and rapidly descended the stairs. When they reached the street they could not find a carriage and began to look for one, shouting after the cabmen passing at a distance.

57   They went toward the Seine in despair, shivering with cold. At last they found on the quay one of those ancient night cabs which, as though they were ashamed to show their shabbiness during the day, are never seen round Paris until after dark.

58   It took them to their dwelling in the Rue des Martyrs, and sadly they mounted the stairs to their flat. All was ended for her. As to him, he reflected that he must be at the ministry at ten o'clock that morning.

59   She removed her wraps before the glass so as to see herself once more in all her glory. But suddenly she uttered a cry. She no longer had the necklace around her neck!

60   "What is the matter with you?" demanded her husband, already half undressed.

61   She turned distractedly toward him.

62   "I have—I have—I've lost Madame Forestier's necklace," she cried.

63   He stood up, bewildered.

64   "What!—how? Impossible!"

65 They looked among the folds of her skirt, of her cloak, in her pockets, everywhere, but did not find it.

66 "You're sure you had it on when you left the ball?" he asked.

67 "Yes, I felt it in the vestibule of the minister's house."

68 "But if you had lost it in the street we should have heard it fall. It must be in the cab."

69 "Yes, probably. Did you take his number?"

70 "No. And you—didn't you notice it?"

71 "No."

72 They looked, thunderstruck, at each other. At last Loisel put on his clothes.

73 "I shall go back on foot," said he, "over the whole route, to see whether I can find it."

74 He went out. She sat waiting on a chair in her ball dress, without strength to go to bed, overwhelmed, without any fire, without a thought.

75 Her husband returned about seven o'clock. He had found nothing.

76 He went to police headquarters, to the newspaper offices to offer a reward; he went to the cab companies—everywhere, in fact, whither he was urged by the least spark of hope.

77 She waited all day, in the same condition of mad fear before this terrible calamity.

78 Loisel returned at night with a hollow, pale face. He had discovered nothing.

79 "You must write to your friend," said he, "that you have broken the clasp of her necklace and that you are having it mended. That will give us time to turn round."

80 She wrote at his dictation.

81 At the end of a week they had lost all hope. Loisel, who had aged five years, declared:

82 "We must consider how to replace that ornament."

83 The next day they took the box that had contained it and went to the jeweler whose name was found within. He consulted his books.

84 "It was not I, madame, who sold that necklace; I must simply have furnished the case."

85 Then they went from jeweler to jeweler, searching for a necklace like the other, trying to recall it, both sick with **chagrin** and grief.

86 They found, in a shop at the Palais Royal, a string of diamonds that seemed to them exactly like the one they had lost. It was worth forty thousand francs. They could have it for thirty-six.

87 So they begged the jeweler not to sell it for three days yet. And they made a bargain that he should buy it back for thirty-four thousand francs, in case they should find the lost necklace before the end of February.

88 Loisel possessed eighteen thousand francs which his father had left him. He would borrow the rest.

89 He did borrow, asking a thousand francs of one, five hundred of another, five louis here, three louis there. He gave notes, took up ruinous obligations, dealt with usurers and all the race of lenders. He compromised all the rest of his life, risked signing a note without even knowing whether he could meet it; and, frightened by the trouble yet to come, by the black misery that was about to fall upon him, by the prospect of all the physical privations and moral tortures that he was to suffer, he went to get the new necklace, laying upon the jeweler's counter thirty-six thousand francs.

90 When Madame Loisel took back the necklace Madame Forestier said to her with a chilly manner:

91 "You should have returned it sooner; I might have needed it."

92 She did not open the case, as her friend had so much feared. If she had detected the substitution, what would she have thought, what would she have said? Would she not have taken Madame Loisel for a thief?

93 Thereafter Madame Loisel knew the horrible existence of the needy. She bore her part, however, with sudden heroism. That dreadful debt must be paid. She would pay it. They dismissed their servant; they changed their lodgings; they rented a garret under the roof.

94 She came to know what heavy housework meant and the odious cares of the kitchen. She washed the dishes, using her dainty fingers and rosy nails on greasy pots and pans. She washed the soiled linen, the shirts and the

dishcloths, which she dried upon a line; she carried the slops down to the street every morning and carried up the water, stopping for breath at every landing. And dressed like a woman of the people, she went to the fruiterer, the grocer, the butcher, a basket on her arm, bargaining, meeting with **impertinence**, defending her miserable money.

95 Every month they had to meet some notes, renew others, obtain more time.

96 Her husband worked evenings, making up a tradesman's accounts, and late at night he often copied manuscript for five sous a page.

97 This life lasted ten years.

98 At the end of ten years they had paid everything, everything, with the rates of usury and the accumulations of the compound interest.

99 Madame Loisel looked old now. She had become the woman of impoverished households—strong and hard and rough. With frowsy hair, skirts askew and red hands, she talked loud while washing the floor with great swishes of water. But sometimes, when her husband was at the office, she sat down near the window and she thought of that gay evening of long ago, of that ball where she had been so beautiful and so admired.

100 What would have happened if she had not lost that necklace? Who knows? who knows? How strange and changeful is life! How small a thing is needed to make or ruin us!

101 But one Sunday, having gone to take a walk in the Champs Elysees to refresh herself after the labors of the week, she suddenly perceived a woman who was leading a child. It was Madame Forestier, still young, still beautiful, still charming.

102 Madame Loisel felt moved. Should she speak to her? Yes, certainly. And now that she had paid, she would tell her all about it. Why not?

103 She went up.

104 "Good-day, Jeanne."

105 The other, astonished to be familiarly addressed by this plain good-wife, did not recognize her at all and stammered:

106 "But—madame!—I do not know—You must have mistaken."

107 "No. I am Mathilde Loisel."

108 Her friend uttered a cry.

109   "Oh, my poor Mathilde! How you are changed!"

110   "Yes, I have had a pretty hard life, since I last saw you, and great poverty—and that because of you!"

111   "Of me! How so?"

112   "Do you remember that diamond necklace you lent me to wear at the ministerial ball?"

113   "Yes. Well?"

114   "Well, I lost it."

115   "What do you mean? You brought it back."

116   "I brought you back another exactly like it. And it has taken us ten years to pay for it. You can understand that it was not easy for us, for us who had nothing. At last it is ended, and I am very glad."

117   Madame Forestier had stopped.

118   "You say that you bought a necklace of diamonds to replace mine?"

119   "Yes. You never noticed it, then! They were very similar."

120   And she smiled with a joy that was at once proud and ingenuous.

121   Madame Forestier, deeply moved, took her hands.

122   "Oh, my poor Mathilde! Why, my necklace was paste! It was worth at most only five hundred francs!"

Please note that excerpts and passages in the StudySync® library and this workbook are intended as touchstones to generate interest in an author's work. The excerpts and passages do not substitute for the reading of entire texts, and StudySync® strongly recommends that students seek out and purchase the whole literary or informational work in order to experience it as the author intended. Links to online resellers are available in our digital library. In addition, complete works may be ordered through an authorized reseller by filling out and returning to StudySync® the order form enclosed in this workbook.

Reading & Writing
Companion   **243**

THINK QUESTIONS

1. What does Mathilde spend much of her time fantasizing about in the beginning of the story? Why do you think de Maupassant describes these thoughts so thoroughly, as part of introducing Mathilde's character? Support your answer with textual evidence.

2. What does Mathilde spend much of her time fantasizing about in the beginning of the story? Why do you think de Maupassant describes these thoughts so thoroughly, as part of introducing Mathilde's character? Support your answer with textual evidence.

3. What kind of person is M. Loisel? How do his personality and character compare to his wife's? Support your answer with textual evidence.

4. Use context to determine the meaning of the word **rapture** as it is used in "The Necklace." Write your definition of "rapture" and explain how you arrived at it.

5. Use context to determine the meaning of the word **chagrin** as it is used in "The Necklace." Write your definition of "chagrin" and describe how you figured it out.

CLOSE READ

Reread the excerpt from *The Necklace*. As you reread, complete the Focus Questions below. Then use your answers and annotations from the questions to help you complete the Writing Prompt.

FOCUS QUESTIONS

1. Reread the first four paragraphs of the story. What kinds of character traits does Mathilde display? What message might the author be trying to send with this description? Highlight specific textual evidence and make annotations to explain what this evidence reveals about her.

2. One of the themes of the story centers on "trying to be something you are not." Highlight examples from the text that illustrate this theme, and make annotations to explain your answers.

3. Reread the passage beginning with "Thereafter Madame Loisel knew the horrible existence..." and ending with "sou by sou." The narrator describes Mathilde's response as "sudden heroism." Make annotations highlighting the behavior that he means, and explain why it might be considered heroic.

4. Examine the four paragraphs at the end of the story, beginning with the line, "Madame Loisel looked old now." Highlight examples that illustrate how she has changed from the beginning of the story, and make annotations to indicate how she compares to her earlier self.

5. By the end of the story, do you think Madame Loisel regrets borrowing the necklace and attending the ball, or does she still think her dream was worth pursuing? Explain your response and make annotations to highlight evidence supporting your position.

WRITING PROMPT

How does Madame Loisel change from the beginning to the end of the story? Does the story imply that she has changed for the better or the worse? Write a response to this question that relates to a theme or themes you identified in the story. Support your answer with evidence from the text.

Please note that excerpts and passages in the StudySync® library and this workbook are intended as touchstones to generate interest in an author's work. The excerpts and passages do not substitute for the reading of entire texts, and StudySync® strongly recommends that students seek out and purchase the whole literary or informational work in order to experience it as the author intended. Links to online resellers are available in our digital library. In addition, complete works may be ordered through an authorized reseller by filling out and returning to StudySync® the order form enclosed in this workbook.

Reading & Writing Companion

245

OF MICE AND MEN

FICTION
John Steinbeck
1937

INTRODUCTION

John Steinbeck's novel, *Of Mice and Men*, is set in northern California during the Great Depression. Two men, George Milton and Lennie Small, move from job to job as ranch hands. Lennie is physically strong but mentally childlike. George takes care of his friend and more than once extricates the two from the trouble Lennie unintentionally causes. As they make camp near their next job, the two share their often-retold dream and plan for better times to come.

"I won't get in no trouble, George. I ain't gonna say a word."

FIRST READ

NOTES

Excerpt from Chapter 1

1   Lennie pleaded, "Come on, George. Tell me. Please, George. Like you done before."

2   "You get a kick outta that, don't you? Awright, I'll tell you, and then we'll eat our supper..."

3   George's voice became deeper. He repeated his words **rhythmically** as though he had said them many times before. "Guys like us, that work on ranches, are the loneliest guys in the world. They got no family. They don't belong no place. They come to a ranch an' work up a stake and then they go into town and blow their stake, and the first thing you know they're poundin' their tail on some other ranch. They ain't got nothing to look ahead to."

4   Lennie was delighted. "That's it—that's it. Now tell how it is with us."

5   George went on. "With us it ain't like that. We got a future. We got somebody to talk to that gives a damn about us. We don't have to sit in no bar room blowin' in our jack jus' because we got no place else to go. If them other guys gets in jail they can rot for all anybody gives a damn. But not us."

6   Lennie broke in. "But not us! An' why? *Because... because I got you to look after me, and you got me to look after you, and that's why.*" He laughed delightedly. "Go on now, George!"

7   "You got it by heart. You can do it yourself."

8   "No, you. I forget some a' the things. Tell about how it's gonna be."

NOTES

9 "O.K. Someday—we're gonna get the jack together and we're gonna have a little house and a couple of acres an' a cow and some pigs and——"

10 *"An' live off the fatta the lan',"* Lennie shouted. "An' have *rabbits*. Go on, George! Tell about what we're gonna have in the garden and about the rabbits in the cages and about the rain in the winter and the stove, and how thick the cream is on the milk like you can hardly cut it. Tell about that, George."

11 "Why'n't you do it yourself? You know all of it."

12 "No... you tell it. It ain't the same if I tell it. Go on... George. How I get to tend the rabbits."

13 "Well," said George, "we'll have a big vegetable patch and a rabbit hutch and chickens. And when it rains in the winter, we'll just say the hell with goin' to work, and we'll build up a fire in the stove and set around it an' listen to the rain comin' down on the roof—Nuts!" He took out his pocket knife. "I ain't got time for no more." He drove his knife through the top of one of the bean cans, sawed out the top and passed the can to Lennie. Then he opened a second can. From his side pocket he brought out two spoons and passed one of them to Lennie.

14 They sat by the fire and filled their mouths with beans and chewed mightily. A few beans slipped out of the side of Lennie's mouth. George gestured with his spoon. "What you gonna say tomorrow when the boss asks you questions?"

15 Lennie stopped chewing and swallowed. His face was **concentrated**. "I... I ain't gonna... say a word."

16 "Good boy! That's fine, Lennie! Maybe you're gettin' better. When we get the coupla acres I can let you tend the rabbits all right. 'Specially if you remember as good as that."

17 Lennie choked with pride. "I can remember," he said.

18 George motioned with his spoon again. "Look, Lennie. I want you to look around here. You can remember this place, can't you? The ranch is about a quarter mile up that way. Just follow the river?"

19 "Sure," said Lennie. "I can remember this. Di'n't I remember about not gonna say a word?"

20 " 'Course you did. Well, look. Lennie—if you jus' happen to get in trouble like you always done before, I want you to come right here an' hide in the **brush**."

21 "Hide in the brush," said Lennie slowly.

22 "Hide in the brush till I come for you. Can you remember that?"

23 "Sure I can, George. Hide in the brush till you come."

24 "But you ain't gonna get in no trouble, because if you do, I won't let you tend the rabbits." He threw his empty bean can off into the brush.

25 "I won't get in no trouble, George. I ain't gonna say a word."

26 "O.K. Bring your **bindle** over here by the fire. It's gonna be nice sleepin' here. Lookin' up, and the leaves. Don't build up no more fire. We'll let her die down."

27 They made their beds on the sand, and as the blaze dropped from the fire the **sphere** of light grew smaller; the curling branches disappeared and only a faint glimmer showed where the trunks were. From the darkness Lennie called, "George—you asleep?"

28 "No. Whatta you want?"

29 "Let's have different color rabbits, George."

30 "Sure we will," George said sleepily. "Red and blue and green rabbits, Lennie. Millions of 'em."

31 "Furry ones, George, like I seen in the fair in Sacramento."

32 "Sure, furry ones."

33 " 'Cause I can jus' as well go away, George, an' live in a cave."

34 "You can jus' as well go to hell," said George. "Shut up now."

35 The red light dimmed on the coals. Up the hill from the river a coyote yammered, and a dog answered from the other side of the stream. The sycamore leaves whispered in a little night breeze.

Excerpted from Of Mice and Men by John Steinbeck, published by the Penguin Group.

THINK QUESTIONS

1. Briefly explain the relationship of the two men in the text. How do they feel about each other? How can you tell? Refer to one or more details from the text to support your answer.

2. How is the present situation of the men different from the vision they imagine in the future? How do they hope their lives will change in the future? Cite details in the text that support your answer.

3. Why do you think Lennie wants George to tell him a story that he already knows by heart? Support your ideas and inferences with details from the text.

4. Use context to determine the meaning of the word **sphere** as it is used in *Of Mice and Men*. Write your definition of "sphere" and tell how you arrived at it.

5. Use the context clues provided in the passage to determine the meaning of **bindle**. Write your definition of "bindle" and tell how you arrived at it.

CLOSE READ

Reread the excerpt from *Of Mice and Men*. As you reread, complete the Focus Questions below. Then use your answers and annotations from the questions to help you complete the Writing Prompt.

FOCUS QUESTIONS

1. Explain how the author uses dialogue and dialect to help readers understand the characters in this excerpt. Highlight dialogue that reveals information about the characters. Make annotations to explain what you can infer about the characters from their words.

2. The author once explained that *Of Mice and Men* was written with a lot of dialogue so that it could easily be performed as a drama. Reread the passage from the point at which Lennie and George begin eating beans up until they get ready for bed. Make annotations marking lines that couldn't be spoken in a stage performance of this text. How would a stage performance of this scene be different from reading the text?

3. Highlight all of the places in the text where George warns Lennie not to get into any trouble. Why do you think this warning needs to be repeated so often? What can readers infer about George and Lennie from this repeated warning?

4. Create a summary of the future that George and Lennie hope to have one day. Where will they live? What will they own? What will they do all day? Highlight textual evidence and make annotations to explain your ideas.

5. What does Lennie and George's final exchange before sleep, in which Lennie says, with hurt feelings, "I can jus' as well go... an' live in a cave," say about their dream of the future? Why are dreams for the future so important to people who are going through tough times? What makes these dreams worth pursuing? Highlight textual evidence and make annotations to explain your ideas.

WRITING PROMPT

George and Lennie travel together, unlike many who are out of work during the Great Depression. Consider the benefits and risks inherent in George and Lennie's partnership. In around 300 words, use examples from the text to explain what their relationship says about the nature of friendship.

Please note that excerpts and passages in the StudySync® library and this workbook are intended as touchstones to generate interest in an author's work. The excerpts and passages do not substitute for the reading of entire texts, and StudySync® strongly recommends that students seek out and purchase the whole literary or informational work in order to experience it as the author intended. Links to online resellers are available in our digital library. In addition, complete works may be ordered through an authorized reseller by filling out and returning to StudySync® the order form enclosed in this workbook.

Reading & Writing Companion   251

SYMPATHY

POETRY
Paul Laurence Dunbar
1899

INTRODUCTION

P aul Laurence Dunbar was one of the first nationally acclaimed African American poets. The child of former slaves, Dunbar was born after the Civil War and the abolition of slavery, but at a time when African Americans continued to face the horrors of racism and discrimination. Dunbar was a gifted writer from a young age and published his first poems when he was only sixteen years old. His poem "Sympathy" includes the famous line "I know why the caged bird sings," the inspiration for the title of Maya Angelou's autobiography.

"I know why the caged bird beats his wing..."

FIRST READ

NOTES

1 I know what the caged bird feels, **alas!**
2 When the sun is bright on the upland slopes;
3 When the wind stirs soft through the springing grass,
4 And the river flows like a stream of glass;
5 When the first bird sings and the first bud opes,
6 And the faint perfume from its **chalice** steals—
7 I know what the caged bird feels!

8 I know why the caged bird beats his wing
9 Till its blood is red on the cruel bars;
10 For he must fly back to his perch and cling
11 When he fain would be on the **bough** a-swing;
12 And a pain still throbs in the old, old scars
13 And they pulse again with a **keener** sting—
14 I know why he beats his wing!

15 I know why the caged bird sings, ah me,
16 When his wing is bruised and his bosom sore,—
17 When he beats his bars and he would be free;
18 It is not a carol of joy or glee,
19 But a prayer that he sends from his heart's deep core,
20 But a plea, that upward to Heaven he flings—
21 I know why the caged bird sings!

THINK QUESTIONS

1. What is the speaker describing in the first stanza, and how does this description help the reader to understand how the caged bird feels? Use evidence from the text to support your response.

2. Use details from the text to write two or three sentences describing the caged bird's feelings and the reasons for his feelings in the second stanza.

3. What is the caged bird's song about, and how do you know this? Support your answer with textual evidence.

4. Use context to determine the meaning of the word alas as it is used in "Sympathy." Write your definition of "alas" and explain its effect in the poem.

5. Use context to determine the meaning of the word **bough** as it is used in "Sympathy." Write your definition of "boughv" and state the clues from the text you used to determine your answer.

CLOSE READ

Reread the poem "Sympathy." As you reread, complete the Focus Questions below. Then use your answers and annotations from the questions to help you complete the Writing Prompt.

FOCUS QUESTIONS

1. Explain how the poet uses words with particular connotations to create a tone in the first stanza. How does his choice of words help you visualize what the stanza describes? Highlight evidence from the text and make annotations to explain your choices.

2. How does the tone of the second stanza differ from the tone of the first stanza? Highlight the words and phrases in the text that help to create this different tone, and make annotations to explain the impact of specific words' connotations. Then describe how the meaning of the stanza might be different if the poet had used neutral words.

3. What words and phrases help you visualize the setting and situation in the third stanza? Highlight these words and phrases and make annotations to identify and explain the connotations of the words.

4. The poet repeats certain phrases throughout the poem. Highlight these phrases in the text and make notes on their effects and significance. Then explain why he repeats those phrases.

5. What is a major theme of the poem? How does the poet's use of figurative language and metaphor help you understand his feelings about pursuing a dream of freedom? Make inferences about the text and its deeper meaning, and then highlight evidence from the text and make annotations to support your explanation.

WRITING PROMPT

Summarize the main ideas conveyed in each stanza of the poem. In your summary, describe the structure and progression of ideas presented in the poem, and discuss the way word connotations help set a tone, develop key ideas, and support themes. Use evidence from the poem to support your response.

Please note that excerpts and passages in the StudySync® library and this workbook are intended as touchstones to generate interest in an author's work. The excerpts and passages do not substitute for the reading of entire texts, and StudySync® strongly recommends that students seek out and purchase the whole literary or informational work in order to experience it as the author intended. Links to online resellers are available in our digital library. In addition, complete works may be ordered through an authorized reseller by filling out and returning to StudySync® the order form enclosed in this workbook.

Reading & Writing Companion   **255**

I KNOW WHY THE CAGED BIRD SINGS

NON-FICTION

Maya Angelou
1969

INTRODUCTION

In her memoir, acclaimed poet Maya Angelou (born Marguerite Johnson) recalls the anguish and hard-won independence of her childhood in Arkansas and her adolescence in Northern slums. This passage is an important turning point for the author. Silenced by a deeply traumatic experience, young Marguerite is coaxed by a neighbor into embracing the healing power of language.

"She opened the first page and I heard poetry for the first time in my life."

 FIRST READ

From Chapter 14

1   For nearly a year, I sopped around the house, the Store, the school, and the church, like an old biscuit, dirty and inedible. Then I met, or rather got to know, the lady who threw me my first lifeline.

2   Mrs. Bertha Flowers was the **aristocrat** of Black Stamps. She had the grace of control to appear warm in the coldest weather, and on the Arkansas summer days it seemed she had a private breeze which swirled around, cooling her. She was thin without the taut look of wiry people, and her printed voile dresses and flowered hats were as right for her as denim overalls for a farmer. She was our side's answer to the richest white woman in town.

3   Her skin was a rich black that would have peeled like a plum if snagged, but then no one would have thought of getting close enough to Mrs. Flowers to ruffle her dress, let alone snag her skin. She didn't encourage familiarity. She wore gloves too.

4   I don't think I ever saw Mrs. Flowers laugh, but she smiled often. A slow widening of her thin black lips to show even, small white teeth, then the slow effortless closing. When she chose to smile on me, I always wanted to thank her. The action was so graceful and inclusively **benign**.

5   She was one of the few gentle women I have ever known, and has remained throughout my life the measure of what a human being can be.

6   One summer afternoon, sweet-milk fresh in my memory, she stopped at the Store to buy provisions. Another Negro woman of her health and age would have been expected to carry the paper sacks home in one hand, but Momma said, "Sister Flowers, I'll send Bailey up to your house with these things."

NOTES

7 She smiled that slow dragging smile, "Thank you, Mrs. Henderson. I'd prefer Marguerite, though." My name was beautiful when she said it. "I've been meaning to talk to her, anyway." They gave each other age-group looks.

8 There was a little path beside the rocky road, and Mrs. Flowers walked in front swinging her arms and picking her way over the stones.

9 She said, without turning her head, to me, "I hear you're doing very good schoolwork, Marguerite, but that it's all written. The teachers report that they have trouble getting you to talk in class." We passed the triangular farm on our left and the path widened to allow us to walk together. I hung back in the separate unasked and unanswerable questions.

10 "Come and walk along with me, Marguerite." I couldn't have refused even if I wanted to. She pronounced my name so nicely. Or more correctly, she spoke each word with such clarity that I was certain a foreigner who didn't understand English could have understood her.

11 "Now no one is going to make you talk—possibly no one can. But bear in mind, language is man's way of communicating with his fellow man and it is language alone which separates him from the lower animals." That was a totally new idea to me, and I would need time to think about it.

12 "Your grandmother says you read a lot. Every chance you get. That's good, but not good enough. Words mean more than what is set down on paper. It takes the human voice to **infuse** them with the shades of deeper meaning."

13 I memorized the part about the human voice infusing words. It seemed so valid and poetic.

14 She said she was going to give me some books and that I not only must read them, I must read them aloud. She suggested that I try to make a sentence sound in as many different ways as possible.

15 "I'll accept no excuse if you return a book to me that has been badly handled." My imagination boggled at the punishment I would deserve if in fact I did abuse a book of Mrs. Flowers'. Death would be too kind and brief.

16 The odors in the house surprised me. Somehow I had never connected Mrs. Flowers with food or eating or any other common experience of common people. There must have been an outhouse, too, but my mind never recorded it.

17 The sweet scent of vanilla had met us as she opened the door.

18 "I made tea cookies this morning. You see, I had planned to invite you for cookies and lemonade so we could have this little chat. The lemonade is in the icebox."

19 It followed that Mrs. Flowers would have ice on an ordinary day, when most families in our town bought ice late on Saturdays only a few times during the summer to be used in the wooden ice-cream freezers.

20 She took the bags from me and disappeared through the kitchen door. I looked around the room that I had never in my wildest fantasies imagined I would see. Browned photographs leered or threatened from the walls and the white, freshly done curtains pushed against themselves and against the wind. I wanted to gobble up the room entire and take it to Bailey, who would help me analyze and enjoy it.

21 "Have a seat, Marguerite. Over there by the table." She carried a platter covered with a tea towel. Although she warned that she hadn't tried her hand at baking sweets for some time, I was certain that like everything else about her the cookies would be perfect.

22 They were flat round wafers, slightly browned on the edges and butter-yellow in the center. With the cold lemonade they were sufficient for childhood's lifelong diet. Remembering my manners, I took nice little ladylike bites off the edges. She said she had made them expressly for me and that she had a few in the kitchen that I could take home to my brother. So I jammed one whole cake in my mouth and the rough crumbs scratched the insides of my jaws, and if I hadn't had to swallow, it would have been a dream come true.

23 As I ate she began the first of what we later called "my lessons in living." She said that I must always be intolerant of ignorance but understanding of illiteracy. That some people, unable to go to school, were more educated and even more intelligent than college professors. She encouraged me to listen carefully to what country people called mother wit. That in those homely sayings was **couched** the collective wisdom of generations.

24 When I finished the cookies she brushed off the table and brought a thick, small book from the bookcase. I had read *A Tale of Two Cities* and found it up to my standards as a romantic novel. She opened the first page and I heard poetry for the first time in my life.

25 "It was the best of times, it was the worst of times. . . ." Her voice slid in and curved down through and over the words. She was nearly singing. I wanted to look at the pages. Were they the same that I had read? Or were there notes, music, lined on the pages, as in a hymn book? Her sounds began cascading gently. I knew from listening to a thousand preachers that she was

nearing the end of her reading, and I hadn't really heard, heard to understand, a single word.

26 "How do you like that?"

27 It occurred to me that she expected a response. The sweet vanilla flavor was still on my tongue and her reading was a wonder in my ears. I had to speak.

28 I said, "Yes, ma'am." It was the least I could do, but it was the most also.

29 "There's one more thing. Take this book of poems and memorize one for me. Next time you pay me a visit, I want you to recite."

30 I have tried often to search behind the sophistication of years for the enchantment I so easily found in those gifts. The essence escapes but its **aura** remains. To be allowed, no, invited, into the private lives of strangers, and to share their joys and fears, was a chance to exchange the Southern bitter wormwood for a cup of mead with *Beowulf* or a hot cup of tea and milk with *Oliver Twist*. When I said aloud, "It is a far, far better thing that I do, than I have ever done . . ." tears of love filled my eyes at my selflessness.

Excerpted from *I Know Why the Caged Bird Sings* by Maya Angelou, published by Bantam Books.

 THINK QUESTIONS

1. What is Mrs. Flowers's plan for helping Marguerite overcome her fear of speaking, and what reason does she give for doing it? Support your response with evidence from the text.

2. Before meeting Mrs. Flowers, Marguerite had refused to speak and also refused any help. Why is Mrs. Flowers able to help her, when others could not? What evidence in the text supports your answer?

3. How does Mrs. Flowers's lesson change the way Marguerite feels about books and words? Support your answer with evidence from the text.

4. Use context to determine the meaning of the word **infuse** as it is used in *I Know Why the Caged Bird Sings*. Write your definition of "infuse" and tell how you arrived at it.

5. Use context to determine the meaning of the word **aura** as it is used in *I Know Why the Caged Bird Sings*. Write your definition of "aura" and tell how you arrived at it.

CLOSE READ

Reread the excerpt from *I Know Why the Caged Bird Sings*. As you reread, complete the Focus Questions below. Then use your answers and annotations from the questions to help you complete the Writing Prompt.

FOCUS QUESTIONS

1. In paragraphs 2 and 3, Angelou describes Mrs. Flowers's appearance and attitude. To what things does Angelou compare her? What is the effect of these descriptions on your impression of Mrs. Flowers? Highlight evidence from the text and make annotations to explain your choices.

2. In paragraph 11, Mrs. Flowers makes a statement about the importance of language. Explain why this statement might have had a strong impact on Marguerite, and how it might relate to a larger theme. Highlight evidence from the text and make annotations to support your response.

3. Reread Mrs. Flowers's statement to Marguerite in paragraph 12. How does Marguerite respond to this comment, and why might Mrs. Flowers consider this a persuasive argument? What is the common theme in everything Mrs. Flowers tells Marguerite? Support your answer with textual evidence and make annotations to explain your response.

4. In several paragraphs, Angelou refers to the way Mrs. Flowers herself uses words. What effect does Mrs. Flowers's own speaking and language have on Marguerite, and how might this make her a good person to help Marguerite? Highlight examples and evidence from the text to support your answer.

5. In your own words, state one of the themes of this passage. How does the influence of Mrs. Flowers in Marguerite's youth affect the pursuit of her dreams later in life? Highlight textual evidence and make annotations to explain your ideas.

WRITING PROMPT

In an essay of at least 300 words, analyze Mrs. Flowers's influence over Marguerite (and later, Maya). How does Angelou's use of figurative language in this passage reflect what she learned from Mrs. Flowers about language? How does the theme developing in this passage relate to Mrs. Flowers's "lessons in living" and Maya's later career as a writer and poet? Refer to specific details and images from the text to support your ideas.

Please note that excerpts and passages in the StudySync® library and this workbook are intended as touchstones to generate interest in an author's work. The excerpts and passages do not substitute for the reading of entire texts, and StudySync® strongly recommends that students seek out and purchase the whole literary or informational work in order to experience it as the author intended. Links to online resellers are available in our digital library. In addition, complete works may be ordered through an authorized reseller by filling out and returning to StudySync® the order form enclosed in this workbook.

Reading & Writing Companion 261

THE JOY LUCK CLUB

FICTION
Amy Tan
1989

INTRODUCTION

Chinese-American author Amy Tan was born in Oakland, California to immigrant parents, and her popular novel *The Joy Luck Club* draws on that background, exploring the relationships between a group of Chinese-American women and their Chinese-immigrant mothers. Structuring the book to resemble a mahjong game, a central activity in the book, Tan weaves together the stories, words and language of multiple characters to provide a compelling portrait of the Chinese-American experience across generations. This excerpt focuses on one mother's high expectations for her daughter, who she envisions as "a Chinese

"In all of my imaginings I was filled with a sense that I would soon become perfect..."

 FIRST READ

 NOTES

Excerpt from "Jing-Mei Woo: Two Kinds"

1   My mother believed you could be anything you wanted to be in America. You could open a restaurant. You could work for the government and get good retirement. You could buy a house with almost no money down. You could become rich. You could become instantly famous.

2   "Of course you can be **prodigy**, too," my mother told me when I was nine. "You can be best anything. What does Auntie Lindo know? Her daughter, she is only best tricky."

3   America was where all my mother's hopes lay. She had come here in 1949 after losing everything in China: her mother and father, her family home, her first husband, and two daughters, twin baby girls. But she never looked back with regret. There were so many ways for things to get better.

4   We didn't immediately pick the right kind of prodigy. At first my mother thought I could be a Chinese Shirley Temple. We'd watch Shirley's old movies on TV as though they were training films. My mother would poke my arm and say, "Ni kan"—You watch. And I would see Shirley tapping her feet, or singing a sailor song, or pursing her lips into a very round O while saying, "Oh my goodness."

5   "Ni kan," said my mother as Shirley's eyes flooded with tears. "You already know how. Don't need talent for crying!"

6   Soon after my mother got this idea about Shirley Temple, she took me to the beauty training school in the Mission District and put me in the hands of a student who could barely hold the scissors without shaking. Instead of getting big fat curls, I emerged with an uneven mass of crinkly black fuzz. My mother dragged me off to the bathroom and tried to wet down my hair.

7   "You look like a Negro Chinese," she lamented, as if I had done this on purpose.

8   The instructor of the beauty training school had to lop off these soggy clumps to make my hair even again. "Peter Pan is very popular these days" the instructor assured my mother. I now had bad hair the length of a boy's, with curly bangs that hung at a slant two inches above my eyebrows. I liked the haircut, and it made me actually look forward to my future fame.

9   In fact, in the beginning I was just as excited as my mother, maybe even more so. I pictured this prodigy part of me as many different images, and I tried each one on for size. I was a dainty ballerina girl standing by the curtain, waiting to hear the music that would send me floating on my tiptoes. I was like the Christ child lifted out of the straw manger, crying with holy **indignity**. I was Cinderella stepping from her pumpkin carriage with sparkly cartoon music filling the air.

10 In all of my imaginings I was filled with a sense that I would soon become perfect: My mother and father would adore me. I would be beyond **reproach**. I would never feel the need to sulk, or to clamor for anything. But sometimes the prodigy in me became impatient. "If you don't hurry up and get me out of here, I'm disappearing for good," it warned. " And then you'll always be nothing."

11 Every night after dinner my mother and I would sit at the Formica topped kitchen table. She would present new tests, taking her examples from stories of amazing children that she read in Ripley's Believe It or Not or Good Housekeeping, Reader's Digest, or any of a dozen other magazines she kept in a pile in our bathroom. My mother got these magazines from people whose houses she cleaned. And since she cleaned many houses each week, we had a great assortment. She would look through them all, searching for stories about remarkable children.

12 The first night she brought out a story about a three-year-old boy who knew the capitals of all the states and even most of the European countries. A teacher was quoted as saying that the little boy could also pronounce the names of the foreign cities correctly. "What's the capital of Finland?" my mother asked me, looking at the story.

13 All I knew was the capital of California, because Sacramento was the name of the street we lived on in Chinatown. "Nairobi!" I guessed, saying the most foreign word I could think of. She checked to see if that might be one way to pronounce Helsinki before showing me the answer.

NOTES

14   The tests got harder - multiplying numbers in my head, finding the queen of hearts in a deck of cards, trying to stand on my head without using my hands, predicting the daily temperatures in Los Angeles, New York, and London. One night I had to look at a page from the Bible for three minutes and then report everything I could remember. "Now Jehoshaphat had riches and honor in **abundance** and... that's all I remember, Ma," I said.

15   And after seeing, once again, my mother's disappointed face, something inside me began to die. I hated the tests, the raised hopes and failed expectations. Before going to bed that night I looked in the mirror above the bathroom sink, and I saw only my face staring back – and understood that it would always be this ordinary face – I began to cry. Such a sad, ugly girl! I made high - pitched noises like a crazed animal, trying to scratch out the face in the mirror. And then I saw what seemed to be the prodigy side of me – a face I had never seen before. I looked at my reflection, blinking so that I could see more clearly. The girl staring back at me was angry, powerful. She and I were the same. I had new thoughts, willful thoughts – or, rather, thoughts filled with lots of won'ts. I won't let her change me, I promised myself. I won't be what I'm not.

16   So now when my mother presented her tests, I performed **listlessly**, my head propped on one arm. I pretended to be bored. And I was. I got so bored that I started counting the bellows of the foghorns out on the bay while my mother drilled me in other areas. The sound was comforting and reminded me of the cow jumping over the moon. And the next day I played a game with myself, seeing if my mother would give up on me before eight bellows. After a while I usually counted only one bellow, maybe two at most. At last she was beginning to give up hope.

Excerpted from *The Joy Luck Club* by Amy Tan, published by the Penguin Group.

THINK QUESTIONS

1. What does the mother in this excerpt want from her daughter? Refer to one or more details from the text to support your response.

2. Shirley Temple was a famous child movie star in the 1930s. Use details from the text to write two or three sentences about the mother's efforts to make her daughter into a "Chinese Shirley Temple."

3. Write two or three sentences about how the daughter's attitude toward becoming a prodigy changes during the selection. Support your answer with textual evidence.

4. Use context to determine the meaning of the word **prodigy** as it is used in *The Joy Luck Club*. Write your definition of "prodigy" and tell how you arrived at it.

5. Use your knowledge of the word "dignity" and the Latin prefix *–in*, which means "not," along with the context clues provided in the passage, to determine the meaning of **indignity**. Write your definition of "indignity" and tell how you arrived at it.

CLOSE READ

Reread the excerpt from *The Joy Luck Club.* As you reread, complete the Focus Questions below. Then use your answers and annotations from the questions to help you complete the Writing Prompt.

FOCUS QUESTIONS

1. Explain who the narrator of this selection is. What is her relationship to the daughter in the story? In what way does this relationship influence how the narrator tells the story? Highlight textual evidence and make annotations to explain your ideas.

2. Why does the mother have such a strong motivation to pursue her dream of success through her daughter? What influence might her past, as described in the third paragraph, have on this goal? Highlight the textual evidence that supports your answer, and make annotations to explain your ideas.

3. How do the daughter's motivations change in the last three paragraphs? What event sparks the change? What decision does she make? Highlight textual evidence and make annotations to explain your answer.

4. How does the daughter force her mother to stop trying to turn her into a prodigy? What clues in the final paragraph tell the reader how the daughter feels as she is doing this? Highlight evidence from the text and make annotations to support your explanation.

5. What lesson about being true to oneself does the child in this excerpt experience? Briefly state this lesson as the author's message or theme for the selection. What conclusion can be made about what makes a dream worth pursuing? Highlight textual evidence and make annotations to explain your ideas.

WRITING PROMPT

In an essay of around 300 words, describe the American Dream that the mother is reaching for and answer this question: Is the mother's dream of making her daughter into a prodigy worth pursuing? Explain why or why not, supporting your writing with evidence from the text. Use your understanding of complex characters and motivations to describe and evaluate the mother and daughter.

ONLY DAUGHTER

NON-FICTION
Sandra Cisneros
1990

INTRODUCTION

Sandra Cisneros is a Mexican-American writer who is best known for her coming-of-age novel *The House on Mango Street*. Cisneros has said that her Mexican-American heritage gives her "two ways of looking at the world" and "twice as many words to pick from." In her autobiographical essay "Only Daughter," which originally appeared in *Glamour* magazine, Cisneros describes what it was like to grow up as the only girl in a family of seven children, and how her traditional father was more concerned with her finding a husband than

"I am the only daughter in a family of six sons. *That* explains everything."

FIRST READ

1 Once several years ago, when I was just starting out my writing career, I was asked to write my own contributor's note for an anthology I was part of. I wrote: "I am the only daughter in a family of six sons. *That* explains everything."

2 Well, I've thought about that ever since, and yes, it explains a lot to me, but for the reader's sake I should have written: "I am the only daughter in a *Mexican* family of six sons." Or even: "I am the only daughter of a Mexican father and a Mexican-American mother." Or: "I am the only daughter of a working-class family of nine." All of these had everything to do with who I am today.

3 I was/am the only daughter and *only* a daughter. Being an only daughter in a family of six sons forced me by **circumstance** to spend a lot of time by myself because my brothers felt it beneath them to play with a *girl* in public. But that aloneness, that loneliness, was good for a would-be writer—it allowed me time to think, to imagine, to read and prepare myself.

4 Being only a daughter for my father meant my destiny would lead me to become someone's wife. That's what he believed. But when I was in fifth grade and shared my plans for college with him, I was sure he understood. I remember my father saying, "Que bueno, *mi'ja*, that's good." That meant a lot to me, especially since my brothers thought the idea **hilarious**. What I didn't realize was that my father thought college was good for girls—for finding a husband. After four years in college and two more in graduate school, and still no husband, my father shakes his head even now and says I wasted all that education.

5 In **retrospect**, I'm lucky my father believed daughters were meant for husbands. It meant it didn't matter if I majored in something silly like English. After all, I'd find a nice profession eventually, right? This allowed me the liberty to putter about **embroidering** my little poems and stories without my father interrupting with so much as a, "What's that you're writing?"

6   But the truth is, I wanted him to interrupt. I wanted my father to understand what it was I was scribbling, to introduce me as "My only daughter, the writer." Not as "This is my only daughter. She teaches. "*Es maestra*—teacher. Not even *profesora*.

7   In a sense, everything I have ever written has been for him, to win his approval even though I know my father can't read English words, even though my father's only reading includes the brown-ink *Esto* sports magazines from Mexico City and the bloody *¡Alarma!* magazines that feature yet another sighting of *La Virgen de Guadalupe* on a tortilla or a wife's revenge on her philandering husband by bashing his skull in with a *molcajete* (a kitchen mortar made of volcanic rock). Or the *fotonovelas*, the little picture paperbacks with tragedy and trauma erupting from the characters' mouths in bubbles.

8   My father represents, then, the public majority. A public who is disinterested in reading, and yet one whom I am writing about and for, and privately trying to woo.

9   When we were growing up in Chicago, we moved a lot because of my father. He suffered periodic bouts of **nostalgia**. Then we'd have to let go our flat, store the furniture with mother's relatives, load the station wagon with baggage and bologna sandwiches, and head south. To Mexico City.

10 We came back, of course. To yet another Chicago flat, another Chicago neighborhood, another Catholic school. Each time, my father would seek out the parish priest in order to get a tuition break, and complain or boast: "I have seven sons."

11 He meant *siete hijos*, seven children, but he translated it as "sons". "I have seven sons." To anyone who would listen. The Sears Roebuck employee who sold us the washing machine. The short-order cook where my father ate his ham-and-eggs breakfasts. "I have seven sons." As if he deserved a medal from the state.

12 My papa. He didn't mean anything by that mistranslation, I'm sure. But somehow I could feel myself being erased. I'd tug my father's sleeve and whisper, "Not seven sons. Six! and one *daughter*."

13 When my oldest brother graduated from medical school, he fulfilled my father's dream that we study hard and use this—our heads, instead of this—our hands. Even now my father's hands are thick and yellow, stubbed by a history of hammer and nails and twine and coils and springs. "Use this," my father said, tapping his head, "and not this," showing us those hands. He always looked tired when he said it.

14 Wasn't college an investment? And hadn't I spent all those years in college? And if I didn't marry, what was it all for? Why would anyone go to college and then choose to be poor? Especially someone who had always been poor.

15 Last year, after ten years of writing professionally, the financial rewards started to trickle in. My second National Endowment for the Arts Fellowship. A guest professorship at the University of California, Berkeley. My book, which sold to a major New York publishing house.

16 At Christmas, I flew home to Chicago. The house was throbbing, same as always; hot tamales and sweet tamales hissing in my mother's pressure cooker, and everybody—my mother, six brothers, wives, babies, aunts, cousins—talking too loud and at the same time, like in a Fellini film, because that's just how we are.

17 I went upstairs to my father's room. One of my stories had just been translated into Spanish and published in an anthology of Chicano writing, and I wanted to show it to him. Ever since he recovered from a stroke two years ago, my father likes to spend his leisure hours horizontally. And that's how I found him, watching a Pedro Infante movie on Galavision and eating rice pudding.

18 There was a glass filmed with milk on the bedside table. There were several vials of pills and balled Kleenex. And on the floor, one black sock and a plastic urinal that I didn't want to look at but looked at anyway. Pedro Infante was about to burst into song, and my father was laughing.

19 I'm not sure if it was because my story was translated into Spanish, or because it was published in Mexico, or perhaps because the story dealt with Tepeyac, the *colonia* my father was raised in, but at any rate, my father punched the mute button on his remote control and read my story.

20 I sat on the bed next to my father and waited. He read it very slowly. As if he were reading each line over and over. He laughed at all the right places and read lines he liked out loud. He pointed and asked questions: "Is this so-and-so?" "Yes," I said. He kept reading.

21 When he was finally finished, after what seemed like hours, my father looked up and asked, "Where can we get more copies of this for the relatives?"

22 Of all the wonderful things that happened to me last year, that was the most wonderful.

THINK QUESTIONS

1. Refer to one or more details from the text to explain how Sandra Cisneros feels about being the only daughter in a family of seven children. Support your response with ideas that are directly stated and ideas that you have inferred from clues in the text.

2. Write two or three sentences explaining how Cisneros's father felt about her plans to go to college and why he felt that way. What does this tell the reader about him? Support your answer with textual evidence.

3. Write two or three sentences exploring the significance of the father's response, at the end of the excerpt, to the story the author had written. Support your answer with textual evidence.

4. Use context to determine the meaning of the word **nostalgia** as it is used in *Only Daughter*. Write your definition of "nostalgia" and tell how you arrived at it.

5. Remembering that the Latin root retro means "backward" and that the Latin root **spec** means "look at," use the context clues provided in the passage to determine the meaning of **retrospect**. Write your definition of "retrospect" and tell how you determined it.

CLOSE READ

Reread the excerpt from *Only Daughter*. As you reread, complete the Focus Questions below. Then use your answers and annotations from the questions to help you complete the Writing Prompt.

FOCUS QUESTIONS

1. Explain how the author uses the first two paragraphs to set up the main focus of this excerpt from her autobiographical essay. Highlight evidence from the text and make annotations to explain your choices.

2. In Paragraphs 4 and 5, the author indicates that from her present-day perspective, being "the only daughter and only a daughter" had certain advantages. Do you think this is how Cisneros felt when she was growing up? Why or why not? What benefits did she see in this situation by the time she wrote this autobiographical essay? Highlight your textual evidence and make annotations to explain your choices.

3. What do paragraphs 6 and 7 reveal about the thing Cisneros wanted most from her father? How does the author tie this desire to her current goals as a writer? Make annotations to support your inferences about the text and its deeper meaning. Support your answer with textual.

4. In paragraph 13, Cisneros describes her father's joy when her oldest brother graduated from medical school. Why was this event so important to her father? What key idea does the author try to communicate about her relationship with her father in paragraph 14? Highlight evidence from the text and make annotations to support your explanation.

5. In the last four paragraphs, Cisneros describes an interaction between her and her father. Why is her father's reaction to the story she has written so meaningful to the author? Do you think she feels her pursuit of her father's recognition has been worthwhile? Highlight textual evidence and make annotations to explain your ideas.

WRITING PROMPT

Write a strong paragraph of 200 to 300 words in which you use your understanding of the Cisneros family, the roles of men and women in their culture, the words and actions of the people described, and Cisneros's own statements to help determine at least one theme that emerges in this passage. Consider which details about Cisneros's family life are most important to developing this theme in the excerpt.

Please note that excerpts and passages in the StudySync® library and this workbook are intended as touchstones to generate interest in an author's work. The excerpts and passages do not substitute for the reading of entire texts, and StudySync® strongly recommends that students seek out and purchase the whole literary or informational work in order to experience it as the author intended. Links to online resellers are available in our digital library. In addition, complete works may be ordered through an authorized reseller by filling out and returning to StudySync® the order form enclosed in this workbook.

Reading & Writing Companion **273**

THE VOICE THAT CHALLENGED A NATION:
MARIAN ANDERSON AND THE STRUGGLE FOR EQUAL RIGHTS

NON-FICTION

Russell Freedman
2011

INTRODUCTION

With a voice "heard only once in a hundred years," contralto Marian Anderson's vocal range spanned from low baritone to high soprano. She bridged other divides as well. The first African American to join the New York Metropolitan Opera, Anderson sang at the presidential inaugurations of Dwight D. Eisenhower and John F. Kennedy, served as a delegate to the United Nations, and received numerous accolades, including the Presidential Medal of Freedom and a Grammy Lifetime Achievement award. Her gift was evident early

"Her classmates would remember her as a shy and often self-conscious young woman who kept to herself..."

FIRST READ

Excerpt from Chapter Two: Twenty-Five Cents a Song

1 While she dreamed of a singing career, [Marian] knew she would have to support herself and help her family when she finished school, so she took the high school's secretarial course, studying bookkeeping, shorthand, and typing. But her heart wasn't in those studies, and after three unhappy years she was able to transfer to the newly established South Philadelphia High School for Girls, where she enrolled in an academic course, emphasizing music. Several years older than any of the other girls, she was one of the school's few black students. Her classmates would remember her as a shy and often self-conscious young woman who kept to herself and concentrated on her musical studies. She was "interested in pretty much nothing else but singing," one student recalled, "not taking part in dances or things like that."

2 During her high school years, Marian continued to sing at church and social events and, increasingly, at concerts out of town. In 1917, just before Christmas, she was invited to take part in a gala concert at the Georgia State Industrial College, a black college in Savannah. She had never visited the Deep South before, and on this trip, for the first time, she experienced the strict **"Jim Crow" laws** that enforced racial segregation throughout the South.

3 She traveled with her mother from Philadelphia to Washington, D.C., where they had to change trains to continue south. At Washington's Union Station black and white passengers were separated. The Andersons' bags were taken to the first coach on the train headed south—the Jim Crow coach reserved for blacks. As Marian recalled, the car was dirty inside and out, the windows were badly in need of washing, and the **ventilation** and lighting were poor. When the air became stuffy and the windows were raised, smoke and soot from the engine directly ahead poured into the car. "I had heard about Jim Crow," Marian wrote later, "but meeting it bit deeply into the soul...

Copyright © BookheadEd Learning, LLC

NOTES

I had looked closely at my people in that train. Some seemed to be embarrassed to the core. Others appeared to accept the situation as if it were beyond repair."

4   Arriving in Savannah after an overnight trip, Marian and her mother were greeted warmly by school officials and were put up at the home of the college president. That evening an audience of nearly a thousand people turned out for the concert in Savannah's new Municipal Auditorium, whites sitting in the boxes and dress circle, blacks in segregated orchestra or gallery seats. "[Marian] Anderson, the soloist, has one of the most remarkable voices ever heard in Savannah," reported the *Savannah Morning News.*

5   By now she was receiving so many invitations that she had trouble keeping up with her high school studies. Roland Hayes invited her to sing on some of his own programs. She traveled to Tennessee, where she gave a week of concerts at black churches and colleges. And she won a **scholarship** to take a six-week summer course at the Chicago Conservatory of Music.

6   In Wilmington, Delaware, at a reception following a concert, she was introduced to a tall young man named Orpheus Fisher, who, like her, was still in high school. He fell for the shy singer with the soft laughter and huge sparkling eyes who was almost as tall as he, and Marian, as she later admitted, was attracted to Orpheus. They saw a good deal of each other. It wasn't long before Orpheus suggested that they run away and get married. But Marian, determined to build a career, wasn't interested in discussing marriage. "I was busy with the beginnings of my concert life," she said later, "and I thought there was no great hurry." Orpheus **persisted**, and in the years that followed he kept in touch with Marian as she traveled around the world. He never gave up hope that one day he would persuade her to marry him.

7   Meanwhile, the principal of Marian's high school, Dr. Lucy Langdon Wilson, had been following the young singer's progress with great interest. Convinced that Marian had a great future ahead of her, Wilson helped arrange an audition with Giuseppe Boghetti, a well-known voice coach who had studios in both Philadelphia and New York. Boghetti was short, stocky, and **dynamic**, a demanding teacher with a vast store of knowledge about vocal technique and a stern manner with his students. More than once students had been seen leaving his studio in tears. He insisted at first that he was much too busy to see Marian. He wanted no new students, he said. But finally, as a favor, he agreed to hear her sing one song.

8   Marian was so nervous when she arrived at Boghetti's studio that she sang her single song, "Deep River," without once looking at him. When she finished, Boghetti seemed stunned. Finally, he turned to her. "I will make room for you

Copyright © BookheadEd Learning, LLC

right away," he said, "and I will need only two years with you. After that, you will be able to go anywhere and sing for anybody."

9   Again there was no money for lessons. Most of Marian's earnings from concert appearances went to her mother, who was still taking in laundry and scrubbing floors, and to her sisters, who were still in school. And again the congregation at Union Baptist Church came to Marian's aid, organizing a benefit concert that raised $566 so that she could study with Boghetti. Despite his prediction, he would remain her voice teacher for many years to come.

Excerpted from *The Voice That Challenged a Nation: Marian Anderson and the Struggle for Equal Rights* by Russell Freedman, published by Clarion Books.

THINK QUESTIONS

1. Refer to one or more details from the text to support your understanding of why the train trip from Washington, D.C., to Savannah was difficult for Marian and her mother—both from ideas that are directly stated and ideas that you have inferred from clues in the text.

2. Use details from the text to write two or three sentences describing the different ways people responded to Marian Anderson's singing.

3. Write two or three sentences describing the type of person that Marian Anderson was in her teen years. Support your answer with textual evidence.

4. Use context to determine the meaning of the phrase **"Jim Crow" laws** as it is used in *The Voice That Challenged a Nation*. Write your definition of "'Jim Crow' laws" and tell how you arrived at it.

5. Remembering that the Latin prefix *per-* means "through," the Latin root sist means "stand," and the *-ed* ending signals use of the past tense, use the context clues provided in the passage to determine the meaning of **persisted**. Write your definition of "persisted" and tell how you arrived at it.

Please note that excerpts and passages in the StudySync® library and this workbook are intended as touchstones to generate interest in an author's work. The excerpts and passages do not substitute for the reading of entire texts, and StudySync® strongly recommends that students seek out and purchase the whole literary or informational work in order to experience it as the author intended. Links to online resellers are available in our digital library. In addition, complete works may be ordered through an authorized reseller by filling out and returning to StudySync® the order form enclosed in this workbook.

Reading & Writing Companion   277

CLOSE READ

Reread the excerpt from *The Voice That Challenged a Nation*. As you reread, complete the Focus Questions below. Then use your answers and annotations from the questions to help you complete the Writing Prompt.

FOCUS QUESTIONS

1. In paragraph 1, the author mentions that Marian was "one of the school's few black students". Why is this information important for the reader to know? Highlight evidence from the text and make annotations to explain your choices.

2. Think about the title of the book from which the excerpt is taken: *The Voice That Challenged a Nation: Marian Anderson and the Struggle for Equal Rights*. How do the events the author describes in this excerpt connect with the title? What kinds of events might the author present in later chapters of the book? Support your answer with textual evidence and make annotations to explain your answer choices.

3. Paragraph 1 describes Marian as "shy and self-conscious." What images come to mind when you think of her? Paragraph 7 describes Guiseppe Boghetti as "dynamic." What images come to mind when you think of him? How might Boghetti's dynamic personality influence Marian when she takes lessons from him? Highlight your textual evidence and make annotations to explain your choices.

4. In paragraph 8, the author includes the detail that Boghetti "seemed stunned" after he heard Marian sing. Why is this an important detail to include? Highlight evidence from the text and make annotations to support your explanation.

5. In paragraph 6, referring to Orpheus's marriage proposal, Marian says, "I was busy with the beginnings of my concert life, and I thought there was no great hurry." How does this statement, as well as her other actions described in this excerpt, relate to the unit theme, "What makes a dream worth pursuing"? Highlight textual evidence and make annotations to explain your ideas.

WRITING PROMPT

How do the informational text elements that Russell Freedman includes in this excerpt from *The Voice That Challenged a Nation* help you understand Marian as a singer? How do they help you understand the social situation of the time? Are there additional text elements that you might find useful? Use your understanding of informational text elements to respond. Support your writing with evidence from the text.

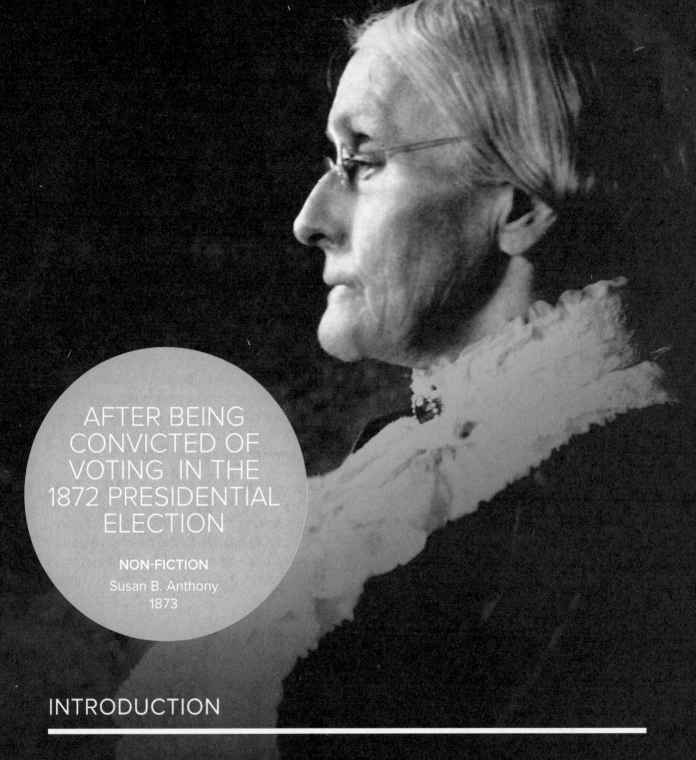

AFTER BEING CONVICTED OF VOTING IN THE 1872 PRESIDENTIAL ELECTION

NON-FICTION
Susan B. Anthony
1873

INTRODUCTION

In the late 1800s, women in the United States did not yet have the right to vote, and famed women's suffrage activist Susan B. Anthony set out to change that. After being arrested for casting an illegal vote in the presidential election of 1872, Anthony drafted a speech arguing that she had committed no crime, and delivered it in each of the 29 postal districts in Monroe County, New York. The speech was so effective that the prosecution requested a change of venue.

"I not only committed no crime, but, instead, simply exercised my citizen's rights..."

 FIRST READ

Stump Speech in all 29 postal districts of Monroe County, New York, in 1873

1   Friends and fellow citizens: I stand before you tonight under **indictment** for the alleged crime of having voted at the last presidential election, without having a lawful right to vote. It shall be my work this evening to prove to you that in thus voting, I not only committed no crime, but, instead, simply exercised my citizen's rights, guaranteed to me and all United States citizens by the National Constitution, beyond the power of any state to deny. ...

2   The preamble of the Federal Constitution says:

3   "We, the people of the United States, in order to form a more perfect union, establish justice, insure domestic tranquility, provide for the common defense, promote the general welfare, and secure the blessings of liberty to ourselves and our **posterity**, do ordain and establish this Constitution for the United States of America."

4   It was we, the people; not we, the white male citizens; nor yet we, the male citizens; but we, the whole people, who formed the Union. And we formed it, not to give the blessings of liberty, but to secure them; not to the half of ourselves and the half of our posterity, but to the whole people—women as well as men. And it is a downright mockery to talk to women of their enjoyment of the blessings of liberty while they are denied the use of the only means of securing them provided by this democratic-republican government—the ballot. ...

5   For any state to make sex a qualification that must ever result in the **disfranchisement** of one entire half of the people, is to pass a bill of attainder, or, an **ex post facto** law, and is therefore a violation of the supreme law of the

NOTES

land. By it the blessings of liberty are forever withheld from women and their female posterity. ...

6 To them this government has no just powers derived from the consent of the governed. To them this government is not a democracy. It is not a republic. It is an odious aristocracy; a hateful **oligarchy** of sex; the most hateful aristocracy ever established on the face of the globe; an oligarchy of wealth, where the rich govern the poor. An oligarchy of learning, where the educated govern the ignorant, or even an oligarchy of race, where the Saxon rules the African, might be endured; but this oligarchy of sex, which makes father, brothers, husband, sons, the oligarchs over the mother and sisters, the wife and daughters, of every household—which ordains all men sovereigns, all women subjects, carries dissension, discord, and rebellion into every home of the nation.

7 Webster, Worcester, and Bouvier all define a citizen to be a person in the United States, entitled to vote and hold office.

8 The only question left to be settled now is: Are women persons? And I hardly believe any of our opponents will have the hardihood to say they are not. Being persons, then, women are citizens; and no state has a right to make any law, or to enforce any old law, that shall abridge their privileges or immunities. Hence, every discrimination against women in the constitutions and laws of the several states is today null and void, precisely as is every one against Negroes.

 THINK QUESTIONS

1. Why does Anthony believe that she has been wrongly accused of a crime? Use your own inferences and evidence from the first paragraph of the speech to support your answer.

2. Why does Anthony quote the preamble to the Constitution? Use your own inferences and examples from the text to support your answer.

3. Why does Anthony believe that voting is also a woman's right? Use inference and examples from the text to support your answer.

4. Use context to determine the meaning of the word **oligarchy** as it is used in "After Being Convicted Of Voting In The 1872 Presidential Election." Write your definition of "oligarchy" and explain how you arrived at it.

5. Remembering that the Latin prefix post- means "after" and the Latin word facto means "the fact," use the context clues provided in the passage to determine the meaning of **ex post facto**. Write your definition of "ex post facto" and explain how you arrived at it.

Please note that excerpts and passages in the StudySync® library and this workbook are intended as touchstones to generate interest in an author's work. The excerpts and passages do not substitute for the reading of entire texts, and StudySync® strongly recommends that students seek out and purchase the whole literary or informational work in order to experience it as the author intended. Links to online resellers are available in our digital library. In addition, complete works may be ordered through an authorized reseller by filling out and returning to StudySync® the order form enclosed in this workbook.

Reading & Writing Companion   **281**

CLOSE READ

Reread Anthony's speech. As you reread, complete the Focus Questions below. Then use your answers and annotations from the questions to help you complete the Writing Prompt.

FOCUS QUESTIONS

1. Explain how Anthony's word choice in the first paragraph adds to the power of her argument, focusing especially on her technical language. Highlight evidence from the text and make annotations to explain your choices.

2. Examine paragraphs 3 and 4. How does Anthony build from the preamble to the Constitution to form her argument? Highlight evidence from the text and make annotations to explain your answer.

3. Explore the connotations of Anthony's word choices in paragraphs 5 and 6. Highlight key words and write down their connotations in this context.

4. The seventh paragraph of the text is a single sentence that stands alone. Why do you think Anthony makes the decision to give the line its own paragraph? Annotate the line to explain your answer.

5. In the final paragraph of the speech, highlight a phrase or sentence that the entire speech has been building up to. Annotate to explain your answer.

6. Recall the Essential Question of this unit: "What makes a dream worth pursuing?" Why do you think Susan B. Anthony believes the dream of voting rights for women is worth pursuing? Give evidence for your answer.

WRITING PROMPT

In an essay of at least 300 words, show how Susan B. Anthony's logic, conviction, and argument build with each paragraph. Be sure to note how her language choices contribute to this forward movement. Quote passages from the text to support your claims.

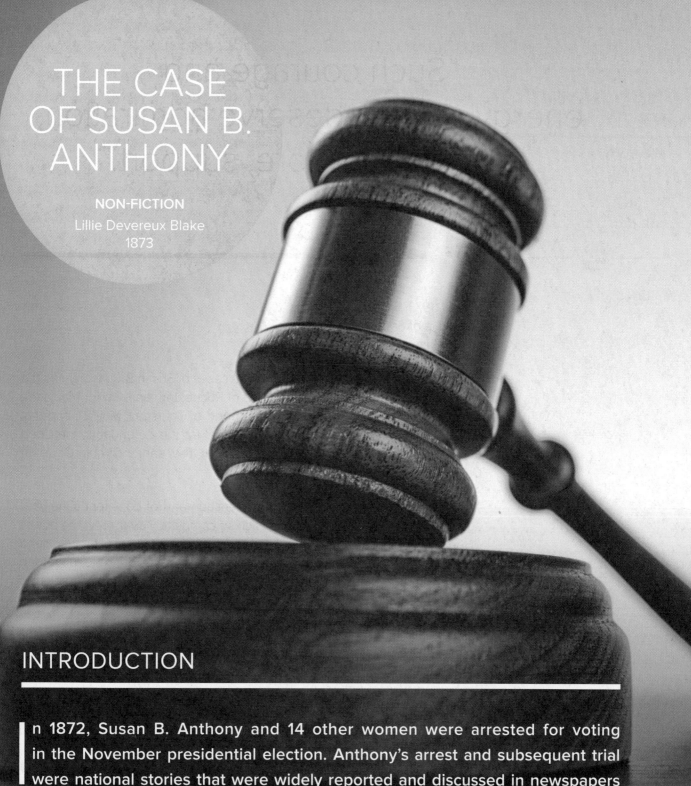

THE CASE OF SUSAN B. ANTHONY

NON-FICTION
Lillie Devereux Blake
1873

INTRODUCTION

In 1872, Susan B. Anthony and 14 other women were arrested for voting in the November presidential election. Anthony's arrest and subsequent trial were national stories that were widely reported and discussed in newspapers across the country. In this letter to the editor of *The New York Times*, supporter Lillie Devereux Blake defends Anthony's actions and attempts to rally others to her cause. Anthony was ultimately convicted of voting illegally in what was to become one of the most famous court cases in American history.

"Such courage and energy as hers deserve admiration, and what is more, support."

 FIRST READ

May 31, 1873
The Case of Susan B. Anthony
To the Editor of the New York Times

1   The papers last week informed us that the cases of Susan B. Anthony and the other women voters of the Eighth Ward of Rochester came up for trial in the United States District Court on the afternoon of Thursday, May 21, and that despite "the strenuous opposition of counsel for the defendants, the Court ordered all the indictments to be tried at the same Circuit Court at Canandaigua."

2   This statement deserved a word of explanation and of comment. One year ago last November, at the election which so completely overthrew the power of the Tweed Ring in this City, Mrs. L.D. Mansfield, the principal of the Rockland Female Institute, of Nyack, and several of her teachers, voted the full reform ticket, were not **molested** in any way at the time, and were not prosecuted afterward as guilty of any crime.

3   Last Fall Miss Anthony, her sister, and several other women, voted the full State and National Republican tickets on the 5th of November. No action in their regard has up to this time been taken by the State or local authorities, although since then Miss Anthony and several others of the original "offenders" have twice cast their ballots, once for State officers, and once at a municipal election. The United States authorities have, however, pursued these women with what may almost be styled **virulence**. Of course, everyone is aware that the essence of crime is entirely absent in their case, as no fraud whatever was practiced. When a man is punished for voting illegally, it is because he has used some deception; he has either **perjured** himself with a false oath as to his residence, or is a repeater, or is guilty of some other violation of the law.

4   No such charge is brought against these women; they took no false oaths; they simply swore that they were citizens of the United States, and as the Fourteenth Amendment to the Constitution declares that "all persons born or naturalized in the United States are citizens thereof," this was surely a correct statement; nor did they attempt to disguise their sex or to deceive the registers in any way. They merely claimed that existing laws give women the right to vote, and at worst this was an error of interpretation and not a crime. They have, however, been prosecuted by the United State authorities, as if they were guilty of a felony. Some weeks after the election Miss Anthony and the fourteen other women were arrested, threatened with imprisonment in the common jail unless they gave bail, and in all respects treated as criminals. That is, they were **ostensibly** so treated; in reality, nearly all the parties concerned in the prosecution showed themselves, to their credit be it said, heartily ashamed of their part in the proceedings.

5   Finding that much annoyance and trouble were likely to come to others beside herself, Miss Anthony, with a rare generosity, although she had not persuaded the other women to vote, though they had done so in most instances without even consulting with her, voluntarily assumed the whole burden of the expenses of the trial.

6   The case, as it stood, became an **anomalous** one—one in which the defendants were to be tried as criminals, not for a crime, but merely for a misinterpretation of the law, although in this misinterpretation they were sustained by the Board of Registers and other officials.

7   As this case was an alleged felony, however, it was, of course, to be brought before a jury and, as the principal offender, Susan B. Anthony, was out on bail, she at once, with indomitable pluck and energy, went to work to stump the county in which the Court was to sit, and thus create a sentiment in her favor. Through the storms and cold of a most inclement March she made her way to every town and village in Monroe County, asking, night after night, large audiences the question "It it a Crime for a United States Citizen to Vote?"

8   The District Attorney hearing of this certainly perfectly justifiable act of self-defense grew very angry, declaring that he could never obtain an impartial jury for the coming trial. In other words, after Miss Anthony had given her opinion of the law, he would be unable to find twelve intelligent men who had not heard both sides of the question.

9   After many delays the celebrated case was at length reached on the Calendar, but not to be brought to a conclusion, not to be fairly tried in the community where the "guilty ones were all known and respected, but only to be put off to another term of the court, to be held in another county. If, however, the District Attorney thinks of these means to bring it among people who had not

NOTES

heard Miss Anthony, he was entirely mistaken, for that dauntless woman has already started on the canvass of Ontario County.

10 Such courage and energy as hers deserve admiration, and what is more, support. The expenses which she has assumed are very heavy and she has no resources to depend upon but what she can earn for herself from day to day. Help ought to be given her by all those who are in sympathy with the cause she represents, and all who simply revere justice and honor [should make] Contribution to the Anthony defense fund to be sent to Mrs. C.S. Lozier, Chairman of the Committee.

THINK QUESTIONS

1. According to Susan B. Anthony and her supporters in 1873, what was the view of the United States Constitution on the issue of women voting? Support your answer with evidence from the text.

2. What view of the District Attorney and prosecutors does the letter present? Cite words or phrases from the text that show this view.

3. What role did letter writer Lillie Devereux Blake play in the voting rights controversy, besides writing the letter to the New York Times? Support your answer with textual evidence.

4. Use context to determine the meaning of the word **perjured** as it is used in "The Case of Susan B. Anthony." Write your definition of "perjured" and tell how you arrived at it.

5. Remembering that the Latin suffix -ence means "the quality or state of," and considering that the Latin root word virus means "poison," use the context clues provided in the passage to determine the meaning of **virulence**. Write your definition of "virulence" and tell how you arrived at it.

CLOSE READ

Reread the excerpt from "The Case of Susan B. Anthony." As you reread, complete the Focus Questions below. Then use your answers and annotations from the questions to help you complete the Writing Prompt.

FOCUS QUESTIONS

1. Why is sequential organization a good structure for the first three paragraphs of the letter? Highlight and annotate evidence for your answer.

2. In one sentence, describe the writer's point of view or perspective in the fourth paragraph of the letter. Support your answer with textual evidence and make annotations to explain your answer choices.

3. In paragraphs 6–9, cite two examples of words and phrases that signal sequential organization. Then cite two examples of words and phrases that signal other types of organization. What type(s) of organization do the latter examples signal? Highlight and annotate your evidence.

4. State two ways in which the author uses comparison and contrast structure in paragraph 9. Highlight and annotate evidence from the text.

5. From Lillie Devereux Blake's point of view, what makes the dream of women's suffrage worth pursuing? Highlight textual evidence and make annotations to explain your response.

WRITING PROMPT

What is the letter writer's point of view, or perspective, on Susan B. Anthony? How does the writer's choice of words and informational text structure help express her point of view? Use your understanding of author's purpose, point of view, text structure, and vivid language to analyze the writer's point of view and how it is made evident in the letter. Support your ideas with quotations from the text.

Please note that excerpts and passages in the StudySync® library and this workbook are intended as touchstones to generate interest in an author's work. The excerpts and passages do not substitute for the reading of entire texts, and StudySync® strongly recommends that students seek out and purchase the whole literary or informational work in order to experience it as the author intended. Links to online resellers are available in our digital library. In addition, complete works may be ordered through an authorized reseller by filling out and returning to StudySync® the order form enclosed in this workbook.

Reading & Writing Companion   **287**

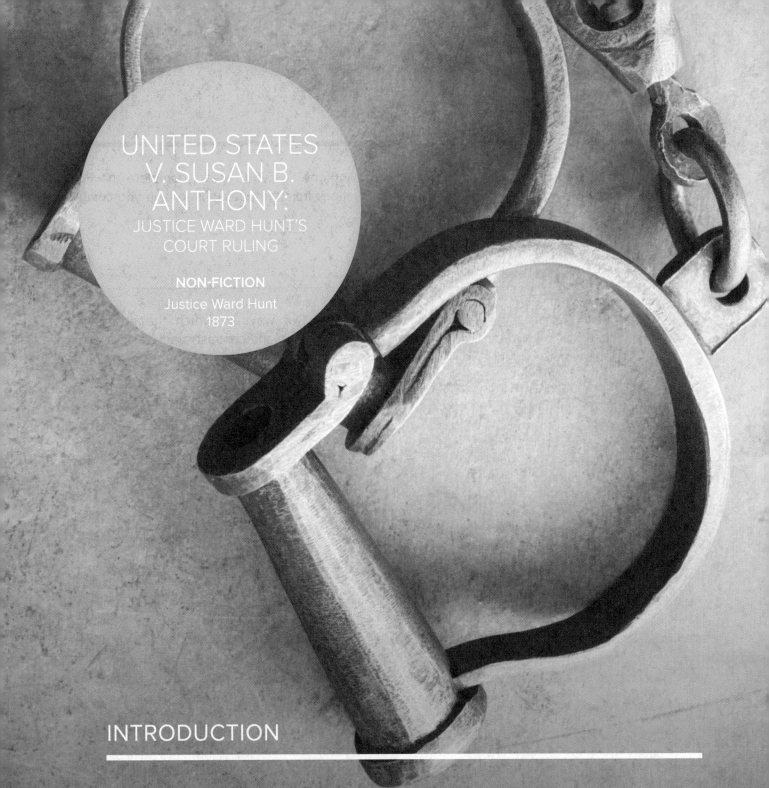

UNITED STATES V. SUSAN B. ANTHONY:
JUSTICE WARD HUNT'S COURT RULING

NON-FICTION
Justice Ward Hunt
1873

INTRODUCTION

Relying on the recently adopted 14th Amendment that addressed citizenship rights and equal protection under the law, women's suffrage activist Susan B. Anthony and several other women attempted to cast votes in the presidential election of 1872. Anthony was subsequently arrested for voting illegally, and her trial in a New York federal circuit court became one of the most famous court cases in American history. The excerpt here is from Justice Ward Hunt's court ruling that found Susan B. Anthony guilty of the crime of voting.

"Miss Anthony knew that she was a woman, and that the constitution of this state prohibits her from voting."

FIRST READ

NOTES

From Justice Ward Hunt's decision:

1   The right of voting, or the privilege of voting, is a right or privilege arising under the constitution of the state, and not under the constitution of the United States. The qualifications are different in the different states. Citizenship, age, sex, residence, are variously required in the different states, or may be so. If the right belongs to any particular person, it is because such a person is entitled to it by the laws of the state where he offers to exercise it, and not because of citizenship of the United States. If the state of New York should provide that no person should vote until he had reached the age of thirty years, or after he had reached the age of fifty, or that no person having gray hair, or who had not the use of all his limbs, should be entitled to vote, I do not see how it could be held to be a violation of any right derived or held under the constitution of the United States. We might say that such regulations were unjust, tyrannical, unfit for the regulation of an intelligent state; but, if rights of a citizen are thereby violated, they are of that fundamental class, derived from his position as a citizen of the state, and not those limited rights belonging to him as a citizen of the United States; and such was the decision in *Corfield* v. *Coryell*.

2   The United States rights appertaining to this subject are those, first, under article 1, § 2, subd. 1, of the United States constitution, which provides, that electors of representatives in congress shall have the qualifications requisite for electors of the most numerous branch of the state legislature; and second, under the fifteenth amendment, which provides, that "the right of citizens of the United States to vote shall not be denied or **abridged** by the United States, or by any state, on account of race, color, or previous condition of **servitude**." If the legislature of the state of New York should require a higher qualification in a voter for a representative in congress than is required for a voter for a member of the house of assembly of the state, this would, I conceive, be a violation of a right belonging to a person as a citizen of the

NOTES

United States. That right is in relation to a federal subject or interest, and is guaranteed by the federal constitution. The inability of a state to abridge the right of voting on account of race, color, or previous condition of servitude, arises from a federal guaranty. Its violation would be the denial of a federal right—that is, a right belonging to the **claimant** as a citizen of the United States. This right, however, exists by virtue of the fifteenth amendment. If the fifteenth amendment had contained the word "sex," the argument of the defendant would have been potent. She would have said, that an attempt by a state to deny the right to vote because one is of a particular sex is expressly prohibited by that amendment. The amendment, however, does not contain that word. It is limited to race, color, or previous condition of servitude. The legislature of the state of New York has seen fit to say, that the franchise of **voting** shall be limited to the male sex. In saying this, there is, in my judgment, no violation of the letter, or of the spirit, of the fourteenth or of the fifteenth amendment.

3   This view is assumed in the second section of the fourteenth amendment, which enacts, that, if the right to vote for federal officers is denied by any state to any of the male inhabitants of such state, except for crime, the basis of representation of such state shall be reduced in a proportion specified. Not only does this section assume that the right of male inhabitants to vote was the especial object of its protection, but it assumes and admits the right of a state, notwithstanding the existence of that clause under which the defendant claims to the contrary, to deny to classes or portions of the male inhabitants the right to vote which is allowed to other male inhabitants. The regulation of the suffrage is thereby conceded to the states as a state's right.

4   The case of *Bradwell* v. *State* decided at the recent term of the supreme court, sustains both of the positions above put forth, viz., first, that the rights referred to in the fourteenth amendment are those belonging to a person as a citizen of the United States and not as a citizen of a state; and second, that a right of the character here involved is not one connected with citizenship of the United States. Mrs. Bradwell made application to be admitted to practice as an attorney and counsellor at law in the courts of Illinois. Her application was denied, and, upon a writ of error, it was held by the supreme court, that, to give jurisdiction under the fourteenth amendment, the claim must be of a right pertaining to citizenship of the United States, and that the claim made by her did not come within that class of cases. Justices Bradley, Swayne, and Field held that a woman was not entitled to a license to practice law. It does not appear that the other judges passed upon that question. The fourteenth amendment gives no right to a woman to vote, and the voting by Miss Anthony was in violation of law.

5   If she believed she had a right to vote, and voted in reliance upon that belief, does that relieve her from the penalty? It is argued, that the knowledge

referred to in the act relates to her knowledge of the illegality of the act, and not to the act of voting; for, it is said, that she must know that she voted. Two principles apply here: First, ignorance of the law excuses no one; second, every person is presumed to understand and to intend the necessary effects of his own acts. Miss Anthony knew that she was a woman, and that the constitution of this state prohibits her from voting. She intended to violate that provision—intended to test it, perhaps, but, certainly, intended to violate it. The necessary effect of her act was to violate it, and this she is presumed to have intended. There was no ignorance of any fact, but, all the facts being known, she undertook to settle a principle in her own person. She takes the risk, and she can not escape the consequences. It is said, and authorities are cited to sustain the position, that there can be no crime unless there is a **culpable** intent, and that, to render one criminally responsible a vicious will must be present. A. commits a trespass on the land of B., and B., thinking and believing that he has a right to shoot an intruder upon his premises, kills A. on the spot. Does B.'s misapprehension of his rights justify his act? Would a judge be justified in charging the jury, that, if satisfied that B. supposed he had a right to shoot A., he was justified, and they should find a verdict of not guilty? No judge would make such a charge. To constitute a crime, it is true that there must be a criminal intent, but it is equally true that knowledge of the facts of the case is always held to supply this intent. An intentional killing bears with it evidence of malice in law. Whoever, without justifiable cause, intentionally kills his neighbor, is guilty of a crime. The principle is the same in the case before us, and in all criminal cases. The precise question now before me has been several times decided, viz., that one illegally voting was bound and was assumed to know the law, and that a belief that he had a right to vote gave no defense, if there was no mistake of fact. [Here Hunt cited five cases from courts in various states.] No system of criminal jurisprudence can be sustained upon any other principle. Assuming that Miss Anthony believed she had a right to vote, that fact constitutes no defense, if, in truth, she had not the right. She voluntarily gave a vote that was illegal, and thus is subject to the penalty of the law.

Please note that excerpts and passages in the StudySync® library and this workbook are intended as touchstones to generate interest in an author's work. The excerpts and passages do not substitute for the reading of entire texts, and StudySync® strongly recommends that students seek out and purchase the whole literary or informational work in order to experience it as the author intended. Links to online resellers are available in our digital library. In addition, complete works may be ordered through an authorized reseller by filling out and returning to StudySync® the order form enclosed in this workbook.

Reading & Writing
Companion

291

THINK QUESTIONS

1. Cite details from the text to show that the judge feels voting is a right or privilege that falls under state, not federal, government authority.

2. Explain why the judge feels the Fifteenth Amendment does not give Susan B. Anthony the right to vote. Cite evidence from the text in your explanation.

3. Write two or three sentences to explain why the judge concludes that the accused "is subject to the penalty of the law." Support your answer with textual evidence.

4. Use context clues to determine the meaning of the word **abridged** as it is used in the second paragraph of the ruling. Write the meaning you determine and explain how you arrived at it. Then check your preliminary determination in a dictionary.

5. Use context clues to determine the meaning of the word **franchise** as it is used in the second paragraph of the ruling. Write the meaning you determine, and explain how you arrived at it. Then check your preliminary determination in a dictionary.

CLOSE READ

Reread Justice Ward Hunt's ruling. As you reread, complete the Focus Questions below. Then use your answers and annotations from the questions to help you complete the Writing Prompt.

FOCUS QUESTIONS

1. Highlight the claim the judge makes in the first paragraph and the facts and examples he uses to support the claim. How does he attempt to strengthen the claim with the hypothetical example in the fifth sentence of the paragraph? Does the example actually strengthen the claim? Reread the paragraph to help you explain your answer.

2. In the second paragraph, highlight and annotate the judge's point about the wording in the Fifteenth Amendment. Explain the logic he uses to make his point about the significance of the wording that the Fifteenth Amendment does— and does not— contain.

3. In the third paragraph, how does the judge's observation about the Fourteenth Amendment strengthen his argument? Highlight and annotate the main points he makes about the content of the Fourteenth Amendment.

4. What kind of evidence is the case of *Bradwell* v. *State*, which the judge cites in the fourth paragraph? Make annotations describing the evidence and what it shows. Then explain how the judge's summary of the case helps lead to his claim in the last sentence of the paragraph.

5. In the final paragraph, highlight the legal term "criminal intent" and make annotations clarifying the meaning of the term from the context of the judge's explanation. How is the term logically connected to earlier details in the paragraph and to the judge's ruling that concludes the paragraph? Read the paragraph more than once to understand the connections.

6. In the legal case cited in the next-to-last paragraph, highlight details that suggest the dream Mrs. Bradwell was pursuing. How does Mrs. Bradwell's dream relate to Susan B. Anthony's dream? What do the legal rulings in both cases show about the women's dreams and whether they were worth pursuing?

WRITING PROMPT

When she voted in the presidential election of 1872, Susan B. Anthony insisted that, as a U.S. citizen, she had the right to do so. How effective is Justice Ward Hunt in refuting her claim? What claims of his own does he make, and what logical reasons and evidence does he use to support them? Use your understanding of arguments and claims to identify and evaluate the case Justice Hunt makes with his ruling. Support your writing with evidence from the text.

WE CHOOSE TO GO TO THE MOON

NON-FICTION

John F. Kennedy

1961

INTRODUCTION

After the Soviet Union's successful launch of its space satellite *Sputnik* in October 1957, the United States started what became known as the "Space Race," quickly forming the National Aeronautics and Space Administration (NASA) and working to launch its own satellites. Within five years, both the U.S. and U.S.S.R. had launched manned spacecraft. The Soviets initially soared ahead, putting the first man in space and successfully penetrating the moon's atmosphere. Landing a man on the moon was the most coveted prize of all, however, and President John F. Kennedy was determined to accomplish that goal first for America. At Houston's Rice University, in September 1962, he spoke of this quest to an audience of 35,000. His impassioned speech ignited the country, inspiring Americans everywhere to embrace the challenge of putting a man on the moon.

"The greater our knowledge increases, the greater our ignorance unfolds."

 FIRST READ

 NOTES

1   We meet at a college noted for knowledge, in a city noted for progress, in a state noted for strength, and we stand in need of all three, for we meet in an hour of change and challenge, in a decade of hope and fear, in an age of both knowledge and ignorance. The greater our knowledge increases, the greater our ignorance unfolds.

2   Despite the striking fact that most of the scientists that the world has ever known are alive and working today, despite the fact that this Nation's own scientific manpower is doubling every 12 years in a rate of growth more than three times that of our population as a whole, despite that, the vast stretches of the unknown and the unanswered and the unfinished still far outstrip our collective comprehension. . . .

3   Surely the opening **vistas** of space promise high costs and hardships, as well as high reward. So it is not surprising that some would have us stay where we are a little longer to rest, to wait. But those who waited and rested and wished to look behind them did not build this city of Houston, this state of Texas, this country of the United States. This country was conquered by those who moved forward—and so will space.

4   . . .[M]an, in his quest for knowledge and progress, is determined and cannot be deterred. The exploration of space will go ahead, whether we join in it or not, and it is one of the great adventures of all time, and no nation which expects to be the leader of other nations can expect to stay behind in this race for space.

5   Those who came before us made certain that this country rode the first waves of the industrial revolution, the first waves of modern invention, and the first wave of nuclear power, and this generation does not intend to **founder** in the backwash of the coming age of space. We mean to be a part of it—we mean

NOTES

to lead it. For the eyes of the world now look into space, to the moon and to the planets beyond, and we have vowed that we shall not see it governed by a hostile flag of conquest, but by a banner of freedom and peace. We have vowed that we shall not see space filled with weapons of mass destruction, but with instruments of knowledge and understanding.

6   Yet the vows of this Nation can only be fulfilled if we in this Nation are first, and, therefore, we intend to be first. In short, our leadership in science and industry, our hopes for peace and security, our obligations to ourselves as well as others, all require us to make this effort, to solve these mysteries, to solve them for the good of all men, and to become the world's leading space-faring nation.

7   We set sail on this new sea because there is new knowledge to be gained, and new rights to be won, and they must be won and used for the progress of all people. For space science, like nuclear science and all technology, has no conscience of its own. Whether it will become a force for good or ill depends on man, and only if the United States occupies a position of pre-eminence can we help decide whether this new ocean will be a sea of peace or a new terrifying theater of war. . . .

8   There is no strife, no prejudice, no national conflict in outer space as yet. Its hazards are hostile to us all. Its conquest deserves the best of all mankind, and its opportunity for peaceful cooperation many never come again. But why, some say, the moon? Why choose this as our goal? And they may well ask why climb the highest mountain? Why, 35 years ago, fly the Atlantic? Why does Rice play Texas?

9   We choose to go to the moon. We choose to go to the moon in this decade and do the other things, not because they are easy, but because they are hard, because that goal will serve to organize and measure the best of our energies and skills, because that challenge is one that we are willing to accept, one we are unwilling to postpone, and one which we intend to win, and the others, too.

10 It is for these reasons that I regard the decision last year to shift our efforts in space from low to high gear as among the most important decisions that will be made during my incumbency in the office of the Presidency. . . .

11 Within these last 19 months at least 45 satellites have circled the earth. Some 40 of them were "made in the United States of America" and they were far more **sophisticated** and supplied far more knowledge to the people of the world than those of the Soviet Union. . . .

12 We have had our failures, but so have others, even if they do not admit them. And they may be less public.

Copyright © BookheadEd Learning, LLC

13   To be sure, we are behind, and will be behind for some time in manned flight. But we do not intend to stay behind, and in this decade, we shall make up and move ahead.

14   The growth of our science and education will be enriched by new knowledge of our universe and environment, by new techniques of learning and mapping and observation, by new tools and computers for industry, medicine, the home as well as the school. Technical institutions, such as Rice, will reap the harvest of these gains.

15   And finally, the space effort itself, while still in its infancy, has already created a great number of new companies, and tens of thousands of new jobs. . . .

16   To be sure, all this costs us all a good deal of money. This year's space budget is three times what it was in January 1961, and it is greater than the space budget of the previous eight years combined. . . .

17   But if I were to say, my fellow citizens, that we shall send to the moon, 240,000 miles away from the control station in Houston, a giant rocket more than 300 feet tall, the length of this football field, made of new metal alloys, some of which have not yet been invented, capable of standing heat and stresses several times more than have ever been experienced, fitted together with a precision better than the finest watch, carrying all the equipment needed for propulsion, **guidance**, control, communications, food and survival, on an untried mission, to an unknown celestial body, and then return it safely to earth, re-entering the atmosphere at speeds of over 25,000 miles per hour, causing heat about half that of the temperature of the sun—almost as hot as it is here today—and do all this, and do it right, and do it first before this decade is out—then we must be bold. . . .

18   Many years ago the great British explorer George Mallory, who was to die on Mount Everest, was asked why did he want to climb it. He said, "Because it is there."

19   Well, space is there, and we're going to climb it, and the moon and the planets are there, and new hopes for knowledge and peace are there. And, therefore, as we set sail we ask God's blessing on the most hazardous and dangerous and greatest adventure on which man has ever **embarked**.

THINK QUESTIONS

1. Refer to one or more details from the speech to make an inference about the objections that Kennedy sees to space travel.

2. Use details from the text to write two or three sentences explaining why Kennedy believes it is vital that the United States should be the leader in space travel.

3. Write two or three sentences exploring Kennedy's feelings about the Soviet Union. Support your answer with textual evidence.

4. Use context to determine the meaning of the word **founder** as it is used in "We Choose to Go to the Moon." From paragraph 5, what meaning would you assign to "founder," and how would its use in the paragraph help you confirm the meaning?

5. Use context clues to determine the meaning of the word **sophisticated** as it is used in "We Choose to Go to the Moon." Write your definition of "sophisticated" and state the clue(s) from the text you used to determine your answer.

CLOSE READ

Reread the speech "We Choose to Go to the Moon." As you reread, complete the Focus Questions below. Then use your answers and annotations from the questions to help you complete the Writing Prompt.

FOCUS QUESTIONS

1. Summarize the first four paragraphs of the speech. How does the speaker make his point of view about space exploration clear, and what rhetorical devices does he use to advance that point of view? Highlight evidence from the text and make annotations to explain your choices.

2. What contrast does Kennedy set up between the United States and the Soviet Union in paragraph 5, and how does he develop that contrast? Highlight words and phrases in this section that support your response, and make annotations to explain how this rhetoric works to persuade people of this point of view.

3. Paragraph 6 focuses on the author's purpose. What rhetorical strategies is he using in this section? Highlight the words and phrases that make the author's purpose clear, and note any examples of persuasive rhetoric.

4. In paragraph 7, highlight examples of figurative language and appeals to emotion and shared values the speaker uses to support his views, and make annotations exploring why these rhetorical devices are (or are not) effective.

5. Summarize the reasons why Kennedy feels that space exploration is a dream worth pursuing. Make annotations noting inferences about the text and its deeper meaning. Highlight evidence from the text to support your explanation.

WRITING PROMPT

Examine the reasons President Kennedy lists for wanting to send Americans to the moon by the end of the 1960s, and consider his point of view. Based on his speech, what do you think motivates Kennedy's point of view? What rhetorical strategies does he use most to advance his way of thinking? Do you find his arguments and rhetoric persuasive? Explain in a response of 300 words, using evidence from the text to support your answer.

Please note that excerpts and passages in the StudySync® library and this workbook are intended as touchstones to generate interest in an author's work. The excerpts and passages do not substitute for the reading of entire texts, and StudySync® strongly recommends that students seek out and purchase the whole literary or informational work in order to experience it as the author intended. Links to online resellers are available in our digital library. In addition, complete works may be ordered through an authorized reseller by filling out and returning to StudySync® the order form enclosed in this workbook.

Reading & Writing
Companion

299

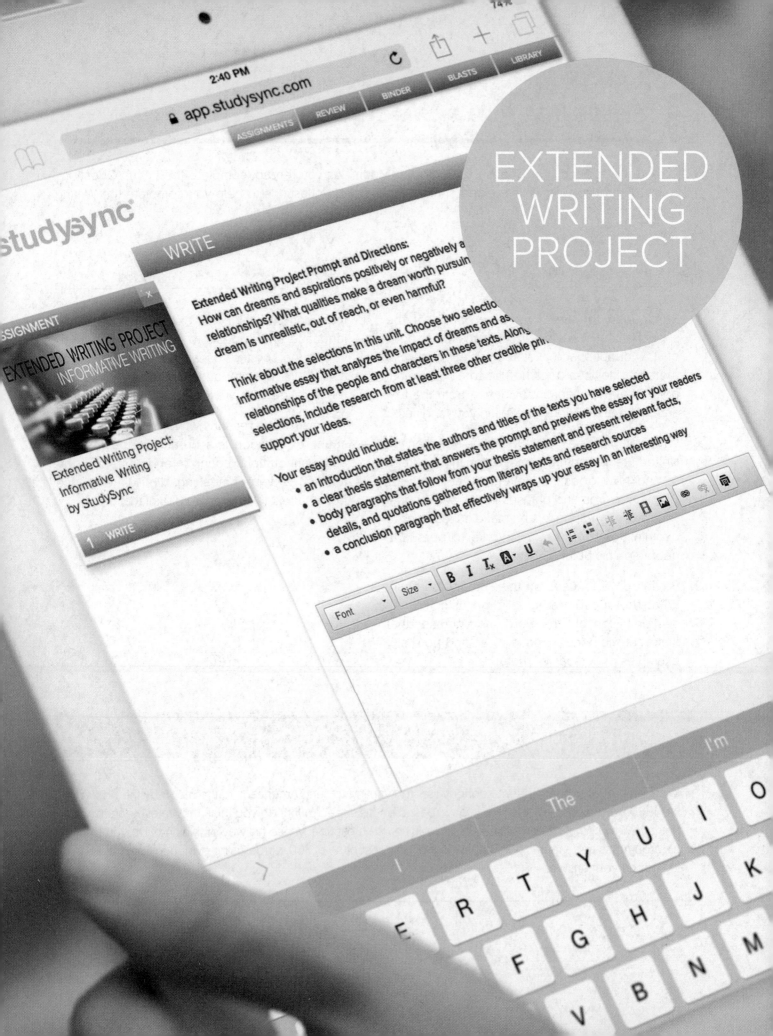

2:40 PM

🔒 app.studysync.com

ASSIGNMENTS   REVIEW   BINDER   BLASTS   LIBRARY

studysync®

WRITE

EXTENDED WRITING PROJECT
INFORMATIVE WRITING

ASSIGNMENT

Extended Writing Project:
Informative Writing
by StudySync

1   WRITE

Extended Writing Project Prompt and Directions:
How can dreams and aspirations positively or negatively a...
relationships? What qualities make a dream worth pursuin...
dream is unrealistic, out of reach, or even harmful?

Think about the selections in this unit. Choose two selectio...
Informative essay that analyzes the impact of dreams and as...
relationships of the people and characters in these texts. Alon...
selections, include research from at least three other credible pri...
support your ideas.

Your essay should include:
• an introduction that states the authors and titles of the texts you have selected
• a clear thesis statement that answers the prompt and previews the essay for your readers
• body paragraphs that follow from your thesis statement and present relevant facts,
  details, and quotations gathered from literary texts and research sources
• a conclusion paragraph that effectively wraps up your essay in an interesting way

Font   Size   B I T_x A▾ U ↑

EXTENDED
WRITING
PROJECT

INFORMATIVE/ EXPLANATORY WRITING

WRITING PROMPT

How can dreams and aspirations positively or negatively affect people's lives and relationships? What qualities make a dream worth pursuing? How do people decide when a dream is unrealistic, out of reach, or even harmful?

Your essay should include:

- an introduction with a clear thesis statement
- body paragraphs with relevant evidence and thorough analysis to support your thesis
- a conclusion paragraph that effectively wraps up your essay

Informative/explanatory writing explains, compares, describes, and informs. The purpose of informative writing is to examine and convey complex information to the reader. Examples of informative writing include scientific studies, reports, research papers, newspaper articles, and non-fiction texts.

Strong informative writing introduces a main idea, often in the form of a thesis statement, and develops that main idea with well-chosen and relevant facts, details, quotations, or other examples. The writing stays focused on the main idea by using transition words to help create flow and make connections among complex ideas and concepts. Though informative writing draws a conclusion based on the facts and information presented, the writing is unbiased, meaning that the writer does not state his/her own opinion.

In some cases, it is important to conduct outside research when writing an informative/explanatory essay. This research can be used to supply necessary historical or factual context for understanding a fictional text. Research may

Please note that excerpts and passages in the StudySync® library and this workbook are intended as touchstones to generate interest in an author's work. The excerpts and passages do not substitute for the reading of entire texts, and StudySync® strongly recommends that students seek out and purchase the whole literary or informational work in order to experience it as the author intended. Links to online resellers are available in our digital library. In addition, complete works may be ordered through an authorized reseller by filling out and returning to StudySync® the order form enclosed in this workbook.

Reading & Writing Companion **301**

also be necessary to provide sufficient facts, definitions, and evidence to fully explain the ideas in the essay to the reader.

The features of informative/explanatory writing include:

- a clear and logical organizational structure
- an introduction with a clear thesis statement
- supporting details, including facts, definitions, quotations, and examples drawn from reliable sources
- precise language and domain-specific (specialized) vocabulary
- a formal and objective tone
- citations of sources
- a concluding statement

During this extended writing project, you will be given more instructions and have opportunities to practice each of the elements of informative writing as you develop your own essay.

 STUDENT MODEL

Before you get started on your own informative/explanatory essay, begin by reading this essay that one student wrote in response to the writing prompt. As you read this student model, highlight and annotate the features of informative writing that the student included in her essay. Note that the student model includes outside research, parenthetical citations, and a works cited page. Parenthetical citations are one method for citing sources, but you will also learn about other methods later in this extended writing project.

The Power of Dreams

Every one of us has felt hopeless at one time or another. But having a dream—something to work toward and hope for—can be the ray of hope shining brightly at the end of a long tunnel of despair. The characters in Of Mice and Men and The Joy Luck Club all had dreams. Lenny and George dreamed of owning their own ranch. Jing-Mei Woo and her mother Suyuan Woo worked to turn Jing-Mei into a child prodigy. These dreams helped them through difficult times and rough transitions. But dreams can also come at a cost, pushing a person too hard and too fast, causing her to give up entirely or lose the people closest to her. Lenny and George in Of Mice and Men and Jing-Mei and Suyuan Woo in The Joy Luck Club pursue dreams that both connect them to and drive them away from the most important people in their lives.

Of Mice and Men, by John Steinbeck, is set in California during the Great Depression. The Great Depression lasted a long ten years, from 1929 through 1939. During this time, up to 15 million Americans were unemployed. Banks across the nation were failing, thanks to bank runs when customers demanded their money back—in cash ("The Great Depression"). Furthermore, the Great Plains states suffered through the Dust Bowl. The Dust Bowl was the result of a seven-year drought and the replacement of natural grasslands with fields of crops. Farmers there watched their land blow away in great dust storms. Very little grew, and many farms went into debt and bankruptcy. Many of the families that lost their farms to the Dust Bowl moved to California, where they hoped to find work. Just like Lenny and George, they were migrant farmers, moving from farm to farm and making barely enough to survive (Fanslow). This period in American history is particularly hopeless and joyless. Lenny and George, living in this bleak time, needed a dream to keep themselves going. Regardless of the dream's specifics, just having a dream helped Lenny and George keep putting one foot in front of the other—the dream was worth pursuing because it kept them alive and hopeful.

Because *Of Mice and Men* is set during the Great Depression, it is a book first and foremost about making plans and having dreams. The title itself refers to a line of poetry by Robert Burns: "The best laid schemes of mice and men often go awry" (SyncTV). The book begins with Lenny and George discussing their "scheme" or dream. Lenny begs George to "[t]ell about how it's gonna be" and George describes their shared vision of their future: "O.K. Someday—we're gonna get the jack together and we're gonna have a little house and a couple of acres an' a cow and some pigs and—" And Lenny knows the story by heart, so he finishes the sentence: *"An' live off the fatta the lan'* . . . An' have *rabbits"* (Steinbeck 13). The tone is wistful and romantic; George and Lenny have co-created a beautiful dream of their future, and each can recite what it will be because they have had this conversation so many times. By constantly discussing their shared dream, George and Lenny give themselves a future to look forward to and work toward when their life in the present is incredibly difficult. It's likely that George knows the dream is unrealistic, as he interrupts the retelling of it to discuss how to keep Lenny out of trouble. He coaches Lenny to not "say a word" so he 'won't get in no trouble" (Steinbeck 5). George knows that keeping Lenny around may ultimately stop George from achieving the dream, but he continues to protect Lenny and hold onto the dream. He has weighed the pros and cons and decided

Please note that excerpts and passages in the StudySync® library and this workbook are intended as touchstones to generate interest in an author's work. The excerpts and passages do not substitute for the reading of entire texts, and StudySync® strongly recommends that students seek out and purchase the whole literary or informational work in order to experience it as the author intended. Links to online resellers are available in our digital library. In addition, complete works may be ordered through an authorized reseller by filling out and returning to StudySync® the order form enclosed in this workbook.

Reading & Writing Companion   **303**

holding onto the dream with Lenny is more valuable than taking his chances alone. The dream is as much about Lenny and George being together as it is about escaping the Great Depression and having a place to call their own. At the end of the day, the dream of owning their own ranch gives Lenny and George a reason to keep going when times are rough and strengthens their friendship in a time that would try even the closest of relationships.

In *The Joy Luck Club*, Suyuan Woo came to America after "losing everything in China," believing "you could be anything you wanted to be in America" *(The Joy Luck Club 132)*. She believed, "You could become rich. You could become instantly famous" *(The Joy Luck Club 132)*. Amy Tan's own mother came to America also after great hardship. Abused by a cruel husband, the young mother of three began a relationship with Tan's father and was thrown in jail for adultery. Now living in America, Tan's father

> prayed that his sweetheart be freed, and sure enough, she was released from prison. Then she cabled my father and asked whether he wanted her to come to America. Shanghai would soon be taken over by the Communists and his answer had to be now or never *(The Opposite of Fate 12–13)*.

This story is not directly translated into the fiction of *The Joy Luck Club*, nor are any of Tan's life experiences. But, she notes, "my life is, I believe, excellent fodder for fiction" *(The Opposite of Fate 33)*. She picks and chooses bits of her life to create the lives of her characters. Thus, the characters in *The Joy Luck Club* struggle with immigration and the hope embedded in moving one's life halfway across the world, just as her mother did. The dream of the immigrant is the dream of a better life. The dream is so powerful that it is worth leaving behind everything they know. And it is worth pursuing because what they have to lose doesn't compare to what they have to gain; what they can hope for in their home country is a sliver of what they could dream of in America.

In *The Joy Luck Club*, Suyuan dreamed that Jing-Mei could become a child prodigy like Shirley Temple. Though not stated directly, the desire behind the dream of Jing-Mei becoming a child prodigy is the dream of success in America. If Jing-Mei were a child prodigy, then the family would have enough money and fame to be respected and successful—her mother would never have to lose everything again. This dream echoes Tan's own experiences of learning—and giving up piano: "What you rather do: play piano and become famous, or play outside and become nobody?" *(The Opposite of Fate 18)*. Initially, Jing-Mei, and presumably Tan, was young enough that she also believed in this dream of fame and success. Jing-Mei said, "in the beginning I was just as excited as my mother, maybe even more so. I pictured this prodigy part of me as many different images, and tried each one on for size. I was a dainty ballerina . . . I was like the Christ child . . . I was Cinderella . . ." *(The Joy Luck Club 133)*. So, mother and daughter worked together tirelessly to achieve this shared dream. Jing-Mei got a makeover from "the beauty training school in the Mission District" and every night Suyuan would drill her with "tests" to make her smart like the other remarkable children she read about in the magazines *(The Joy Luck Club 133–134)*. But as much as the dream of becoming a child prodigy brought mother and daughter together in a shared project, eventually it worked just as hard to drive them apart. While Suyuan still believed Jing-Mei could become a prodigy, Jing-Mei became more and more disheartened as she realized the dream was unrealistic. "[S]omething inside me began to die," she said, because she never passed her mother's tests. She "performed listlessly" on purpose on those tests and watched to see when her mother would finally give up *(The Joy Luck Club 134–135)*. "I got so bored that I started counting the bellows of the foghorns . . . seeing if my mother would give up on me before eight bellows," she said *(The Joy Luck Club 135)*. Eventually, Suyuan gives up on Jing-Mei after only one or two bellows: the dream was finally dying for both of them. In the end, Suyuan's dream of Jing-Mei becoming a child prodigy does more to drive them apart than it did to bring them together.

Whether they drive people apart—as in *The Joy Luck Club*—or bring them together—as in *Of Mice and Men*—dreams are part of being human. Having something to look forward to and work towards gives people a purpose in life. Without that purpose, how are we to keep putting one foot in front of the other? Lenny and George in *Of Mice and Men* hold onto their dream to keep them hopeful in a time without hope. Even Jing-Mei and Suyuan in *The Joy Luck Club*, find closeness and commonality thanks to a shared dream. That dream ultimately drives them apart, but it also shows that dreams can bring people together. No matter the dream, no matter the situation, people's dreams affect their relationships, for good and for ill.

THINK QUESTIONS

1. What is the central idea of this essay?

2. How does the text in "The Power of Dreams" compare and contrast *Of Mice and Men* and *The Joy Luck Club?*

3. What are the writer's thoughts about the dream Jing-Mei and Suyuan share? What evidence do they use to explain their thoughts?

4. Thinking about the writing prompt, which selections or other resources would you like to use to create your own informative essay? What types of resources do you think will help you to construct your thesis?

5. Based on what you have read, listened to, or researched, how would you answer the question: *How can dreams and aspirations positively or negatively affect people's lives and relationships? What are some ways dreams can be helpful? How can they be damaging?*

NOTES

PREWRITE

WRITING PROMPT

How can dreams and aspirations positively or negatively affect people's lives and relationships? What qualities make a dream worth pursuing? How do people decide when a dream is unrealistic, out of reach, or even harmful?

Your essay should include:

- an introduction with a clear thesis statement
- body paragraphs with relevant evidence and thorough analysis to support your thesis
- a conclusion paragraph that effectively wraps up your essay

In addition to studying techniques authors use to convey information, you have been reading and learning about stories that feature dreams and deal with how those dreams affect people and their relationships. Now you will use those informational writing techniques to compose your own informative essay. During this prewriting stage, you may choose to record your thoughts and ideas using such strategies as free writing, mind mapping, and list making.

Since your informative essay will analyze how dreams affect people's lives and relationships, you'll want to think about the specific dreams of the people and characters you've read about and how those dreams affected their lives and relationships. Think back to what you read about Lenny and George in *Of Mice and Men:* What dream did Lenny and George share? Why did they consider this dream worth pursuing? Did Lenny and George ever consider the dream unrealistic or harmful? How did their shared dream affect their relationship?

Please note that excerpts and passages in the StudySync® library and this workbook are intended as touchstones to generate interest in an author's work. The excerpts and passages do not substitute for the reading of entire texts, and StudySync® strongly recommends that students seek out and purchase the whole literary or informational work in order to experience it as the author intended. Links to online resellers are available in our digital library. In addition, complete works may be ordered through an authorized reseller by filling out and returning to StudySync® the order form enclosed in this workbook.

Reading & Writing Companion   **307**

Make a list of the answers to these questions for *Of Mice and Men*. Then adapt and answer the questions for at least one other text you've read in this unit. Use this model to help you get started with your own prewriting:

Text: *Of Mice and Men* by John Steinbeck

Dream: Lenny and George dream about having their own ranch, where they live "off the fatta the lan'."

Positive aspects of the dream: It gives them something to hope for in a hopeless time.

Negative aspects of the dream: George won't leave Lenny, who is a danger to both of them. Lenny's habit of getting into trouble makes it even less likely they will achieve their dream.

Effects on their relationship: The dream strengthens George and Lenny's friendship, confirming their care for each other and George's desire to protect Lenny from the wider world.

After you have brainstormed answers to the preceding questions for at least two texts, look for patterns to emerge. Do the dreams have anything in common? Do the characters or people? What ideas are repeated throughout? Looking for these patterns may help you solidify the ideas you want to discuss in your essay. Use the "Prewriting: Dreams and Their Impacts Graphic Organizer" to compare and contrast the dreams. Add an extra circle to the Venn Diagram if you have brainstormed three texts.

After you have completed your diagramming, consider your answers and ideas as you work through the following Skills lessons to help you map out your essay.

SKILL:
RESEARCH AND
NOTE-TAKING

 DEFINE

If you have completed research presentations in previous units or this unit, you have already been learning about research. **Research** is the process of generating questions and gathering answers to those questions from a variety of sources, both electronic and print. During this process, you may see that you are finding too much information and need to limit the scope of your research project by narrowing the questions. Or you may find that your questions are too narrow, leaving you without many sources to consult, and you have to broaden the questions to provide a full view of your topic. As you begin researching, the questions will guide you to sources and those sources will, in turn, lead you to refine or redirect your questions.

During the research process, it is important to consult multiple sources. **Sources** are the documents and information that an author uses to research his or her writing. Some sources are **primary sources.** A primary source is a first-hand account of thoughts or events by the individual who experienced them. Other sources are **secondary sources.** A secondary source analyzes and interprets primary sources. It isn't enough to find sources, though; you must confirm that they are **authoritative,** or reliable on the subject, and relevant to the task, purpose, and audience.

Note-taking is just what it sounds like: writing down the information you collect from your sources that answers your research question(s). It also includes writing down details about the sources themselves, including the authors, titles, and publishers, as well as other details.

••• IDENTIFICATION AND APPLICATION

- The first step in researching is generating one or more research questions. These questions focus research by giving writers something specific to search for.

- As writers research, they continue to refine their research questions.

NOTES

> If writers find too much information in too many places, they narrow their search by writing more specific research questions or by eliminating some questions entirely.
> If writers don't find enough information, they broaden their search by writing more general research questions or adding related questions to their search.
> Writers use electronic databases to conduct research using advanced search terms. To use advanced search terms, they combine more than one search term in a single search. For example, instead of using a general search term such as "Great Depression," they use an advanced search term such as "Great Depression AND migrant farmers" or "Great Depression AND California."

- As writers research, they consult a variety of sources. Sources can be primary or secondary. Sources also come in a variety of media: print sources, like books and magazines; electronic resources, like internet articles or podcasts; audio-visual sources, such as photographs and films; and living sources, such as anyone you may interview yourself.

- Primary sources are first-hand accounts, artifacts, or other original materials. Examples of primary sources include:
  > letters or other correspondence
  > photographs
  > official documents
  > diaries or journals
  > autobiographies or memoirs
  > eyewitness accounts and interviews
  > audio recordings and radio broadcasts
  > works of art
  > literature, including novels, short stories, poems, and dramas.
  > artifacts, or objects

- Secondary sources are usually text. Secondary sources are the written interpretation and analysis of primary source materials. Some examples of secondary sources include:
  > encyclopedia articles
  > textbooks
  > commentary or criticisms
  > histories
  > documentary films
  > news analyses

- Whether sources are primary or secondary, they must be **authoritative,** which means they are credible and accurate. Writers of informative/

NOTES

explanatory texts look for sources from experts in the topic they are writing about.

> When researching online, they look for URLs that contain ".gov" (government agencies), ".edu" (colleges and universities), and ".org" (museums and other non-profit organizations).

> Writers also use respected print and online news and information sources.

- In addition, to determine whether sources are authoritative, writers assess whether the source is appropriate to the task they are engaged with. The source should answer the task, suit the purpose of the writing, and be appropriate for the intended audience.

- While researching, writers take many notes. They use the following strategies while taking notes:

> Keeping note cards: Writers use physical note cards or a computer program that mimics note cards. Writers use one note card for each idea, example, definition, fact, or quotation they find useful.

> Keeping notebooks: Writers may also use a notebook—physical or electronic—to keep track of their notes. Notes in a notebook should include the same information as those on note cards.

> Paraphrasing and quoting: It is important to paraphrase, or use your own words, as you take notes while researching. If writers do write down a direct quotation while taking notes, they put quotation marks around the text so they will cite it correctly later. Writers also avoid plagiarizing by carefully noting the name of the source along with the relevant idea or quotation.

> Recording sources: When researching, writers must keep careful track of the sources they consult. If using note cards, they create one note card with the details for each source they intend to use. If using a notebook, they may keep a running log of sources. This information is crucial later in the research process, when creating citations and works cited pages. When noting sources, be sure to write down:

- author name

- title of article

- title of entire work

- relevant page numbers

- publisher

- city of publication

- date of publication

- medium (print, web, etc.)

- date of access (if electronic)

MODEL

The writer of the student model essay "The Power of Dreams" supported her analysis of *Of Mice and Men* by researching the Great Depression. See her research note cards below:

Bibliography Card: **Source 1**		**Bibliography Card:** **Source 2**
Article: "The Great Depression" Website name: History.com Publication date: 2009 Publisher: A+E Networks Date Accessed: 14 October 2014 Medium: Web		Article: "The Migrant Experience" Author: Robin A. Fanslow Website name: American Memory: Voices from the Dust Bowl Publication date: 6 April 1998 Publisher: American Folklife Center, Library of Congress Date Accessed: 14 October 2014 Medium: Web
Great Depression, Background Source 1 lasted from 1929 to 1939		**Great Depression, Background** Source 1 Up to 15 million were unemployed
Great Depression, Background Source 1 Banks failed. Lots of bank runs when customers demanded their money back—in cash.		**Great Depression, Migrant Farmers** Source 2 Families who lost their farms moved to California to find work.

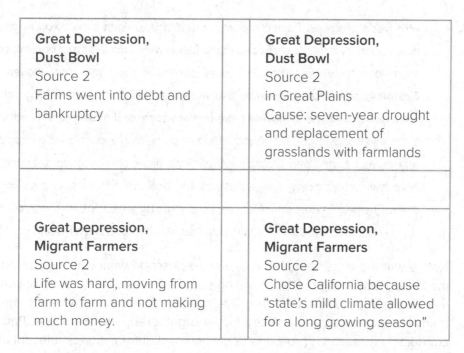

Great Depression, Dust Bowl Source 2 Farms went into debt and bankruptcy	Great Depression, Dust Bowl Source 2 in Great Plains Cause: seven-year drought and replacement of grasslands with farmlands
Great Depression, Migrant Farmers Source 2 Life was hard, moving from farm to farm and not making much money.	Great Depression, Migrant Farmers Source 2 Chose California because "state's mild climate allowed for a long growing season"

Notice there are two types of cards in her notes: bibliography cards and note cards. The bibliography cards include details about the sources themselves and give those sources numbers. By creating a bibliography card for each source and numbering her sources, the writer saves herself the effort of writing the source details on every note card she makes. By numbering her sources, she can refer to the bibliography card when writing her essay and works cited page.

Each note card has a subject at the top, the number of the relevant source, and one fact, idea, quotation, example or definition. The writer includes a subject at the top of each card and only includes one piece of information per note card to make organizing her research later easier. By using one note card per idea, she will be able to shuffle the ideas regardless of which source they came from.

Now, let's see how the writer used her research notes to write the first body paragraph of "The Power of Dreams":

Of Mice and Men, by John Steinbeck, is set in California during the Great Depression. The Great Depression lasted a long ten years, **from 1929 through 1939**. During this time, up to **15 million Americans were unemployed. Banks across the nation were failing, thanks to bank runs when customers demanded their money back—in cash** ("The Great Depression"). Furthermore, the **Great Plains states suffered through the Dust Bowl. The Dust Bowl was the result of a seven-year drought and the replacement of natural grasslands** with fields of crops. Farmers there watched their land blow away in great dust storms. Very little grew, and many **farms went into debt and bankruptcy**. Many of the families that lost their farms to the Dust Bowl **moved to California, where they hoped to find work**. Just like Lenny and George, they were migrant farmers, moving from farm to farm and making barely enough to survive (Fanslow). This period in American history is particularly hopeless and joyless. Lenny and George, living in this bleak time, needed a dream to keep themselves going. Regardless of the dream's specifics, just having a dream helped Lenny and George keep putting one foot in front of the other—the dream was worth pursuing because it kept them alive and hopeful.

Notice that the writer uses her research to describe what was happening in the United States in general, providing context for the specific story of Lenny and George in *Of Mice and Men*. The facts she found in her research are in bold. The writer didn't use every fact she gathered, and that's fine. Part of conducting a research project is deciding which information is relevant and important and which information should be left out of the essay. Notice also that the writer cited her sources by putting the name of the website or author in parentheses after explaining the facts. (We will look at creating MLA style citations and works cited pages later in the unit.)

SKILL:
THESIS
STATEMENT

DEFINE

In informative writing, the thesis statement expresses the writer's central idea about a topic. The thesis statement is usually in the introductory paragraph, often as its last sentence. It is the most important sentence in an informative/explanatory essay because it tells the reader what the writer will discuss. It also determines which details the writer will include in the body of the essay; if a detail or idea does not relate to the thesis statement, it does not belong in the essay. The writer supports the thesis statement by providing facts, evidence, examples, definitions, text quotations, and other supporting details in the body paragraphs that make up the bulk of the essay.

IDENTIFICATION AND APPLICATION

A thesis statement:

- presents the essay's topic
- responds to the informative/explanatory prompt
- makes a clear statement of the writer's central idea about the essay's topic
- previews what will appear in the body of the essay
- reflects the writer's understanding of the subject based on the sources the writer has researched
- appears in the introduction paragraph, often as its last sentence

The following is the introduction paragraph from the student model informative/explanatory essay "The Power of Dreams":

> Every one of us has felt hopeless at one time or another. But having a dream—something to work toward and hope for—can be the ray of hope shining brightly at the end of a long tunnel of despair. The characters in *Of*

Please note that excerpts and passages in the StudySync® library and this workbook are intended as touchstones to generate interest in an author's work. The excerpts and passages do not substitute for the reading of entire texts, and StudySync® strongly recommends that students seek out and purchase the whole literary or informational work in order to experience it as the author intended. Links to online resellers are available in our digital library. In addition, complete works may be ordered through an authorized reseller by filling out and returning to StudySync® the order form enclosed in this workbook.

Reading & Writing Companion   **315**

Mice and Men and *The Joy Luck Club* all had dreams. Lenny and George dreamed of owning their own ranch. Jing-Mei Woo and her mother Suyuan Woo worked to turn Jing-Mei into a child prodigy. These dreams helped them through difficult times and rough transitions. But dreams can also come at a cost, pushing a person too hard and too fast, causing her to give up entirely or lose the people closest to her. **Lenny and George in *Of Mice and Men* and Jing-Mei and Suyuan Woo in *The Joy Luck Club* pursue dreams that both connect them to and drive them away from the most important people in their lives.**

Notice the boldfaced thesis statement. This student's thesis statement presents the essay's topic, dreams and how they affect people's relationships, and it also answers the prompt. It makes a clear statement about her central idea, which is that dreams can connect us to or drive us apart from important people in our lives. It previews her supporting details, which will relate to the characters in *Of Mice and Men* and *The Joy Luck Club*. Finally, it is the last sentence in the introductory paragraph.

 PRACTICE

Write a thesis statement for your informative essay that states your central idea in relation to the essay prompt. When you are finished, trade with a partner and offer each other feedback. How clear was your partner's main point or idea? Is it obvious what this essay will focus on? Does it specifically address the prompt? Offer each other suggestions, and remember that they are most helpful when they are constructive.

SKILL:
ORGANIZE
INFORMATIVE
WRITING

DEFINE

The purpose of writing an informative/explanatory text is to explain a topic in detail and/or inform readers about the topic. To do this effectively, writers need to organize and present their ideas, facts, details, and other information in a logical sequence that's easy to understand.

Experienced authors choose an **organizational structure** suited to their topic and purpose before they begin to write. They often use an outline or another graphic organizer to visualize their organizational structure and to help them express their ideas effectively.

Writers of informative/explanatory texts can choose from many organizational structures, including **comparison-contrast, cause-effect, problem-solution, order of importance, chronological order, definition, and classification.**

IDENTIFICATION AND APPLICATION

- When selecting an organizational structure for an informative/explanatory essay, writers must consider their central idea. Then they need to determine the best way to present the evidence they will use to support that central idea. They might ask themselves the following questions:
  › What is the central idea I'd like to convey?
  › Is my central idea the cause of a series of effects? Or is it an effect with a number of causes?
  › How can I compare and contrast ideas or details in the text to further examine their significance?
  › Is there an order of importance to my evidence? Is some stronger and suited to being presented first? Or is all the evidence equally strong?
  › Can I elaborate on the evidence by asking a question or posing a problem and then offering answers or solutions?
  › Does presenting events in chronological order make sense?

Copyright © BookheadEd Learning, LLC

- Writers often use word choice to create connections between details and hint at the organizational structure being used:
  › Compare-contrast: *like, unlike, also, both, similarly, although, while, but, however*
  › Order of importance: *most important, least important, first, best, mainly*
  › Problem-solution: *problem, solution, why, how*
  › Cause-effect: *because, accordingly, as a result, effect, so, therefore*
  › Chronological order: *first, next, then, finally, last, initially, ultimately*

- Sometimes, within the overall structure, writers may find it necessary to organize individual paragraphs using other structures—a cause and effect paragraph within an essay that uses chronological order, for instance. This should not affect the overall organization.

Looking over the prewriting notes and the notes gathered in the student model during the research process, the writer of the student model essay decided to focus on two texts, *Of Mice and Men* and *The Joy Luck Club*, because they have both important similarities and differences. These similarities and differences suggest to her a compare-contrast organizational structure.

In her thesis statement in the introduction of the student model, the writer uses the signal word "both" to indicate that she will compare the two texts:

> Lenny and George in *Of Mice and Men* and Jing-Mei and Suyuan Woo in *The Joy Luck Club* pursue dreams that **both** connect them to and drive away the most important people in their lives.

Because the writer knew that she was comparing and contrasting the dreams in two texts, during prewriting she used a three-column chart to organize her ideas about the impact of dreams.

NOTES

	OF MICE AND MEN	THE JOY LUCK CLUB
How the dream brings the characters closer together:	Strengthens friendship by giving them something to look forward to; helps them fight the hopelessness of living in the Great Depression. Great Depression was a hopeless time because of unemployment. Migrant farmers lived unpleasant lives.	Work together to make Jing-Mei a prodigy by making over her appearance, building up her knowledge through quizzes. Tan's mother encouraged to play piano to become "famous," too.
How the dream drives the characters apart:	*Could* separate them if George decides living out the dream himself is worth more than keeping Lenny out of trouble.	Jing-Mei realizes becoming a prodigy is hopeless and stops trying so hard. Suyuan is disappointed in Jing-Mei and slowly gives up, too. They drift apart. Tan's mother was never happy, making their relationship difficult.

 PRACTICE

Using an *Organize Informative/Explanatory Writing* Three Column Chart like the one you have just studied, organize the information you gathered in the Prewrite stage of writing your essay.

SUPPORTING DETAILS

sync•skills
Writing

SKILL:
SUPPORTING
DETAILS

 DEFINE

Informative/explanatory essays state a central idea and then explain that idea in detail. The success of the essay's explanation depends on the quality of the **supporting details** the writer uses. Supporting details form the body of the essay and work together to develop and support the central idea. They include facts, extended definitions, concrete details, direct quotations from texts or other media, and any other information or example that elaborates the central idea.

To write a successful informative/explanatory essay, a writer must use relevant details that are sufficient to fully develop the topic. To be relevant, the details must be directly related to the central idea. If the detail does not develop or expand the central idea it is irrelevant and should be discarded. For supporting details to be sufficient, the writer must include enough details to fully explain the central idea. Outside research conducted for an informative/explanatory essay can be doubly helpful: it can provide relevant and sufficient supporting details and help the writer refine his or her central idea.

 IDENTIFICATION AND APPLICATION

Step 1:

Review the thesis statement you have already written. To identify relevant supporting details from your outside research and the texts you are analyzing, ask this question: What is my central idea about dreams and their effects on characters? The writer of the Student Model, for example, developed this thesis statement:

> Lenny and George in *Of Mice and Men* and Jing-Mei and Suyuan Woo in *The Joy Luck Club* pursue dreams that both connect them to and drive them away from the most important people in their lives.

Copyright © BookheadEd Learning, LLC

Step 2:

Ask what a reader needs to know about the topic in order to understand your central idea. This thesis presents the writer with two supporting examples that require explanation. Let's look at how the writer develops her first supporting example. What does the reader need to know to understand Lenny and George's dream and how it brings them together and/or drives them apart? These details, from the writer's *Organize Informative/Explanatory Writing* Three-Column Chart are relevant and sufficient:

- The **dream brings them together** by giving them something they each look forward to.
- The dream **could drive them apart** if Lenny can't stay out of trouble, in which case George might pursue the dream on his own.
- During the Great Depression, millions were unemployed and migrant farmers lived hard lives.

Why is the last detail about the Great Depression relevant? This detail is from the writer's outside research and requires a little extra explanation to make it relevant to the topic of dreams:

- Because the Great Depression was so difficult to live through, Lenny and George **needed a dream** to give them hope.

Note that the evidence gathered from the outside research helps the writer more fully explain the supporting details she collected from the literary text *Of Mice and Men*. In this way, outside research helps a writer obtain and integrate sufficient evidence. When conducting outside research, be aware of using only the evidence that helps you develop your central idea. In order to maintain the flow of your essay, use only the best evidence and weave it in with the discussion of your central idea.

Step 3:

Continue to examine your sources—literary texts and outside research sources—to look for concrete details, quotations, facts, extended definitions, and other examples that develop your thesis statement. These supporting details will strengthen the thesis statement. Writing an essay is a building process, and you have to evaluate each piece of evidence to be sure it supports the structure of the essay. To do this, ask yourself:

- Does this information help the reader understand the topic?
- Does this information support the central idea presented in my thesis statement?
- Is there stronger evidence that makes the same point?
- Have I provided enough evidence to fully develop my central idea?

In the following excerpt from "The Voice that Challenged a Nation," by Russell Freedman, Freedman's central idea is that Marian Anderson's goal in life was to pursue a career in singing.

> While **she dreamed of a singing career**, she knew she would have to support herself and help her family when she finished school, so she took the high school's secretarial course, studying bookkeeping, shorthand, and typing. But **her heart wasn't in those studies**, and after three unhappy years she was able to transfer to the newly established South Philadelphia High School for Girls, where she enrolled in an academic course, emphasizing music. Several years older than any of the other girls, she was one of the school's few black students. Her classmates would remember her as a shy and often self-conscious young woman who **kept to herself and concentrated on her musical studies. She was "interested in pretty much nothing else but singing,"** one student recalled, "not taking part in dances or things like that."
>
> During her high school years, **Marian continued to sing at church and social events** and, increasingly, **at concerts out of town**. In 1917, just before Christmas, she was invited **to take part in a gala concert** at the Georgia State Industrial College, a black college in Savannah. She had never visited the Deep South before, and on this trip, for the first time, she experienced the strict "Jim Crow" laws that enforced racial segregation throughout the South.

In the first sentence, Freedman states that Anderson "dreamed of a singing career." His thesis is echoed by one of Anderson's classmates, who remembered Anderson was "interested in pretty much nothing else but singing."

Freedman provides supporting details to explain Anderson's desire to have a singing career, including:

- she took secretarial course but "her heart wasn't in those studies"
- she "concentrated on her musical studies" instead of making friends
- throughout high school, she sang anywhere she could, including "church and social events . . . concerts out of town" and even "a gala concert at the Georgia State Industrial college"

 PRACTICE

Use the Supporting Details Organizer to evaluate the supporting details you gathered from your outside research and the literary texts you chose.

PLAN

WRITING PROMPT

How can dreams and aspirations positively or negatively affect people's lives and relationships? What qualities make a dream worth pursuing? How do people decide when a dream is unrealistic, out of reach, or even harmful?

Your essay should include:

- an introduction with a clear thesis statement
- body paragraphs with relevant evidence and thorough analysis to support your thesis
- a conclusion paragraph that effectively wraps up your essay

Review your thesis statement and the supporting details you evaluated and recorded in your Supporting Details Organizer. This information will help you to create a road map to use for writing your essay. You may also wish to consult the graphic organizers you completed during the Prewrite and Organize Informative Writing lessons.

Consider the following questions as you develop your main paragraph topics and their supporting details in the road map:

- What dreams did the characters pursue in the texts you chose?
- What qualities made those dreams worth pursuing?
- How did the characters decide if the dream was unrealistic or harmful? What did they do then?
- What impact did these dreams have on the characters' lives? On their relationships?

NOTES

• What details from your outside research can you use to further explain and/or give context for your analysis of the literary texts

As you outline your essay, list the supporting details you want to use in the order you want to use them. Remember to combine details from your outside research with the details you draw from the literary texts.

Use this model to get started with your outline:

INFORMATIVE/EXPLANATORY ESSAY ROAD MAP

> **THESIS STATEMENT:** Lenny and George in *Of Mice and Men* and Jing-Mei and Suyuan Woo in *The Joy Luck Club* pursue dreams that both connect them to and drive them away from the most important people in their lives.
>
> a. **Paragraph 1 Topic:** The Great Depression
>   i. *Supporting Detail #1:* Paraphrase basic facts of Great Depression from History.com.
>   ii. *Supporting Detail #2:* Paraphrase facts about migrant farmers from Fanslow.
>   iii. *Supporting Detail #3:* Lenny and George needed a dream to survive this hopeless time.
>
> b. **Paragraph 2 Topic:** How Lenny and George's dream connected them
>   i. *Supporting Detail #1:* Quote *Of Mice and Men* and explain Lenny and George's dream.
>   ii. *Supporting Detail #2:* Analyze dream through discussion of tone.
>   iii. *Supporting Detail #3:* Quote *Of Mice and Men* to explain how Lenny's constant troubles endanger the dream and could drive the two apart.
>
> c. **Paragraph 3 Topic:** Importance of dreams for immigrants
>   i. *Supporting Detail #1:* Quote *The Joy Luck Club* about Suyuan losing everything and coming to America to improve her fortunes.
>   ii. *Supporting Detail #2:* Quote *The Opposite of Fate* to draw parallel between Suyuan and Tan's own mother.
>   iii. *Supporting Detail #3:* Explain how Tan uses her own life for fiction and how immigrants come to America to follow their dreams
>
> d. **Paragraph 4 Topic:** How Suyuan and Jing-Mei's dream drove them apart
>   i. *Supporting Detail #1:* Analyze reasons motivating the dream: ex. the desire to never lose everything again.

ii. *Supporting Detail #2:* Quote *The Opposite of Fate* to show how Tan's life mirrored the lives of her characters'.

iii. *Supporting Detail #3:* Quote *The Joy Luck Club* about Jing-Mei's excitement in beginning and explain how it changed.

iv. *Supporting Detail #4:* Quote *The Joy Luck Club* about Jing-Mei's giving up on the dream and explain how it leads Suyuan to giving up, too.

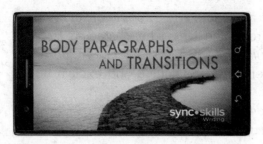

SKILL:
BODY
PARAGRAPHS
AND TRANSITIONS

 DEFINE

The **introduction** is the opening paragraph or section of a nonfiction text. In an informative/explanatory text, the introduction provides readers with important information by **introducing the topic** and **stating the thesis** that will be developed in the body of the text. A strong introduction also generates interest in the topic by engaging readers in an interesting or attentive way.

 IDENTIFICATION AND APPLICATION

- **Body paragraphs** make up the bulk of an informative/explanatory essay; they come between the introduction and conclusion paragraphs. Body paragraphs support the central idea in a thesis statement by providing and explaining evidence drawn from the assigned texts and outside research. Typically, each body paragraph focuses on one main reason or example that supports the central idea. This structure makes the essay easy to follow for readers.

- Following a clear structure for the body paragraphs is important. Here is one strategy for structuring a body paragraph for a literary analysis:

- **Topic sentence:** The topic sentence is the first sentence of your body paragraph and clearly states the main idea of the paragraph. It is important that your topic sentence supports the central idea in your thesis statement.

- **Supporting details:** It is essential to support your topic sentence with details. These supporting details can be relevant facts, definitions, concrete details, quotations, or other valid information and examples.

- **Analysis/Explanation:** After presenting a supporting detail, you will need to analyze the detail and explain how it supports your topic sentence and, in turn, the central idea in your thesis.

- **Repeat as needed:** Continue to develop your paragraph's topic sentence with more supporting details and explanations.

- **Concluding sentence:** After you present all the supporting details in your paragraph, it is a good idea to wrap up in a concluding sentence, either by restating your topic sentence or transitioning to the next paragraph.

- A body paragraph may present a number of supporting details. To keep the paragraph a digestible length, though, if it contains more than four supporting details, consider deleting some details or breaking the paragraph in half.

- **Transitions** are words and phrases that connect ideas in a text and clarify the relationships among them. Transitions work at three different levels: across the overall organizational structure, between paragraphs, and within a sentence. In informative/explanatory writing, transitions help readers recognize the overall organizational structure, whether it is cause-effect, comparison-contrast, or some other structure. Transitions help readers make connections between the major sections of the text: the central idea, the supporting details, and the analysis of those details. Transitions between paragraphs guide readers smoothly through the text. Transitions within a sentence—conjunctions such as *and, or,* and *but* as well as prepositions such as *with, beyond,* and *inside*—show the relationships between words and help readers understand meaning.

The student model uses a comparison-contrast body paragraph structure to develop supporting details that prove the central idea of the essay. The Student Model uses transitions to help the reader understand the relationships among the central idea, the supporting details, and the analysis of those details.

Read the first two body paragraphs from the Student Model essay, "The Power of Dreams." Look closely at the structure and note the transition words in bold. Think about the purpose of the information presented. Are supporting details stated in each body paragraph? Does the analysis explain the relevance of the details? How do the transition words help you to understand the information within and between paragraphs?

> *Of Mice and Men,* by John Steinbeck, is set in California during the Great Depression. The Great Depression lasted a long ten years, from 1929 through 1939. **During this time,** up to 15 million Americans were unemployed. Banks across the nation were failing, thanks to bank runs when customers demanded their money back—in cash (History.com). **Furthermore,** the Great Plains states suffered through the Dust Bowl. The Dust Bowl was the result of a seven-year drought and replacing natural grasslands with fields of crops. Farmers there watched their land blow away in great dust storms. Very little grew, **and** many farms went into debt and bankruptcy. Many of the families that lost their farms to the Dust Bowl moved to California,

Please note that excerpts and passages in the StudySync® library and this workbook are intended as touchstones to generate interest in an author's work. The excerpts and passages do not substitute for the reading of entire texts, and StudySync® strongly recommends that students seek out and purchase the whole literary or informational work in order to experience it as the author intended. Links to online resellers are available in our digital library. In addition, complete works may be ordered through an authorized reseller by filling out and returning to StudySync® the order form enclosed in this workbook.

Reading & Writing Companion   **327**

NOTES

where they hoped to find work. **Just like** Lenny and George, they were migrant farmers, moving from farm to farm and making barely enough to survive (Fanslow). This period in American history is particularly hopeless and joyless. Lenny and George, living in this bleak time, needed a dream to keep themselves going. Regardless of the dream's specifics, just having a dream helped Lenny and George keep putting one foot in front of the other—the dream was worth pursuing because it kept them alive and hopeful.

Because *Of Mice and Men* is set during the Great Depression, it is a book first and foremost about making plans and having dreams. The title itself refers to a line of poetry by Robert Burns: "The best laid schemes of mice and men often go awry" (SyncTV). The book **begins** with Lenny and George discussing their "scheme" or dream. Lenny begs George to "[t]ell about how it's gonna be" and George describes their shared vision of their future: "O.K. Someday—we're gonna get the jack together and we're gonna have a little house and a couple of acres an' a cow and some pigs and—" And Lenny knows the story by heart, **so** he finishes the sentence: *"An' live off the fatta the lan'... An' have rabbits"* (Steinbeck 13). The tone is wistful and romantic; George and Lenny have co-created a beautiful dream of their future, and each can recite what it will be because they have had this conversation so many times. By constantly discussing their shared dream, George and Lenny give themselves a future to look forward to and work toward when their life in the present is incredibly difficult. It's likely that George knows the dream is unrealistic, as he interrupts the retelling of it to discuss how to keep Lenny out of trouble. He coaches Lenny not "say a word" so he "won't get in no trouble" (Steinbeck 5). George knows that keeping Lenny around may ultimately stop him from achieving the dream, **but** he continues to protect Lenny and hold onto the dream. He has weighed the pros and cons and decided holding onto the dream with Lenny is more valuable than taking his chances alone. The dream is as much about Lenny and George being together as it is about escaping the Great Depression and having a place to call their own. **At the end of the day**, the dream of owning their own ranch gives Lenny and George a reason to keep going when times are rough and strengthens their friendship in a time that would try even the closest of relationships.

In body paragraph 1, the Student Model states, "*Of Mice and Men*, by John Steinbeck, is set in California during the Great Depression." This **topic**

NOTES

sentence clearly establishes the topic of the paragraph, which is the Depression-era setting of *Of Mice and Men*. This main idea supports the central idea of the essay because it provides context to explain why having a dream was particularly important to Lenny and George and why it would bring them closer together.

The writer goes on to provide **details** gathered from outside research sources to describe the Great Depression and migrant farm work in California during that time period. She uses the transition word "furthermore" to indicate that the information from the second research source builds on the information from the first. When she is finished describing the Great Depression in general, she uses the transitional phrase "Just like" to draw a connection between the real world of the Great Depression and the lives of the characters Lenny and George. She then explains why the context provided by the research is relevant to her central idea: George and Lenny needed a dream because their lives would be otherwise hopeless, thanks to the Great Depression.

Body paragraph 2 begins with the transition word "Because," signaling that the writer will be using a cause and effect structure within this paragraph: Because the book is set during the Great Depression, as discussed in body paragraph 1, the book deals with dreams, as will be discussed in paragraph 2.

 PRACTICE

Using the outline you generated in the Plan lesson, draft one body paragraph for your informative/explanatory essay that follows the suggested format. Structure your paragraph as described in the Define section, and use appropriate transition words. When you are finished, trade papers with a partner and offer each other feedback. How effective is the topic sentence at stating the main point of the paragraph? How strong are the supporting details used to back up the topic sentence? Are all quotes and paraphrased ideas cited properly? Are the supporting details relevant and sufficient enough to support the topic sentence? Offer each other suggestions and remember to be constructive!

NOTES

DRAFT

WRITING PROMPT

How can dreams and aspirations positively or negatively affect people's lives and relationships? What qualities make a dream worth pursuing? How do people decide when a dream is unrealistic, out of reach, or even harmful?

Your essay should include:

- an introduction with a clear thesis statement
- body paragraphs with relevant evidence and thorough analysis to support your thesis
- a conclusion paragraph that effectively wraps up your essay

In addition to studying techniques authors use to convey information, you have been reading and learning about stories that characters striving toward their dreams. Now you will use those informational/explanatory writing techniques to compose your own informative essay.

You've already made progress toward writing your informative/explanatory essay. You have thought about your purpose, audience, and topic. You have carefully examined the unit's texts and selected the two you want to discuss. You have consulted outside sources and gathered more facts and supporting details during the research process. Based on your analysis of textual evidence, you have identified what you want to say about the texts' characters and how their dreams impacted their lives and relationships. You have decided how to structure your essay as a whole and how to organize and order relevant supporting details. Now it is time to write a draft of your informative/explanatory essay.

Use your graphic organizers and your other prewriting materials to help you as you write. Remember that an informative/explanatory essay begins with an introduction and presents a central idea in the thesis statement. Body paragraphs develop the central idea in the thesis statement with supporting details, including facts, extended definitions, quotations, and other relevant information and explanations drawn from the texts and your outside research. Transitions help the reader understand the relationships among the thesis statement, supporting details, and text evidence. They also help readers follow the flow of information. A concluding paragraph restates or reinforces the central idea in your thesis statement. An effective conclusion can also do more—it can leave a lasting impression on your readers.

When drafting, ask yourself these questions:

- How can I improve my hook, or the way of grabbing readers' attention?
- What can I do to clarify the central idea in my thesis statement? Does my thesis provide a road map to the body of the essay?
- What supporting details—including relevant facts, strong details, and interesting quotations in each body paragraph—prove the central idea in the thesis statement?
- Would more precise language or different details about the characters, their dreams, and the impact of those dreams make my informative essay more exciting and vivid?
- How well have I communicated each text's portrayal of dreams and their impact on characters?
- What final thought do I want to leave with my readers?

Before you submit your draft, read it over carefully. You want to be sure that you have responded to all aspects of the prompt.

NOTES

SKILL: SOURCES AND CITATIONS

DEFINE

When writing any essay that uses ideas and quotations from other texts, it is important to include **citations** throughout the essay and a **works cited page** at the end of the essay to acknowledge those other texts. Citations are notes in the body of an essay that give information about the sources an author used in his or her writing. Citations are required whenever authors quote others' words or paraphrase others' ideas in their writing. They let readers know who originally came up with those words and ideas.

The works cited page is a list at the end of the essay that collects and organizes every text the author cited within the body of the essay. If an author cites a text within the essay, he or she must then include details about that text on the works cited page. While citations are brief references to the original source, the works cited page includes more detailed bibliographic information for those sources. This way readers can independently find the exact source the writer cited.

There are many styles for citing sources, including MLA (Modern Language Association) and APA (American Psychological Association). Regardless of the style, all citation methods require the same fundamental elements: author, title, publisher, publication date, city of publication, date accessed, medium, and page numbers. This lesson will focus on MLA style, which is the accepted form in English language arts and humanities courses.

IDENTIFICATION AND APPLICATION

- Whenever a writer uses words from another source exactly as they are written, the words must appear in quotation marks. Quotation marks show that the words are not the author's own words but are borrowed from another source. In the Student Model essay, the writer uses quotation marks around words taken directly from the source *Of Mice and Men*:

Copyright © BookheadEd Learning, LLC

And Lenny knows the story by heart, so he finishes the sentence:
"An' live off the fatta the lan' . . . An' have rabbits" (Steinbeck 13).

- Citations are also necessary when a writer borrows ideas from another source, even if the writer paraphrases, or puts those ideas in his or her own words. For instance, if you summarize facts you uncovered during the research process, you cite the source even if you do not directly quote the text. Citations credit the source, but they also help readers discover where they can learn more.

- When citing your sources, be sure to consult the style guide required by your teacher. Popular styles include MLA, APA, and Chicago (University of Chicago) styles. While each style uses the same information (author, title, publisher, publication date, etc.), each requires a slightly different format for presenting that information. When citing sources for essays and research papers, a writer should always have the appropriate style guide close by.

- There are several different ways to cite a source **in the body** of your essay.

  › Use parenthetical citations within the body of the essay. Put the author's last name in parentheses (followed by a page number if available) at the end of the sentence in which the quote appears. This is what the writer of the Student Model essay does after the quotation under the first bullet.

  › Alternatively, include the author's name in the context of the sentence (with a page number, if available, in parentheses at the end of the sentence). For example, the writer of the Student Model could also have written the sentence under the first bullet like this:

    Steinbeck has Lenny finish the sentence, as he knows the story by heart: *"An' live off the fatta the lan' . . . An' have rabbits."* **(13)**

  › Use the title of an article when there is no known author, as in this example:

    Banks across the nation were failing, thanks to bank runs when customers demanded their money back—in cash ("The Great Depression").

  › When citing more than one text by the same author, as seen in the following example, cite the title of the work. Also note the page number cited in parentheses:

    This dream echoes Tan's own experiences of learning—and giving up piano: "What you rather do: play piano and become famous, or play outside and become nobody?" (*The Opposite of Fate* **18**).

  › Use superscript numbers after quoted or paraphrased text to indicate endnotes, bibliographic information listed at the end of the text.

Please note that excerpts and passages in the StudySync® library and this workbook are intended as touchstones to generate interest in an author's work. The excerpts and passages do not substitute for the reading of entire texts, and StudySync® strongly recommends that students seek out and purchase the whole literary or informational work in order to experience it as the author intended. Links to online resellers are available in our digital library. In addition, complete works may be ordered through an authorized reseller by filling out and returning to StudySync® the order form enclosed in this workbook.

Reading & Writing
Companion

333

NOTES

Footnotes are similar, but they appear in a different place. See the following example:

> **He coaches Lenny not "say a word" so he "won't get in no trouble."[1]**

› In the case of an endnote, the following bibliographic note would appear at the end of the essay on a separate page titled "Notes." In the case of a footnote, this bibliographic note would appear at the bottom of the page that the superscript number is on. Notice that the number of the footnote or endnote matches the superscript number within the body of the essay:

> **1. John Steinbeck, *Of Mice and Men* (New York: Penguin, 2002) 5.**

• To properly cite sources, a writer must include a full works cited page in addition to using in-text citation. The works cited page includes full bibliographical details about the sources cited in the essay. This page allows readers to find the sources for themselves.

  › The works cited page lists all the sources in alphabetical order.
  › The format for citing a source depends on the type of source: print book, magazine article, online encyclopedia, etc. Consult the MLA Handbook (or other required style guide) or the MLA Style Guide online at the Purdue University Online Writing Lab (https://owl.english.purdue.edu/owl/section/2/11/).

In this excerpt from the student model essay, the writer uses quotations from *The Joy Luck Club* and *The Opposite of Fate*, another book by Amy Tan she read as part of her outside research. She includes parenthetical citations to cite her sources.

In The Joy Luck Club, Suyuan dreamed that Jing-Mei could become a child prodigy like Shirley Temple. Though not stated directly, the desire behind the dream of Jing-Mei becoming a child prodigy is the dream of success in America. If Jing-Mei were a child prodigy, then the family would have enough money and fame to be respected and successful—her mother would never have to lose everything again. **This dream echoes Tan's own experiences of learning—and giving up piano: "What you rather do: play piano and become famous, or play outside and become nobody?" (*The Opposite of Fate* 18).** *Initially, Jing-Mei, and presumably Tan, was young enough that she also believed in this dream of fame and success.* **Jing-Mei said, "in the beginning I was just as excited as my mother, maybe even more so. I pictured this prodigy part of me as many different images, and tried each one on for size. I was a dainty ballerina . . . I was like the Christ child . . . I was Cinderella . . ."**

(*The Joy Luck Club* **133**). So, mother and daughter worked together tirelessly to achieve this shared dream. Jing-Mei got a makeover from "the beauty training school in the Mission District" and every night Suyuan would drill her with "tests" to make her smart like the other remarkable children she read about in the magazines (*The Joy Luck Club* 133–134). But as much as the dream of becoming a child prodigy brought mother and daughter together in a shared project, eventually it worked just as hard to drive them apart. While Suyuan still believed Jing-Mei could become a prodigy, Jing-Mei became more and more disheartened as she realized the dream was unrealistic. "[S]omething inside me began to die," she said, because she never passed her mother's tests. She "performed listlessly" on purpose on those tests and watched to see when her mother would finally give up (*The Joy Luck Club* 134–135). "I got so bored that I started counting the bellows of the foghorns . . . seeing if my mother would give up on me before eight bellows," she said (*The Joy Luck Club* 135). Eventually, Suyuan gives up on Jing-Mei after only one or two bellows: the dream was finally dying for both of them. In the end, Suyuan's dream of Jing-Mei becoming a child prodigy does more to drive them apart than it did to bring them together.

Notice that when the writer uses portions of text from the source material, that text appears in quotations. The student has cited material with the titles of the books in parentheses after each quotation, as she is citing two works by the same author.

In this excerpt from the student model, the writer ends her paper with a works cited page:

Works Cited

Fanslow, Robin A. "The Migrant Experience." *American Memory: Voices from the Dust Bowl.*

American Folklife Center: Library of Congress, 6 April 6 1998. Web. 13 Oct. 2014

"The Great Depression." *History.com.* A+E Networks, 2009. Web. 13 October 2014.

Steinbeck, John. *Of Mice and Men.* New York: Penguin, 2002. Print.

"SyncTV: *Of Mice and Men.*" Online video clip. *StudySync.* BookheadEd Learning, 2014. Web. 9 Oct. 2014.

Please note that excerpts and passages in the StudySync® library and this workbook are intended as touchstones to generate interest in an author's work. The excerpts and passages do not substitute for the reading of entire texts, and StudySync® strongly recommends that students seek out and purchase the whole literary or informational work in order to experience it as the author intended. Links to online resellers are available in our digital library. In addition, complete works may be ordered through an authorized reseller by filling out and returning to StudySync® the order form enclosed in this workbook.

Reading & Writing Companion **335**

Tan, Amy. *The Joy Luck Club*. New York: Putnam, 1989. Print.

—. *The Opposite of Fate*. New York: Putnam, 2003. Print.

Note that the sources are formatted according to MLA style, appear in alphabetical order, and are double-spaced with a hanging indent

NOTES

EXTENDED WRITING PROJECT
REVISE

REVISE

WRITING PROMPT

How can dreams and aspirations positively or negatively affect people's lives and relationships? What qualities make a dream worth pursuing? How do people decide when a dream is unrealistic, out of reach, or even harmful?

Your essay should include:

- an introduction with a clear thesis statement
- body paragraphs with relevant evidence and thorough analysis to support your thesis
- a conclusion paragraph that effectively wraps up your essay

You have written a draft of your informative/explanatory essay. You have also received input from your peers about how to improve it. Now you are going to revise your draft.

Here are some recommendations to help you revise:

- Review the suggestions made by your peers.
- Focus on maintaining a formal style. A formal style suits your purpose—giving information about literary and informational texts. It also fits your audience—students, teachers, and other readers interested in learning more about your topic.
  - › As you revise, eliminate any slang.
  - › Look for imprecise language. Can you substitute a more precise word for a word that is general or dull?
  - › Remove any first-person pronouns such as "I," "me," or "mine" or instances of addressing readers as "you." These are more suitable to a writing style that is informal, personal, and conversational.

Please note that excerpts and passages in the StudySync® library and this workbook are intended as touchstones to generate interest in an author's work. The excerpts and passages do not substitute for the reading of entire texts, and StudySync® strongly recommends that students seek out and purchase the whole literary or informational work in order to experience it as the author intended. Links to online resellers are available in our digital library. In addition, complete works may be ordered through an authorized reseller by filling out and returning to StudySync® the order form enclosed in this workbook.

> If you include personal opinions or anecdotes, even if they relate to the prompt, remove them. Your essay should be clear, direct, and focused on the texts you discuss.

- After you have revised elements of style, think about whether there is anything else you can do to improve your essay's information or organization.

  › Do you need to add any new supporting details to your essay? Is there a detail about a character's dream that readers might find interesting? Is there a detail you uncovered in your research that would support your analysis of a literary text?

  › Do you need to refine the order in which you present facts and details from your outside research and the literary texts? Does one fact flow seamlessly to the next?

  › Consider your organization. Would your essay flow better if you strengthened the transitions between paragraphs?

- Double-check all your citations and your works cited page.

  › Have you cited all direct quotations and paraphrased ideas within the body of the essay?

  › Is every source you cited in the body of your essay included on your works cited page?

  › Is there a source listed on your works cited page that you did not include in the essay? Delete that source from the list.

  › Are your internal citations and works cited page formatted appropriately according to the assigned style (MLA, APA, or Chicago)?

- As you add new details or change information, check your grammar and punctuation.

  › Check that you have used parallel structure in sentences that include a series.

  › Be sure to punctuate restrictive and nonrestrictive phrases and clauses correctly.

  › Check carefully for misspelled words.

NOTES

EDIT,
PROOFREAD,
AND PUBLISH

WRITING PROMPT

How can dreams and aspirations positively or negatively affect people's lives and relationships? What qualities make a dream worth pursuing? How do people decide when a dream is unrealistic, out of reach, or even harmful?

Your essay should include:

- an introduction with a clear thesis statement
- body paragraphs with relevant evidence and thorough analysis to support your thesis
- a conclusion paragraph that effectively wraps up your essay

You have revised your informative/explanatory essay and received input from your peers on that revision. Now it's time to edit and proofread your essay to produce a final version. Have you included all the valuable suggestions from your peers? Ask yourself: Have I fully developed the central idea in my thesis statement with strong supporting details and relevant facts drawn from outside research? Have I accurately cited my sources? What more can I do to improve my essay's information and organization?

When you are satisfied with your work, move on to proofread it for errors. For example, check that you have used correct punctuation for quotations, citations, restrictive/nonrestrictive phrases and clauses, and compound sentences. Have you used correct parallel structure in sentences with series? Have you misspelled any words?

Please note that excerpts and passages in the StudySync® library and this workbook are intended as touchstones to generate interest in an author's work. The excerpts and passages do not substitute for the reading of entire texts, and StudySync® strongly recommends that students seek out and purchase the whole literary or informational work in order to experience it as the author intended. Links to online resellers are available in our digital library. In addition, complete works may be ordered through an authorized reseller by filling out and returning to StudySync® the order form enclosed in this workbook.

Reading & Writing Companion **339**

STUDYSYNC LIBRARY | **Extended Writing Project**

NOTES

Once you have made all your corrections, you are ready to submit and publish your work. You can distribute your writing to family and friends, hang it on a bulletin board, or post it on your blog. If you publish online, create links to your sources and citations. That way, readers can follow-up on what they've learned from your essay and read more on their own.

studysync®

Reading & Writing Companion

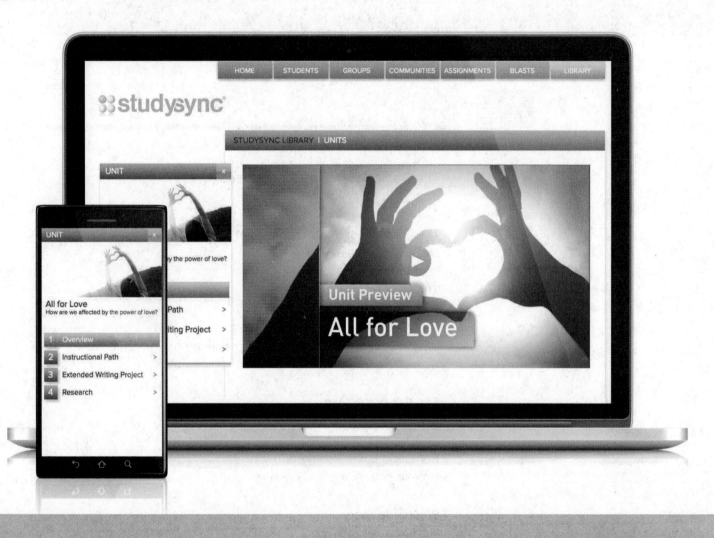

How are we affected by the power of love?

All for Love

All for Love

TEXTS

TEXTS

EXTENDED WRITING PROJECT

462

Text Fulfillment through StudySync

THE TRAGICAL HISTORY OF ROMEUS AND JULIET

FICTION

Arthur Brooke

1562

INTRODUCTION

Shakespeare's play *Romeo and Juliet* dramatizes the story of two young lovers who die as a result of misunderstandings amidst a family feud. This tale of ill-fated love was well known at Shakespeare's time. There were many versions, but Shakespeare's primary source was Arthur Brooke's narrative poem *The Tragical History of Romeus and Juliet*. This particular excerpt from Brooke's poem, in which Romeus and Juliet meet at her window and confess their love, inspired the famous balcony scene in Shakespeare's *Romeo and Juliet*.

"For love is fearful oft where is no cause of fear..."

FIRST READ

NOTES

Lines 457–517: Romeus and Juliet have been secretly meeting at night at Juliet's house, but for several days they keep missing each other, and Juliet fears that Romeus might be dead. One night, while leaning out her window, Juliet sees Romeus and her fear is instantly relieved.

457   He doth keep back his forward foot from passing there by day;
458   But when on earth the Night her mantle black hath spread;
459   Well armed he walketh forth alone, ne dreadful foes doth dread.
460   Whom maketh Love not bold, nay, whom makes he not blind?
461   He reaveth danger's dread oft-times out of the lover's mind.
462   By night he passeth here, a week or two in vain;
463   And for the missing of his mark his grief hath him nigh slain.
464   And Juliet that now doth lack her heart's relief,
465   Her Romeus' pleasant eyne, I mean, is almost dead for grief.
466   Each day she changeth hours (for lovers keep an hour
467   When they are sure to see their love in passing by their **bower)**.
468   Impatient of her **woe,** she happed to lean one night
469   Within her window, and anon the moon did shine so bright
470   That she espied her love: her heart revivéd sprang;
471   And now for joy she claps her hands, which erst for woe she wrang.
472   Eke Romeus, when he saw his long desiréd sight,
473   His mourning cloak of moan cast off, hath clad him with delight.
474   Yet dare I say, of both that she rejoicéd more:
475   His care was great, hers twice as great was all the time before;
476   For whilst she knew not why he did himself absent,
477   Aye doubting both his health and life, his death she did lament
478   For love is fearful oft where is no cause of fear,
479   And what love fears, that love laments, as though it chancéd were.
480   Of greater cause alway is greater work y-bred;
481   While he nought doubteth of her health, she dreads lest he be dead.

Please note that excerpts and passages in the StudySync® library and this workbook are intended as touchstones to generate interest in an author's work. The excerpts and passages do not substitute for the reading of entire texts, and StudySync® strongly recommends that students seek out and purchase the whole literary or informational work in order to experience it as the author intended. Links to online resellers are available in our digital library. In addition, complete works may be ordered through an authorized reseller by filling out and returning to StudySync® the order form enclosed in this workbook.

Reading & Writing Companion   **345**

NOTES

482 When only absence is the cause of Romeus' smart,
483 By happy hope of sight again he feeds his fainting heart.
484 What wonder then if he were wrapped in less annoy?
485 What marvel if by sudden sight she fed of greater joy
486 His smaller grief or joy no smaller love do prove;
487 Ne, for she passed him in both, did she him pass in love:
488 But each of them alike did burn in equal flame,
489 The well-beloving knight and eke the well-beloved dame.
490 Now whilst with bitter tears her eyes as fountains run,
491 With whispering voice, y-broke with sobs, thus is her tale begun:
492 "O Romeus, of your life too lavas sure you are,
493 That in this place, and at this time, to hazard it you dare.
494 What if your deadly foes, my kinsmen, saw you here?
495 Like lions wild, your tender parts **asunder** would they tear.
496 In ruth and in disdain, I, weary of my life,
497 With cruel hand my mourning heart would pierce with bloody knife.
498 For you, mine own, once dead, what joy should I have here?
499 And eke my honour stained, which I than life do hold more dear."
500 "Fair lady mine, dame Juliet, my life," quod he,
501 "Even from my birth committed was to fatal sisters three.
502 They may in spite of foes draw forth my lively thread;
503 And they also, whoso saith nay, asunder may it shred.
504 But who to reave my life, his rage and force would bend,
505 Perhaps should try unto his pain how I it could defend.
506 Ne yet I love it so, but always for your sake,
507 A sacrifice to death I would my wounded corpse betake.
508 If my mishap were such, that here before your sight,
509 I should restore again to death, of life, my borrowed light,
510 This one thing and no more my parting sprite would rue,
511 That part he should before that you by certain trial knew
512 The love I owe to you, the **thrall** I languish in,
513 And how I dread to lose the gain which I do hope to win;
514 And how I wish for life, not for my proper ease,
515 But that in it you might I love, you honour, serve and please,
516 Till deadly pangs the sprite out of the corpse shall send."
517 And thereupon he sware an oath, and so his tale had end.

Lines 518–565: Juliet tells Romeus that she would leave her family to marry him, but if he is not being honest in his intentions, she wants him to leave her alone. Romeus assures her of his love and his desire to marry her.

518 Now love and pity boil in Juliet's ruthful breast;
519 In window on her leaning arm her weary head doth rest;
520 Her bosom bathed in tears, to witness inward pain,
521 With dreary cheer to Romeus thus answered she again:

Copyright © BookheadEd Learning, LLC

522 "Ah, my dear Romeus, keep in these words," quod she,

523 "For lo, the thought of such mischance already maketh me

524 For pity and for dread well-nigh to yield up breath;

525 In even balance peiséd are my life and eke my death.

526 For so my heart is knit, yea, made one self with yours,

527 That sure there is no grief so small, by which your mind endures,

528 But as you suffer pain, so I do bear in part,

529 Although it lessens not your grief, the half of all your smart.

530 But these things overpast, if of your health and mine

531 You have respect, or pity aught my teary, weeping eyne,

532 In few unfained words your hidden mind unfold,

533 That as I see your pleasant face, your heart I may behold.

534 For if you do intend my honour to defile,

535 In error shall you wander still, as you have done this while;

536 But if your thought be chaste, and have on virtue ground,

537 If wedlock be the end and mark which your desire hath found,

538 Obedience set aside, unto my parents due,

539 The quarrel eke that long ago between our households grew,

540 Both me and mine I will all whole to you betake,

541 And following you whereso you go, my father's house forsake.

542 But if by wanton love and by unlawful suit

543 You think in ripest years to pluck my maidenhood's dainty fruit,

544 You are **beguiled;** and now your Juliet you beseeks

545 To cease your suit, and suffer her to live among her likes."

546 Then Romeus, whose thought was free from foul desire,

547 And to the top of virtue's height did worthily aspire,

548 Was filled with greater joy than can my pen express,

549 Or, till they have enjoyed the like, the hearer's heart can guess.

550 And then with joined hands, heaved up into the skies,

551 He thanks the Gods, and from the heavens for vengeance down he cries

552 If he have other thought but as his lady spake;

553 And then his look he turned to her, and thus did answer make:

554 "Since, lady, that you like to honour me so much

555 As to accept me for your spouse, I yield myself for such.

556 In true witness whereof, because I must depart,

557 Till that my deed do prove my word, I leave in pawn my heart.

558 To-morrow eke betimes before the sun arise,

559 To Friar Laurence will I wend, to learn his sage advice.

560 He is my ghostly sire, and oft he hath me taught

561 What I should do in things of weight, when I his aid have sought.

562 And at this self-same hour, I plight you here my faith,

563 I will be here, if you think good, to tell you what he saith."

564 She was contented well; else favour found he none

565 That night at lady Juliet's hand, save pleasant words alone.

THINK QUESTIONS

1. What do Romeus and Juliet do in the hope of seeing each other? What does Juliet do to improve her chances of seeing Romeus? Cite evidence from the text to support your answer.

2. According to the text of Brooke's poem, which of the two lovers is more excited when they finally see each other? Why? Explain your answer by citing evidence from the text.

3. What does Juliet ask Romeus to promise? How does Romeus respond to Juliet's request? Write two or three sentences to explain your answers. Support your answers with textual evidence.

4. Use context to determine the meaning of the word **asunder** as it is used in *The Tragical History of Romeus and Juliet*. Write your definition of "asunder" and tell how you arrived at it.

5. Remembering that the Latin prefix be- means "thoroughly" and the French root *guile* means "trick," use the context clues in the passage and your knowledge of word parts to determine the meaning of **beguiled.** Write your definition of "beguiled" and tell how you arrived at it.

CLOSE READ

Reread the excerpt from *The Tragical History of Romeus and Juliet*. As you reread, complete the Focus Questions below. Then use your answers and annotations from the questions to help you complete the Writing Prompt.

FOCUS QUESTIONS

1. Explain how the poet uses the first eighteen lines of the excerpt (lines 457 to 473) to set up the plot and develop the characters of Romeus and Juliet. Highlight details from the text and make annotations to support your explanation.

2. The speaker states that when Romeus and Juliet finally saw each other, Juliet "rejoicéd more" (line 474). Why would this make sense, given the circumstances of the two characters? Make annotations explaining your inferences about the meaning of the text.

3. In lines 491 to 499, how does Juliet respond to the dangers that she knows Romeus faces? In lines 500 to 507, what is his response to her feelings? What do the characters' responses reveal about them, and how might these responses foreshadow later events? Highlight evidence from the text and make annotations to support your answers.

4. What does Juliet ask Romeus to prove about himself in lines 530 to 533, and why is this important to her? What is Juliet willing to do if she is satisfied by his demonstration? Predict how the characters' desires and actions will affect the development of the story's plot. Base your answers on textual evidence.

5. How would you describe the effect of love on Romeus and Juliet? What does their love make them think and do? How might their love for each other affect others around them? Support your ideas with textual evidence and inferences.

WRITING PROMPT

What do you learn about Romeus and Juliet, the two main characters in the poem, from what the speaker says about them directly and from what they say to each other? In a brief essay, describe their traits, their desires, and the situation they are in. Also, make a prediction about their future, based on their dialogue. Throughout your response, give textual evidence to support your ideas.

THE TRAGEDY OF ROMEO AND JULIET
(ACT II, SCENE II)

DRAMA
William Shakespeare
1592

INTRODUCTION

The love story of *Romeo and Juliet* is among Shakespeare's most famous plays. The volatile family feud between the Montagues and Capulets has broken out in violence in the streets of Verona, Italy. With his two friends, Romeo, the son of Lord Montague, attends a party held by Lord Caplulet. A mask hides Romeo's identity. There, he meets and falls in love with the beautiful Juliet, a Capulet. Later that night he finds her standing at her balcony, thinking aloud about the boy she met that evening. Based on the plot of a previous story, Shakespeare's tragic tale of "star-crossed" lovers who are convinced that love can conquer all remains as popular today as it was when written in the late 16th Century.

"O Romeo, Romeo! wherefore art thou Romeo?"

FIRST READ

Act II, Scene II

1   *[Enter Romeo.]*

2   ROMEO: He jests at scars that never felt a wound.

3   *[Enter Juliet above at a window.]*

4   But soft! What light through yonder window breaks?
5   It is the East, and Juliet is the sun!
6   Arise, fair sun, and kill the envious moon,
7   Who is already sick and pale with grief
8   That thou her maid art far more fair than she.
9   Be not her maid, since she is envious.
10   Her vestal livery is but sick and green,
11   And none but fools do wear it. Cast it off.
12   It is my lady; O, it is my love!
13   O that she knew she were!
14   She speaks, yet she says nothing. What of that?
15   Her eye discourses; I will answer it.
16   I am too bold; 'tis not to me she speaks.
17   Two of the fairest stars in all the heaven,
18   Having some business, do **entreat** her eyes
19   To twinkle in their spheres till they return.
20   What if her eyes were there, they in her head?
21   The brightness of her cheek would shame those stars
22   As daylight doth a lamp; her eyes in heaven
23   Would through the airy region stream so bright
24   That birds would sing and think it were not night.
25   See how she leans her cheek upon her hand!

26   O that I were a glove upon that hand,
27   That I might touch that cheek!

28 JULIET: Ay me!

29 ROMEO: She speaks.
30   O, speak again, bright angel! for thou art
31   As glorious to this night, being o'er my head,
32   As is a winged messenger of heaven
33   Unto the white-upturned wond'ring eyes
34   Of mortals that fall back to gaze on him
35   When he bestrides the lazy-pacing clouds
36   And sails upon the bosom of the air.

37 JULIET: O Romeo, Romeo! wherefore art thou Romeo?
38   Deny thy father and refuse thy name!
39   Or, if thou wilt not, be but sworn my love,
40   And I'll no longer be a Capulet.

41 ROMEO: *[aside]* Shall I hear more, or shall I speak at this?

42 JULIET: 'Tis but thy name that is my enemy.
43   Thou art thyself, though not a Montague.
44   What's Montague? it is nor hand, nor foot,
45   Nor arm, nor face, nor any other part
46   Belonging to a man. O, be some other name!
47   What's in a name? That which we call a rose
48   By any other name would smell as sweet.
49   So Romeo would, were he not Romeo call'd,
50   Retain that dear perfection which he owes
51   Without that title. Romeo, doff thy name;
52   And for that name, which is no part of thee,
53   Take all myself.

54 ROMEO: I take thee at thy word.
55   Call me but love, and I'll be new baptiz'd;
56   Henceforth I never will be Romeo.

57 JULIET: What man art thou that, thus bescreen'd in night,
58   So stumblest on my counsel?

59 ROMEO: By a name
60   I know not how to tell thee who I am.
61   My name, dear saint, is hateful to myself,
62   Because it is an enemy to thee.
63   Had I it written, I would tear the word.

NOTES

64 JULIET: My ears have yet not drunk a hundred words
65   Of that tongue's **utterance,** yet I know the sound.
66   Art thou not Romeo, and a Montague?

67 ROMEO: Neither, fair saint, if either thee dislike.

68 JULIET: How cam'st thou hither, tell me, and wherefore?
69   The orchard walls are high and hard to climb,
70   And the place death, considering who thou art,
71   If any of my kinsmen find thee here.

72 ROMEO: With love's light wings did I o'erperch these walls;
73   For stony limits cannot hold love out,
74   And what love can do, that dares love attempt.
75   Therefore thy kinsmen are no let to me.

76 JULIET: If they do see thee, they will murther thee.

77 ROMEO: Alack, there lies more peril in thine eye
78   Than twenty of their swords! Look thou but sweet,
79   And I am proof against their **enmity.**

80 JULIET: I would not for the world they saw thee here.

81 ROMEO: I have night's cloak to hide me from their sight;
82   And but thou love me, let them find me here.
83   My life were better ended by their hate
84   Than death prorogued, wanting of thy love.

85 JULIET: By whose direction found'st thou out this place?

86 ROMEO: By love, that first did prompt me to enquire.
87   He lent me counsel, and I lent him eyes.
88   I am no pilot; yet, wert thou as far
89   As that vast shore wash'd with the farthest sea,
90   I would adventure for such merchandise.

91 JULIET: Thou knowest the mask of night is on my face;
92   Else would a maiden blush bepaint my cheek
93   For that which thou hast heard me speak to-night.
94   Fain would I dwell on form- fain, fain deny
95   What I have spoke; but farewell compliment!
96   Dost thou love me, I know thou wilt say 'Ay';
97   And I will take thy word. Yet, if thou swear'st,
98   Thou mayst prove false. At lovers' perjuries,
99   They say Jove laughs. O gentle Romeo,

100 If thou dost love, pronounce it faithfully.
101 Or if thou thinkest I am too quickly won,
102 I'll frown, and be perverse, and say thee nay,
103 So thou wilt woo; but else, not for the world.
104 In truth, fair Montague, I am too fond,
105 And therefore thou mayst think my haviour light;
106 But trust me, gentleman, I'll prove more true
107 Than those that have more cunning to be strange.
108 I should have been more strange, I must confess,
109 But that thou overheard'st, ere I was ware,
110 My true-love passion. Therefore pardon me,
111 And not **impute** this yielding to light love,
112 Which the dark night hath so discovered.

113 ROMEO: Lady, by yonder blessed moon I swear,
114 That tips with silver all these fruit-tree tops-

115 JULIET: O, swear not by the moon, th' inconstant moon,
116 That monthly changes in her circled orb,
117 Lest that thy love prove likewise variable.

118 ROMEO: What shall I swear by?

119 JULIET: Do not swear at all;
120 Or if thou wilt, swear by thy gracious self,
121 Which is the god of my **idolatry,**
122 And I'll believe thee.

123 ROMEO: If my heart's dear love-

124 JULIET: Well, do not swear. Although I joy in thee,
125 I have no joy of this contract to-night.
126 It is too rash, too unadvis'd, too sudden;
127 Too like the lightning, which doth cease to be
128 Ere one can say 'It lightens.' Sweet, good night!
129 This bud of love, by summer's ripening breath,
130 May prove a beauteous flow'r when next we meet.
131 Good night, good night! As sweet repose and rest
132 Come to thy heart as that within my breast!

133 ROMEO: O, wilt thou leave me so unsatisfied?

134 JULIET: What satisfaction canst thou have to-night?

135 ROMEO: Th' exchange of thy love's faithful vow for mine.

NOTES

136 JULIET: I gave thee mine before thou didst request it;
137   And yet I would it were to give again.

138 ROMEO: Would'st thou withdraw it? For what purpose, love?

139 JULIET: But to be frank and give it thee again.
140   And yet I wish but for the thing I have.
141   My bounty is as boundless as the sea,
142   My love as deep; the more I give to thee,
143   The more I have, for both are infinite.
144 *[Nurse calls within.]*
145   I hear some noise within. Dear love, adieu!
146   Anon, good nurse! Sweet Montague, be true.
147   Stay but a little, I will come again. *[Exit above.]*

148 ROMEO: O blessed, blessed night! I am afeard,
149   Being in night, all this is but a dream,
150   Too flattering-sweet to be substantial.
151 *[Enter Juliet above.]*

152 JULIET: Three words, dear Romeo, and good night indeed.
153   If that thy bent of love be honourable,
154   Thy purpose marriage, send me word to-morrow,
155   By one that I'll procure to come to thee,
156   Where and what time thou wilt perform the rite;
157   And all my fortunes at thy foot I'll lay
158   And follow thee my lord throughout the world.

159 NURSE: *[within]* Madam!

160 JULIET: I come, anon.- But if thou meanest not well,
161   I do beseech thee-

162 NURSE: *[within]* Madam!

163 JULIET: By-and-by I come.-
164   To cease thy suit and leave me to my grief.
165   To-morrow will I send.

166 ROMEO: So thrive my soul-

167 JULIET: A thousand times good night! *[Exit Above.]*

168 ROMEO: A thousand times the worse, to want thy light!
169   Love goes toward love as schoolboys from their books;
170   But love from love, towards school with heavy looks.
171 *[Enter Juliet again, above.]*

172 JULIET: Hist! Romeo, hist! O for a falconer's voice

173   To lure this tassel-gentle back again!

174   Bondage is hoarse and may not speak aloud;

175   Else would I tear the cave where Echo lies,

176   And make her airy tongue more hoarse than mine

177   With repetition of my Romeo's name.

178   Romeo!

179 ROMEO: It is my soul that calls upon my name.

180   How silver-sweet sound lovers' tongues by night,

181   Like softest music to attending ears!

182 JULIET: Romeo!

183 ROMEO: My dear?

184 JULIET: At what o'clock to-morrow

185   Shall I send to thee?

186 ROMEO: By the hour of nine.

187 JULIET: I will not fail. 'Tis twenty years till then.

188   I have forgot why I did call thee back.

189 ROMEO: Let me stand here till thou remember it.

190 JULIET: I shall forget, to have thee still stand there,

191   Rememb'ring how I love thy company.

192 ROMEO: And I'll still stay, to have thee still forget,

193   Forgetting any other home but this.

194 JULIET: 'Tis almost morning. I would have thee gone-

195   And yet no farther than a wanton's bird,

196   That lets it hop a little from her hand,

197   Like a poor prisoner in his twisted gyves,

198   And with a silk thread plucks it back again,

199   So loving-jealous of his liberty.

200 ROMEO: I would I were thy bird.

201 JULIET: Sweet, so would I.

202   Yet I should kill thee with much cherishing.

203   Good night, good night! Parting is such sweet sorrow,

204   That I shall say good night till it be morrow.

205   *[Exit Above.]*

206 ROMEO: Sleep dwell upon thine eyes, peace in thy breast!

207   Would I were sleep and peace, so sweet to rest!

208   Hence will I to my ghostly father's cell,

209   His help to crave and my dear hap to tell.

210 *[Exit].*

 THINK QUESTIONS

1. What details tell you where and when Act II, Scene II takes place? Where are the characters in relation to each other? What time of day is it?

2. In Juliet's second speech (beginning on line 37), what does she say is the central problem that exists between her and Romeo? In her mind, how could this problem be solved? Support your answer with textual evidence.

3. In Juliet's long speech beginning with line 91, what vow does she ask Romeo to make in order to prove his love? What does she promise to do in exchange for this vow? Cite evidence from the text to support your answers.

4. Use context to determine the meaning of the word **entreat** as it is used in Romeo's first speech. Write your definition of "entreat" and tell how you arrived at it.

5. Look again at the word **idolatry** as it is used in line 121. You may recognize the root word **idol**, and you may recall seeing other words that end in -*try*, such as "bigotry" and "gallantry." The suffix -*ry* means "practice of" and turns a word into an abstract noun. From your knowledge of word parts, what do you think is the meaning of "idolatry"? Explain your reasoning.

CLOSE READ

Reread the excerpt from *The Tragedy of Romeo and Juliet*. As you reread, complete the Focus Questions below. Then use your answers and annotations from the questions to help you complete the Writing Prompt.

FOCUS QUESTIONS

1. To what different things does Romeo compare Juliet in his opening speech? What does this figurative language express about his feelings toward Juliet? Highlight evidence from the text and make annotations to explain your answers.

2. Explain what Juliet means by saying in lines 47–48, "What's in a name? That which we call a rose / By any other name would smell as sweet." What is the connection to her situation? Highlight textual evidence and make annotations to explain your ideas.

3. In her speech beginning with line 91, what concern does Juliet express about the words that Romeo overheard her speak? In her later speech beginning on line 152, what does she say will satisfy her, and under what condition? Support your answers with textual evidence and make annotations to explain your interpretations.

4. How does falling in love with Juliet affect Romeo's behavior? How does falling in love with Romeo affect Juliet's behavior? What effect might the danger of their situation have on their feelings for each other? Highlight evidence from the text and make annotations to explain your answers.

5. Compare and contrast this excerpt from Shakespeare's *Romeo* and *Juliet* with Arthur Brooke's poem *The Tragedy of Romeus and Juliet*. Summarize the similarities and differences you see in plot, characterization, and language. Why do you think Shakespeare's version is considered "better"? Offer evidence from both texts to support your ideas.

WRITING PROMPT

The nighttime setting is very important in Act II, Scene II. In a brief essay, explain how it affects the way Romeo's and Juliet's feelings are revealed, the figurative language Romeo uses to describe Juliet, and the level of threat Romeo faces from Juliet's kinsmen. Give your opinion about whether the scene could have been as effective if it had taken place in broad daylight. Support your ideas with evidence from the text.

THE RAVEN

POETRY
Edgar Allan Poe
1845

INTRODUCTION

A bizarre bird, a disturbed narrator, and the relentlessly repeated "Nevermore" have made Edgar Allan Poe's "The Raven" one of the best-known poems in the English language. In his essay "The Philosophy of Composition," Poe explains that he wrote "The Raven" logically and methodically to appeal to both critical and popular tastes. Try reading it aloud to experience

"Quoth the Raven 'Nevermore.'"

FIRST READ

1 Once upon a midnight dreary, while I pondered, weak and weary,
2 Over many a quaint and curious volume of forgotten lore —
3 While I nodded, nearly napping, suddenly there came a tapping,
4 As of some one gently rapping, rapping at my chamber door.
5 "'Tis some visitor," I muttered, "tapping at my chamber door —
6 Only this and nothing more."

7 Ah, distinctly I remember it was in the bleak December;
8 And each separate dying ember **wrought** its ghost upon the floor.
9 Eagerly I wished the morrow;—vainly I had sought to borrow
10 From my books **surcease** of sorrow—sorrow for the lost Lenore —
11 For the rare and radiant maiden whom the angels name Lenore —
12 Nameless here for evermore.

13 And the silken, sad, uncertain rustling of each purple curtain
14 Thrilled me—filled me with fantastic terrors never felt before;
15 So that now, to still the beating of my heart, I stood repeating
16 "'Tis some visitor entreating entrance at my chamber door —
17 Some late visitor entreating entrance at my chamber door; —
18 This it is and nothing more."

19 Presently my soul grew stronger; hesitating then no longer,
20 "Sir," said I, "or Madam, truly your forgiveness I **implore;**
21 But the fact is I was napping, and so gently you came rapping,
22 And so faintly you came tapping, tapping at my chamber door,
23 That I scarce was sure I heard you"—here I opened wide the door;—
24 Darkness there and nothing more.

25 Deep into that darkness peering, long I stood there wondering, fearing,
26 Doubting, dreaming dreams no mortal ever dared to dream before;
27 But the silence was unbroken, and the stillness gave no token,

28 And the only word there spoken was the whispered word, "Lenore?"
29 This I whispered, and an echo murmured back the word, "Lenore!"
30 Merely this and nothing more.

31 Back into the chamber turning, all my soul within me burning,
32 Soon again I heard a tapping somewhat louder than before.
33 "Surely," said I, "surely that is something at my window lattice;
34 Let me see, then, what thereat is, and this mystery explore —
35 Let my heart be still a moment and this mystery explore; —
36 'Tis the wind and nothing more!"

37 Open here I flung the shutter, when, with many a flirt and flutter,
38 In there stepped a stately Raven of the saintly days of yore;
39 Not the least obeisance made he; not a minute stopped or stayed he;
40 But with mien of lord or lady, perched above my chamber door —
41 Perched upon a bust of Pallas just above my chamber door —
42 Perched, and sat, and nothing more.

43 Then this ebony bird beguiling my sad fancy into smiling,
44 By the grave and stern decorum of the **countenance** it wore,
45 "Though thy crest be shorn and shaven, thou," I said, "art sure no craven,
46 Ghastly grim and ancient Raven wandering from the Nightly shore —
47 Tell me what thy lordly name is on the Night's Plutonian shore!"
48 Quoth the Raven "Nevermore."

49 Much I marvelled this ungainly fowl to hear discourse so plainly,
50 Though its answer little meaning—little relevancy bore;
51 For we cannot help agreeing that no living human being
52 Ever yet was blessed with seeing bird above his chamber door —
53 Bird or beast upon the sculptured bust above his chamber door,
54 With such name as "Nevermore."

55 But the Raven, sitting lonely on the placid bust, spoke only
56 That one word, as if his soul in that one word he did outpour.
57 Nothing farther then he uttered—not a feather then he fluttered —
58 Till I scarcely more than muttered "Other friends have flown before —
59 On the morrow he will leave me, as my Hopes have flown before."
60 Then the bird said "Nevermore."

61 Startled at the stillness broken by reply so aptly spoken,
62 "Doubtless," said I, "what it utters is its only stock and store
63 Caught from some unhappy master whom unmerciful Disaster
64 Followed fast and followed faster till his songs one burden bore —
65 Till the dirges of his Hope that melancholy burden bore
66 Of 'Never—nevermore.'"

67 But the Raven still beguiling my sad fancy into smiling,
68 Straight I wheeled a cushioned seat in front of bird, and bust and door;
69 Then, upon the velvet sinking, I betook myself to linking
70 Fancy unto fancy, thinking what this ominous bird of yore —
71 What this grim, ungainly, **ghastly,** gaunt, and ominous bird of yore
72 Meant in croaking "Nevermore."

73 This I sat engaged in guessing, but no syllable expressing
74 To the fowl whose fiery eyes now burned into my bosom's core;
75 This and more I sat divining, with my head at ease reclining
76 On the cushion's velvet lining that the lamp-light gloated o'er,
77 But whose velvet-violet lining with the lamp-light gloating o'er,
78 She shall press, ah, nevermore!

79 Then, methought, the air grew denser, perfumed from an unseen censer
80 Swung by seraphim whose foot-falls tinkled on the tufted floor.
81 "Wretch," I cried, "thy God hath lent thee—by these angels he hath sent thee
82 Respite—respite and nepenthe from thy memories of Lenore;
83 Quaff, oh quaff this kind nepenthe and forget this lost Lenore!"
84 Quoth the Raven "Nevermore."

85 "Prophet!" said I, "thing of evil!—prophet still, if bird or devil! —
86 Whether Tempter sent, or whether tempest tossed thee here ashore,
87 Desolate yet all undaunted, on this desert land enchanted —
88 On this home by Horror haunted—tell me truly, I implore —
89 Is there—is there balm in Gilead?—tell me—tell me, I implore!"
90 Quoth the Raven "Nevermore."

91 "Prophet!" said I, "thing of evil!—prophet still, if bird or devil!
92 By that Heaven that bends above us—by that God we both adore —
93 Tell this soul with sorrow laden if, within the distant Aidenn,
94 It shall clasp a sainted maiden whom the angels name Lenore —
95 Clasp a rare and radiant maiden whom the angels name Lenore."
96 Quoth the Raven "Nevermore."

97 "Be that word our sign of parting, bird or fiend!" I shrieked, upstarting —
98 "Get thee back into the tempest and the Night's Plutonian shore!
99 Leave no black plume as a token of that lie thy soul hath spoken!
100 Leave my loneliness unbroken!—quit the bust above my door!
101 Take thy beak from out my heart, and take thy form from off my door!"
102 Quoth the Raven "Nevermore."

103 And the Raven, never flitting, still is sitting, still is sitting
104 On the pallid bust of Pallas just above my chamber door;

105 And his eyes have all the seeming of a demon's that is dreaming,
106 And the lamp-light o'er him streaming throws his shadow on the floor;
107 And my soul from out that shadow that lies floating on the floor
108 Shall be lifted—nevermore!

 THINK QUESTIONS

1. Refer to one or more details from the text to support your understanding of what the speaker was doing and what state of mind he was in when the encounter with the Raven occurred.

2. Who or what does the speaker originally think is tapping at his door? Use quotes from the text to support your answer.

3. Explain what the speaker hopes the Raven will tell him. Support your answer with textual evidence.

4. Use context to determine the meaning of the word **implore** as it is used in "The Raven." Write your definition of "implore" and tell how you arrived at it.

5. Use context to determine the meaning of the word **surcease** as it is used in "The Raven." Write your definition of "surcease" and tell how you arrived at it.

CLOSE READ

Reread the poem "The Raven." As you reread, complete the Focus Questions below. Then use your answers and annotations from the questions to help you complete the Writing Prompt.

FOCUS QUESTIONS

1. Explain how the author uses the first three stanzas to establish and develop the setting and tone of the poem. Highlight evidence from the text and make annotations to explain your choices.

2. How does the author use rhyme, rhythm, and repetition in the first half of the poem to establish a mood, or feeling? How does that mood change by the end of the poem? Highlight evidence of repetition and rhyme at the beginning and at the end of the text, and make annotations to explain how they contribute to the different moods.

3. Stanza 4 shows the author responding to the tapping by getting up and opening his door, only to find no one there. Several words in this stanza share related connotations. What are the most telling words in this section, and what

connotations do they offer? How do these connotations work together to reveal the theme of the poem? Highlight your textual evidence and make annotations to explain your choices.

4. Readers first see the Raven in stanza 7. In the following stanzas, the Raven is described with several different words. What are some of the words Poe uses to describe the Raven? What sort of connotations do these words share? Highlight evidence from the text and make annotations to support your explanation.

5. This unit focuses on how human beings are affected by the power of love. How does love play a role in the speaker's life and in this story? Was love a positive or negative aspect in his life? Highlight textual evidence and make annotations to explain your ideas.

WRITING PROMPT

Poe claimed to have written "The Raven" very logically and methodically. Write an essay in which you explore the poem's structure and language, and explain how these elements suggest that Poe was making careful choices in his writing. Use your understanding of poetic structure and connotation, and how both can contribute to a poem's theme and mood, when answering the question. Support your ideas with evidence from the text.

WHY WE LOVE:
THE NATURE AND CHEMISTRY OF ROMANTIC LOVE

NON-FICTION
Helen Fisher
2004

INTRODUCTION

Biological anthropologist Dr. Helen Fisher is a member of the Center for Human Evolutionary Studies at Rutgers University, and also serves as chief scientific advisor to the popular internet dating website, Match.com. In her book *Why We Love*, Fisher discusses the universal nature of romantic love and explores the possible evolutionary path that led humans to experience love. In this excerpt, she describes the role that the brain chemicals dopamine, norepinephrine, and serotonin play in the process.

"Central to romantic love is the lover's preference for the beloved."

FIRST READ

From Chapter 3: Chemistry of Love: Scanning the Brain "in Love"

1   "There is the heat of Love, the pulsing rush of Longing, the lover's whisper, irresistible—magic to make the sanest man go mad." This magic that Homer sang of in *The Iliad* has started wars, sired dynasties, topped kingdoms, and generated some of the world's finest literature and art. People sing for love, work for love, kill for love, live for love, and die for love. What causes this sorcery?

2   As you know, I have come to believe that romantic love is a universal human feeling, produced by specific chemicals and networks in the brain. But exactly which ones? Determined to shed some light on this magic that can make the sanest man go mad, I launched a multipart project in 1996 to collect scientific data on the chemistry and brain circuitry of romantic love. I assumed that many chemicals must be involved in one way or another. But I focused my investigation on dopamine and norepinephrine, as we as a related brain substance, serotonin.

3   I looked into the nature of these chemicals for two reasons: the attraction animals feel for particular mates is linked with elevated levels of dopamine and/or norepinephrine in the brain. More important, all three of these chemicals produce many of the sensations of human romantic passion.

Rock On, Sweet Dopamine

4   Take dopamine. Elevated levels of dopamine in the brain produce extremely focused attention, as well as unwavering motivation and goal-directed behaviors. These are central characteristics of romantic love. Lovers intensely focus on the beloved, often to the exclusion of all around them. Indeed, they concentrate so relentlessly on the positive qualities of the adored one that

they easily overlook his or her negative traits, they even dote on specific events and objects shared with this sweetheart.

5   **Besotted** lovers also regard the beloved as novel and unique. And dopamine has been associated with learning about novel stimuli.

6   Central to romantic love is the lover's preference for the beloved. As you recall from chapter two, among prairie voles, this favoritism is associated with heightened levels of dopamine in specific brain regions. And it is not a leap of logic to suggest that if dopamine is associated with mate preference in prairie voles, it can play a role in partiality in people. As you recall, all mammals have basically the same brain machinery, although size, shape, and placement of brain parts definitely vary.

7   **Ecstasy** is another outstanding trait of lovers. This, too, appears to be associated with dopamine. Elevated concentrations of dopamine in the brain produce exhilaration, as well as many of the other feelings that lovers report— including increased energy, hyperactivity, sleeplessness, loss of appetite, trembling, a pounding heart, accelerated breathing, and sometimes mania, anxiety, or fear.

8   Dopamine involvement may even explain why love-stricken men and women become so dependent on their romantic relationship and why they crave emotional union with their beloved. Dependency and craving are symptoms of addiction—and all of the major addictions are associated with elevated levels of dopamine. Is romantic love an addiction? Yes; I think it is—a blissful dependency when one's love is returned, a painful, sorrowful, and often destructive craving when one's love is spurned.

9   In fact, dopamine may fuel the frantic effort a lover musters when he/she feels the love affair is in jeopardy. When a reward is delayed, dopamine-producing cells in the brain increasetheir work, pumping out more of this natural stimulant to energize the brain, focus attention, and drive the pursuer to strive even harder to acquire a reward: in this case, winning one's sweetheart. Dopamine, thy name is persistence.

10 Even the craving for sex with the beloved may be indirectly related to elevated levels of dopamine. As dopamine increases in the brain, it often drives up levels of testosterone, the hormone of sexual desire.

Norepinephrine's High

11 Norepinephrine, a chemical derived from dopamine, may also contribute to the lover's high. The effects of norepinephrine are varied, depending on the part of the brain it activates. Nevertheless, increasing levels of this stimulant

Copyright © BookheadEd Learning, LLC

generally produce exhilaration, excessive energy, sleeplessness, and loss of appetite—some of the basic characteristics of romantic love.

12   Increasing levels of norepinephrine could also explain why the lover can remember the smallest details of the beloved's actions and cherished moments spent together. This liquor is associated with increased memory for new stimuli.

13   A third chemical may also be involved in that "irresistible" feeling of magic Homer spoke of: serotonin.

Serotonin

14   A striking symptom of romantic love is incessant thinking about the beloved. Lovers cannot turn off their racing thoughts. Indeed, this single aspect of being in love is so intense that I use it as the litmus test of romantic passion. The first thing I ask anyone who tells me they are "in love" is, "What percentage of your waking hours do you think about your sweetheart?" Many say "over 90 percent." Some bashfully admit they never stop thinking about "him" or "her."

15   Lovers are obsessed. And doctors who treat individuals with most forms of obsessive-compulsive disorder prescribe SSRIs (selective serotonin reuptake inhibitors) such as Prozac or Zoloft, substances that *elevate* levels of serotonin in the brain. So I came to suspect that the lover's persistent, involuntary, irresistible **ruminations** about a sweetheart might be associated with low levels of some type (there are at least fourteen variations) of this chemical compound.

16   There is some support for my reasoning. In 1999, scientists in Italy studied sixty individuals: twenty were men and women who had fallen in love in the previous six months; twenty others suffered from unmedicated obsessive-compulsive disorder (OCD); twenty more were normal, healthy individuals who were not in love and were used as controls. Both the in-love participants and those suffering from OCD were found to have significantly lower levels of serotonin than did the controls.

17   These scientists examined serotonin levels in components of the blood, however, rather than the brain. Until scientists document the activity of serotonin in specific brain regions, we cannot be sure of the role of serotonin in romantic love. Nevertheless, this experiment has established, for the first time, a possible connection between romantic love and lowlevels of bodily serotonin.

18 All those countless hours when your mind races like a mouse upon a treadmill may be associated with reduced levels of serotonin coursing through the highways of the brain.

19 And as a love affair intensifies, this irresistible, obsessive thinking can increase—due to a negative relationship between serotonin and its relatives, dopamine and norepinephrine. As levels of dopamine and norepinephrine climb, they can cause serotonin levels to plummet. This could explain why a lover's increasing romantic ecstasy actually intensifies the compulsion to daydream, fantasize, muse, ponder, obsess about a romantic partner.

A "Working" Hypothesis

20 Given the properties of these three related chemicals in the brain—dopamine, norepinephrine, and serotonin—I began to suspect that all played a role in human romantic passion.

21 The feelings of euphoria, sleeplessness, and loss of appetite, as well as the lover's intense energy, focused attention, driving motivation, and goal-oriented behaviors, his/her tendency to regard the beloved as novel and unique, and the lover's increased passion in the face of adversity might all be caused, in part, by heightened levels of dopamine and/or norepinephrine in the brain. And the lover's obsessive **cogitation** about the beloved might be due to decreased brain levels of some type of serotonin.

22 Now for the **caveats.** This theory is complicated by many facts: different doses of these chemicals can produce different effects. These substances do different things in different brain parts. Each interacts with the others in different ways under different circumstances. And each harmonizes with many other bodily systems and brain circuits, setting up complex chain reactions. Moreover, passionate romantic love takes a variety of graded forms, from pure elations when one's love is reciprocated to feelings of emptiness, despair, and often rage when one's love is thwarted. These chemicals undoubtedly vary in their concentrations and combinations as the relationship ebbs and flows.

23 Nevertheless, the distinct correlation between numerous characteristics of romantic love and the effects of these three brain substances led me to the following hypothesis: this fire in the mind is caused by elevated levels of either dopamine or norepinephrine or both, as well as decreased levels of serotonin. These chemicals form the backbone of obsessive, passionate, romantic love.

Excerpted from *Why We Love: The Nature and Chemistry of Romantic Love* by Helen Fisher, published by Henry Holt and Company.

THINK QUESTIONS

1. Refer to one or more details from the text to explain why the author chose to look specifically at dopamine, norepinephrine, and serotonin in her study of romantic love.

2. Use details from the text to write two or three sentences about the author's theory of how romantic love is similar to addiction. How does this idea connect to the descriptions of love in the first paragraph of the article?

3. Write two or three sentences explaining what scientists in Italy discovered about OCD patients and people in love and what the author concludes from this. Support your answer with textual evidence.

4. Use context to determine the meaning of the word **ruminations** as it is used in *Why We Love*. Write your definition of "ruminations" and tell how you determined it.

5. The word **caveats** comes directly from Latin. Use context to determine the meaning of "caveats" as it is used in *Why We Love*. Write your definition of "caveats" and explain how you derived it.

Copyright © BookheadEd Learning, LLC

CLOSE READ

Reread the excerpt from *Why We Love: The Nature and Chemistry of Romantic Love.* As you reread, complete the Focus Questions below. Then use your answers and annotations from the questions to help you complete the Writing Prompt.

FOCUS QUESTIONS

1. Reread the first section of the text, under the heading "From Chapter 3: Chemistry of Love: Scanning the Brain 'in Love.'" Then, locate the next three headings and make annotations to explain how those three sections connect to the first section, using evidence from the text.

2. Reread paragraph 6, which compares the behavior of prairie voles to the behavior of humans. What connection is the author drawing? Highlight and make annotations to support your explanation with evidence from the text.

3. In paragraph 9, the author uses the technical term "stimulant" to refer to dopamine. Based on the context in the paragraph, what does she probably mean by "stimulant"? Highlight the context clues you identify, and make annotations to explain how you determined the meaning from the text evidence.

4. Explain how the author takes the properties of three chemicals and ties them to her hypothesis in the final section of the excerpt, "A Working Hypothesis." Highlight and make annotations to support your explanations with evidence from the text.

5. In this article, Helen Fisher addresses *why* we are affected by love, on a chemical level, and *how* this chemical process of love affects us. Think about the portrayals of people in love that you have seen in films or television shows, or read in fiction. Do these portrayals sound similar to the chemical "love" effects described by Fisher? Explain why or why not, supporting your answers with evidence from the text.

WRITING PROMPT

In a short essay, explain how author Helen Fisher uses this passage to ask and answer a question about romantic love. How does she organize the text in a way that develops and supports her ideas? How does technical language add to the effectiveness of her explanations? Use evidence from the text to support your analysis, and include technical language from the text to make your analysis specific and clear.

Please note that excerpts and passages in the StudySync® library and this workbook are intended as touchstones to generate interest in an author's work. The excerpts and passages do not substitute for the reading of entire texts, and StudySync® strongly recommends that students seek out and purchase the whole literary or informational work in order to experience it as the author intended. Links to online resellers are available in our digital library. In addition, complete works may be ordered through an authorized reseller by filling out and returning to StudySync® the order form enclosed in this workbook.

Reading & Writing Companion   371

THE GIFT OF THE MAGI

FICTION
O. Henry
1906

INTRODUCTION

Known for his trademark surprise endings, American writer O. Henry penned over 400 short stories, often at the rate of one a day, before passing away at age 47. One of his most beloved stories is "The Gift of the Magi," about Della and Jim, a young couple living in New York City, struggling to make ends meet—and hoping to have enough left over to buy each other Christmas presents.

"Of all who give and receive gifts, such as they are wisest."

 FIRST READ

 NOTES

1 ONE dollar and eighty-seven cents. That was all. And sixty cents of it was in pennies. Pennies saved one and two at a time by bulldozing the grocer and the vegetable man and the butcher until one's cheeks burned with the silent imputation of parsimony that such close dealing implied. Three times Della counted it. One dollar and eighty-seven cents. And the next day would be Christmas.

2 There was clearly nothing to do but flop down on the shabby little couch and howl. So Della did it. Which instigates the moral reflection that life is made up of sobs, sniffles, and smiles, with sniffles **predominating.**

3 While the mistress of the home is gradually subsiding from the first stage to the second, take a look at the home. A furnished flat at $8 per week. It did not exactly beggar description, but it certainly had that word on the lookout for the mendicancy squad.

4 In the vestibule below was a letter-box into which no letter would go, and an electric button from which no mortal finger could coax a ring. Also appertaining thereunto was a card bearing the name "Mr. James Dillingham Young."

5 The "Dillingham" had been flung to the breeze during a former period of prosperity when its possessor was being paid $30 per week. Now, when the income was shrunk to $20, though, they were thinking seriously of contracting to a modest and unassuming D. But whenever Mr. James Dillingham Young came home and reached his flat above he was called "Jim" and greatly hugged by Mrs. James Dillingham Young, already introduced to you as Della. Which is all very good.

6 Della finished her cry and attended to her cheeks with the powder rag. She stood by the window and looked out dully at a gray cat walking a gray fence

NOTES

in a gray backyard. Tomorrow would be Christmas Day, and she had only $1.87 with which to buy Jim a present. She had been saving every penny she could for months, with this result. Twenty dollars a week doesn't go far. Expenses had been greater than she had calculated. They always are. Only $1.87 to buy a present for Jim. Her Jim. Many a happy hour she had spent planning for something nice for him. Something fine and rare and sterling— something just a little bit near to being worthy of the honor of being owned by Jim.

7   There was a pier glass between the windows of the room. Perhaps you have seen a pier glass in an $8 flat. A very thin and very agile person may, by observing his reflection in a rapid sequence of longitudinal strips, obtain a fairly accurate conception of his looks. Della, being slender, had mastered the art.

8   Suddenly she whirled from the window and stood before the glass. Her eyes were shining brilliantly, but her face had lost its color within twenty seconds. Rapidly she pulled down her hair and let it fall to its full length.

9   Now, there were two possessions of the James Dillingham Youngs in which they both took a mighty pride. One was Jim's gold watch that had been his father's and his grandfather's. The other was Della's hair. Had the queen of Sheba lived in the flat across the airshaft, Della would have let her hair hang out the window some day to dry just to **depreciate** Her Majesty's jewels and gifts. Had King Solomon been the janitor, with all his treasures piled up in the basement, Jim would have pulled out his watch every time he passed, just to see him pluck at his beard from envy.

10 So now Della's beautiful hair fell about her rippling and shining like a cascade of brown waters. It reached below her knee and made itself almost a garment for her. And then she did it up again nervously and quickly. Once she faltered for a minute and stood still while a tear or two splashed on the worn red carpet.

11 On went her old brown jacket; on went her old brown hat. With a whirl of skirts and with the brilliant sparkle still in her eyes, she fluttered out the door and down the stairs to the street.

12 Where she stopped the sign read: "Mme. Sofronie. Hair Goods of All Kinds." One flight up Della ran, and collected herself, panting. Madame, large, too white, chilly, hardly looked the "Sofronie."

13 "Will you buy my hair?" asked Della.

14 "I buy hair," said Madame. "Take yer hat off and let's have a sight at the looks of it."

15 Down rippled the brown cascade.

16 "Twenty dollars," said Madame, lifting the mass with a practised hand.

17 "Give it to me quick," said Della.

18 Oh, and the next two hours tripped by on rosy wings. Forget the hashed metaphor. She was **ransacking** the stores for Jim's present.

19 She found it at last. It surely had been made for Jim and no one else. There was no other like it in any of the stores, and she had turned all of them inside out. It was a platinum fob chain simple and chaste in design, properly proclaiming its value by substance alone and not by meretricious ornamentation—as all good things should do. It was even worthy of The Watch. As soon as she saw it she knew that it must be Jim's. It was like him. Quietness and value—the description applied to both. Twenty-one dollars they took from her for it, and she hurried home with the 87 cents. With that chain on his watch Jim might be properly anxious about the time in any company. Grand as the watch was, he sometimes looked at it on the sly on account of the old leather strap that he used in place of a chain.

20 When Della reached home her intoxication gave way a little to **prudence** and reason. She got out her curling irons and lighted the gas and went to work repairing the ravages made by generosity added to love. Which is always a tremendous task, dear friends—a mammoth task.

21 Within forty minutes her head was covered with tiny, close-lying curls that made her look wonderfully like a truant schoolboy. She looked at her reflection in the mirror long, carefully, and critically.

22 "If Jim doesn't kill me," she said to herself, "before he takes a second look at me, he'll say I look like a Coney Island chorus girl. But what could I do—oh! what could I do with a dollar and eighty-seven cents?"

23 At 7 o'clock the coffee was made and the frying-pan was on the back of the stove hot and ready to cook the chops.

24 Jim was never late. Della doubled the fob chain in her hand and sat on the corner of the table near the door that he always entered. Then she heard his step on the stair away down on the first flight, and she turned white for just a moment. She had a habit of saying a little silent prayer about the simplest everyday things, and now she whispered: "Please God, make him think I am still pretty."

25   The door opened and Jim stepped in and closed it. He looked thin and very serious. Poor fellow, he was only twenty-two—and to be burdened with a family! He needed a new overcoat and he was without gloves.

26   Jim stopped inside the door, as immovable as a setter at the scent of quail. His eyes were fixed upon Della, and there was an expression in them that she could not read, and it terrified her. It was not anger, nor surprise, nor disapproval, nor horror, nor any of the sentiments that she had been prepared for. He simply stared at her fixedly with that peculiar expression on his face.

27   Della wriggled off the table and went for him.

28   "Jim, darling," she cried, "don't look at me that way. I had my hair cut off and sold because I couldn't have lived through Christmas without giving you a present. It'll grow out again—you won't mind, will you? I just had to do it. My hair grows awfully fast. Say 'Merry Christmas!' Jim, and let's be happy. You don't know what a nice—what a beautiful, nice gift I've got for you."

29   "You've cut off your hair?" asked Jim, **laboriously,** as if he had not arrived at that patent fact yet even after the hardest mental labor.

30   "Cut it off and sold it," said Della. "Don't you like me just as well, anyhow? I'm me without my hair, ain't I?"

31   Jim looked about the room curiously.

32   "You say your hair is gone?" he said, with an air almost of idiocy.

33   "You needn't look for it," said Della. "It's sold, I tell you—sold and gone, too. It's Christmas Eve, boy. Be good to me, for it went for you. Maybe the hairs of my head were numbered," she went on with sudden serious sweetness, "but nobody could ever count my love for you. Shall I put the chops on, Jim?"

34   Out of his trance Jim seemed quickly to wake. He enfolded his Della. For ten seconds let us regard with discreet scrutiny some inconsequential object in the other direction. Eight dollars a week or a million a year—what is the difference? A mathematician or a wit would give you the wrong answer. The magi brought valuable gifts, but that was not among them. This dark assertion will be illuminated later on.

35   Jim drew a package from his overcoat pocket and threw it upon the table.

36   "Don't make any mistake, Dell," he said, "about me. I don't think there's anything in the way of a haircut or a shave or a shampoo that could make me like my girl any less. But if you'll unwrap that package you may see why you had me going a while at first."

37   White fingers and nimble tore at the string and paper. And then an ecstatic scream of joy; and then, alas! a quick feminine change to hysterical tears and wails, necessitating the immediate employment of all the comforting powers of the lord of the flat.

38   For there lay The Combs—the set of combs, side and back, that Della had worshipped long in a Broadway window. Beautiful combs, pure tortoise shell, with jewelled rims—just the shade to wear in the beautiful vanished hair. They were expensive combs, she knew, and her heart had simply craved and yearned over them without the least hope of possession. And now, they were hers, but the tresses that should have adorned the coveted adornments were gone.

39   But she hugged them to her bosom, and at length she was able to look up with dim eyes and a smile and say: "My hair grows so fast, Jim!"

40   And then Della leaped up like a little singed cat and cried, "Oh, oh!"

41   Jim had not yet seen his beautiful present. She held it out to him eagerly upon her open palm. The dull precious metal seemed to flash with a reflection of her bright and ardent spirit.

42   "Isn't it a dandy, Jim? I hunted all over town to find it. You'll have to look at the time a hundred times a day now. Give me your watch. I want to see how it looks on it."

43   Instead of obeying, Jim tumbled down on the couch and put his hands under the back of his head and smiled.

44   "Dell," said he, "let's put our Christmas presents away and keep 'em a while. They're too nice to use just at present. I sold the watch to get the money to buy your combs. And now suppose you put the chops on."

45   The magi, as you know, were wise men—wonderfully wise men—who brought gifts to the Babe in the manger. They invented the art of giving Christmas presents. Being wise, their gifts were no doubt wise ones, possibly bearing the privilege of exchange in case of duplication. And here I have lamely related to you the uneventful chronicle of two foolish children in a flat who most unwisely sacrificed for each other the greatest treasures of their house. But in a last word to the wise of these days let it be said that of all who give gifts these two were the wisest. Of all who give and receive gifts, such as they are wisest. Everywhere they are wisest. They are the magi.

Please note that excerpts and passages in the StudySync® library and this workbook are intended as touchstones to generate interest in an author's work. The excerpts and passages do not substitute for the reading of entire texts, and StudySync® strongly recommends that students seek out and purchase the whole literary or informational work in order to experience it as the author intended. Links to online resellers are available in our digital library. In addition, complete works may be ordered through an authorized reseller by filling out and returning to StudySync® the order form enclosed in this workbook.

Reading & Writing Companion   377

THINK QUESTIONS

1. Refer to details from the text or inferences you have drawn from text details to support your understanding of why Della wanted to buy a special Christmas present for Jim.

2. Use details from the text to write two or three sentences describing the financial situation of the young couple and its effect on them.

3. Write two or three sentences exploring how the gifts affect Della and Jim's relationship. Support your answer with textual evidence.

4. Use context to determine the meaning of the word **depreciate** as it is used in "The Gift of the Magi." Write your definition of "depreciate" and tell how you arrived at it.

5. Remember that the Latin prefix *pre-* can mean "in front of," and then think about the meaning of the word "dominate." Use the context clues provided in the passage to determine the meaning of **predominating.** Write your definition of "predominating" and tell how you arrived at it.

CLOSE READ

Reread the short story "The Gift of the Magi." As you reread, complete the Focus Questions below. Then use your answers and annotations from the questions to help you complete the Writing Prompt.

FOCUS QUESTIONS

1. Explain how the author uses the first three paragraphs to indicate Della's feelings about the poverty the couple are experiencing. Highlight evidence from the text and make annotations to explain your choices.

2. Paragraphs 4–5 describe the change in the couple's finances. How has this change affected Jim emotionally? What is the textual evidence that the financial change has also changed how he views himself? Make inferences about Jim's emotions, and annotate your thoughts. Support your answer with textual evidence.

3. Paragraph 10 makes a brief break from the action as the narrator reveals the two possessions that Della and Jim most treasure. Why is this information important to the story? What possible problem could these possessions cause for the young couple? Highlight your textual evidence and make annotations to explain your choices.

4. In the last four paragraphs of the story, Jim realizes that both gifts are now useless. What does Jim's reaction to the situation reveal about his nature? Use your inference skills to answer the question. Highlight evidence from the text and make annotations to support your answer.

5. How has love affected the couple's life together? Consider ways in which it has created or lessened problems. Highlight textual evidence and make annotations to support your ideas.

WRITING PROMPT

Describe what the story reveals about how love affects Jim and Della. How does love motivate the actions of both characters? What message about love would you identify as the story's theme? Support your writing with text evidence.

Please note that excerpts and passages in the StudySync® library and this workbook are intended as touchstones to generate interest in an author's work. The excerpts and passages do not substitute for the reading of entire texts, and StudySync® strongly recommends that students seek out and purchase the whole literary or informational work in order to experience it as the author intended. Links to online resellers are available in our digital library. In addition, complete works may be ordered through an authorized reseller by filling out and returning to StudySync® the order form enclosed in this workbook.

Reading & Writing Companion

379

ROMANTIC LOVE: REALITY OR MYTH?

NON-FICTION

2014

INTRODUCTION

The authors of these two short passages dispute the concept of romantic love—an idea that has been part of the human experience since the dawn of civilization. One writer argues that falling in love is a biological phenomenon—an impulse of the brain with a scientific basis. The other claims that romantic love is a cultural construct, created by society because it makes a good foundation for a story. Each passage presents strong arguments and supports its claims with evidence. Which argument do you feel is more convincing?

"The fairy tale of romantic love is one that we all want to believe."

FIRST READ

Point: Romantic Love Is Real!

1   Most people who have experienced romantic love—and many who haven't—will insist that it is undeniably real. However, a few unbelievers still see romantic love as a cultural **phenomenon;** some even have the audacity to compare love to other cultural concepts such as popular music and manners. Fortunately, we don't have to rely on anecdotal evidence to prove the doubters wrong. A look at science and history proves that romantic love is indeed a real biological phenomenon. In fact, romantic love is more similar to the human ability to walk on two legs than it is to manners!

2   Romantic love evolved for humans in the same way that upright posture evolved. Humans evolved to walk upright because it freed their hands for reaching and carrying food, tools, and their young. This adaptation helped early humans survive, and therefore the trait was passed on to subsequent generations of humans. By the same token, the children of parents who were paired monogamously survived better than the children whose parents did not stay together. This is because monogamous pairs were more likely to work together to raise their children successfully. So what motivated parents to pair monogamously in the first place? The brain must have evolved to feel the very real emotion of romantic love. Therefore it makes sense that the capacity for romantic love is just as much a biological concept for humans as the ability to walk upright. Both of these biological adaptations were important for early humans to evolve into what they are today.

3   Another piece of evidence that romantic love is a product of evolution rather than culture is that romantic love has existed for a very long time. Culture is fluid and ever-changing. Although biology does change through evolution, that change is very gradual. The speed at which romantic love has developed and changed over time points to biology rather than culture. Romantic love

has been around for much longer than other cultural concepts, such as manners. Plato wrote about the infinite nature of romantic love thousands of years ago. Romantic love was a driving force in both the *Iliad* and the *Odyssey,* also written in ancient times. Now compare this to the cultural phenomena we mentioned earlier: popular music and manners. Popular music and manners have changed so much over thousands of years that they are almost unrecognizable from what they were in the time of Plato or Homer. Romantic love has remained the same, and this proves that it cannot be a by-product of culture.

4 If these logical explanations don't convince you, there is also scientific proof that romantic love is real. Modern scientists are able to use magnetic resonance imaging scans (MRIs) to capture pictures of what happens in the body in the presence of certain **stimuli.** One stimulus that was studied is love. These studies have proven that when a person feels love, a network of a dozen brain regions are working together to create these feelings. According to a *Scientific American* article about love, "the network releases neurotransmitters and other chemicals in the brain and blood that create the sensations of attraction, arousal, pleasure... and obsession." This is just one more piece of evidence that proves that romantic love is a biological concept.

5 Although we can all agree that love has a very important place in our culture, its roots are biological rather than cultural. We only need to consult science and history to find proof. The historical and scientific evidence is **emphatic:** humans evolved to feel romantic love as a way to help the species survive, and the impulse to love still exists in the human brain today. Those who have experienced romantic love will probably agree: it is not only real, but it is one of the most amazing things about being human. To claim that romantic love is only a cultural concept is to diminish the importance of love in the history of the human species.

Counterpoint: Romantic Love Is a Fairy Tale

6 Some people truly believe that romantic love is a biological phenomenon. They may point to anecdotal evidence about their parents, or even their own relationships, as proof. But the logical thinkers of the world know that anecdotal evidence is not scientific proof. The people who believe in romantic love may also point to **dubious** scientific studies where brain scans "prove" that when humans feel romantic love they respond biologically. These studies are not reliable; even many scientists are skeptical about their results. According to Dr. Sally Satel of the American Enterprise Institute, activity in a small area of the brain called the insula has been used to prove that one can both "love" one's smartphone *and* feel "disgust" for a former political candidate who was involved in a scandal. How can activity in one area of the brain prove both love and disgust? How can scientists tell that the person

doesn't love the former political candidate and feel disgust at the smartphone? The only thing that these brain scan studies prove is that science can be twisted to support whatever the scientist or writer believes.

7   Other attempts to prove that romantic love is real have also failed. One reason for this is that love is not easily defined. It means different things to different people. Think about some of the biological concepts that can be measured, such as hormone levels or blood type. These concepts can be measured with specific words and numbers. Now try to define love with words or numbers. It's not so easy! Even other emotions are more concrete than love. If you ask a group of people what anger or frustration feels like, you will probably get the same answer from most of them. If you ask a group of people what romantic love feels like, you will probably get many different answers. The fact that love can't be defined proves that it is not a real biological concept, but rather an invention of our culture.

8   It is understandable that many people believe in romantic love. The concept is so entwined with human culture that it is difficult to tell that it is a cultural invention rather than a biological phenomenon. Romantic love is **depicted** in almost every childhood fairy tale, and it continues to frame the narrative of our lives all the way into adulthood. When you examine the history of the human species, it makes sense that culture evolved this way. Families are at the root of the organization of human civilization, and as humans became more organized, they promoted the idea that there was some force holding these family units together. That force, of course, is romantic love. Because the family unit was advantageous for human survival, it became a way of life. Then the romantic love that held the parents together became a centerpiece of human culture.

9   Another reason that romantic love is so prominent in human culture is that people are in love with the *idea* of falling in love. One of the things that makes the human brain special is its ability to create a fantasy world that may be very different from a person's tangible surroundings. Our fantasies have very real implications for our behavior in daily life. For example, if we dream of living in a nice house and driving a fancy car, this motivates us to work hard, so we can afford to buy those things in reality. Similarly, we imagine a partnered relationship that fits the concept of "romantic love" and then we try to create that relationship in the real world. Just as the importance of a nice house and a fancy car is dictated by culture, the same is true of romantic love. The world around us tells us that a partnered relationship is something to strive for, and we internalize that idea as the truth.

10   The fairy tale of romantic love is one that we all want to believe. Who wouldn't want to live in a world where we all have one true mate who will complete us and make us happy? But wanting to believe in the stories of Cinderella or

Sleeping Beauty doesn't make them true. In reality, the concept of romantic love is one that comes from our culture, rather than some biological need to find a romantic partner.

THINK QUESTIONS

1. What connection do both passages make between the idea of romantic love and the importance of the family unit in human society? Support your answer with details from the text of both passages.

2. Use details from both passages to explain the use both writers make of examples of romantic love in literature.

3. Identify the basic sources that both writers use in their arguments about romantic love. Use specific details from both passages in your answer.

4. Use context to determine the meaning of the word **dubious** as it is used in "Romantic Love Is a Fairy Tale." Write your definition of "dubious" and explain how you arrived at it.

5. Remembering that the Latin prefix *de-* means "of" and the Latin root *pict* means "image," use the context clues provided in the passage to determine the meaning of **depicted.** Write your definition of "depicted" and explain how you arrived at it.

CLOSE READ

Reread the debate "Romantic Love: Reality or Myth?" As you reread, complete the Focus Questions below. Then use your answers and annotations from the questions to help you complete the Writing Prompt.

FOCUS QUESTIONS

1. Both authors reference sources they used to write their passages. As far as you can judge without actually consulting these sources, are the sources reputable, and do they appear likely to provide accurate information? How does your analysis of the sources affect your opinion of the persuasiveness of each essay? Use specific details from the passages in your response.

2. Choose one example in either passage of weak, poorly-thought-out, or irrelevant evidence, and analyze what makes this evidence weak, faulty, or beside the point. How does the writer's choice to include this evidence affect your overall impression of the passage, and why? Use specific details from the passage to support your answer.

3. Compare and contrast the arguments made in the two passages. Which writer do you think makes a stronger case for his or her main point? What makes this essay stronger? If you think neither one makes a good case, or that both make an equally good case, explain why. Use specific details from both passages to support your answer. (Hint: You can agree with the author's main point and still argue that his or her passage does not make a strong argument.)

4. The word "love" is repeated many times in both passages. Analyze the denotation(s) and connotation(s) of the word love. Does it have more than one meaning? Are the connotations positive, negative or both? Do the passages seem to understand the word "love" in its fullest possible meaning, or do they only use it in a narrow sense? How does your analysis of this word affect your opinion of the persuasiveness of the arguments made in the passages?

5. Throughout this unit, you have been asked to consider how people are affected by the power of love. How do you think the writers of each of the passages are affected by the power of love? What evidence in both passages supports your answer?

WRITING PROMPT

Both passages agree that the phenomenon of romantic love is very powerful in human experience. If it's true that "Romantic Love Is a Fairy Tale," how do you account for its power in human civilization from ancient times to the present day? Use details from both passages to support your response.

WEST SIDE STORY

FICTION
Arthur Laurents
1957

INTRODUCTION

Arthur Laurents' *West Side Story* is an American musical inspired by the tale of Romeo and Juliet. The play is set in New York City in the 1950s. Against the backdrop of violence between the two gangs, Tony, a member of the Polish-American Jets, falls in love with Maria, the sister of Bernardo, leader of the rival Puerto Rican Sharks. Laurents' take on the ill-fated love story is a dark one, reimagining the relevance of the tale in the light of contemporary social problems. In this excerpt, Tony and Maria secretly meet at her window.

"See only me."

 FIRST READ

From Act I, Scene VI, Balcony Scene

A Back Alley - 11:00 p.m.

1   (Maria appears at the window above him which opens onto the escape.)

2   TONY: Maria, Maria. . .

3   MARIA: Ssh!

4   TONY: Maria!

5   MARIA: Quiet!

6   TONY: Come down!

7   MARIA: No!

8   TONY: Maria. . .

9   MARIA: Please if Bernardo!

10   TONY: He's at the dance. Come down!

11   MARIA: He will soon bring Anita home!

12   TONY: Just for a minute. . .

13   MARIA (smiles): A minute is not enough

14   TONY (smiles): For an hour then. . .

15   MARIA: I cannot!

16   TONY: For ever!

17   MARIA: Ssh!

18   TONY: Then I'm coming up

19   WOMAN'S VOICE (from the offstage apartment): Maria!

20   MARIA: *Momentito*, Mama. . .

21   TONY (climbing up): Maria, Maria. . .

22   MARIA: *Caladito!* (reaching her hand out to stop him) Ssh!

23   TONY (grabbing her hand): Ssh!

24   MARIA: It is dangerous.

25   TONY: I'm not "one of them."

26   MARIA: You are; but to me, you are not. Just as I am one of them. . . (gestures inside)

27   TONY: To me, you are all the. . . (She covers his mouth with her hand.)

28   MAN'S VOICE (from the unseen apartment): *Maruca!*

29   MARIA: *Si, ya vengo, Papa!*

30   TONY: *Maruca?*

31   MARIA: His pet name for me.

32   TONY: I like him. He will like me.

33   MARIA: No. He is like Bernardo: afraid. Imagine being afraid of you!

34   TONY: You see?

35   MARIA (touching his face): I see you.

36   TONY: See only me.

Excerpted from *West Side Story* by Arthur Laurents, published by Random House.

THINK QUESTIONS

1. Refer to one or more details from the text to support your understanding of why Maria keeps telling Tony to be quiet and go away. Why does she not want anyone to see him on her balcony? Support your answer with textual evidence.

2. Why does Maria say her father will not like Tony? Why might Tony think that her father will like him? Support your answer with textual evidence.

3. Write two or three sentences exploring the dialogue in this excerpt from *West Side Story*. What does the dialogue tell you about the characters' situation in this scene? How does the conversation in this excerpt reflect Tony and Maria's relationship? Support your answer with textual evidence.

4. This excerpt from *West Side Story* contains a number of Spanish words and phrases. Use a bilingual dictionary to determine the correct pronunciation and definitions of **momentito, caladito,** and **ya vengo.** Then write your definitions and explain how knowing the meanings of these terms helps increase a reader's understanding of the excerpt.

5. Maria says the word her father calls her, *Maruca*, is a "pet name." Some synonyms for "pet name" include *nickname, epithet,* and *tag.* Even though these words all share the same denotation, they have different connotations, or emotional associations. Explain the denotations and connotations of the word "pet name," and why Maria might use this term instead of a synonym.

Please note that excerpts and passages in the StudySync® library and this workbook are intended as touchstones to generate interest in an author's work. The excerpts and passages do not substitute for the reading of entire texts, and StudySync® strongly recommends that students seek out and purchase the whole literary or informational work in order to experience it as the author intended. Links to online resellers are available in our digital library. In addition, complete works may be ordered through an authorized reseller by filling out and returning to StudySync® the order form enclosed in this workbook.

Reading & Writing Companion **389**

CLOSE READ

Reread the excerpt from *West Side Story*. As you reread, complete the Focus Questions below. Then use your answers and annotations from the questions to help you complete the Writing Prompt.

FOCUS QUESTIONS

1. In *Romeo and Juliet,* Act II, Scene II, we hear Romeo's words before he spots Juliet. How is this scene in *West Side Story* different, and what is the effect of that difference? Do you think Tony feels the same way about Maria as Romeo feels about Juliet? Why or why not? Annotate your inferences about the text and its deeper meaning. Support your answer with textual evidence, and make annotations to explain your answer choices.

2. Compare and contrast Romeo and Tony. How are they alike? How are they different? Highlight evidence of Tony's personality, feelings, and motivations, and make annotations to explain how they are similar to or different from Romeo's. Remember to always support your explanations with textual evidence from both works.

3. How are the writing styles different in *Romeo and Juliet* and *West Side Story*? How are they the same? Highlight evidence from the text and make annotations to support your explanation.

4. How do you think the relationship between Tony and Maria will turn out in the end? Is "happily ever after" possible for them? Why or why not?

5. Do you think *Romeo and Juliet* and *West Side Story* are still relevant today? Are most humans still as affected by the power of love as Romeo and Tony, and Juliet and Maria? Which of their actions and words are still something that rings true today about the power of love to control our behavior? Highlight textual evidence and make annotations to explain your ideas.

WRITING PROMPT

Read *Romeo and Juliet* Act II, Scene II, and then reread the balcony scene from *West Side Story*. In around 300 words, write a response comparing and contrasting the scenes across each version. Cite evidence from the texts to support your response.

ANGELA'S ASHES

NON-FICTION
Frank McCourt
1996

INTRODUCTION

In his Pulitzer Prize-winning autobiography *Angela's Ashes*, Frank McCourt tells the sometimes humorous and sometimes sad tale of his poverty-stricken childhood. Born in New York in 1930, McCourt and his family returned to Ireland during the Great Depression, ultimately settling in the slums of Limerick. The excerpt below focuses on McCourt's experience as a typhoid patient in a hospital in Ireland. During his stay, young Frank befriends the girl in the neighboring room, filling their time by reading poetry and annoying their nurse, Sister Rita.

"She says I'll have plenty of time to reflect on my sins in the big ward upstairs..."

 FIRST READ

From Chapter VIII

1   The room next to me is empty till one morning a girl's voice says, Yoohoo, who's there?

2   I'm not sure if she's talking to me or someone in the room beyond.

3   Yoohoo, boy with the typhoid, are you awake?

4   I am.

5   Are you better?

6   I am.

7   Well, why are you here?

8   I don't know. I'm still in the bed. They stick needles in me and give me medicine.

9   What do you look like?

10 I wonder, What kind of a question is that? I don't know what to tell her.

11 Yoohoo, are you there, typhoid boy?

12 I am.

13 What's your name?

14 Frank.

Copyright © BookheadEd Learning, LLC

15   That's a good name. My name is Patricia Madigan. How old are you?

16   Ten.

17   Oh. She sounds disappointed.

18   But I'll be eleven in August, next month.

19   Well, that's better than ten. I'll be fourteen in September. Do you want to know
     why I'm in the Fever Hospital?

20   I do.

21   I have diphtheria and something else.

22   What's something else?

23   They don't know. They think I have a disease from foreign parts because my
     father used to be in Africa. I nearly died. Are you going to tell me what you
     look like?

24   I have black hair.

25   You and millions.

26   I have brown eyes with bits of green that's called hazel.

27   You and thousands.

28   I have stitches on the back of my right hand and my two feet where they put
     in the soldier's blood.

29   Oh, God, did they?

30   They did.

31   You won't be able to stop marching and saluting.

32   There's a swish of habit and click of beads and then Sister Rita's voice. Now,
     now, what's this? There's to be no talking between two rooms especially
     when it's a boy and a girl. Do you hear me, Patricia?

33   I do, Sister.

34   Do you hear me, Francis?

35   I do, Sister.

Please note that excerpts and passages in the StudySync® library and this workbook are intended as touchstones to generate interest in an author's work. The excerpts and passages do not substitute for the reading of entire texts, and StudySync® strongly recommends that students seek out and purchase the whole literary or informational work in order to experience it as the author intended. Links to online resellers are available in our digital library. In addition, complete works may be ordered through an authorized reseller by filling out and returning to StudySync® the order form enclosed in this workbook.

Reading & Writing
Companion   393

NOTES

36 You could be giving thanks for your two remarkable recoveries. You could be saying the rosary. You could be reading *The Little Messenger of the Sacred Heart* that's beside your beds. Don't let me come back and find you talking.

37 She comes into my room and wags her finger at me. Especially you, Francis, after thousands of boys prayed for you at the Confraternity. Give thanks, Francis, give thanks.

38 She leaves and there's silence for awhile. Then Patricia whispers, Give thanks, Francis, give thanks, and say your rosary, Francis, and I laugh so hard a nurse runs in to see if I'm all right. She's a very stern nurse from the County Kerry and she frightens me. What's this, Francis? Laughing? What is there to laugh about? Are you and that Madigan girl talking? I'll report you to Sister Rita. There's to be no laughing for you could be doing serious damage to your **internal apparatus.**

39 She plods out and Patricia whispers again in a heavy Kerry accent, No laughing, Francis, you could be doin' serious damage to your internal apparatus. Say your rosary, Francis, and pray for your internal apparatus.

    . . .

40 Every day I can't wait for the doctors and nurses to leave me alone so I can learn a new verse from Patricia and find out what's happening to the highwayman and the landlord's red-lipped daughter. I love the poem because it's exciting and almost as good as my two lines of Shakespeare. The redcoats are after the highwayman because they know he told her, I'll come to thee by moonlight, though hell should bar the way.

41 I'd love to do that myself, come by moonlight for Patricia in the next room, though hell should bar the way. She's ready to read the last few verses when in comes the nurse from Kerry shouting at her, shouting at me, I told ye there was to be no talking between room. Diphtheria is never allowed to talk to typhoid and visa versa. I warned ye. And she calls out, Seamus, take this one. Take the by. Sister Rita said one more word out of him and upstairs with him. We gave ye a warning to stop the **blathering** but ye wouldn't. Take the by, Seamus, take him.

42 Ah, now nurse, sure isn't he harmless. 'Tis only a bit o' poetry.

43 Take that by, Seamus, take him at once.

44 He bends over me and whispers, Ah, God, I'm sorry, Frankie. Here's your English history book. He slips the book under my shirt and lifts me from the bed. He whispers that I'm a feather. I try to see Patricia when we pass through her room but all I can make out is a blur of dark head on a pillow.

45 Sister Rita stops us in the hall to tell me I'm a great disappointment to her, that she expected me to be a good boy after what God had done for me, after all the prayers said by hundreds of boys at the Confraternity, after all the care from the nuns and nurses of the Fever Hospital, after the way they let my mother and father in to see me, a thing rarely allowed, and this is how I repaid them lying in the bed reciting silly poetry back and forth with Patricia Madigan knowing very well there was a ban on all talk between typhoid and diphtheria. She says I'll have plenty of time to reflect on my sins in the big ward upstairs and I should beg God's forgiveness for my disobedience reciting a **pagan** English poem about a thief on a horse and a maiden with red lips who commits a terrible sin when I could have been praying or reading the life of a saint. She made it her business to read that poem so she did and I'd be well advised to tell the priest in confession.

46 The Kerry nurse follows us upstairs gasping and holding on to the banister. She tells me I better not get the notion she'll be running up to this part of the world every time I have a little pain or a **twinge.**

47 There are twenty beds in the ward, all white, all empty. The nurse tells Seamus put me at the far end of the ward against the wall to make sure I don't talk to anyone who might be passing the door, which is very unlikely since there isn't another soul on this whole floor. She tells Seamus this was the fever ward during the Great Famine long ago and only God knows how many died here brought in too late for anything but a wash before they were buried and there are stories of cries and moans in the far reaches of the night. She says 'twould break your heart to think of what the English did to us, that if they didn't put the blight on the potato they didn't do much to take it off. No pity. No feeling at all for the people that died in this very ward, children suffering and dying here while the English feasted on roast beef and guzzled the best of wine in their big houses, little children with their mouths all green from trying to eat the grass in the fields beyond, God bless us and save us and guard us from future famines.

48 Seamus says 'twas a terrible thing indeed and he wouldn't want to be walking these halls in the dark with all the little green mouths gaping at him. The nurse takes my temperature, 'Tis up a bit, have a good sleep for yourself now that you're away from the chatter with Patricia Madigan below who will never know a gray hair.

49 She shakes her head at Seamus and he gives her a sad shake back.

50 Nurses and nuns never think you know what they're talking about. If you're ten going on eleven you're supposed to be simple like my uncle Pat Sheehan who was dropped on his head. You can't ask questions. You can't show you understand what the nurse said about Patricia Madigan, that she's going to die, and you can't show you want to cry over this girl who taught you a lovely poem which the nun says is bad.

Excerpted from *Angela's Ashes: A Memoir* by Frank McCourt, published by Simon & Schuster.

 THINK QUESTIONS

1. Refer to one or more details from the text to support your understanding of where the narrator of the text is situated at the beginning of the text—both from ideas that are directly stated and ideas that you have inferred from clues in the text.

2. Use details from the text to draw two or three conclusions about the society and cultural context in which the narrative occurs.

3. Write two or three sentences exploring the relationship between the Irish and English, as demonstrated in the text. Support your answer with textual evidence.

4. Use context to determine the meaning of the word **twinge** as it is used in *Angela's Ashes*. Write your definition of "twinge" and tell how you arrived at it. Then, use a dictionary to check your meaning.

5. Use context to determine the meaning of the word **pagan.** Write your definition of "pagan" and tell how you determined its meaning.

CLOSE READ

Reread the excerpt from *Angela's Ashes*. As you reread, complete the Focus Questions below. Then use your answers and annotations from the questions to help you complete the Writing Prompt.

FOCUS QUESTIONS

1. Reread the first section of dialogue in the passage and explain how the author's choice of words and sentence structures help create the tone of the selection. Highlight evidence from the text and make annotations to explain your choices.

2. Reread Sister Rita's first appearance in the passage. How does the author establish a tone that demonstrates his attitude toward the Sister, and her attitude towards the author (as a child)? Make annotations about your inferences about the text and its deeper meaning. Support your answer with textual evidence.

3. Reread the paragraphs in which Frank describes his time spent with Patricia (beginning with "Every day I can't. . ."). What central idea or ideas does the author seem to be developing in the interactions between Frank and Patricia? Highlight textual evidence and make annotations to explain your response.

4. What is the central idea being developed by the paragraph in which Sister Rita stops the protagonist (and Seamus) in the hall? Highlight evidence from the text and make annotations to support your explanation.

5. Does the selection provide any insight into how people are affected by the power of love? Who demonstrates love in this excerpt, and what or whom do they love? Highlight textual evidence and make annotations to explain your ideas.

WRITING PROMPT

How does the language of the selection and its use of vocabulary contribute to an overall tone or multiple tones? How does the tone of the selection help to increase your understanding of the themes, and help reveal the social and political context of the era in which the narrative takes place? Support your answer with evidence from the text.

Please note that excerpts and passages in the StudySync® library and this workbook are intended as touchstones to generate interest in an author's work. The excerpts and passages do not substitute for the reading of entire texts, and StudySync® strongly recommends that students seek out and purchase the whole literary or informational work in order to experience it as the author intended. Links to online resellers are available in our digital library. In addition, complete works may be ordered through an authorized reseller by filling out and returning to StudySync® the order form enclosed in this workbook.

Reading & Writing Companion   397

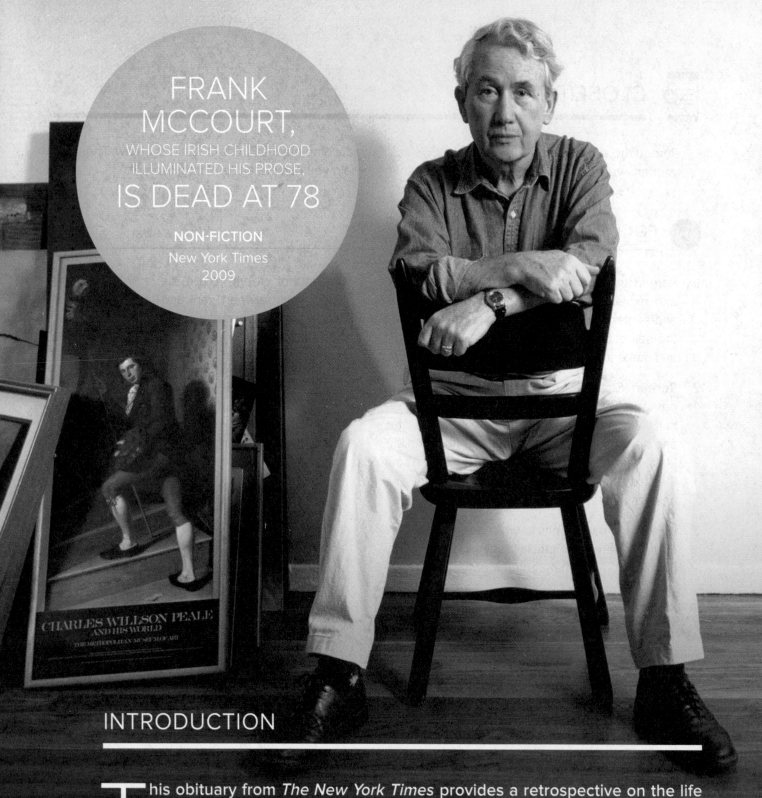

FRANK McCOURT,
WHOSE IRISH CHILDHOOD
ILLUMINATED HIS PROSE,
IS DEAD AT 78

NON-FICTION

New York Times
2009

INTRODUCTION

This obituary from *The New York Times* provides a retrospective on the life and accomplishments of acclaimed Irish-American teacher and writer Frank McCourt. Born in Brooklyn, New York, McCourt's family moved back to Ireland during the Great Depression, and ultimately settled in a rain-soaked Limerick slum. McCourt drew heavily upon his impoverished childhood in writing

"When I look back on my childhood, I wonder how I survived at all."

 FIRST READ

 NOTES

1 Frank McCourt, a former New York City schoolteacher who turned his miserable childhood in Limerick, Ireland, into a **phenomenally** popular, Pulitzer Prize-winning memoir, "Angela's Ashes," died in Manhattan on Sunday. He was 78 and lived in Manhattan and Roxbury, Conn.

2 The cause was metastatic melanoma, said Mr. McCourt's brother, the writer Malachy McCourt.

3 Mr. McCourt, who taught in the city's school system for nearly 30 years, had always told his writing students that they were their own best material. In his mid-60s, he decided to take his own advice, sitting down to commit his childhood memories to paper and producing what he described as "a modest book, modestly written."

4 In it Mr. McCourt described a childhood of terrible **deprivation.** After his alcoholic father abandoned the family, his mother — the Angela of the title — begged on the streets of Limerick to keep him and his three brothers meagerly fed, poorly clothed and housed in a basement flat with no bathroom and a thriving population of vermin. The book's clear-eyed look at childhood misery, its incongruously lilting, buoyant prose and its heartfelt urgency struck a remarkable chord with readers and critics.

5 "When I look back on my childhood, I wonder how I survived at all," the book's second paragraph begins in a famous passage. "It was, of course, a miserable childhood: The happy childhood is hardly worth your while. Worse than the ordinary miserable childhood is the miserable Irish childhood, and worse yet is the miserable Irish Catholic childhood.

6 "People everywhere brag and whimper about the woes of their early years, but nothing can compare with the Irish version: the poverty; the shiftless

Please note that excerpts and passages in the StudySync® library and this workbook are intended as touchstones to generate interest in an author's work. The excerpts and passages do not substitute for the reading of entire texts, and StudySync® strongly recommends that students seek out and purchase the whole literary or informational work in order to experience it as the author intended. Links to online resellers are available in our digital library. In addition, complete works may be ordered through an authorized reseller by filling out and returning to StudySync® the order form enclosed in this workbook.

Reading & Writing
Companion

399

loquacious alcoholic father; the pious defeated mother moaning by the fire; pompous priests; bullying schoolmasters; the English and all the terrible things they did to us for 800 long years."

7 "Angela's Ashes," published by Scribner in 1996, rose to the top of the best-seller lists and stayed there for more than two years, selling four million copies in hardback. The next year, it won the Pulitzer Prize for biography and the National Book Critics Circle Award.

8 Two more installments of his life story followed: "'Tis" (1999), which described his struggle to gain a foothold in New York, and "Teacher Man" (2005), an account of his misadventures and small victories as a public-school teacher. Both, although best sellers, did not achieve anything like the runaway success of Mr. McCourt's first book, which the British director Alan Parker brought to the screen in 1999.

9 Not to be outdone, Mr. McCourt's younger brother Malachy, an actor, brought out two volumes of his own memoirs: "A Monk Swimming" (1998), which also made the best-seller list, and "Singing My Him Song" (2000). Then, when it seemed that the McCourt tale had been well and truly told, Conor McCourt, Malachy's son, gathered the four brothers, got them talking and filmed two television documentaries, "The McCourts of Limerick" and "The McCourts of New York."

10 It was "Angela's Ashes" that loomed over all things McCourt, however, and constituted a **transformative** experience for its author.

11 Speaking to students at Bay Shore High School on Long Island in 1997, he said, "I learned the significance of my own insignificant life."

Born in New York

12 Francis McCourt was born Aug. 19, 1930, on Classon Avenue on the edge of the Bedford-Stuyvesant section of Brooklyn, where his Irish immigrant parents had hoped to make a better life. It was not to be, largely because his father, Malachy, usually spent his scant laborer's earnings at the local bar. Beaten, the family returned to Limerick when Frank was 4, and the pattern repeated itself.

13 Three of Mr. McCourt's six siblings died in early childhood. The family's circumstances were so dire, he later told a student audience, that he often dreamed of becoming a prison inmate so that he would be guaranteed three meals a day and a warm bed. At home, the staple meal was tea and bread, which his mother jokingly referred to as a balanced diet: a solid and a liquid.

14   When Frank was 11, his father went to work in a munitions factory in Britain and disappeared from the picture. Frank stole bread and milk, which became the family's principal means of support. After dropping out of school at 13, he delivered telegrams and earned extra income writing letters for a local landlady.

15   In 1949, Mr. McCourt, at 19, gathered his savings and boarded a ship for New York and a new life, which began unpromisingly. Finding a job at the Biltmore Hotel in Midtown Manhattan, he was put in charge of the 60 caged canaries in the public rooms. Thirty-nine of them died, whereupon Mr. McCourt taped the lifeless bodies to their perches. The ruse did not work.

16   A series of laboring jobs followed, interrupted by the Korean War. Drafted into the Army, Mr. McCourt served as a dog trainer and later a clerk in West Germany.

A Career as a Teacher

17   Despite his lack of formal schooling, Mr. McCourt won admission to New York University, where he earned a degree in English education in 1957. A year later he began teaching at McKee Vocational High School on Staten Island, an eye-opening experience that he recalled, in often hilarious detail, in his third volume of memoirs, "Teacher Man."

18   In his first week, an unruly student threw a homemade sandwich on the floor, an act that astonished Mr. McCourt not so much for its brazenness as for the waste of good food. After appraising the sandwich with a connoisseur's eye, he picked it up and ate it.

19   Mr. McCourt developed an idiosyncratic teaching style that found a somewhat more receptive audience at the elite Stuyvesant High School, where he taught creative writing after earning a master's degree in English from Brooklyn College in 1967. He had students sing Irish songs to break down their resistance to poetry. After discovering a sheaf of written excuses from past years, he recognized an unexplored literary genre and asked students to write, say, an excuse letter from Adam or Eve to God, explaining why he or she should not be punished for eating the apple.

20   He even had students test themselves. "When they wrote their own tests, they asked questions they wanted answers to and then they answered them," Mr. McCourt told the journal Instructor. "It was grand."

Testing Literary Waters

21   On the side, Mr. McCourt made fitful stabs at writing. He contributed articles on Ireland to The Village Voice. He kept notebooks. But at the Lion's Head in

NOTES

Greenwich Village, where he became friends with Pete Hamill and Jimmy Breslin, he felt like an interloper, he said. They were writers. He was just a teacher.

22 "I had no idea he had the ambition, much less the ability to carry it off in such spectacular fashion," Mr. Hamill, who first met Mr. McCourt at the Lion's Head in the 1960s, said in a telephone interview.

23 In 1977, Mr. McCourt and his brother Malachy, who was acting and bartending in New York, **cobbled** together a series of autobiographical sketches into a two-man play, "A Couple of Blaguards," which opened off Off Broadway at the Billymunk Theater on East 45th Street. They performed a revised version at the Village Gate in 1984 and again at the Billymunk in 1986 and took their show to several other cities.

24 This excursion into the past, along with his nagging sense that a writing teacher should write, motivated Mr. McCourt to undertake his childhood memoirs after he retired from teaching in 1987. An early attempt, when he was studying at New York University, had fizzled out, but three decades later, he said, he had worked through his awkward, self-conscious James Joyce phase and had gotten beyond the crippling anger that darkened his memories.

25 "After 20 pages of standard omniscient author, I wrote something that I thought was just a note to myself, about sitting on a seesaw in a playground, and I found my voice, the voice of a child," he told The Providence Journal in 1997. "That was it. It carried me through to the end of the book."

26 Still, his plans were vague. "I didn't know what I was going to do with it, but I had to write it anyway," he said in another interview. "I had to get it out of my system."

27 A persistent friend demanded to see what Mr. McCourt was writing, then turned the pages over to a literary agent, Molly Friedrich, who submitted the incomplete manuscript to Scribner. It was bought immediately.

28 Critics, enchanted by Mr. McCourt's language and gripped by his story, delivered the kind of reviews that writers can only dream of. But the book was ultimately a word-of-mouth success.

29 An instant celebrity, Mr. McCourt did his utmost to resist becoming the designated spokesman for all things Irish, "from agriculture to the decline in the consumption of claret in the West of Ireland," as he once joked.

30 In Ireland itself, the reaction was mixed. "When the book was published in Ireland, I was **denounced** from hill, pulpit and barstool," he told the online magazine Slate in 2007. "Certain citizens claimed I had disgraced the fair

NOTES

name of the city of Limerick, that I had attacked the church, that I had despoiled my mother's name and that if I returned to Limerick, I would surely be found hanging from a lamppost."

31 Time healed at least some wounds. Mr. McCourt was awarded an honorary doctorate by Limerick University, and curious tourists can now take "Angela's Ashes" tours of the city.

A Translation to Film

32 In 1999, the British director Alan Parker translated the memoir to the screen, with Emily Watson as Angela (who died in 1981), Robert Carlyle as Malachy Sr. (who died in 1985) and three actors in the roles of Mr. McCourt as a small, medium-size and grown boy.

33 For the Irish Repertory Theater, Mr. McCourt devised a history lesson disguised as an evening of storytelling and singing, titled "The Irish . . . and How They Got That Way." It opened in 1997 to less than rapturous reviews. His second volume of memoirs, " 'Tis," which began with his arrival in New York, also encountered rough weather from critics still giddy from the memory of "Angela's Ashes." Although his storytelling gifts were in full evidence, Mr. McCourt was taken to task by many critics for being bitter and self-pitying, a marked contrast to the stoic tone of "Angela's Ashes," putting off many readers.

34 With "Teacher Man," Mr. McCourt rallied. Although criticized as lumpy and episodic, the book was praised for its humane inquiry into the role of the teacher and the possibilities of education.

35 Mr. McCourt's first two marriages ended in divorce. In 1994 he married Ellen Frey McCourt. She survives him, as do his brothers Malachy and Alphie, both of Manhattan, and his brother Mike, of San Francisco; his daughter, Maggie McCourt of Burlington, Vt.; and three grandchildren.

36 "I think there's something about the Irish experience — that we had to have a sense of humor or die," Mr. McCourt once told an interviewer. "That's what kept us going — a sense of absurdity, rather than humor.

37 "And it did help because sometimes you'd get desperate," he continued. "And I developed this habit of saying to myself, 'Oh, well.' I might be in the midst of some misery, and I'd say to myself, 'Well, someday you'll think it's funny.' And the other part of my head will say: 'No, you won't — you'll never think this is funny. This is the most miserable experience you've ever had.' But later on you look back and you say, 'That was funny, that was absurd.'"

THINK QUESTIONS

1. How was *Angela's Ashes* originally received in Ireland, and why did people react this way? Why do you think people eventually changed their minds about it?

2. According to the article, why was *Angela's Ashes* so successful? Why does the article say that McCourt's other books were less successful, and why might this have affected audiences? Use evidence from the text to support your answer.

3. Write two or three sentences about what McCourt believed it took to survive tough circumstances. Support your answer with textual evidence.

4. Use context to determine the meaning of the word **denounced** as it is used in the passage. Write your definition of "denounced" and tell how you arrived at it.

5. Use context and your knowledge of word parts and prefixes to determine the meaning of **transformative** as it is used in the passage. Write your definition and explain how you determined it.

CLOSE READ

Reread Frank McCourt's obituary. As you reread, complete the Focus Questions below. Then use your answers and annotations from the questions to help you complete the Writing Prompt.

FOCUS QUESTIONS

1. Reread the first paragraph and explain how the author uses informational text elements to set up the main focus of this obituary. Highlight evidence from the text and make annotations to explain your choices.

2. Reread paragraphs 6 through 9. What purpose does the information in this section serve? Why might the author have wanted to include information about McCourt's relatives in the obituary for Frank McCourt?

3. Reread the section entitled "Born in New York." What details does Grimes include about McCourt's childhood? What purpose do you think these details serve? Highlight your textual evidence and annotate to explain your choices.

4. In the section "A Career as a Teacher," what information does Grimes include about McCourt's teaching days? How does the author connect this information to the rest of McCourt's life? Highlight your textual evidence and annotate to explain your choices.

5. From the information given in his obituary, what could a reader infer about the power of love in McCourt's life? Is this influence stated directly, or does it need to be read from "between the lines"? Highlight evidence from the text and annotate to support your answer.

WRITING PROMPT

In the obituary, Grimes quotes McCourt saying that, in writing *Angela's Ashes,* "I learned the significance of my own insignificant life." In a short essay, explore the meaning of this statement. How does the obituary describe McCourt's significance, and how might McCourt describe it? What details does Grimes use to convey the significance of McCourt's life with this obituary, and how does the obituary make connections between McCourt's life and his work's impact? Support your writing with textual evidence that refers to the obituary's informational text elements.

Please note that excerpts and passages in the StudySync® library and this workbook are intended as touchstones to generate interest in an author's work. The excerpts and passages do not substitute for the reading of entire texts, and StudySync® strongly recommends that students seek out and purchase the whole literary or informational work in order to experience it as the author intended. Links to online resellers are available in our digital library. In addition, complete works may be ordered through an authorized reseller by filling out and returning to StudySync® the order form enclosed in this workbook.

Reading & Writing Companion   **405**

'ANGELA'S ASHES' AUTHOR FRANK MCCOURT DIES AT 78

NON-FICTION
PBS
2009

INTRODUCTION

Frank McCourt, the Pulitzer Prize-winning author of *Angela's Ashes*, died in 2009 at the age of 78. Born in New York, McCourt endured an impoverished childhood in the slums of Limerick, Ireland before returning to the United States and eventually finding success as a writer. In this video transcript, McCourt recounts his impressions upon arriving back in New York at age 19, and American writer Roger Rosenblatt speaks with PBS NewsHour correspondent Margaret

"...he told it in this beautiful, plain language, that brought you to your knees."

 FIRST READ

1   JIM LEHRER: And finally tonight, remembering author Frank McCourt. He was profiled and interviewed on the NewsHour when he rose to fame in the 1990s. Margaret Warner has our appreciation.

2   MARGARET WARNER: "Angela's Ashes," Frank McCourt's memoir of growing up poor in Ireland, became a publishing phenomenon. It hit the best-seller list in 1996 and remained there for 115 weeks.

3   "Angela's Ashes" **chronicled** with wit and compassion what McCourt called his "miserable Irish Catholic childhood," abandoned by an alcoholic father, losing three siblings to disease and malnutrition, and stealing to support his mother and remaining brothers.

4   Our Elizabeth Farnsworth spoke with McCourt when his book won the Pulitzer Prize in 1997. She asked him to read an excerpt.

5   FRANK MCCOURT: "I think my father is like the Holy Trinity with three people in him: the one in the morning with the paper, one at night with the stories and the prayers, and then the one who does the bad thing and comes home with the smell of whiskey and wants us to die for Ireland."

6   "I feel sad over the bad thing, but I can't back away from him because the one in the morning is my real father. And if I were in America, I could say, 'I love you, Dad,' the way they do in the films. But you can't say that in Limerick for fear you might be laughed at."

7   ELIZABETH FARNSWORTH: You must have been very angry for quite a while after this experience, losing so many members of your family, you being humiliated over and over again. Were you angry?

NOTES

8   FRANK MCCOURT: Well, when I arrived in America at 19, I was a time bomb, and I continued like that for a long time. I couldn't engage in any civilized discussion of anything because, if anybody opposed me, I would simply erupt. And I was always getting into trouble over this.

9   It took me years — I think it was in the classroom as a high school teacher — I finally became a civilized human being that had to listen to other points of view and present mine in a reasonable way.

10   MARGARET WARNER: McCourt published a new book in 1999 and spoke with the NewsHour's Terence Smith.

11   TERENCE SMITH: We took Frank McCourt back to the old Stuyvesant high school in New York where he taught English for 18 years to talk about his new book.

12   Now, "Angela's Ashes" ended as the young Frank McCourt arrived in the United States, and the last word of the book was word of the book was "'Tis."

13   FRANK MCCOURT: Yes.

14   TERENCE SMITH: Do you remember your first impressions when you came to this country?

15   FRANK MCCOURT: Of New York?

16   TERENCE SMITH: And of New York, but. . .

17   FRANK MCCOURT: Oh, God. Gold, that was the main thing, because I sailed in on an October morning, one of those glorious autumn mornings, coming in—that's before the Verrazano Bridge was built. You sail into the harbor, and Staten Island is on your left, and then you see the Statue of Liberty.

18   This is what everyone in the world has dreams of when they think about New York. And I thought, "My God, I'm in heaven. I'll be dancing down Fifth Avenue like Fred Astaire with Ginger Rogers." That was going to be my life.

19   TERENCE SMITH: How much money did you have in your pocket?

20   FRANK MCCOURT: Fifty dollars, less than $50. I had spent some of it.

21   TERENCE SMITH: And today, a mere 40 years later. . .

22   FRANK MCCOURT: Yes.

NOTES

23 TERENCE SMITH: . . . it is made of gold.

24 FRANK MCCOURT: It is made of gold, but it took a long time. And what has happened to me is beyond the wildest imagination of any screenwriter, any novelist. It's certainly beyond my imagination, because I never expected this. I never expected to write a book about a slum in Ireland that was going to catapult me, as they say, into some kind of—onto the best-seller list.

25 MARGARET WARNER: Frank McCourt died yesterday in New York. He was 78 years old.

26 And some further thoughts now about Frank McCourt from another writer who knew him. Author and former NewsHour essayist Roger Rosenblatt joins me from New York.

27 Hello, Roger. Frank McCourt, your friend, we know and late in life was wildly successful writer. How significant a writer do you think he was in literary terms?

28 ROGER ROSENBLATT: I think he was a very significant writer. He wrote probably the best memoir of recent years and established the fact that a memoir was a work of literature—a work of high literature and thus joined other Irish writers of other eras in giving us original language and beautiful thought on the subject of poverty and suffering and things that were hard to swallow, except in the hands of a first-class writer.

29 MARGARET WARNER: Now, he taught creative writing for decades to high school students, yet he struggled. He was unable to write his own memoir until very late in his life. Did he ever talk to you about what it was that unlocked him, that enabled him to write such a painful story in such a graceful way?

30 ROGER ROSENBLATT: Graceful is the key word. The idea of writing about so difficult a subject, such hard times, is not to write it with any self-pity or anything self-reflective or solipsistic or narcissistic, surely, but just to say, "This happened, and that happened."

31 When you have the goods, you don't need to dress up what you're writing. And I think it took awhile for Frank to understand that neither anger nor self-reflection were the ways into his story. His story was good enough on its own. And then, once he told it in this beautiful, plain language, that brought you to your knees.

32 MARGARET WARNER: Yes, and he once said he wrote it actually in the voice of a young boy and that that had also, I remember, he said, helped him. Tell us what he was like as a person.

Copyright © BookheadEd Learning, LLC

33 ROGER ROSENBLATT: He was like a young boy as a person. There was nobody who would make you laugh more than Frank. When he smiled, he was like a little boy, smiling. And when he would make himself laugh, which was unprofessional to be sure in a reading, but still, he would do it, then everybody just roared, because he would just surrender himself to the helplessness of laughter, the way a child does.

34 At the same time, as a friend, he was a most loyal friend. And you could count on him for anything. He was hardly without discriminations, but he was somebody who, if you had a cause worth supporting, if you had an event worth appearing at, he never thought of how he would look at that event or supporting that cause. He'd do it because it was the right thing to do. He was the person you never had to look around to see where he was. He was always with you.

35 MARGARET WARNER: Now, of course, when you knew him, he was by then rich and famous, but were there still traces or more than traces of this **impoverished** kid from Limerick?

36 ROGER ROSENBLATT: He never would think of himself as rich and famous. He used to make a joke of it. He said, "I'm a big shot now," he would say, thus shooting down all the big shots of history.

37 And as for fame, he used it in the best possible way, to meet people and make his literature go abroad, and help other lives, and **ennoble** other lives, and make the world more beautiful.

38 He was wonderful, Margaret, to watch with an audience in a reading. You could see him foreign for the words as if he'd never said them before. He had said them before. But it was a kind of innocence with which he viewed the world, which, of course, made any kind of pride or foolish reaction to his own success out of the question.

39 MARGARET WARNER: Now, as we just heard, he talked with Elizabeth about still the anger that certainly he'd had when he arrived and that he struggled with all his life. Did you still see traces of that?

40 ROGER ROSENBLATT: He could get angry at the right things. He could get angry at injustice. He could get angry at just the unfairness of a situation or of a **calamity** or of poverty itself.

41 But he wouldn't put anger in the writing. If you put anger in the writing, then it's like an actor crying on stage. The audience will not cry with the actor and in some way inure itself against the emotion.

42 But if you just say what's happening and say, in effect, here is why one might get angry at such facts, then he gives to the audience all the emotions that he has withheld from the prose.

43 MARGARET WARNER: And, briefly, before we go, his Irishness, how central to his identity as a writer and a man?

44 ROGER ROSENBLATT: He hated the idea of the stage Irishman, although he would make fun of it. But he really was Irish in the sense of the -- in the best sense, in terms of being a great talker, because the Irish talk English better than anyone else.

45 And he was in the tradition of the Irish literary revival of Yates and of Joyce and later of O'Casey, John Millington Synge, and Lady Gregory, Behan. All the great Irish writers were able to make the world more beautiful through original language, and that's what Frank did.

46 MARGARET WARNER: Roger, Roger Rosenblatt, thank you so much.

47 ROGER ROSENBLATT: Pleasure.

Used by permission of NewsHour Productions, LLC.

 THINK QUESTIONS

1. In two or three sentences, describe the character of Frank McCourt, based on your viewing of this television program. Cite evidence from the video to support your answer.

2. What is the attitude of interviewer Margaret Warner toward McCourt? Support your answer with evidence from the video.

3. Give two or more reasons why Roger Rosenblatt was a good choice of interviewee for a program about Frank McCourt. Support your answer with evidence from the video.

4. Use context to determine the meaning of the word **catapult** as it is used in *"Angela's Ashes" Author Frank McCourt Dies at 78*. Write your definition of "catapult" and tell how you found it.

5. Keeping in mind that the prefix *en-* indicates a verb meaning "to cause to be," use the context clues provided in the passage to determine the meaning of **ennoble.** Write your definition of "ennoble" and tell how you got it.

CLOSE READ

Reread the interview about Frank McCourt's death. As you reread, complete the Focus Questions below. Then use your answers and annotations from the questions to help you complete the Writing Prompt.

FOCUS QUESTIONS

1. At 0:33–0:50 of the video, journalist Margaret Walker discusses the fact that "Angela's Ashes chronicled with wit and compassion what McCourt called his 'miserable Irish Catholic childhood.'" What additional impact does the visual add to Walker's discussion? Provide evidence from the two versions, highlighting and using annotations to cite details from the written version.

2. From 0:58–1:28 in the video, Frank McCourt reads a passage from Angela's Ashes beginning "I think my father is like the Holy Trinity," and ending "for fear you might be laughed at." Discuss how the experience of listening to the reading might be different from reading the printed version. How might the audience's perception of McCourt's feelings about his father change from one medium to the other? Highlight or annotate details from the text to support your response.

3. Rewatch the portion of the video in which McCourt travels with a journalist to the high school in New York City where he used to teach (2:07–3:35). The two men discuss McCourt's early experiences in New York. Give one reason why changing the setting of the interview to the high school is a good choice for the video and one reason why it isn't a good choice. Cite specific details from the video or passage to support your answer.

4. The second half of the program is devoted to an interview with a friend of McCourt, writer Roger Rosenblatt. In your opinion, is the interview more effective in print or on video? Explain why, highlighting or annotating specific passages from the interview to support your response.

5. Based on your reading of all the selections by or about Frank McCourt in this unit, how do McCourt's life and work show the power of love? Use the highlight and annotation tools to provide evidence from the texts, and cite details from the video to support your answer.

Copyright © BookheadEd Learning, LLC

WRITING PROMPT

You have encountered "Angela's Ashes Author Frank McCourt Dies at 78" both as a written text and as a video. How might a version in the medium of radio (or an audio podcast) compare and contrast with those two versions? Remember that radio can include only words and sound effects, not visuals. Use your understanding of media to help you analyze how an all-audio medium would affect the information presented and the audience's understanding of that information. Your essay should also evaluate what would be gained and what would be lost in switching to this medium.

SONNET 73

POETRY
William Shakespeare
1609

INTRODUCTION

I n *Sonnet 73*, William Shakespeare practiced his art of masterful, lyrical storytelling in the shorter form of a 14-line sonnet poem. His inspired imagery takes us on a journey through life's final season, that passage toward "the twilight of such day / As after sunset fadeth in the west, / Which by and by black night doth take away.". The poem tells of the passage of youth, the waning of love, the approach of death. For each of the four-line stanzas, we are carried along by Shakespeare's visual metaphors, until the final two lines when the narration shifts from introspection into invitation, enticing readers to participate and reach their own conclusions.

"To love that well which thou must leave ere long."

NOTES

FIRST READ

1 That time of year thou mayst in me behold

2 When yellow leaves, or none, or few, do hang

3 Upon those boughs which shake against the cold,

4 Bare ruin'd choirs, where late the sweet birds sang.

5 In me thou seest the twilight of such day

6 As after sunset fadeth in the west,

7 Which by and by black night doth take away,

8 Death's second self, that seals up all in rest.

9 In me thou see'st the glowing of such fire

10 That on the ashes of his youth doth lie,

11 As the death-bed **whereon** it must **expire**

12 Consumed with that which it was **nourish'd** by.

13   This thou **perceivest,** which makes thy love more strong,

14   To love that well which thou must leave **ere** long.

THINK QUESTIONS

1. What time of life is the speaker in the poem discussing? Use evidence from the text to support your answer.

2. To what things does the speaker compare himself? What do each of these comparisons have in common? Support your response with evidence from the text.

3. Write two or three sentences about what Shakespeare is saying about mortality and love. How do death and love relate? Support your answer with textual evidence.

4. Use context to determine the meaning of the word nourish'd as it is used in the passage. Write your definition of **"nourish'd"** and tell how you found it. Then, find the word's meaning in a dictionary and compare it to your response.

5. Use context to determine the meaning of the word **perceivest** as it is used in the passage, and determine synonyms for this word. Write your synonyms of "perceivest" and tell how you found them.

CLOSE READ

Reread the poem "Sonnet 73." As you reread, complete the Focus Questions below. Then use your answers and annotations from the questions to help you complete the Writing Prompt.

 FOCUS QUESTIONS

1. What theme is Shakespeare exploring in the first four lines of the poem? How does the structure of the poem, including the rhyme scheme and the line arrangement, help to reveal this theme? Highlight evidence from the text and make annotations to support your answers.

2. What do you think Shakespeare means by the figure of speech "Death's second self"? How does this term change the tone of the metaphor in which he uses it? Support your answer with textual evidence and make annotations to explain your answer choices.

3. How does the tone of the poem change within the last six lines? What other elements of the poem and its structure shift in these lines?

Highlight evidence from the text and make annotations to support your answers.

4. The scope of something refers to how far it reaches. For example, the scope of a football field is 100 yards; the scope of a lifetime is about 100 years. How does the scope of the poet's metaphors about aging change throughout the poem? Highlight evidence from the text and make annotations to support your answers.

5. How does Shakespeare's statement in the last two lines of the sonnet illustrate the power of love in the face of lost youth, or even death? Highlight textual evidence and make annotations to support and explain your ideas.

WRITING PROMPT

In "Sonnet 73," Shakespeare describes old age through a series of metaphors. In an essay of at least 300 words, describe how these metaphors work within the poem's structure to tell a story of the process of aging. What is the tone the speaker takes toward aging, and how is that tone created by the progression of metaphors, the rhythm of the lines, and the rhyming words in the poem? Remember to cite evidence from the poem to support your ideas.

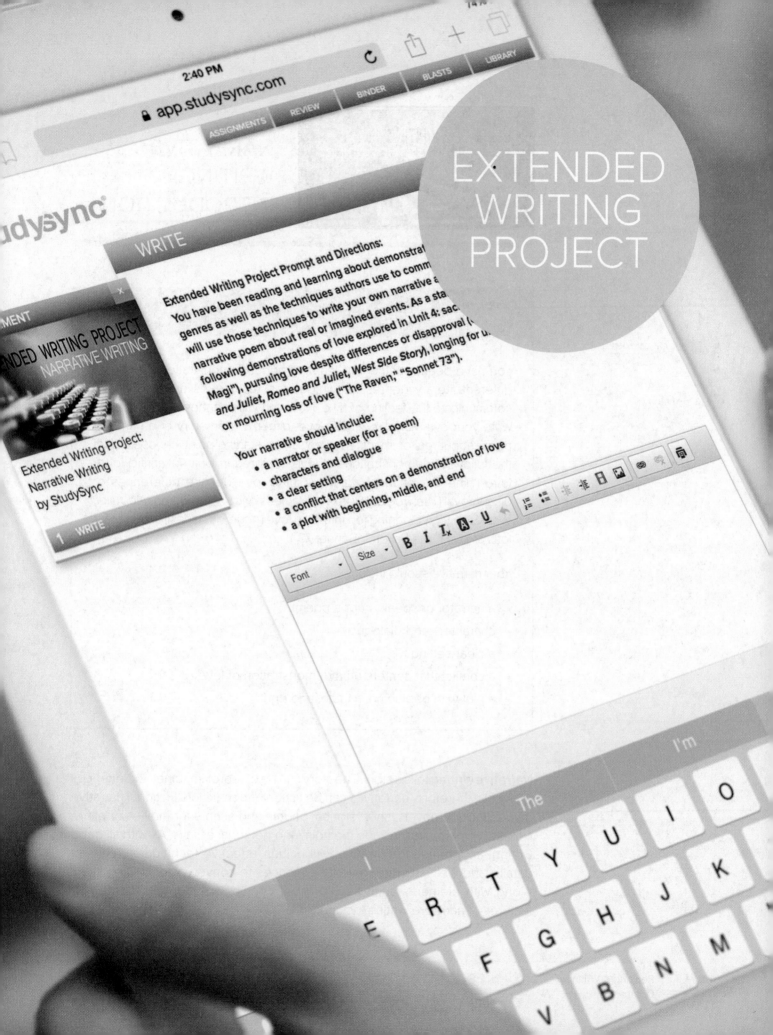

2:40 PM

app.studysync.com

REVIEW · BINDER · BLASTS · LIBRARY

ASSIGNMENTS

EXTENDED WRITING PROJECT

studysync®

WRITE

EXTENDED WRITING PROJECT
NARRATIVE WRITING

Extended Writing Project:
Narrative Writing
by StudySync

1 WRITE

Extended Writing Project Prompt and Directions:
You have been reading and learning about demonstrat...
genres as well as the techniques authors use to comm...
will use those techniques to write your own narrative a...
narrative poem about real or imagined events. As a sta...
following demonstrations of love explored in Unit 4: sac...
Magi"), pursuing love despite differences or disapproval (...
and Juliet, Romeo and Juliet, West Side Story), longing for u...
or mourning loss of love ("The Raven," "Sonnet 73").

Your narrative should include:
- a narrator or speaker (for a poem)
- characters and dialogue
- a clear setting
- a conflict that centers on a demonstration of love
- a plot with beginning, middle, and end

NARRATIVE WRITING: INTRODUCTION

WRITING PROMPT

You have been reading and learning about demonstrations of love in different literary genres, as well as the techniques authors use, to communicate the feeling of love. Now you will use those techniques to write your own narrative about love--either a short story or a narrative poem about real or imagined events. As a starting point, choose one of the following demonstrations of love explored in Unit 4: sacrificing for love ("The Gift of the Magi"), pursuing love despite differences or disapproval (*The Tragical History of Romeus and Juliet, Romeo and Juliet, West Side Story*), longing for unfulfilled love (*Angela's Ashes*), or mourning loss of love ("The Raven," "Sonnet 73").

Your narrative should include:

- a narrator or speaker (for a poem)
- characters and dialogue
- a clear setting
- a conflict that centers on a demonstration of love
- a plot with beginning, middle, and end

Narrative writing tells a story. The story can be of real or imagined experiences or events; therefore, narratives can be fiction or non-fiction. Fictional narrative genres include novels, short stories, poems and scripts for movies or plays. Non-fiction narratives include memoirs and personal essays. As with all good writing, an interesting narrative will include effective techniques, relevant details, and well-structured event sequences to convey a compelling story. Along with elements such as character, conflict, setting, and theme, the features of narrative writing include:

Copyright © BookheadEd Learning, LLC

- a narrator
- dialogue
- transitions
- conclusion

 STUDENT MODEL

Before you get started on your own narrative love story or narrative poem, read this narrative that one student wrote in response to the Writing Prompt. As you read the model, highlight and annotate the features of narrative writing that this student included in the story.

The Drop

At the end of every school year, the sophomores at Washington High take a trip to Wild World, a large amusement park about 45 minutes away and the sort of place that adds a new, more terrifying ride each year. To understand this story, you need to know that the sophomores' year-end outing was more than an average field trip. Somehow, somewhere in the legend and lore of Washington High, this Wild World trip had become the place where you told someone you liked them. It was the moment when you took that plunge and either crashed and burned or ended up "going out for the summer." So, as you might guess, on this particular outing, everyone spent time watching to see who was talking to each other, who had "coincidentally" gotten in line next to someone, and who switched buses to ride home together at the end of the day. So Wild World was not your average trip, and, fittingly, the rides were not your average rides.

The ride Wild World had added this year was a ridiculous, new roller coaster, which the park's marketers dubbed the "Moment of Truth." With the largest single drop in North America, a drop that plummeted riders over 500 feet at a near-vertical angle while reaching speeds of close to 140 miles per hour, this ride was no joke.

Of course, the drop was only the beginning, followed by the requisite number of inversions, twists and plunges to make the entire experience one breathless ordeal. But the drop was all people saw. At least that's all John saw, and all he needed to see before he blurted out, "That is just plain stupid. You've got to be out of your mind to ride that thing."

Now, that is definitely what John said. Those were his words. Pat and Ken and Zin all heard him. You can ask them. There's just no question about it. So, with that fact firmly established, the real question arises, why was John now standing deep in the middle of the line to ride the Moment of Truth? The astute observer, being fully informed of Washington High's annual trip to Wild World, would not have to look far to find the answer. Kaitlyn Ross was standing next to him.

Kaitlyn Ross was about the most beautiful girl that John had ever seen. Kaitlyn Ross was smart. Kaitlyn Ross laughed at jokes and played basketball and got good grades. Kaitlyn Ross was so special that whenever John spoke of her, he called her Kaitlyn Ross; calling her just plain Kaitlyn would be like referring to George Washington as George, or Thomas Jefferson as "Tom." She was not just a girl named Kaitlyn; she was Kaitlyn Ross, and she was standing in line next to him as he was about to do the scariest thing he had ever done in his life. Why was he standing in line to do the scariest thing he had ever done in his life? Why? Because Kaitlyn Ross had seen him with his friends, and Kaitlyn Ross had said, "Hey, we're going to go ride that," and she had pointed at the drop. And then Kaitlyn Ross had asked, "Do you want to go?"

Now they were in line together, and about every three minutes, another ground-shaking roar and another blast of screams would fly over their heads, stirring John's stomach up even more, then fading off into a distant rumble as a new group of riders sped along through their own moment of truth.

It was hot. The line was packed. But she wanted to ride this, and he wanted to be near her. So he made the sacrifice. He was doing this for her. He was doing this because he wanted to sit next to her. He would never have gone anywhere near this ride if not for her. Maybe he would touch her hand. This really was the moment of truth, and he was here because of her.

And then they were sitting next to each other.

And then they were buckled in and moving.

Is this love? John thought to himself, *this sudden lift, this loss of control and pure, exhilarating free-fall? This drop from reality? This stomach-lurching, twist and turning, upside down and round and round, mad, fantastic ride?* An unexpected left. Another drop. *How long will this last? Oh, another drop. Is this fun? It feels fun—in a terrifying sort of way. Did her hand just touch mine? Whoa! Are we upside down?* John tried to look at Kaitlyn, but could barely turn his head. He had the sense she was smiling. Or maybe she was frowning—they were upside down. He tried to smile. *Are you kidding me? Oh wow.* Upside down again. *And here we go, another turn. And...we're back. It's over. I can breathe.* John breathed deeply, but only briefly. Because when the restraints were lifted, Kaitlyn Ross, the Kaitlyn Ross, did something that would make John's mind flip loops of its own for quite some time. Kaitlyn Ross suddenly hugged John and shouted, "That was awesome!"

"Yeah," he stammered, "that was awesome."

"You were holding on for dear life," she laughed.

"Yes, I was," he said and laughed, too.

And so after she went off with her friends, and he went off with Ken, and Pat and Zin, John's thoughts spent the rest of the day on their own wild ride. *Was that a friendly hug or something more? What did she mean by that? Was she just excited? What am I supposed to do now? Was that an accident? Was it on purpose? What was that? OK, it was nothing. Or was it?*

That night John lay in bed, still thinking, *Should I call her? Should I text her? What should I do? I don't know what to do.*

In truth, there was something else John did not know. As the class was leaving Wild World, Kaitlyn Ross had texted him to see if he wanted to ride the same bus back to school with her; then, when she got home, having never heard back, she had texted him again to say how much fun she'd had with him. She finished her text with "call me." And then she waited. And waited. And now, not being able to take it any longer, she was calling him, and she was wondering why he wouldn't respond.

Every year the sophomores at Washington High take a trip to Wild World. Every year, Wild World adds a new ride. Just this very day, a boy had ridden that ride for one purpose, to be next to a certain girl. He would never have even considered it, except she asked him, and he wanted to spend time with her. He rode that ride so he could be near her. He rode it so he could get to know her. He rode it with the long-shot hope that she might actually like him. He rode it only for her. Now that girl was calling him. And somewhere in the dark, in the middle of that amusement park, deep in the bushes directly beneath the biggest loop of that newest, most terrifying ride, the boy's phone was ringing. . . and ringing. . . and ringing.

THINK QUESTIONS

1. What is the main conflict, or problem, of the story? How did this student engage the reader by setting out that problem?

2. How did the student establish point of view? Does the student maintain the same point of view throughout the story?

3. Who is the narrator? Does the narrator have a personality? What techniques did the student use to develop the character of the narrator?

4. What techniques did the student use to develop the characters of Kaitlyn and John? How does the writer help us get to know them better? How might you use similar techniques to develop the characters in your own story or narrative poem?

5. What are some of the techniques that the student used to create a smooth progression of experiences or events? What ideas might you borrow for your own narrative?

NOTES

SKILL:
ORGANIZE
NARRATIVE
WRITING

DEFINE

Every narrative plot contains a **narrator, characters,** and details that introduce the driving **conflict** behind a story. **Conflict** forms the core, or main problem, of the story, and its details are developed and revealed throughout the course of the narrative. Conflicts can be external, such as a knight having to kill a dragon, or internal, such as that same knight having to grapple with his fear of killing the dragon.

The **narrator** is the voice of the story, relaying its events to the reader. The most common types of narrator are first-person and third-person. The first-person narrator is a character in the story who tells us the events from his or her perspective. The third-person narrator tells the story from outside of the events, often with full access to the thoughts, emotions and motivations of some or all of the characters.

The **characters** take the actions that create the plot of a story, moving the narrative forward through the decisions they make. Characters are defined by many attributes, including appearance, background, emotions, and speech, but characters are defined primarily by the actions they take (or don't take, in some instances).

IDENTIFICATION AND APPLICATION

- A story's narrator introduces characters and conflict through details that help bring the story to life.
- Narrators provide information about characters over time, sometimes through the character's thoughts, often through the character's speech, and always through the character's actions.
- Writers present a conflict that they hope will be interesting, then they build their story around that conflict.

- As the story proceeds, the narrator provides more and more details that build the problem and make the reader engage with the characters even more.
- In a love story, these details will also often strengthen the bond between the main characters.
- Stories build to a climax at which the characters must make a decision and take action (or, in some instances, refuse to take action).

MODEL

The Gift of the Magi is a fiction narrative told from the perspective of a third-person narrator. Pay close attention to how the narrator uses specific details to introduce the conflict that the characters are facing:

> **ONE dollar and eighty-seven cents.** That was all. And sixty cents of it was in pennies. Pennies saved one and two at a time by bulldozing the grocer and the vegetable man and the butcher until one's cheeks burned with the silent imputation of parsimony that such close dealing implied. Three times Della counted it. One dollar and eighty-seven cents. And the next day would be Christmas.
>
> There was clearly nothing to do but flop down on the **shabby little couch and howl.** So Della did it. Which instigates the moral reflection that life is made up of sobs, sniffles, and smiles, with sniffles predominating.
>
> While the mistress of the home is gradually subsiding from the first stage to the second, take a look at the home. **A furnished flat at $8 per week.** It did not exactly beggar description, but it certainly had that word on the lookout for the mendicancy squad.

Here, the author has introduced the conflict: it's Christmas Eve and Della doesn't have enough money to purchase a present. We don't yet know for whom she wants to buy one, but we see her clearly in distress. Note that the author, O. Henry, shows us the problem; he doesn't simply tell us they're poor. He starts his story with a very specific detail, "One dollar and eighty-seven cents," then builds more details around that (it's in pennies; Della had to haggle with the grocer, the vegetable man, and the butcher to amass even that much; she flops down on a "shabby little couch" in order to paint the picture of their particular dilemma. The story continues:

> In the vestibule below was a letter-box into which no letter would go, and an electric button from which no mortal finger could coax a ring. Also appertaining thereunto was a card bearing the name **"Mr. James Dillingham Young."**

The "Dillingham" had been flung to the breeze during a former period of prosperity when its possessor was being paid $30 per week. Now, when **the income was shrunk to $20,** though, they were thinking seriously of contracting to a modest and unassuming D. But **whenever Mr. James Dillingham Young came home and reached his flat above he was called "Jim" and greatly hugged by Mrs. James Dillingham Young,** already introduced to you as Della. Which is all very good.

Della finished her cry and attended to her cheeks with the powder rag. She stood by the window and looked out dully at a gray cat walking a gray fence in a gray backyard. Tomorrow would be Christmas Day, and she had only $1.87 with which to buy Jim a present. She had been saving every penny she could for months, with this result. Twenty dollars a week doesn't go far. Expenses had been greater than she had calculated. They always are. **Only $1.87 to buy a present for Jim.** Her Jim. Many a happy hour she had spent planning for something nice for him. Something fine and rare and sterling—something just a little bit near to being worthy of the honor of being owned by Jim.

Now the narrator has told us that it's her husband whom Della wants to buy a present for, and he's told us the husband's name as well, James Dillingham Young.

Through the details, we know that Jim only makes $20 a week, and $8 of that goes to their rent. Notice how the narrator begins to heighten the conflict: "Many a happy hour she had spent planning for something nice for him." He also introduces the emotional bond Della feels for her husband: "Only $1.87 to buy a present for Jim. Her Jim," and "whenever Mr. James Dillingham Young came home and reached his flat above he was called 'Jim' and greatly hugged by Mrs. James Dillingham Young." So within the first few paragraphs, O. Henry's narrator has used details to set up the conflict of the love story. As we read on, the conflict is heightened by the fact that Jim himself faces the same dilemma of not having enough to make a purchase worthy of Della, until we reach O. Henry's famous surprise ending in which each character has made a very personal sacrifice in order to express their love for the other.

 PRACTICE

Write a basic outline for your narrative love story or poem that includes: who the narrator or speaker will be and what kind of narrator it is (first or third-person), a possible conflict (driving problem of the story), the setting of the story (time of day, year, or period in history, and location—house, town, country, society, or natural surroundings) and a description of at least one character (age, sex, appearance, what they think or how they feel about the conflict). When you are finished, trade outlines with a partner and offer each other feedback. How has your partner described each basic story element mentioned? How will each of these elements help to drive the plot of the story? Offer each other suggestions, and remember that they are most helpful when they are constructive.

PREWRITE

WRITING PROMPT

You have been reading and learning about demonstrations of love in different literary genres, as well as the techniques authors use, to communicate the feeling of love. Now you will use those techniques to write your own narrative about love--either a short story or a narrative poem about real or imagined events. As a starting point, choose one of the following demonstrations of love explored in Unit 4: sacrificing for love ("The Gift of the Magi"), pursuing love despite differences or disapproval (*The Tragical History of Romeus and Juliet, Romeo and Juliet, West Side Story*), longing for unfulfilled love (*Angela's Ashes*), or mourning loss of love ("The Raven," "Sonnet 73").

Your narrative should include:

- a narrator or speaker (for a poem)
- characters and dialogue
- a clear setting
- a conflict that centers on a demonstration of love
- a plot with beginning, middle, and end

In addition to studying techniques authors use to engage and entertain readers, you have been reading and learning about stories that center on demonstrations of love. In the extended writing project, you will use these narrative writing techniques to compose your own narrative love story.

Authors frequently take notes about story ideas before they sit down to actually start writing the story. These notes may include ideas about characters, conflict, theme, setting, and so on. Authors may also write down actual sentences, lines of dialogue, or descriptions that will later appear in their story as they are writing it. Sometimes an author might start with a specific character, the conflict, the plot, or even the setting as his or her initial inspiration.

Thinking about what you've learned thus far about how authors organize narrative writing, what kind(s) of problem(s) do you want your characters to face in your love story? What types of characters would you like to write about? Thinking about the student model, "The Drop," in which the roller coaster plays a major role in the plot, how might the setting of your story affect your characters and the conflict in which they're involved? From whose point of view should your story be told, and why?

Answer these questions for yourself by completing the "Prewrite: Narrative Writing" graphic organizer. Brainstorm and record your ideas about narrator, character, conflict, and setting on the chart. Next, examine your ideas and choose the ones you feel will work best for your narrative. Use a chart like the one that follows, completed by the writer of the student example, as a model to help guide your own prewriting:

PREWRITE – NARRATIVE WRITING			
Characters *What type of characters would I like to write about?*	**Conflict** *What types of problems might these characters face?*	**Setting** *How might the setting affect the characters and the problem?*	**Narrator** *From which point of view should this story be told? Why?*

Copyright © BookheadEd Learning, LLC

PREWRITE – NARRATIVE WRITING

Two high school kids Their friends (just a little bit) Their school (not too much, just as background to understand the field trip) ~~Their parents~~ ~~Their teachers~~	The boy and girl like each other but are afraid to say ~~Her friends don't like him~~ ~~Their parents don't want them to go out~~ The real conflict is that the boy is a little intimidated by the girl and is afraid to talk to her, let alone ask her out or anything. ~~Friends don't get along~~ After they ride the roller coaster, she "makes the first move" by calling him, but he doesn't know this because he's lost his phone.	A "thrill-ride" amusement park that the high school goes to every year. The roller coaster is where his phone falls out of his pocket.	~~First-person, from the boy's perspective~~ Can't be first-person, because then we won't know where the phone is or that the girl is calling him Third-person narrator (so that the reader can know things the characters don't)

Please note that excerpts and passages in the StudySync® library and this workbook are intended as touchstones to generate interest in an author's work. The excerpts and passages do not substitute for the reading of entire texts, and StudySync® strongly recommends that students seek out and purchase the whole literary or informational work in order to experience it as the author intended. Links to online resellers are available in our digital library. In addition, complete works may be ordered through an authorized reseller by filling out and returning to StudySync® the order form enclosed in this workbook.

Reading & Writing
Companion

429

SKILL:
INTRODUCTIONS

 ## DEFINE

The **introduction** is the beginning of the story, which sets the stage for the events to come. Because the introduction of a narrative is the reader's first experience with a particular story, writers often include elements of **exposition**—essential information such as character, setting, and problem—in the opening paragraphs of the story. A story's introduction should be engaging, capture a reader's attention, and tempt the reader to move forward into the story with interest. After reading a story's introduction, a reader should want to know more, and think, "What will happen in this story? I'd like to keep reading to discover more about these characters and explore this place." A good introduction will hook a reader with precise language and sensory details that transport a reader into the world of the story.

 ## IDENTIFICATION AND APPLICATION

- Writers often work vivid sensory details into their narrative introductions to draw readers into a story.

- Writers make precise word choices in story introductions, to help the reader visualize the characters and setting.

- A narrative introduction should provide the reader with a strong sense of time and place.

- Writers often introduce main characters in the opening paragraphs of a story.

- The opening scene of a story may contain an action that sets a sequence of events in motion.

- A writer may present the story's conflict in the introductory paragraphs in an effort to engage the reader with the events to come.

MODEL

In the opening paragraphs of a narrative, a writer aims to orient and engage the reader with specific details. These details are often expository elements that reveal important information about character, setting, and the central problem or conflict in the story. The student author of "The Drop" wrote the following introduction to the story:

At the end of every school year, the sophomores at Washington High take a trip to Wild World, a large amusement park about 45 minutes away and the sort of place that adds a new, more terrifying ride each year. To understand this story, you need to know that the sophomores' year-end outing was more than an average field trip. Somehow, somewhere in the legend and lore of Washington High, **this Wild World trip had become the place where you told someone you liked them. It was the moment when you took that plunge and either crashed and burned or ended up "going out for the summer."** So, as you might guess, on this particular outing, everyone spent time watching to see who was talking to each other, who had "coincidentally" gotten in line next to someone, and who switched buses to ride home together at the end of the day. So Wild World was not your average trip, and, fittingly, the rides were not your average rides.

The ride Wild World had added this year was a ridiculous, new roller coaster, which the park's marketers dubbed the "Moment of Truth." **With the largest single drop in North America, a drop that plummeted riders over 500 feet at a near-vertical angle while reaching speeds of close to 140 miles per hour, this ride was no joke.**

Of course, the drop was only the beginning, followed by the requisite number of inversions, twists and plunges to make the entire experience one breathless ordeal. But the drop was all people saw. **At least that's all John saw, and all he needed to see before he blurted out, "That is just plain stupid. You've got to be out of your mind to ride that thing."**

Now, that is definitely what John said. Those were his words. Pat and Ken and Zin all heard him. You can ask them. There's just no question about it. **So, with that fact firmly established, the real question arises, why was John now standing deep in the middle of the line to ride the Moment of Truth?** The astute observer, being fully informed of Washington High's annual trip

NOTES

to Wild World, would not have to look far to find the answer. **Kaitlyn Ross was standing next to him.**

Notice how the opening of the first paragraph provides essential and engaging details about the setting and characters of the story. The reader learns that the story takes place at a large amusement park near Washington High at the end of the school year and that the characters are the sophomores at the school. Furthermore, the author introduces another central fact that sets up an important plot element—the park adds a new "terrifying ride" each year. All these expository details are revealed to the reader in the first sentence, "At the end of every school year, the sophomores at Washington High take a trip to Wild World, a large amusement park about 45 minutes away and the sort of place that adds a new, more terrifying ride each year." Each detail is clearly and concisely described, and each adds to the picture of the world the story takes place in.

In the first paragraph, the reader also learns that the annual trip to Wild World amusement park had become legendary among the sophomores at Washington High. It was on this trip "where you told someone you liked them. It was the moment when you took that plunge and either crashed and burned or ended up 'going out for the summer.'"

The second and third paragraphs of the introduction are brief and are focused on details about the new ride, "The Moment of Truth." The reader learns that "With the largest single drop in North America, a drop that plummeted riders over 500 feet at a near-vertical angle while reaching speeds of close to 140 miles per hour, this ride was no joke." The description of the ride is clearly intended to grab the reader's interest. A reader might ask: "Is this a ride I might enjoy or is it a ride I might be afraid of? Why is it named 'The Moment of Truth?' Does the name have anything to do with the central problem of the story?" By the end of the third paragraph, the reader has learned more about the new ride and is introduced to one of the main characters of the story, John, who blurts out, "That is just plain stupid. You've got to be out of your mind to ride that thing."

John's comment leads directly to the fourth introductory paragraph in which the reader learns that, despite John's assessment, "the real question arises, why was John now standing deep in the middle of the line to ride the Moment of Truth?" We quickly learn the answer: "Kaitlyn Ross was standing next to him." Thus, in just a few short paragraphs consisting of several hundred words, the writer has created a complete story world. The reader knows a great deal about the characters, the setting, and the central problem of the story. Because of the precise and intriguing details, the reader is likely hooked, wanting to know more about what will happen to John and Kaitlyn on the ride—will they ride home together, and "go out for the summer," or will their relationship "crash and burn"? In short, what will their moment of truth be like?

 PRACTICE

Write an introduction for your narrative love story or poem that deals with demonstrations of love. In your introduction, be sure to include information about the setting, characters, and something about the central problem or conflict of the story. When you are finished, trade with a partner and offer each other feedback. How precise is the language used in your partner's introduction? Do the details help you to picture the setting and characters? What information about the characters is revealed in the introduction? Were you interested in what would happen next? Offer each other suggestions, and remember that they are most helpful when they are constructive.

NOTES

SKILL: NARRATIVE TECHNIQUES AND SEQUENCING

 DEFINE

To write a story, authors use a variety of tools to develop the plot and characters, create the setting, and engage the reader. **Narrative techniques** include dialogue, pacing, description, reflection, and the sequencing of events. **Dialogue,** what the characters say to one another, is often used to develop characters and move the plot forward. Writers often manipulate the **pacing** of a narrative, or the speed with which events occur, to build tension or avoid tedious narration. Writers use **description** to build story details and reveal information about character, setting, and plot. Narrators and characters often engage in **reflection,** the act of pondering the events that have occurred so far in the story. Every narrative contains a **sequence of events,** which is carefully planned and controlled by the author as the story unfolds.

The beginning part of a story is called the **introduction** or **exposition.** This is the part of the story in which the writer provides the reader with essential information, such as:

- Characters – the people or figures in a narrative, often the heroes or villains
- Setting – the time and place in which the action occurs
- Problem – the conflict the characters must face

As the story continues, the writer includes details and events to develop the conflict and move the story forward. These events—known as the **rising action** of the story—build until the story reaches the **climax,** the turning point in the story. This is where the most exciting and intense action in the story takes place, and characters are forced to face the conflict head-on.

The writer then focuses on details and events that lead to the **resolution** of the conflict. These details and events make up the **falling action** of the story— everything that happens after the climax and leads to the resolution. These elements make up a story's **conclusion,** which also often contains a message or final thought for the reader. Authors use these narrative techniques to create engaging stories that keep readers hooked from beginning to end.

 IDENTIFICATION AND APPLICATION

- Writers plan a sequence of events that will occur in a narrative, from the story's introduction to its conclusion.
- Writers use pacing to control the speed at which the events of a narrative unfold or are revealed to the reader.
- Writers use dialogue and description to develop characters and advance the action of the plot.
- Reflection slows down the forward motion of the story and gives writers a chance to further develop characters and plot.

 MODEL

In the story "The Drop," the student author uses narrative techniques and sequencing to present plot events and develop characters. Look at this excerpt, which centers on John and Kaitlyn's ride on "The Moment of Truth."

Kaitlyn Ross was about the most beautiful girl that John had ever seen. Kaitlyn Ross was smart. Kaitlyn Ross laughed at jokes and played basketball and got good grades. Kaitlyn Ross was so special that whenever John spoke of her, he called her Kaitlyn Ross; calling her just plain Kaitlyn would be like referring to George Washington as George, or Thomas Jefferson as "Tom." She was not just a girl named Kaitlyn; she was Kaitlyn Ross, and she was standing in line next to him as he was about to do the scariest thing he had ever done in his life. Why was he standing in line to do the scariest thing he had ever done in his life? Why? Because Kaitlyn Ross had seen him with his friends, and Kaitlyn Ross had said, "Hey, we're going to go ride that," and she had pointed at the drop. And then Kaitlyn Ross had asked, "Do you want to go?"

The student author makes effective use of descriptive language and repetition to reveal John's feelings for Kaitlyn Ross. He begins by cataloguing all the things that make her so special. "Kaitlyn Ross was about the most beautiful girl that John had ever seen. Kaitlyn Ross was smart. Kaitlyn Ross laughed at jokes and played basketball and got good grades. Kaitlyn Ross was so special that whenever John spoke of her, he called her *Kaitlyn Ross*. . . She was not just a girl named Kaitlyn; she was Kaitlyn Ross. . ." The author then builds suspense as the two main characters stand in line, waiting for their turn to ride.

> **Now they were in line together, and about every three minutes, another ground-shaking roar and another blast of screams would fly over their heads,** stirring John's stomach up even more, then fading off into a distant rumble **as a new group of riders sped along through their own moment of truth.**
>
> **It was hot. The line was packed. But she wanted to ride this, and he wanted to be near her. So he made the sacrifice.** He was doing this for her. He was doing this because he wanted to sit next to her. He would never have gone anywhere near this ride if not for her. Maybe he would touch her hand. **This really was the moment of truth, and he was here because of her.**
>
> **And then they were sitting next to each other.**
>
> **And then they were buckled in and moving.**

Notice how the writer shares the urgency of the moment by pacing the description of the passing time: "Now they were in line together, and about every three minutes, another ground-shaking roar and another blast of screams would fly over their heads. . . as a new group of riders sped along through their own moment of truth." John reiterates that he is there, only because she wants him to be there—"It was hot. The line was packed. But she wanted to ride this, and he wanted to be near her. So he made the sacrifice." Then the pace of the scene builds up with emphasis, "And then they were sitting next to each other. And then they were buckled in and moving."

In the next paragraph, the author describes John's experience while riding "The Moment of Truth." Notice that the description is both physical and emotional. The writer lets the reader experience the ride as John physically does, but the writer also uses the physical description to introduce John's thoughts about the significance of the ride and his feelings for Kaitlyn Ross.

> *Is this love?* John thought to himself, *this sudden lift, this loss of control and pure, exhilarating free-fall? This drop from reality? This stomach-lurching, twist and turning, upside down and round and round, mad, fantastic ride?* An unexpected left. Another drop. *How long will this last?* Oh, another drop. *Is this fun? It feels fun—in a terrifying sort of way. Did her hand just touch mine? Whoa! Are we upside down?* John tried to look at Kaitlyn, but could

barely turn his head. **He had the sense she was smiling. Or maybe she was frowning—they** *were* **upside down.** He tried to smile. *Are you kidding me? Oh wow. Upside down again. And here we go, another turn. And. . .we're back. It's over. I can breathe.* John breathed deeply. But only briefly. **Because when the restraints were lifted, Kaitlyn Ross,** *the* **Kaitlyn Ross, did something that would make John's mind flip loops of its own for quite some time. Kaitlyn Ross suddenly hugged John and shouted, "That was awesome!"**

The end of this paragraph leads into a brief dialogue between Kaitlyn and John. This is followed by a reflection by John as he tries to figure the significance of what has happened.

> "Yeah," he stammered, "that was awesome."
>
> "You were holding on for dear life," she laughed.
>
> "Yes, I was," he said and laughed too.
>
> And so after she went off with her friends, and he went off with Ken, and Pat and Zin, John's thoughts spent the rest of the day on their own wild ride. **Was that a friendly hug or something more? What did she mean by that?** *Was she just excited? What am I supposed to do now? Was that an accident? Was it on purpose? What* <u>was</u> *that? OK, it was nothing. Or was it?*
>
> That night John lay in bed, still thinking, *Should I call her? Should I text her? What should I do? I don't know what to do.*

The author has skillfully satisfied the reader's interest in what happened on the ride; however, the actual events—the hug, the statement "That was awesome"—just lead John to further question the significance of the events. *"Was that a friendly hug or something more? What did she mean by that?"* John knows what has happened, but he doesn't know what the events actually reveal about Kaitlyn's feelings for him. The reader, like John, is propelled into further introspection and self-reflection. "That night John lay in bed, still thinking, *Should I call her? Should I text her? What should I do? I don't know what to do.*" Having carefully controlled the sequence of events in rising action, while picking up the pace of events from the slow wait in line to the frenetic ride itself to the unexpected outcome, the author has taken both John and the reader back to a slower reflective pace while keeping the reader "hooked" and interested in finding out what will happen next.

Please note that excerpts and passages in the StudySync® library and this workbook are intended as touchstones to generate interest in an author's work. The excerpts and passages do not substitute for the reading of entire texts, and StudySync® strongly recommends that students seek out and purchase the whole literary or informational work in order to experience it as the author intended. Links to online resellers are available in our digital library. In addition, complete works may be ordered through an authorized reseller by filling out and returning to StudySync® the order form enclosed in this workbook.

Reading & Writing Companion   **437**

NOTES

PRACTICE

Write a short section for your love story or love poem that focuses on one of the narrative techniques you have been studying in this lesson. For example, you might create a short dialogue between two main characters, or you might write a description that builds story details and reveals information about character, setting, and plot. Perhaps you would prefer to write a brief scene where a main character reflects on some important event that has happened. When you are finished, trade with a partner and offer each other feedback. Offer each other suggestions, and remember that they are most helpful when they are constructive.

PLAN

WRITING PROMPT

You have been reading and learning about demonstrations of love in different literary genres, as well as the techniques authors use, to communicate the feeling of love. Now you will use those techniques to write your own narrative about love--either a short story or a narrative poem about real or imagined events. As a starting point, choose one of the following demonstrations of love explored in Unit 4: sacrificing for love ("The Gift of the Magi"), pursuing love despite differences or disapproval (*The Tragical History of Romeus and Juliet, Romeo and Juliet, West Side Story*), longing for unfulfilled love (*Angela's Ashes*), or mourning loss of love ("The Raven," "Sonnet 73").

Your narrative should include:

- a narrator or speaker (for a poem)
- characters and dialogue
- a clear setting
- a conflict that centers on a demonstration of love
- a plot with beginning, middle, and end

Consider the elements of narrative outline you explored in the Narrative Techniques and Sequencing lesson. What details and events are most important in the exposition of a story? What story developments should take place during the rising action of a story? What is the purpose of a story's climax? How do writers lead readers toward a resolution of a story? What narrative techniques are the most effective?

Please note that excerpts and passages in the StudySync® library and this workbook are intended as touchstones to generate interest in an author's work. The excerpts and passages do not substitute for the reading of entire texts, and StudySync® strongly recommends that students seek out and purchase the whole literary or informational work in order to experience it as the author intended. Links to online resellers are available in our digital library. In addition, complete works may be ordered through an authorized reseller by filling out and returning to StudySync® the order form enclosed in this workbook.

Reading & Writing Companion   **439**

NOTES

Use the StudySync "Narrative Writing Plot Diagram" to plan a sequence of events for your narrative love story or love poem. Use this plot diagram, completed by the writer of the student model narrative, to help guide your planning:

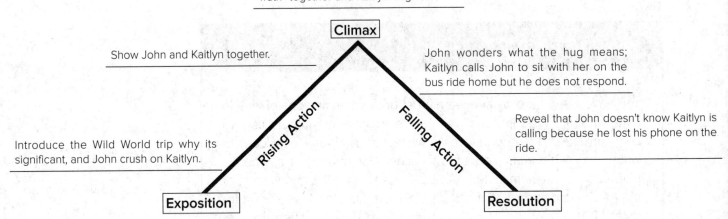

John and Kaitlyn ride the "Moment of Truth" together and Kaitlyn hugs John.

Climax

Show John and Kaitlyn together.

John wonders what the hug means; Kaitlyn calls John to sit with her on the bus ride home but he does not respond.

Rising Action

Falling Action

Reveal that John doesn't know Kaitlyn is calling because he lost his phone on the ride.

Introduce the Wild World trip why its significant, and John crush on Kaitlyn.

Exposition

Resolution

SKILL:
WRITING
DIALOGUE

 DEFINE

When writing a story, authors use a variety of tools to develop the plot and characters, create the setting, and engage the reader. Dialogue is one of the primary tools of narrative writing.

Dialogue is a written verbal exchange between two or more characters. Dialogue is not only used to create an interaction between characters, but it can also provide essential details by illuminating a character's personality, advancing the plot, offering insight into the driving conflict, or showcasing setting by using a regional dialect.

There are two different types of dialogue: direct and indirect. **Direct dialogue** is speech within a narrative using a character's *exact* words. In this case, quotation marks are used. Direct dialogue allows characters to speak for themselves without relying on anyone else to express their sentiments for them. **Indirect dialogue** is a second-hand report of something that was said or written but *not* the exact words in their original form. This second-hand report can come from either the narrator of the story or another character within the narrative.

No matter the type of dialogue, it is essential that punctuation is used appropriately and the reader understands who is speaking (unless the particular scene is intentionally ambiguous).

 IDENTIFICATION AND APPLICATION

Though every writer's style can differ, there are a few basic guidelines to follow when using **direct dialogue** in your narrative:

- Use open (") and closed (") quotation marks to indicate the words that are spoken by the characters.

- Always begin a new paragraph when the speaker changes.

NOTES

- Make sure the reader knows who is saying what.
- When crafting an interaction between characters, the author can use more phrases than simply "he said", "she said", or "they said." Depending on the nature of the character's quotation, it can be followed by stronger verbs, adjectives, or adverbs.
- Use correct punctuation marks and capitalization.

Use **indirect dialogue** without quotation marks:

- when the exact words spoken are not important enough to the narrative to be showcased, but the occurrence and details of the dialogue are important for the reader to know
- if one character is describing or paraphrasing an interaction with another character

Writers can use both direct and indirect dialogue to develop characters by showcasing the characters' opinions, reactions, emotions, experiences, personalities, and even appearances through:

- what the characters say (direct or indirect speech)
- how the characters say it (their speech patterns; the expressions and language they use)
- the tone the characters use ("said happily," "yelled angrily," etc.)
- The characters' body language as they are speaking
- The characters' actions as they are speaking
- The characters' thoughts as they are speaking

 MODEL

Read the following excerpt from "The Gift of the Magi" to see how the author effectively uses direct dialogue to develop plot events and reveal characters' motivations:

On went her old brown jacket; on went her old brown hat. With a whirl of skirts and with the brilliant sparkle still in her eyes, she fluttered down the stairs to the street.

Where she stopped the sign read: "Mme. Sofronie. Hair Goods of All Kinds." One flight up Della ran, and collected herself, panting. Madame, large, too white, chilly, hardly looked the "Sofronie."

"Will you buy my hair?" asked Della.

"I buy hair," said Madame. "Take yer hat off and let's have a sight at the looks of it."

Down rippled the brown cascade.

"Twenty dollars," said Madame, lifting the mass with a practiced hand.

"Give it to me quick," said Della.

Oh, and the next two hours tripped by on rosy wings. Forget the hashed metaphor. She was ransacking the stores for Jim's present.

In this excerpt, we see that O. Henry has followed all of the technical guidelines regarding direct dialogue. He sets off the direct speech of each character with open quotation marks. He also places the closed quotation mark outside the end punctuation of the quote, while the rest of the sentence has its own end punctuation. O. Henry begins a new paragraph whenever the speaker changes (as indicated by the indentation before an open quotation mark). After each direct quotation of speech, O. Henry makes sure the reader knows who is saying what with phrases such as "asked Della," "said Madame," and "said Della."

This excerpt also provides a good example of how dialogue is used to develop the characters. We know that Della is in a hurry. Having made her decision to sell her hair, she doesn't want to have second thoughts, so she moves quickly to put on her coat and hat and get to the hair salon as fast as possible. Della is direct with Madame Sofronie when she asks, "Will you buy my hair?" Notice that Madame replies, "I buy hair." She is a business woman, so it is not in her interest to simply tell Della, "Yes." Instead she says, "Take yer hat off and let's have a sight at the looks of it." This short piece of dialogue helps the reader realize that Madame Sofronie is probably a foreigner who has learned English as an adult. Madame Sofronie speaks clearly enough to be understood, but with an accent ("yer") and with nonstandard grammar and usage ("let's have a sight at the looks of it").

When Madame Sofronie offers Della "twenty dollars," she does so while "lifting the mass with a practiced hand." With this descriptive phrase, O. Henry provides the reader with new information about Madame Sofronie's character. She is clearly is an *experienced* business woman who knows that Della's hair is worth more than the money she is offering. Della's response tells a lot about her character—she is young and somewhat naive; her single goal is to get enough money to buy Jim a nice Christmas present. Notice that Della doesn't try to bargain with Madame Sofronie—"Give it to me quick" is her immediate response.

Dialogue is a useful narrative tool in short stories, novels, plays, and movies. Poets also use dialogue, especially in long narrative poems that tell a story. Notice how Edgar Allan Poe uses dialogue to move the plot of "The Raven" and create a sense of mystery.

> Open here I flung the shutter, when, with many a flirt and flutter,
> In there stepped a stately Raven of the saintly days of yore:
> Not the least obeisance made he; not a minute stopped or stayed he;
> But with mien of lord or lady, perched above my chamber door —
> Perched upon a bust of Pallas just above my chamber door —
> Perched, and sat, and nothing more.
> Then this ebony bird beguiling my sad fancy into smiling
> By the grave and stern decorum of the countenance it wore,
> **"Though thy crest be shorn and shaven, thou," I said, "art sure no craven,**
> **Ghastly grim and ancient Raven wandering from the Nightly shore —**
> **Tell me what thy lordly name is on the Night's Plutonian shore!"**
> **Quoth the Raven "Nevermore."**
>
> Much I marvelled this ungainly fowl to hear discourse so plainly;
> Though its answer little meaning—little relevancy bore;
> For we cannot help agreeing that no living human being
> Ever yet was blessed with seeing bird above his chamber door —
> Bird or beast upon the sculptured bust above his chamber door,
> With such a name as "Nevermore."
>
> But the Raven, sitting lonely on the placid bust, spoke only
> That one word, as if his soul in that one word he did outpour.
> Nothing farther then he uttered—not a feather then he fluttered —
> Till I scarcely more than muttered "Other friends have flown before —
> On the morrow he will leave me, as my Hopes have flown before."
> Then the bird said "Nevermore."

In the second stanza of this excerpt, the speaker of the poem talks directly to his unexpected and unusual guest and asks him, "...Tell me what thy lordly name is on the Night's Plutonian shore!" The Raven responds, "Nevermore." This same structure is repeated in the fourth stanza. This time the speaker mutters "Other friends have flown before — / On the morrow he will leave me, as my Hopes have flown before." Although not speaking directly to the Raven, nonetheless, "Then the bird said 'Nevermore.'" This repetitive structure wherein the speaker addresses the bird (or speaks aloud so the bird hears him), only to get the same one word response is used to build mystery, suspense, and ultimately a sense of despair in the speaker.

PRACTICE

Write a scene for your love story or your narrative love poem in which two or more characters engage in both direct and indirect dialogue. When you are finished, trade scenes with a partner and offer each other feedback. Has the writer followed the technical guidelines relating to direct dialogue? Do you see areas where the indirect dialogue can be improved? How does the dialogue help develop character? Does the dialogue reveal information about the plot? Offer each other suggestions, and remember that they are most helpful when they are constructive.

Please note that excerpts and passages in the StudySync® library and this workbook are intended as touchstones to generate interest in an author's work. The excerpts and passages do not substitute for the reading of entire texts, and StudySync® strongly recommends that students seek out and purchase the whole literary or informational work in order to experience it as the author intended. Links to online resellers are available in our digital library. In addition, complete works may be ordered through an authorized reseller by filling out and returning to StudySync® the order form enclosed in this workbook.

Reading & Writing Companion   **445**

SKILL:
CONCLUSIONS

DEFINE

A narrative **conclusion** is the story's end. The conclusion occurs after the climax and includes the final moments of falling action in a story. A strong conclusion not only ends all action within the plot, but it also must provide a resolution of the conflict; in other words, show how the problem faced by the characters is resolved. This resolution does not always result in a positive outcome for the characters; rather, it solves the problem at hand and reveals how the characters, setting, and plot may have changed since the beginning of the story. A story's conclusion often communicates a lesson that the characters have learned—either directly or indirectly—one that will benefit a reader to learn as well. Because the conclusion is the author's farewell to the reader, an author must consider how the conclusion will affect the reader, as well as how to leave the reader with a lasting impression of the story.

IDENTIFICATION AND APPLICATION

- An effective narrative conclusion presents a resolution of the conflict in the story.
- A narrative conclusion relates the final actions and events in the story, possibly including:
  › A final interaction between characters that have faced the main problem in the story.
  › A speech or soliloquy delivered by a character that tells how the events came to an end.
  › The final thoughts of the character(s) and/or narrator.

- Authors often use descriptive details to draw out an emotional response from the reader upon a narrative's conclusion.
- A narrative conclusion often includes an author's message to the reader.
- A strong narrative conclusion leaves the reader with a lasting impression of the story.

MODEL

In the opening lines of O. Henry's story "The Gift of the Magi," the reader is introduced to one of the two main characters, the setting, and the central problem of the story. It is Christmas Eve in a shabby $8 a week furnished flat. Despite her careful attempts to save money, Della has only $1.87 to spend on a gift for her beloved husband Jim. The reader immediately is hooked: What can Della do to resolve this problem?

As the action of the story rises, we learn of Della's solution. She sells her most precious item—her beautiful long brown hair—in order to raise money to buy Jim's gift, a beautiful watch chain. Jim's watch is his most prized possession, a family heirloom that has come down to him from his father who had received it earlier from his father. These facts make the significance of Della's action even more meaningful. She is willing to sacrifice her most precious possession to give the man she loves something that will enhance the emotional value of his most precious possession.

Readers over the past hundred years have marveled at the cleverness with which O. Henry then twists the plot of this famous story as a means of revealing its true message of love. Jim, it turns out, has sold his precious watch to buy a set of beautiful hair combs that Della has long wanted. Here is the conclusion of the story.

> **Jim had not yet seen his beautiful present.** She held it out to him eagerly upon her open palm. The dull precious metal seemed to flash with a reflection of her bright and ardent spirit.
>
> **"Isn't it a dandy, Jim? I hunted all over town to find it. You'll have to look at the time a hundred times a day now. Give me your watch. I want to see how it looks on it."** Instead of obeying, Jim tumbled down on the couch and put his hands under the back of his head and smiled.
>
> **"Dell," said he, "let's put our Christmas presents away and keep 'em a while. They're too nice to use just at present. I sold the watch to get the money to buy your combs. And now suppose you put the chops on."**

The magi, as you know were wise men—wonderfully wise men—who brought gifts to the Babe in the manger. **They invented the art of giving Christmas presents.** Being wise, their gifts were no doubt wise ones, possibly bearing the privilege of exchange in case of duplication. **And here I have lamely related to you the uneventful chronicle of two foolish children in a flat who most unwisely sacrificed for each other the greatest treasures of their house. But in a last word to the wise of**

Please note that excerpts and passages in the StudySync® library and this workbook are intended as touchstones to generate interest in an author's work. The excerpts and passages do not substitute for the reading of entire texts, and StudySync® strongly recommends that students seek out and purchase the whole literary or informational work in order to experience it as the author intended. Links to online resellers are available in our digital library. In addition, complete works may be ordered through an authorized reseller by filling out and returning to StudySync® the order form enclosed in this workbook.

Reading & Writing Companion   447

these days let it be said that of all who give gifts these two were the wisest. Of all who give and receive gifts, such as they are wisest. Everywhere they are wisest. They are the magi.

Notice how O. Henry presents the falling action of the story as well as its ultimate message in the last four short paragraphs of the story. We learn that "Jim had not yet seen his beautiful present." We learn of Della's excitement at being able to give Jim a gift that will enhance his most cherished possession—"Isn't it a dandy, Jim? I hunted all over town to find it. You'll have to look at the time a hundred times a day now. Give me your watch. I want to see how it looks on it."

Then comes the final ironic twist as we learn that "Instead of obeying, Jim tumbled down on the couch and put his hands under the back of his head and smiled." O. Henry chooses his words precisely because he wants to make sure readers understand Jim's reaction. Jim is not angry or upset in any way. Jim is happy, content in the realization that he and Della had given each other the best possible Christmas gift: a demonstration of their willingness to sacrifice something they cared deeply about for the love of the other person.

In the final paragraph of the conclusion, the author offers the reader a message or moral, a lesson that sums up the point he is making in relating the events of his narrative. The magi, he notes, "invented the art of giving Christmas presents." The author goes out of his way to stress a very important point. "And here I have *lamely* related to you the *uneventful chronicle* of two *foolish children* in a flat who most *unwisely sacrificed* for each other *the greatest treasures of their house.*" In fact, each italicized word is spoken ironically, for the story isn't lame, it isn't an uneventful chronicle, and the characters aren't foolish, nor are they children, and most certain of all, they didn't unwisely sacrifice the greatest treasures of their house. O. Henry brings home this point in a powerful conclusion, intended to make a lasting impression about the real meaning of his message: "But in a last word to the wise of these days let it be said that of all who give gifts these two were the wisest. Of all who give and receive gifts, such as they are wisest. Everywhere they are wisest. They are the magi."

Narrative poems contain the same basic elements of character, setting, plot, and conflict that are found in short stories and other prose narratives. While the structure of narrative poems is often enhanced through the use of rhyme, figurative language, and other poetic devices, narrative poems must also deal with the basics of rising action that eventually climaxes and resolves some emotional or thematic conflict. Notice how Arthur Brooke deals with many of these issues in this excerpt from his narrative poem, *The Tragical History of Romeus and Juliet*. Here, Romeus expresses his joy that Juliet has agreed to marry him.

Copyright © BookheadEd Learning, LLC

NOTES

Then Romeus, whose thought was free from foul desire,
And to the top of virtue's height did worthily aspire,
Was filled with greater joy than can my pen express,
Or, till they have enjoyed the like, the hearer's heart can guess.
And then with joined hands, heaved up into the skies,
He thanks the Gods, and from the heavens for vengeance down he cries
If he have other thought but as his lady spake;
And then his look he turned to her, and thus did answer make:
"Since, lady, that you like to honour me so much
As to accept me for your spouse, I yield myself for such.
In true witness whereof, because I must depart,
Till that my deed do prove my word, I leave in pawn my heart.
To-morrow eke betimes before the sun arise,
To Friar Laurence will I wend, to learn his sage advice.
He is my ghostly sire, and oft he hath me taught
What I should do in things of weight, when I his aid have sought.
And at this self-same hour, I plight you here my faith,
I will be here, if you think good, to tell you what he saith."
She was contented well; else favour found he none
That night at lady Juliet's hand, save pleasant words alone.

Romeus is so thrilled by Juliet's declaration of love that "with joined hands, heaved up into the skies, / He thanks the Gods. . ." Romeus then describes what actions he will take next so the conflict can be resolved by their marriage on the next day. "Since, lady, that you like to honour me so much / As to accept me for your spouse, I yield myself for such. / In true witness whereof, because I must depart, / Till that my deed do prove my word, I leave in pawn my heart. /To-morrow eke betimes before the sun arise, / To Friar Laurence will I wend, to learn his sage advice." Romeus promises to return to Juliet the next day with news of Friar Laurence's advice and details of the plan for their marriage. The conclusion of this section of the narrative poem ends with what appears will soon be the resolution of the central problem. We learn that as a result of Romeus's statement, "She [Juliet] was contented well; else favour found he none / That night at lady Juliet's hand, save pleasant words alone." All is well, until the next section of the narrative begins.

 PRACTICE

Write a draft of a conclusion to your narrative love story or narrative love poem. Refer to your plot diagram from the Plan lesson to review and show how you plan to conclude your story. Note which details from the rising action of your story eventually lead to the narrative's climax. Include details of the falling action and resolution that occur after the climax.

When you are finished, trade your draft with a partner and offer each other feedback. How does the conclusion effectively bring resolution to the experiences of the characters or the events of your love narrative? Do the details of the conclusion cause an emotional reaction from you as a reader? Why or why not? Do you feel as though you can take away a final message from the overall narrative? Why or why not? Were you satisfied that the narrative had a decisive end? Offer each other suggestions, and remember that they are most helpful when they are constructive.

DRAFT

Copyright © BookheadEd Learning, LLC

WRITING PROMPT

You have been reading and learning about demonstrations of love in different literary genres, as well as the techniques authors use, to communicate the feeling of love. Now you will use those techniques to write your own narrative about love--either a short story or a narrative poem about real or imagined events. As a starting point, choose one of the following demonstrations of love explored in Unit 4: sacrificing for love ("The Gift of the Magi"), pursuing love despite differences or disapproval (*The Tragical History of Romeus and Juliet, Romeo and Juliet, West Side Story*), longing for unfulfilled love (*Angela's Ashes*), or mourning loss of love ("The Raven," "Sonnet 73").

Your narrative should include:

- a narrator or speaker (for a poem)
- characters and dialogue
- a clear setting
- a conflict that centers on a demonstration of love
- a plot with beginning, middle, and end

You've already made progress toward writing your love story or poem. You've planned your writing and thought about how writers use descriptive details to enhance and support a narrative. You've drafted your introductory paragraphs and paragraphs containing dialogue, and you've practiced writing the elements of a strong and effective conclusion. Now it's time to write a draft of your narrative love story or poem.

Use your prewriting graphic organizer, plot diagram, and other prewriting materials to help you as you write. Remember that in the rising action of a narrative, writers introduce characters, setting, and conflict and begin to develop characters and plot. The rising action leads to the story's climax, the turning point in the story, where the most exciting action takes place. The falling action of a story occurs after the climax and leads to the resolution of the conflict and the story's conclusion. Keep readers in mind as you write, and aim to keep your audience engaged and thinking about love.

When drafting, ask yourself these questions:

- What can I do to improve my introduction so that readers understand expository information early on in my story?
- How can I use dialogue to reveal information about characters and advance the plot?
- How will my characters demonstrate love in the story?
- What details can I improve and expand on to create a vivid reading experience for readers?
- How will I resolve the story's conflict in a way that is memorable to readers?

Before you submit your draft, read it over carefully. You want to be sure that you've responded to all aspects of the prompt.

TRANSITIONS

sync•skills
Writing

SKILL:
TRANSITIONS

 DEFINE

Transitions clarify the relationship of words and ideas. The use of transition words, clauses, and phrases helps readers understand and follow the structure of a narrative. Writers use time-order words and phrases and clauses (for example, *first, the following day*, and *soon after*) to transition from one event to the next. Transitions can also signal a change in the setting, or where a story takes place. Spatial transitions such as *on top of, behind, near,* and *to the left* help describe the settings of actions and the spatial relationships of objects or people. Transitional phrases such as *but, in addition, on the other hand,* and *as a result,* when they appear at the beginning of a paragraph, show how ideas are related to those in the previous paragraph.

 IDENTIFICATION AND APPLICATION

- Transitions act like bridges between sentences or paragraphs.
- Narrative writers use transitions to signal shifts in time or setting.
- Transitions help writers to convey sequence of events in a story.
- Writers can also use transitions to show the relationships among character experiences and story events.

 MODEL

This excerpt from "The Drop" contains transitions that help the reader understand the setting and sequence of events. Read the passages to identify the transitions the author used.

Please note that excerpts and passages in the StudySync® library and this workbook are intended as touchstones to generate interest in an author's work. The excerpts and passages do not substitute for the reading of entire texts, and StudySync® strongly recommends that students seek out and purchase the whole literary or informational work in order to experience it as the author intended. Links to online resellers are available in our digital library. In addition, complete works may be ordered through an authorized reseller by filling out and returning to StudySync® the order form enclosed in this workbook.

Reading & Writing
Companion

453

Now they were in line together, and about every three minutes, another ground-shaking roar and another blast of screams would fly over their heads, stirring John's stomach up even more, then fading off into a distant rumble as a new group of riders sped along through their own moment of truth.

It was hot. The line was packed. But she wanted to ride this, and he wanted to be near her. So he made the sacrifice. He was doing this for her. He was doing this because he wanted to sit next to her. He would never have gone anywhere near this ride if not for her. Maybe he would touch her hand. This really was the moment of truth, and he was here because of her.

And then they were sitting next to each other.

And then they were buckled in and moving.

In this excerpt of the story, the author uses the word "now" to indicate that they have moved forward in time from the moment when John said that it'd be crazy to go on that ride. The "now" shows that as time passed, he changed his mind and he's in line with Kaitlyn. In the last two lines, the repetition of "And then" transitions between settings and indicates the passage of time. They change settings, moving from waiting in line to being on the ride, and they move forward in time.

 PRACTICE

Write one body paragraph for your narrative love story or narrative love poem that uses transition words, clauses, and/or phrases. When you are finished, trade with a partner and offer each other feedback. How effective are the transitions in indicating the passing of time or change in setting? How well do the transitions show relationships among character experiences and story events? Offer each other constructive, helpful suggestions for revision.

NOTES

REVISE

Copyright © BookheadEd Learning, LLC

WRITING PROMPT

You have been reading and learning about demonstrations of love in different literary genres, as well as the techniques authors use, to communicate the feeling of love. Now you will use those techniques to write your own narrative about love--either a short story or a narrative poem about real or imagined events. As a starting point, choose one of the following demonstrations of love explored in Unit 4: sacrificing for love ("The Gift of the Magi"), pursuing love despite differences or disapproval (*The Tragical History of Romeus and Juliet, Romeo and Juliet, West Side Story*), longing for unfulfilled love (*Angela's Ashes*), or mourning loss of love ("The Raven," "Sonnet 73").

Your narrative should include:

- a narrator or speaker (for a poem)
- characters and dialogue
- a clear setting
- a conflict that centers on a demonstration of love
- a plot with beginning, middle, and end

You have written a draft of your narrative love story or poem. You have also received input from your peers about how to improve it. Now you are going to revise your draft.

Here are some recommendations to help you revise:

- Review the suggestions made by your peers.
- Examine the introduction to your narrative.
  - Do your introductory paragraphs contain expository information about your characters and setting?

Please note that excerpts and passages in the StudySync® library and this workbook are intended as touchstones to generate interest in an author's work. The excerpts and passages do not substitute for the reading of entire texts, and StudySync® strongly recommends that students seek out and purchase the whole literary or informational work in order to experience it as the author intended. Links to online resellers are available in our digital library. In addition, complete works may be ordered through an authorized reseller by filling out and returning to StudySync® the order form enclosed in this workbook.

Reading & Writing Companion   **455**

> › Does your story's introduction orient the reader to the time and place of your story's setting?
> › Have you introduced the conflict in the introductory paragraphs of your narrative?
> › Does your introduction contain details that are interesting and engaging to readers?

- Evaluate the sequencing of events in your narrative.
  › Do the events in your narrative follow a logical order?
  › Have you used transition words to signal shifts in time or setting?
  › Does the order of events in your narrative help build and develop the conflict in your story?

- Examine the prose you have used to tell your story.
  › Have you included descriptive details that help readers visualize the characters, setting, and events in your narrative?
  › Do your transitions show the relationships among character experiences and story events?
  › Have you used language that is engaging and exciting for readers?

- Look at the dialogue in your story.
  › Do your characters address one another in direct dialogue?
  › Does the dialogue reveal details about the characters?
  › Does the dialogue help build the conflict and advance the plot?
  › Does the dialogue reveal additional information about the setting of your narrative?
  › Have you followed the technical guidelines for writing direct and indirect dialogue?
  › When characters converse in your story, is it clear to readers who is speaking?

- Evaluate the conclusion of your story.
  › Does the conclusion present a logical resolution of the conflict?
  › Do you think readers will feel satisfied and entertained after reading your story's conclusion?
  › Have you crafted a conclusion that will leave the reader with a lasting impression of your story?
  › Does your conclusion contain elements that will elicit an emotional response from a reader?

Use these questions to help you evaluate your narrative love story or poem to determine areas that should be strengthened or improved. Then revise these elements of your narrative.

EDIT,
PROOFREAD,
AND PUBLISH

WRITING PROMPT

You have been reading and learning about demonstrations of love in different literary genres, as well as the techniques authors use, to communicate the feeling of love. Now you will use those techniques to write your own narrative about love--either a short story or a narrative poem about real or imagined events. As a starting point, choose one of the following demonstrations of love explored in Unit 4: sacrificing for love ("The Gift of the Magi"), pursuing love despite differences or disapproval (*The Tragical History of Romeus and Juliet, Romeo and Juliet, West Side Story*), longing for unfulfilled love (*Angela's Ashes*), or mourning loss of love ("The Raven," "Sonnet 73").

Your narrative should include:

- a narrator or speaker (for a poem)
- characters and dialogue
- a clear setting
- a conflict that centers on a demonstration of love
- a plot with beginning, middle, and end

You have revised your narrative love story or poem and received input from your peers on that revision. Now it's time to edit and proofread your story or poem to produce a final version. Have you included all the valuable suggestions from your peers? Ask yourself: Have I created a cohesive plot with a beginning, middle, and end? Have I included precise details to convey the setting of my story? Have I developed my characters with descriptive details and dialogue? Does my story have a clear demonstration of love?

When you are satisfied with your work, move on to proofread it for errors. For example, check that you have formatted dialogue correctly. Have you punctuated your transitions properly? Have you spelled words correctly, using appropriate suffixes? Have you chosen the correct words to support the meaning you intended? Are your verbs precise and full of energy?

Once you have made all your corrections and have given your story a title, you are ready to submit and publish your work. You can distribute your writing to family and friends, post it on your blog, or submit it to a literary magazine or contest.

Powered by BookheadEd Learning, LLC

Text Fulfillment
Through StudySync

If you are interested in specific titles, please fill out the form below and we will check availability through our partners.

ORDER DETAILS

Date:

TITLE	AUTHOR	Paperback/ Hardcover	Specific Edition *If Applicable*	Quantity

SHIPPING INFORMATION

Contact:

Title:

School/District:

Address Line 1:

Address Line 2:

Zip or Postal Code:

Phone:

Mobile:

Email:

BILLING INFORMATION   ☐ *SAME AS SHIPPING*

Contact:

Title:

School/District:

Address Line 1:

Address Line 2:

Zip or Postal Code:

Phone:

Mobile:

Email:

PAYMENT INFORMATION

☐ CREDIT CARD

Name on Card:

Card Number: Expiration Date: Security Code:

☐ PO

Purchase Order Number:

StudySync Text Fulfillment, BookheadEd Learning, LLC
610 Daniel Young Drive | Sonoma, CA 95476